NORTHEAST MILAN
Pages 104–123
Street Finder maps 3, 4

HISTORIC CENTRE
Pages 42–59
Street Finder maps 9, 10

SOUTHEAST MILAN
Pages 92–103
Street Finder maps 7, 8

NORTHEAST
MILAN

HISTORIC
CENTRE

SOUTHEAST
MILAN

0 metres   600

0 yards   600

EYEWITNESS TRAVEL

MILAN
& THE LAKES

DK

LONDON, NEW YORK,
MELBOURNE, MUNICH AND DELHI
www.dk.com

Produced by Fabio Ratti
Editoria Libraria e Multimediale, Milan, Italy

PROJECT EDITORS Barbara Cacciani, Giovanni Francesio
EDITORS Emanuela Damiani, Mattia Goffetti,
Alessandra Lombardi, Marco Scapagnini
DESIGNERS Oriana Bianchetti, Silvia Tomasone

Dorling Kindersley Ltd
PROJECT EDITOR Fiona Wild
SENIOR ART EDITOR Marisa Renzullo
DTP DESIGNERS Maite Lantaron, Samantha Borland,
Sarah Meakin
PRODUCTION Marie Ingledew

CONTRIBUTOR
Monica Torri

ILLUSTRATORS
Giorgia Boli, Alberto Ipsilanti,
Daniela Veluti, Nadia Viganò

ENGLISH TRANSLATION
Richard Pierce

Film output by Quadrant Typesetters, London
Reproduced by Lineatre, Milan

Printed and bound in China by L. Rex Printing Co., Ltd

First American Edition, 2000
07 08 09 10 9 8 7 6 5 4 3 2 1

Published in the United States by Dorling Kindersley Publishing,
Inc., 375 Hudson Street, New York 10014

Reprinted with revisions 2003, 2005, 2007

Published in Great Britain by Dorling Kindersley Limited.

A CATALOGING IN PUBLICATION RECORD IS
AVAILABLE FROM THE LIBRARY OF CONGRESS.

ISSN 1542-1554
ISBN 978-0-75662-443-9

FLOORS ARE REFERRED TO THROUGHOUT IN ACCORDANCE WITH
EUROPEAN USAGE; IE THE "FIRST FLOOR" IS THE FLOOR ABOVE GROUND LEVEL.

Front cover main image: Cathedral at dusk, Milan

**The information in this
Dorling Kindersley Travel Guide is checked regularly.**
Every effort has been made to ensure that this book is as up-to-date as
possible at the time of going to press. Some details, however,
such as telephone numbers, opening hours, prices, gallery hanging
arrangements and travel information are liable to change. The publishers
cannot accept responsibility for any consequences arising from the use of
this book, nor for any material on third party websites, and cannot
guarantee that any website address in this
book will be a suitable source of travel information. We value the views
and suggestions of our readers very highly. Please write to: Publisher, DK
Eyewitness Travel Guides, Dorling Kindersley,
80 Strand, London, WC2R 0RL, Great Britain.

CONTENTS

HOW TO USE
THIS GUIDE 6

Statue at the entrance to the
Pinacoteca di Brera *(see pp114–7)*

INTRODUCING MILAN AND THE LAKES

FOUR GREAT DAYS IN
MILAN & THE LAKES
10

PUTTING MILAN ON
THE MAP 12

THE HISTORY
OF MILAN 16

MILAN AT
A GLANCE 28

MILAN THROUGH
THE YEAR 36

Naviglio Grande, in the southern
district of Milan *(see p89)*

Leonardo da Vinci's *Last Supper*, in Santa Maria delle Grazie *(see pp72–3)*

MILAN AREA BY AREA

HISTORIC CENTRE 42

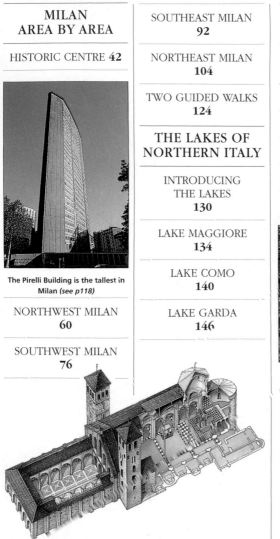

The Pirelli Building is the tallest in Milan *(see p118)*

NORTHWEST MILAN 60

SOUTHWEST MILAN 76

SOUTHEAST MILAN 92

NORTHEAST MILAN 104

TWO GUIDED WALKS 124

THE LAKES OF NORTHERN ITALY

INTRODUCING THE LAKES 130

LAKE MAGGIORE 134

LAKE COMO 140

LAKE GARDA 146

Sant'Ambrogio Basilica dating from the 4th century *(see pp84–7)*

THE SMALLER LAKES 154

TRAVELLERS' NEEDS

WHERE TO STAY 158

WHERE TO EAT 168

BARS & CAFES 184

SHOPS & MARKETS 188

ENTERTAINMENT 196

Shopping in Via Montenapoleone *(see pp106–7)*

SURVIVAL GUIDE

PRACTICAL INFORMATION 208

TRAVEL INFORMATION 214

STREET FINDER 224

GENERAL INDEX 238

W TO USE THIS GUIDE

ide helps you to get the
t out of your visit to Milan
d the lakes of Northern Italy
viding detailed descriptions of
s, practical information and
ert advice. *Introducing Milan,* the
st chapter, sets the city in its geo-
graphical and historical context, and
Milan at a Glance provides a brief
overview of the architecture and cultural background. *Milan Area by Area*
describes the main sightseeing areas
in detail, with maps, illustrations and
photographs. A special section is

dedicated to the lakes of Northern
Italy, which are all within easy travelling distance of Milan's city centre.
Information on hotels, restaurants,
bars, cafés, shops, sports facilities and
entertainment venues is covered in
the chapter *Travellers' Needs,* and the
Survival Guide section contains inval-
uable practical advice on everything
from personal security to using the
public transport system. The guide
ends with a detailed Street Finder map
and a map of the public transport
network in Milan.

FINDING YOUR WAY AROUND THE SIGHTSEEING SECTION

The city of Milan is divided into five
sightseeing areas, each with its own colour-
coded thumb tab. Each area has its own
chapter, which opens with a numbered list
of the sights described. The lakes of

Northern Italy are covered in a separate
chapter, also colour coded. The chapter on
the lakes opens with a road map of the
region. The major sights are numbered for
easy reference.

1 Introduction to the Area
*On this page the major sights are
numbered, listed by category and
plotted on an area map, which also
shows where public transport stops,
taxi ranks and car parks are located.*

A locator map shows where you
are in relation to the other areas
of the city.

Locator map

Each area has a colour-coded thumb tab.

The area shaded pink is
shown in greater detail on
the Street-by-Street map.

2 Street-by-Street Map
*This gives a bird's-eye
view of the most interesting
parts of each sightseeing
area. The numbering of the
sights ties in with the area
map on the preceding page
as well as with the fuller
descriptions provided on
the pages that follow.*

A suggested route for a walk
covers the most interesting
streets in the area.

MILAN AREA BY AREA

The five coloured areas shown on this map *(see pp14–15)* correspond to the main sightseeing areas of Milan – each of which is covered by a full chapter in the *Milan Area by Area* section *(see pp40–123)*. These areas are also highlighted on other maps, for example in the section *Milan at a Glance (see pp28–35)*. The colours on the margins of each area correspond to those on the colour-coded thumb tabs.

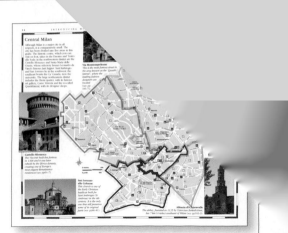

Numbers refer to each sight's position on the area map and its place in the chapter.

Practical information provides everything you need to know to visit the sights, including map references to the *Street Finder (see pp224–37)*.

3 Detailed Information on Each Sight

All the most important monuments and other sights are described individually. They are listed in order, following the numbering on the area map. The key to the symbols used is shown on the back flap for easy reference.

The story boxes discuss particular aspects of the places described.

Stars indicate the features you should not miss.

4 The Top Sights

All the most important sights are described individually in two or more pages. Historic buildings and churches are dissected to reveal their interiors, and museums and galleries have colour-coded floorplans to help you locate the major works on exhibit.

The Visitors' Checklist provides all the practical information needed to plan your visit.

INTRODUCING
MILAN

ALLI LETTORI·
Quanto la nobilißima Città di Milano sia bella, grande, forte, e populata, e
d'acquei per le quali anco uengono barche abondantißima, ei d'ogni sorti d'arti
piena, e d'il suo territorio fertilißimo: Ciascuno che l' habbia uisto, o praticato, o
che leggera chi di essa ne ha scritto facilmente lo può sapere: e pero qui si lassa
di narrarlo, ma solo si metterà nell'altro spatio quello che di essa più
notabile ne appare.

FOUR GREAT DAYS IN MILAN
AND THE LAKES 10–11

PUTTING MILAN ON THE MAP 12–15

THE HISTORY OF MILAN 16–27

MILAN AT A GLANCE 28–35

MILAN THROUGH THE YEAR 36–39

FOUR GREAT DAYS IN MILAN AND THE LAKES

A couple of days in Milan will give you a good idea of the city's riches. Two of the itineraries below focus on attractions such as Leonardo's *Last Supper*, the Duomo, the Brera art gallery and the fashion boutiques. If you need a change of pace,

La Scala's
Museo Teatrale

head to the lakes. The trips to Lake Como and Lake Maggiore will show why these locations are such sought-after retreats, drawing everyone from Catullus to Hemingway. The price guides given include travel, food and admission costs.

ART AND SHOPPING IN CENTRAL MILAN

- **Galleries of Old Masters**
- **Fashion boutiques**
- **Atop the Duomo**
- **Opera at Teatro alla Scala**

TWO ADULTS allow at least €99

Morning
Start at 10am with the Old Masters – Leonardo, Raphael, Caravaggio – in the **Pinacoteca Ambrosiana** *(see pp56–9)*. Then work your way east to Via Torino and the **Piazza del Duomo** *(see pp44–5)*. Ascend to the roof of Italy's second-largest cathedral *(see pp46–9)* and wander amid the spires for views of the city. Pause for lunch at **Caffè Zucca** *(see p187)*, then browse around Milan's splendid 19th-century shopping mall, **Galleria Vittorio Emanuele II** *(see p50)*.

Afternoon
Piazza della Scala is flanked by the world-renowned **Teatro alla Scala** opera house *(see pp52–3)* and its **Museo Teatrale**, devoted to luminaries such as Verdi and Toscanini. If available, buy tickets for tonight's performance – the season runs year-round.

Nearby is the Quadrilatero d'Oro, a "Golden Rectangle" (bounded by Via Manzoni, Via Montenapoleone, Via S Andrea and Via della Spiga) of boutiques by the likes of Dolce & Gabbana, Gucci and Ferragamo. If you prefer art to shopping, two excellent museums in the area, **Poldi Pezzoli** *(see p108)* and **Bagatti Valsecchi** *(see p109)*, showcase the private collections of Milan's 19th-century elite. Finish up at the **Pinacoteca di Brera** *(see pp114–7)*, which lies in the Brera district, packed with lively bars.

Gothic spires of the Duomo, the second-largest cathedral in Italy

The fountain in front of the Castello Sforzesco

MEDIEVAL AND RENAISSANCE MILAN

- **Leonardo's *Last Supper***
- **Ancient churches**
- **Roman remains**
- **Trendy Navigli district**

TWO ADULTS allow at least €83

Morning
Start at 9am with the collections of sculpture (including Michelangelo's *Pietà*) and Renaissance paintings at the medieval **Castello Sforzesco** *(see pp64–7)*. Pop into the **Museo Archeologico** *(see p74)* to ponder Milan's early history while you await your scheduled noon entry time – reserved at least two weeks in advance – to Leonardo's *Last Supper*, in the refectory of **Santa Maria delle Grazie** *(see pp72–3)*. Double back along Corso Magenta to the corner with Via Carducci to enjoy a light lunch at the **Art Nouveau Bar Magenta** *(see p186)*.

Afternoon

Visit the glorious 4th-century church of **Sant'Ambrogio** *(see pp84–7)* and then head for **Museo della Scienza** *(see p88)*, which holds replicas of some of Leonardo's inventions. Afterwards make your way along the Parco delle Basiliche where you will find another 4th-century church, **San Lorenzo** *(see pp80–81)*, preceded by a row of Roman columns; the **Museo Diocesano** *(see p90)*, a repository for art from church treasuries across Lombardy; and **Sant'Eustorgio** *(see p90)*, a church filled with early Renaissance frescoes. Finish in the nearby Navigli area, with its many busy bars and restaurants.

A FAMILY DAY ON LAKE MAGGIORE

- Island-hop by ferry
- Explore glorious gardens
- Lunch by the lakeside
- Breathtaking panoramas

FAMILY OF 4 allow at least €116

Morning

The best way to enjoy Lake Maggiore is by flitting between its three tiny **Borromean Islands** *(see p137)*. Start island-hopping at the lakeside town of **Stresa** *(see p137)*. Spend the morning at Isola Bella and Isola Madre, where peacocks wander the exotic gardens and the palace rooms are filled with quirky exhibits, including marionette stages and

A view of Lake Maggiore and snow-capped mountains from Stresa

liveried mannequins. Then head to the village on Isola dei Pescatori for a leisurely lunch by the lake.

Afternoon

Hop off the ferry heading to Stresa at the Mottarone stop, where you can take a cable car (open daily) to the top of Monte Mottarone. You will be rewarded with spectacular views. It is a three-hour trek back down, so you may want to buy a return ticket. Stresa's cafés are a 20-minute stroll back along a lakeside path lined with crumbling villas.

Those with a car might find time to stop outside the town of **Arona** *(see p136)* to climb the 35-m (115-ft) high statue of San Carlo Borromeo. Kids (aged eight plus only) love to clamber up the spiral staircase inside the statue to the head, and peer out of the eyes or nostrils at a lake panorama.

A DAY ON ELEGANT LAKE COMO

- Lavishly decorated Duomo
- Ornate gardens
- Lakeside strolls
- Palatial villas

TWO ADULTS allow at least €48

Morning

Begin the day at **Como** *(see p142)*, on the southwest arm of the lake. Wander along the lakeside promenade, browse the silk outlets, and visit the impressive Duomo and the museum of notable scientist Alessandro Volta. Then head up to the lovely resort town of **Bellagio** *(see p145)*. The tip of Bellagio's promontory is occupied by the grounds of Villa Serbelloni, which you can visit only by guided tour (sign up at the tourist office).

Afternoon

Take a ferry to **Varenna** *(see p144)*, on the eastern shore, and stop for lunch. Then tour the formal gardens at Villa Cipressi and Villa Monastero, or hike up to the ruins of medieval Castello di Vezio for stunning lake views. Afterwards cross by ferry to the western shore and the town of **Tremezzo** *(see p143)*, home to the 18th-century Villa Carlotta, with its terraced gardens and works by Canova and Hayez. Return to Bellagio for a leisurely evening stroll through its pretty alleyways.

Villa Monastero, one of many elegant lakeside villas on Lake Como

...g Milan on the Map

...s the capital of Lombardy (Lombardia), the most densely populated and ...omically developed region in Italy. The population of Milan is over ...00,000 (second only to Rome). This figure does not include the many people ...no live in the suburbs – which have spread outwards over the years – who ...depend on the city both for work (there are large numbers of commuters) and ...entertainment. The city lies in the middle of the Po river valley (Valle Padana) and has always been a key commercial centre. Today it forms part of an industrial triangle with the cities of Turin and Genoa. Milan's position makes it an ideal starting point for visits to the Alpine lakes. Lake Maggiore and Lake Como are close to Milan, whereas Lake Garda is further east, with the western shore part of Lombardy, the eastern part of the Veneto.

Sondr
S38

Lago Maggiore

Lago di Como

Lago di Lecco

Lago di Lugano

Pennine Alps

Toce

S34

Lago d'Orta

Varese

Lecco

Lago di Varese

A9

A8

Como

Berga

Aosta

VALLE D'AOSTA

A5

Valle di Locana

Canavese

A32

Rivoli

Pinerolo

Biella

A6

Busto Arsizio

Monza

A4

MILAN

L O M B A

Ivrea

A4

Cervo

Novara

A5

Vigevano

Lodi

Cre

Vercelli

Lomellina

Pavia

Lambro

Adda

Casale Monferrato

PO

A21

Piacenza

Torino

A26

Casteggio

Moncalieri

Asti

A21

Alessandria

Tortona

Scrivia

Trebbia

Belbo

Orba

A6

Tanaro

P I E M O N T E

Alba

A7

Ottone

A26

Appennino

Ligure

EUROPE

FINLAND

NORWAY

SWEDEN

ESTONIA

LATVIA

DENMARK

LITHUANIA

BELARUS

REP OF IRELAND

U.K.

NETHERLANDS

GERMANY

POLAND

BELGIUM

CZECH REP.

SLOVAKIA

UKRAINE

SWITZERLAND

AUSTRIA

HUNGARY

FRANCE

SLOVENIA

CROATIA

ROMANIA

Milan

SERBIA & MONTENEGRO

BULGARIA

ITALY

SPAIN

GREECE

PORTUGAL

MOROCCO

ALGERIA

TUNISIA

Genova

LIGURIA

Rapallo

A12

Sestri Levante

Golfo di Genova

La Spezia

Europe

The international airport, Malpensa 2000, in addition to Linate airport, has brought Milan even closer to the other European capitals. Train connections are also excellent.

Liguria
Sea

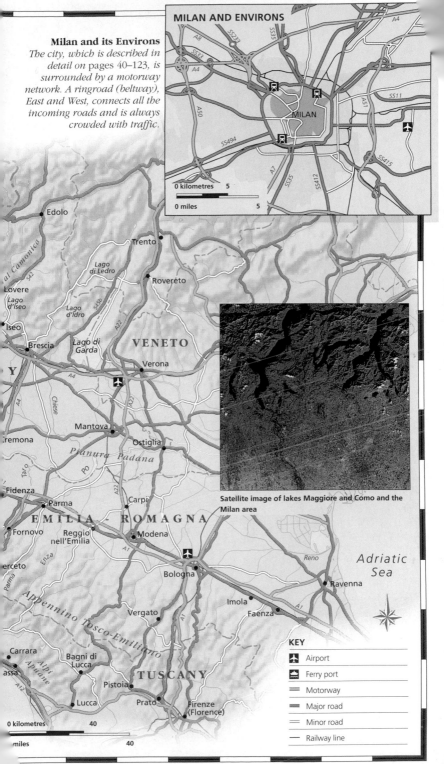

Milan and its Environs
The city, which is described in detail on pages 40–123, is surrounded by a motorway network. A ringroad (beltway), East and West, connects all the incoming roads and is always crowded with traffic.

MILAN AND ENVIRONS

MILAN

0 kilometres   5

0 miles   5

Edolo

Trento

Lago di Ledro

Rovereto

al Camonica

Lovere

Lago d'Iseo

Lago d'Idro

Iseo

Brescia

Lago di Garda

VENETO

Verona

Chiese

Mantova

Ostiglia

Cremona

Pianura Padana

PO

Fidenza

Carpi

Taro

Parma

EMILIA - ROMAGNA

Fornovo

Reggio nell'Emilia

Modena

Enza

erceto

Reno

Adriatic Sea

Bologna

Ravenna

Parma

Appennino Tosco-Emiliano

Imola

Faenza

Vergato

Carrara

Bagni di Lucca

Albi Apuane

assa

TUSCANY

Pistoia

Lucca

Prato

Firenze (Florence)

0 kilometres   40

miles   40

Satellite image of lakes Maggiore and Como and the Milan area

KEY

✈ Airport

⚓ Ferry port

━ Motorway

━ Major road

═ Minor road

— Railway line

Central Milan

Although Milan is a major city in all respects, it is comparatively small. The city has been divided into five areas in this guide. The historic centre, which you can visit on foot, takes in the Duomo and Teatro alla Scala; in the northwestern district are the Castello Sforzesco and Santa Maria delle Grazie, whose refectory houses Leonardo da Vinci's famous *Last Supper*. Sant'Ambrogio and San Lorenzo lie in the southwest; the southeast boasts the Ca' Granda, now the university. The large northeastern district includes the Brera quarter, with its famous art gallery, Corso Venezia and the so-called Quadrilateral, with its designer shops.

Via Montenapoleone
This is the most famous street in the area known as the "Quadri-lateral", where the leading fashion designers are located (see pp 106–7).

Castello Sforzesco
The Visconti built this fortress in 1368 and it was later rebuilt by the Sforza dynasty, creating one of Europe's most elegant Renaissance residences (see pp64–7).

San Lorenzo alle Colonne
This church is one of the Early Christian basilicas built for Sant'Ambrogio (St Ambrose) in the 4th century. It is the only one that still preserves some of its original parts (see pp80–81).

0 metres 600
0 yards 600

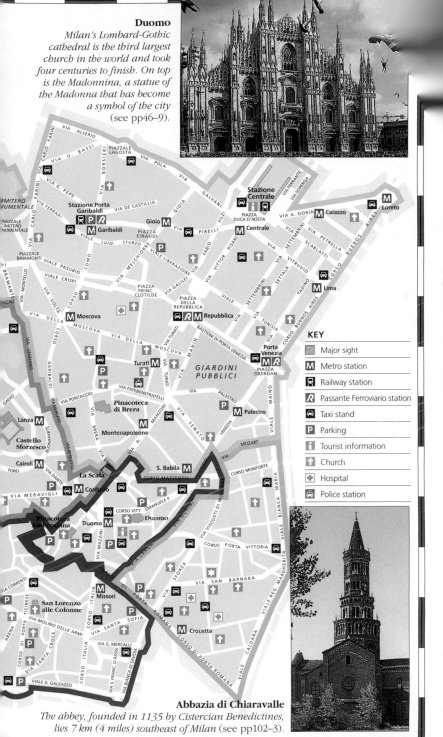

Duomo
Milan's Lombard-Gothic cathedral is the third largest church in the world and took four centuries to finish. On top is the Madonnina, a statue of the Madonna that has become a symbol of the city (see pp46–9).

KEY

	Major sight
M	Metro station
R	Railway station
R	Passante Ferroviario station
🚕	Taxi stand
P	Parking
i	Tourist information
✝	Church
✛	Hospital
🚓	Police station

Abbazia di Chiaravalle
The abbey, founded in 1135 by Cistercian Benedictines, lies 7 km (4 miles) southeast of Milan (see pp102–3).

THE HISTORY OF MILAN

*A*ccording to the words of a 17th-century ambassador, "Milan never fails to be a great city, and when it declines it soon becomes great again". The sentiments encapsulate one of the characteristics of the city – its ability to rise from the ruins of wars, epidemics, sieges and bombings suffered over the centuries, and to regain dynamism and prosperity once more.

THE PREHISTORIC AND ROMAN CITY

In the 3rd–2nd millennium BC, the area covered by Milan today was inhabited by the Ligurians. It was later settled by Indo-European populations and then, in the 5th century BC, by the Etruscans. Around the lakes, archaeologists have unearthed fascinating pre-Roman objects that reveal the presence of a Celtic civilization in the 9th–6th centuries BC. Milan itself was founded in the early 4th century BC when the Gallic Insuber tribes settled there.

Slab with a relief of the half-woolly boar, once the city emblem

The origins of the city are somewhat obscure, as is its name, which most scholars say derives from *Midland* (or "middle of the plain"), while others say it derives from *scrofa semilanuta* (half-woolly boar), the city emblem in ancient times. In 222 BC the Romans, led by the consuls Cnaeus Cornelius Scipio and Claudius Marcellus, defeated the Celts and conquered the Po river valley and its cities. Milan soon became a flourishing commercial centre and in the Imperial era attained political and administrative independence. In AD 286 it became the capital of the Western Roman Empire (until 402) and was the residence of Emperor Maximian. By the late Imperial era Milan was the most important city in the West after Rome and it became a leading religious centre after Constantine's Edict of Milan in 313, which officially recognized Christianity as a religion. Sant'Ambrogio (Ambrose) exerted great influence at this time. He was the first great figure in Milan's history: a Doctor of the Church, he built four basilicas (San Simpliciano, Sant'Ambrogio, San Lorenzo, San Nazaro) and was a leading opponent of the Arian heresy (which denied the divinity of Christ). Sant'Ambrogio was the first in a long series of bishops who ran the city's affairs in the early Middle Ages. Roman Milan was a substantial size: the Republican walls, enlarged to the northeast during the Imperial Age, defined an area that was roughly the same size as the present-day city centre.

TIMELINE

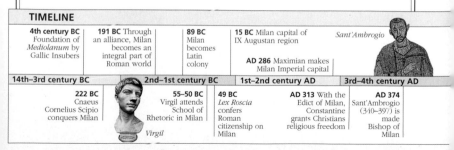

14th–3rd century BC	2nd–1st century BC	1st–2nd century AD	3rd–4th century AD
4th century BC Foundation of *Mediolanum* by Gallic Insubers	**191 BC** Through an alliance, Milan becomes an integral part of Roman world	**89 BC** Milan becomes Latin colony	**15 BC** Milan capital of IX Augustan region	*Sant'Ambrogio*
			AD 286 Maximian makes Milan Imperial capital	
222 BC Cnaeus Cornelius Scipio conquers Milan	**55–50 BC** Virgil attends School of Rhetoric in Milan *Virgil*	**49 BC** *Lex Roscia* confers Roman citizenship on Milan	**AD 313** With the Edict of Milan, Constantine grants Christians religious freedom	**AD 374** Sant'Ambrogio (340–397) is made Bishop of Milan

◁ The *Sforzesca Altarpiece* (1494), now in the Brera art gallery, with portraits of Beatrice d'Este and Lodovico il Moro

THE EARLY MIDDLE AGES AND THE COMMUNE OF MILAN

The 5th and 6th centuries marked a period of decline for Milan. In 402 it lost its status as Imperial capital, was sacked by Attila's Huns in 452, conquered by the Germanic Eruli in 476 and then by Ostrogoths in 489. During the war between the Greek Byzantines and Goths, the city, allies of the former, was attacked by the Goths and utterly destroyed. Reconstruction began in 568, when the city was reconquered by the Byzantine general Narses, who was forced to cede it to the Lombards in the following year. Milan was then ruled by the city of Pavia. The few remaining citizens, led by their bishop Honorius, fled to Liguria: what had been one of the most prosperous cities in the Western Roman Empire was reduced to ruins in the 6th and 7th centuries. The Edict of Rothari of 643 describes in detail Lombard administrative structures of the time.

Emperor Frederick Barbarossa at the Battle of Legnano (1176) in a 1308 miniature

In 774, the Franks defeated the Lombards and conquered Northern Italy. The archbishops regained power and there was a revival of the economy with the rise of an artisan and merchant class, which in the 11th century led to the birth of the commune. After centuries in which Monza and Pavia had been the focal points of Lombardy, Milan was once again the political centre of the region. The aristocrats and mercantile classes struggled for power in the 11th century, but then joined forces

King Rothari proclaims his edict (643), miniature, Codex Legum Longobardorum

to defend the city against the emperor. Once again the city was led by a series of archbishops, some of whom, such as Ariberto d'Intimiano (1018–45), were both bishops and generals. In 1042 the free commune of Milan was founded and a new city wall built. It was demolished in 1162 when, after a siege, the Milanese were forced to open their gates to Frederick Barbarossa: for the second time the city was burned to the ground. Milan and other northern communes together formed the Lombard League, which defeated Barbarossa's troops at Legnano in 1176. Seven years later the Treaty of Constance sanctioned the freedom of these communes.

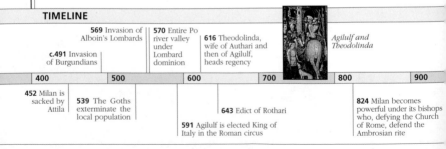

In the 13th century, Milan created a formidable canal network, the Navigli, which linked the city to Ticino in Switzerland. However, power struggles among the leading families sapped the strength of the entire city and foreshadowed its decline.

THE GREAT DYNASTIES

In 1277 at Desio, the Visconti, under Archbishop Ottone, overthrew the Torriani family. The Visconti then summoned the leading artists of the time, including Giotto, to Milan to embellish the city and its palazzi, and they commissioned new buildings such as the Castello and the Duomo *(see pp46 –9)*. The height of Visconti power was achieved under Gian Galeazzo, who became duke in 1395 and undertook an ambitious policy of expansion. Milan soon ruled most of Northern Italy and even controlled some cities in Tuscany, but the duke's dream of a united Italy under his lead came to

Coat of arms of the Visconti family

an end with his death in 1402. Visconti dynasty died out in 14 and for three years the city enjoye self-government under the Ambrosian Republic. In 1450 the *condottiere* Francesco Sforza initiated what was perhaps the most felicitous period in the history of Milan: he abandoned the Visconti expansionist policy and secured lasting peace for the city, which flourished and grew to a population of 100,000. The Visconti castle was rebuilt and became the Castello Sforzesco *(see pp64– 7)*, while architects such as Guiniforte Solari and Filarete began work on the Ospedale Maggiore, better known as Ca' Granda *(see p97)*. However, Milan's cultural golden age came with Lodovico Sforza, known as "il Moro" (1479– 1508). He was an undisciplined politician but a great patron of the arts. His policy of alliances and strategic decisions marked the end of freedom for Milan, which in 1499 fell under French dominion, yet during his rule Milanese arts and culture were second only to Medici Florence. From 1480 on, great men such as Bramante and Leonardo da Vinci were active in Milan. The former restored numerous churches and designed Santa Maria delle Grazie *(see p71)*, in whose refectory Leonardo painted *The Last Supper (see pp72–3)*, one of his many masterpieces. Leonardo also worked on major city projects such as the Navigli network of canals.

Milan in a 15th-century print

◄000	1100	1200	1300	1400	1500
1038 Archbishop Ariberto d'Intimiano leads Milanese against Corrado II and uses *Carroccio* cart with city banner as symbol of Milan	**1158** Barbarossa lays siege to Milan. In 1162 the city is destroyed by Imperial troops	**1277** Rise of the Visconti		**1447–50** Ambrosian Republic	**1482–99** Leonardo da Vinci in Milan
			1395 Gian Galeazzo Visconti becomes duke		**1499** Lodovico cedes duchy to Louis XII
1057 The Pataria vement abuses clergy	**1154** Frederick Barbarossa suppresses commune at Roncaglia	**1176** Lombard League defeats Barbarossa at Legnano	*Frederick Barbarossa*	**1450** Rise of the Sforza	**1525** Sforza return to power
			1494 Lodovico il Moro rules		**1535** Charles V takes over duchy

The Visconti and Sforza

The period of the Signorie, or family lordships, from the late 13th to the early 16th century, was one of the most successful in the history of Milan. The Visconti dynasty succeeded – especially during Gian Galeazzo's rule – in expanding the city's territories, albeit for a brief span of time. The Sforza dukedom is best known for the cultural and artistic splendour commissioned by Lodovico il Moro, who invited the leading artists and architects of the time to his court.

Gian Galeazzo
imprisoned his uncle Bernabò in 1385 and became sole ruler of Milan. He was made a duke by Emperor Wenceslaus ten years later.

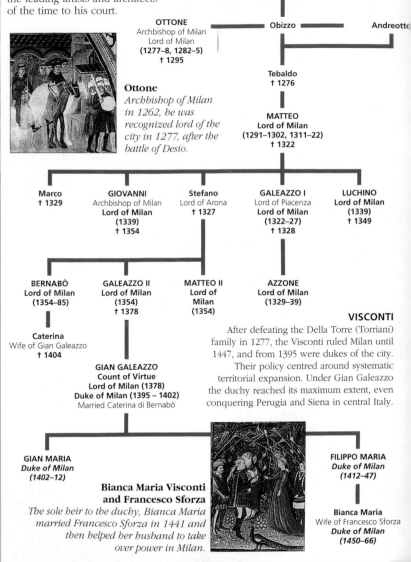

Ottone
Archbishop of Milan in 1262, he was recognized lord of the city in 1277, after the battle of Desio.

Umberto
† before 1248

OTTONE
Archbishop of Milan
Lord of Milan
(1277–8, 1282–5)
† 1295

Obizzo

Andreotto

Tebaldo
† 1276

MATTEO
Lord of Milan
(1291–1302, 1311–22)
† 1322

Marco
† 1329

GIOVANNI
Archbishop of Milan
Lord of Milan
(1339)
† 1354

Stefano
Lord of Arona
† 1327

GALEAZZO I
Lord of Piacenza
Lord of Milan
(1322–27)
† 1328

LUCHINO
Lord of Milan
(1339)
† 1349

BERNABÒ
Lord of Milan
(1354–85)

GALEAZZO II
Lord of Milan
(1354)
† 1378

MATTEO II
Lord of
Milan
(1354)

AZZONE
Lord of Milan
(1329–39)

Caterina
Wife of Gian Galeazzo
† 1404

GIAN GALEAZZO
Count of Virtue
Lord of Milan (1378)
Duke of Milan (1395 – 1402)
Married Caterina di Bernabò

VISCONTI

After defeating the Della Torre (Torriani) family in 1277, the Visconti ruled Milan until 1447, and from 1395 were dukes of the city. Their policy centred around systematic territorial expansion. Under Gian Galeazzo the duchy reached its maximum extent, even conquering Perugia and Siena in central Italy.

GIAN MARIA
Duke of Milan
(1402–12)

Bianca Maria Visconti and Francesco Sforza
The sole heir to the duchy, Bianca Maria married Francesco Sforza in 1441 and then helped her husband to take over power in Milan.

FILIPPO MARIA
Duke of Milan
(1412–47)

Bianca Maria
Wife of Francesco Sforza
Duke of Milan
(1450–66)

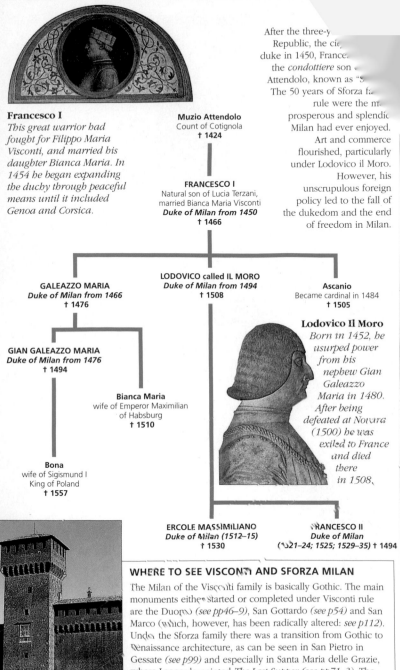

Francesco I
This great warrior had fought for Filippo Maria Visconti, and married his daughter Bianca Maria. In 1454 he began expanding the duchy through peaceful means until it included Genoa and Corsica.

After the three-y...
Republic, the ci...
duke in 1450, France...
the *condottiere* son...
Attendolo, known as "S...
The 50 years of Sforza fa...
rule were the m...
prosperous and splendi...
Milan had ever enjoyed.
Art and commerce
flourished, particularly
under Lodovico il Moro.
However, his
unscrupulous foreign
policy led to the fall of
the dukedom and the end
of freedom in Milan.

Muzio Attendolo
Count of Cotignola
† 1424

FRANCESCO I
Natural son of Lucia Terzani,
married Bianca Maria Visconti
Duke of Milan from 1450
† 1466

GALEAZZO MARIA
Duke of Milan from 1466
† 1476

LODOVICO called IL MORO
Duke of Milan from 1494
† 1508

Ascanio
Became cardinal in 1484
† 1505

GIAN GALEAZZO MARIA
Duke of Milan from 1476
† 1494

Bianca Maria
wife of Emperor Maximilian
of Habsburg
† 1510

Lodovico Il Moro
Born in 1452, he usurped power from his nephew Gian Galeazzo Maria in 1480. After being defeated at Novara (1500) he was exiled to France and died there in 1508.

Bona
wife of Sigismund I
King of Poland
† 1557

ERCOLE MASSIMILIANO
Duke of Milan (1512–15)
† 1530

FRANCESCO II
Duke of Milan
(1521–24; 1525; 1529–35) † 1494

The Castello Storzesco *is one of the symbols of the Signoria period in Milan.*

WHERE TO SEE VISCONTI AND SFORZA MILAN

The Milan of the Visconti family is basically Gothic. The main monuments either started or completed under Visconti rule are the Duomo *(see pp46–9)*, San Gottardo *(see p54)* and San Marco (which, however, has been radically altered: *see p112*). Under the Sforza family there was a transition from Gothic to Renaissance architecture, as can be seen in San Pietro in Gessate *(see p99)* and especially in Santa Maria delle Grazie, where Leonardo painted *The Last Supper (see pp71–3)*. The Ospedale Maggiore, or Ca' Granda *(see p97)* was designed by Filarete for Francesco Sforza, and the Castello Sforzesco *(see pp64–7)* was built by the Visconti but enlarged and embellished by the Sforza, hence the name.

...D SPAIN

...ance petered
...16th century
...followed by a
...eriod of decline.
...was greatly affected
...ne loss of political and
...itary importance on the
...art of the Italian states,
now battlefields for other
European powers, and
because of its wealth and
strategic position the city
was a key target. The
presence of foreign troops
was so common that it
gave rise to a bitterly sarcastic
proverb: "Franza o Spagna purché
se magna" (France or Spain, it
doesn't matter, as long as we have
something on our platter). When
Francesco Sforza died in 1535,
Emperor Charles V appointed a
governor for Milan and the city thus
officially became an Imperial
province. However, the city
nonetheless con-

Charles V in a portrait
by Titian (1532–3)

tinued to thrive and the
population grew to
130,000. Its territory
expanded and from 1548
to 1560 new city walls
were built (called the
Spanish walls) corres-
ponding to today's inner
ring road. The walls were
the most important public
works undertaken during
Spanish rule. All that is
left now is Porta Romana
arch, though not in its
original position. Many
Baroque buildings, such
as Palazzo Durini and those facing
Corso di Porta Romana, were also
built in this period. Among the
leading figures in Spanish Milan was
San Carlo Borromeo (1538–84),
cardinal and archbishop of Milan,
patron of the arts and benefactor,
who rebuilt many churches and was
one of the leading figures in the
Counter Reformation. His nephew
Federico (1564–1631) was also later
archbishop of Milan
and was immortalized
in Manzoni's novel *I
Promessi Sposi (The
Betrothed)*, a wide-
ranging portrait of
Milan under Spanish
rule. Economic and
social decline reached
its lowest point with
the 1630 plague,
which brought the
city's population down
to 60,000.

ENLIGHTENMENT MILAN
Spanish rule ended in
1706, when during the
War of Spanish Succes-

Title page of a rare
1827 edition of
Manzoni's novel

**ALESSANDRO MANZONI'S
THE BETROTHED**

Considered one of the greatest novels
in Italian literature and a masterpiece
of 19th-century European narrative,
The Betrothed (I Promessi Sposi) is
also a splendid portrait of Milan
under Spanish rule in the 1600s.
Manzoni rewrote it several times and
had three different editions published
(1820, with the title *Fermo e Lucia*,
1827 and 1840). The novel is set in
1628–31 and portrays different phases
of Milanese life. In chapter 12 the
hero Renzo is involved in the bread
riots (in Corso Vittorio Emanuele, a
plaque marks the site of the bakery), while from chapter
31 onwards there are vivid descriptions of the city
devastated by the plague of 1630.

TIMELINE

1548 Construction
of the Spanish
walls begins

1576–7 The so-
called San Carlo
plague spreads

1609 Foundation of the
Biblioteca Ambrosiana

*Original nucleus of the
Biblioteca Ambrosiana*

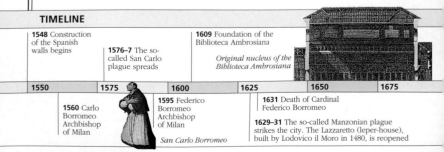

1550	1575	1600	1625	1650	1675

1560 Carlo
Borromeo
Archbishop
of Milan

1595 Federico
Borromeo
Archbishop
of Milan

San Carlo Borromeo

1631 Death of Cardinal
Federico Borromeo

1629–31 The so-called Manzonian plague
strikes the city. The Lazzaretto (leper-house),
built by Lodovico il Moro in 1480, is reopened

French troops at the city walls

sion Austrian troops occupied the city. Milan remained part of the Austro-Hungarian Empire until 1859, except for the Napoleonic period and the Cinque Giornate rebellion *(see pp24–5)*. Economic and, in particular, cultural revival marked the 18th century. Milan was one of the capitals of the Enlightenment, encouraged by Maria Theresa's wise administration (1740–80). From June 1764 to May 1766 a group of Milanese intellectuals, including Cesare Beccaria and the Verri brothers, published the periodical *Il Caffè*, influencing Italian cultural life by propounding the ideas of the French "Encyclopedists".

The lead. Giuseppe . the Teatro a. rebuilt Palazz Classical style, p renewal of the hist designed the Corso Ve. The city's flourishing cult not diminish even when the had to flee from Napoleon's in 1796. As the capital of the s. lived Cisalpine Republic, Milan w the setting for Napoleon's coronation in the Cathedral (1804) and witnessed the construction of various new building projects, including the Foro Bonaparte, the Arena and the Arco della Pace. After Napoleon's defeat, the Congress of Vienna handed Milan back to the Habsburgs, whose government, however, was quite different from the one under Maria Theresa. There were many abortive revolts, and Milan became one of the focal points of Romanticism and the struggle for Italian independence and unity as propounded in the local periodical *Il Conciliatore*. The publication was repressed by censors and its main exponents (Pellico, Confalonieri and Maroncelli) were imprisoned. The independence movement continued to grow, with the help of the operas of Verdi, and reached its peak with the revolt known as the *Cinque Giornate di Milano*, when the Milanese succeeded, albeit briefly, in driving the Austrian troops out of the city.

Maria Theresa of Austria

Abbé Longo, Alessandro Verri, Giovanni Battista Biffi and Cesare Beccaria, the founders of *Il Caffè*

Eugene of drives out last sh governor		**1778** Inauguration of La Scala opera house	**1796** French troops enter Milan		**1848** Cinque Giornate revolt
	1740 Beginning of Maria Theresa's rule in Milan		**1805** Italic Kingdom proclaimed	**1820** Pellico imprisoned by Austrians	**1848** Radetzky occupies Milan
1725	**1750**	**1775**	**1800**	**1825**	**1850**
1714 Treaty of Utrecht: Lombardy ceded to Austria	*Cesare Beccaria*	**1764–66** Pietro Verri publishes *Il Caffè* **1764** Cesare Beccaria publishes *On Crimes and Punishment*	**1818** *Il Conciliatore* published **1797** Cisalpine Republic	**1839** Cattaneo founds *Il Politecnico* **1849** Austria-Piedmont peace treaty	**1859** Milan liberated by French-Piedmontese troops

...ate Revolt

... event was preceded by ... king strike", held during the ...ee days of 1848, when the ...nese refused to buy tobacco as a ...otest against Austrian taxation. The "Five Days" revolt began on 18 March 1848. Clashes broke out after a demonstration and continued in a disorderly fashion for two days, during which ...Austrians, led by Field Marshal Radetzky, were ...tially besieged inside the Castello Sforzesco. After the formation of a War Council and a Provisional Government on 22 March at Porta Tosa, the Imperial troops were defeated and driven out of Milan.

Carlo Cattaneo (1801–69)
Cattaneo was one of the leaders in the Cinque Giornate, and later went into exile in Switzerland.

Carlo Alberto's Proclamation
With this declaration, Carlo Alberto, king of Sardinia, put himself at the head of the revolt. Yet when the opportune occasion arose he failed to attack the Austrians and in August 1848 he was forced to cede Milan to the Austrian Radetzky.

Behind the barricades were people from all social classes, demonstrating the unity of the Milanese in the battle for independence.

The Austrian Army
Field Marshal Radetzky had some 74,000 men (about a third of them Italians) at his disposal, divided into two army corps. The first and larger one was stationed in Milan.

PORTA TOSA

This painting by Carlo Canella, now in the Museo di Milano, represents the *Battle at Porta Tosa,* when the Milanese dealt the final blow to the Austrian troops on 22 March. After this historic event, the city gate, which is situated in the eastern part of the city, was renamed Porta Vittoria (Victory Gate).

Pasquale Sottocorno
Despite being crippled, this 26-year-old shoemaker managed to set fire to the military engineers' building where the enemy troops were barracked, and capture the hospital of San Marco, which was another Austrian stronghold.

ABITANTI DE

Alla testa del prode e vittorioso e
vostro suolo come il liberator vostro d
zionaria e tirannica. Molti di voi, sedot.
hanno dimenticato i sacri doveri verso il
no. Tornate devoti sotto lo scettro benigno
tore e Re. Io vi offro la mano a sincera conc
Abitanti in Lombardia, ascoltate il benevo
Confidenti accogliete le brave mie Truppe. Esse .
al cittadino pacifico ogni maggior sicurezza della pe
la proprietà, ma contro chi si ostinasse nel cieco de.
ribellione procederanno irremissibilmente con tutta la .
della legge marziale;
A voi sta la scelta; a me l'impegno di esattamente ade
pire la mia parola.
Dal Quartier-Generale di Folleggio 27 Luglio 1848.

RADETZKY

The Austrians, forced into retreat

The Austrians Return
After he had defeated King Carlo Alberto at Custoza (25 July), Radetzky returned to Lombardy, as announced in this proclamation of 27 July. He recaptured Milan on 6 August.

Over 1,600 barricades were set up throughout the city during the insurrection.

The Soldier's Widow
In Italy the struggle for independence was closely linked to Romanticism, as can be seen in works dating from this period, such as this 1851 sculpture by Giovanni Pandiani.

THE CINQUE GIORNATE REVOLT

Radetzky	The revolt spreads throughout the city and barricades are built everywhere		Radetzky proposes an armistice but is rejected	
18 March	**19 March**	**20 March**	**21 March**	**22 March**
Demonstration in the Monforte district for freedom of the press and the establishment of a Civil Guard. Radetzky is besieged in the Castello Sforzesco		Formation of the War Council and Provisional Government *Guardia Nobile helmet*		The Imperial troops suffer defeat in the last battle at Porta Tosa (renamed Porta Vittoria) and abandon Milan

ITALY'S UNIFICATION ...ulation of Milan was ...ch shows how much ... grown under Austrian ...wever, the real demo-...xplosion was yet to come. ...gh Milan did not become the ...cal capital after the unification Italy, it became the economic and cultural capital of the country. Infrastructures created by the Austrians were exploited to the full and by 1920 the city had developed into a thriving industrial metropolis. Business was booming, *Corriere della Sera*, the leading Italian daily newspaper, was founded, the city increased in size and the population exploded (there were 850,000 inhabitants in 1923). This over-rapid growth inevitably brought major social consequences: the first trade union centre was founded, and socialist groups grew in strength. Strikes and demonstrations became more and more frequent, and social tensions exploded in 1898, when a protest against the high cost of living was violently repressed by cannon fire, on the orders of General Bava Beccaris. The early 20th century witnessed the rise of an important avant-garde movement in Milan (the

A *Corriere della Sera* poster

The 1898 demonstration quelled by Bava Beccaris

second in the city after the Scapigliatura movement of the second half of the 19th century): Futurism, which was founded by Filippo Tommaso Marinetti (a plaque in Corso Venezia commemorates the event). The Futurists were not only important from an artistic standpoint, but also because their ideas and actions fitted in perfectly with the cultural temper of the times, characterized by the pro-intervention attitude regarding World War I and then the rise of Fascism. In fact, Fascism and Mussolini had a very close relationship with Milan. The original nucleus of the movement was founded in Milan in 1919. In 1943, after the fall of the regime and the foundation of the Repubblica Sociale puppet government, Milan – severely damaged by bombing raids – was the last large Italian city to remain under the control of the remaining Fascists and the Germans. On 26 April 1945, the story of Mussolini and Italian Fascism played out its final moments in Milan: the corpses of il Duce, his mistress Claretta Petacci and some party officials were put on display in Piazzale

Milan after the 1943 bombings

TIMELINE

1860	1870	1880	1890	1900	1910	1920	1930
	1866–7 Mengoni builds the Galleria Vittorio Emanuele II	**1876** Foundation of *Corriere della Sera*	**1900** Umberto I assassinated by Gaetano Bresci		**1919** Fascists meet in Piazza San Sepolcro		
	1872 Pirelli company founded	**1873** Alessandro Manzoni dies	**1898** Insurrection thwarted by Bava Beccaris	**1906** Falck firm founded	*Fiera poster*	**1920** Fiera di Milano founded	
			1901 Verdi dies at the Grand Hotel et de Milan				

Loreto, exactly the same place where some partisans had been executed a few weeks earlier.

THE POSTWAR PERIOD

On 11 May 1946, Arturo Toscanini conducted a concert celebrating the re-opening of the Teatro alla Scala, which had been destroyed by bombs during the war.

Logo of Teatro alla Scala

This historic event demonstrated the desire for recovery and recon-struction that characterized postwar Milan. The linchpin of an industrial triangle with Turin and Genoa, Milan now had 1,800,000 inhabitants. This period of secure growth, disturbed only by student protests in 1968, ended on 12 December 1969, when the explosion of a terrorist bomb in a bank in Piazza Fontana, causing a massacre, began the long, grim period of terrorist activity. The 1980s saw the development of the fashion industry that has made Milan one of the world leaders in this field. The most recent significant event in the city's history was the 199. corruption investigations v forced many members of the r parties to step down from power.

PRESENT-DAY MILAN

Thanks to the dyna-mism, productivity and inventiveness of its people, today's Milan is a leading European city, but it still has a number of problems: the decline in population, now 1.36 million, is proof of a growing dissatisfaction with a city that is con-sidered, for example, unsuitable for children. The rapid increase in com-muter traffic has not been matched by adequate long-distance public transport, which is why the city is frequently blocked by heavy traffic. Last, although Milan is probably the most multicultural city in Italy, clandestine immigration causes its own social problems. Despite this, Milan is an avant-garde city by all standards, a financial, professional and cultural leader in Italian life.

THE GROWTH OF MILAN

This map shows the growth of Milan from the original Roman city to the present-day metropolis.

KEY

- The Roman city
- The medieval city
- Up to the 18th century
- The 19th century
- The early 20th century
- Present-day Milan

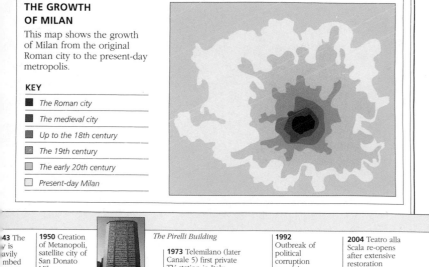

43 The y is avily mbed

1950 Creation of Metanopoli, satellite city of San Donato Milanese

The Pirelli Building

1973 Telemilano (later Canale 5) first private TV station in Italy

1992 Outbreak of political corruption scandal

2004 Teatro alla Scala re-opens after extensive restoration

| 1950 | 1960 | 1970 | 1980 | 1990 | 2000 | 2010 |

1946 Toscanini conducts the opening concert of he restored Scala

1955–60 The Pirelli Building is constructed

1969 Bomb at Piazza Fontana

1973 Bomb in Via Fatebenefratelli

1997 Dario Fo, actor and playwright, wins Nobel Prize for Literature

2000 "Needle, Thread and Knot" sculpture erected in Piazza Cadorna

MILAN AT A GLANCE

One of the many clichés about Milan is that it is a practical, industrious, even drab city, wholly dedicated to work and the world of commercial gain. In fact, besides being a leading metropolis in Europe from a financial standpoint and in terms of productivity, it is also rich in history and culture, architecture and art. The historic centre has no single dominating architectural style, and the buildings are perhaps more varied than any other city centre in Italy. The museums and galleries are among the finest in Northern Italy, and many of the leading figures in the fields of Italian art, design, culture and politics were either born in Milan or achieved success here. The following eight pages will provide brief descriptions of some of the major aspects of the city, while below is a selection of top attractions that no visitor to Milan should miss.

MILAN'S TOP TEN ATTRACTIONS

Sant'Ambrogio
See pp84–7

Teatro alla Scala
See pp52–3

Pinacoteca Ambrosiana
See pp56–9

Ca' Granda
See p97

San Lorenzo alle Colonne
See pp80–1

Abbazia di Chiaravalle
See pp102–3

Duomo
See pp46–9

Castello Sforzesco
See pp64–7

Pinacoteca di Brera
See pp114–7

The Last Supper
See pp72–3

◁ Statues decorating the exterior of the Duomo

Famous Residents and Visitors

Many leading figures in Italian cultural life are connected in some way with Milan, from intellectuals, journalists and politicians to composers, writers and poets. The Italian novelist Alessandro Manzoni was born in Milan, and many other artists have been drawn here, hoping to make their fortune (an illustrious example is Giuseppe Verdi) or, more simply, to find work. One of the most widespread, and perhaps most accurate, sayings about Milan is that it is an open, receptive city ready to give strangers and foreigners a sincere, if brusque, welcome.

Carlo Emilio Gadda (1893–1973)
Milanese by birth, Gadda was one of the great 20th-century authors. One of his major works, L'Adalgis *celebrates the lives of middle-class Milanese and ends with the hero cleaning the tombs in the Monumental Cemetery*

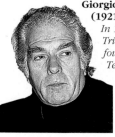

Giorgio Strehler (1921–97)
In 1947 the great Trieste-born director founded the Piccolo Teatro della Città di Milano with Paolo Grassi. It was the first permanent theatre in Italy

NORTHWEST
(see pp60–75)

Leonardo da Vinci (1452–1519)
In 1482 Lodovico il Moro invited Leonardo da Vinci to his court in Milan, where he remained for almost 20 years. He left a number of works, including the Codex Atlanticus, *now in the Biblioteca Ambrosiana and* The Last Supper, *in Santa Maria delle Grazie (see pp72–3).*

SOUTHWES
(see pp76–9)

| 0 metres | 700 |
| 0 yards | 700 |

Benito Mussolini (1883–1945)
In 1919, in Milan's Piazza San Sepolcro, Mussolini founded the Fasci Nazionali di Combattimento, *the first nucleus of the future Fascist movement. On 16 December 1944 Mussolini gave his last speech at the Teatro Lirico in Milan. A few months later, on 26 April 1945, his corpse was hung upside down in Piazzale Loreto.*

Giuseppe Verdi (1813–1901)

Born in Busseto, in the province of Parma, Verdi moved to Milan at a very early age. His third opera, Nabucco *(1842), brought him fame. He died at the Grand Hotel et de Milan, which he had made his home.*

Alessandro Manzoni (1785–1873)

Manzoni wrote what is considered the greatest Italian novel, The Betrothed, *as well as plays and poetry. His house in Piazza Belgioioso (see p51) is open to the public.*

Cesare Beccaria (1738–94)

A leading exponent of the Enlightenment movement in Milan, Beccaria wrote its most representative work, On Crimes and Punishment. *In the square named after him is a monument in his honour.*

NORTHEAST
(see pp104–23)

SOUTHEAST
(see pp92–103)

The Verri Brothers

Pietro (1728–97) and Alessandro (1741–1816) Verri met other noted Enlightenment figures at the Caffè Greco, opposite the Duomo, where they conceived the influential periodical Il Caffè.

Carlo Porta (1775–1821)

A poet who wrote in Milanese dialect, Porta offered a vivacious description of his time in his satirical poems. There is a monument in his honour in Piazza Santo Stefano, which was the setting for one of his best-known works, Ninetta del Verzee.

Milan's Best: Churches and Basilicas

The churches of Milan are built in two basic architectural styles: Lombard Romanesque, which can be seen elsewhere in the region, and the Counter-Reformation Mannerism of Milan under the Borromeos. The only exception is the Duomo, a splendid example of Lombard Gothic. There are very few examples of older styles. This is partly the result of destructive invasions and time, but is mostly due to the fact that the city is built just above the water table, and older buildings had to be demolished to make way for new ones.

Santa Maria delle Grazie
Besides being home to Leonardo's Last Supper, this church designed by Solari and Bramante, is a marvellous example of Renaissance architecture (see pp71–3).

Basilica of Sant'Ambrogio
The famous church founded by Sant'Ambrogio has a long architectural history, culminating in the restoration carried out to repair damage caused by the bombs of World War II (see pp84–7).

NORTHWEST
(see pp60–75)

SOUTHW
(see pp76

Basilica of San Lorenzo
This late 4th-century basilica still has some original architectural elements, such as the columns that surround the courtyard (see pp80–81).

Basilica of Sant'Eustorgio
Inside this 9th-century basilica are several aristocratic chapels, including the Cappella Portinari, one of the great examples of Renaissance architecture in Milan (see p90).

San Marco
The basic structure is 13th-century
Romanesque, while the Neo-Gothic façade
was built in 1871. The three statues depicting
San Marco between Sant'Ambrogio and
Sant'Agostino (above) are works of the
Campionese school (see p112).

San Fedele
This typical example of Counter-
Reformation architecture was
begun in 1569. Pellegrini's original
design was completed by Bassi,
who built the façade, and by
Richini (see p50).

NORTHEAST
(see pp104–23)

HISTORIC
CENTRE
(pp42–55)

SOUTHEAST
(see pp92–103)

Duomo
Milan's cathedral is the third largest church in the
world (see pp46–9). It was begun by the Visconti
family in 1386 and finished by Napoleon in 1805
– more than four centuries later.

0 metres	700
0 yards	700

Basilica of San Nazaro Maggiore
Founded by Sant'Ambrogio towards the
end of the 4th century, the basilica has
been altered many times, but recent
restoration work has revived its original
austere beauty. Do not miss the Trivulzio
Chapel (see p96).

Milan's Best: Museums and Galleries

17th-century clock,
Museo della Scienza e
della Tecnica

Besides housing priceless works of art, the museums and art galleries of Milan also reflect the history of the city. The Pinacoteca di Brera was founded at the height of the Enlightenment period and the Ambrosiana is the result of the patronage of religious art by the Borromeo family. The Castello Sforzesco collections date from the period of the *Signorie*, while the Galleria d'Arte Moderna is a sign of civic commitment to fine arts. Last, the Museo Bagatti Valsecchi and Poldi Pezzoli, private collections, are typical manifestations of the Milanese love of art.

Pinacoteca di Brera
One of Northern Italy's largest art galleries has works from the 14th to the 19th century. Above, Pietà by Giovanni Bellini (see pp114–7).

Musei del Castello
The Castello Sforzesco museums are rich in sculpture, furniture and applied arts and also include a gallery with works by great artists, such as this Madonna and Child with the Infant St John *the Baptist by Correggio (see pp64–7).*

NORTHWEST
(see pp60–75)

Museo Nazionale della Scienza e della Tecnica
The Science and Technology Museum has wooden models of Leonardo's inventions and a section given over to clocks, computers and means of communication and transport (see p88).

SOUTHWEST
(see pp76–9)

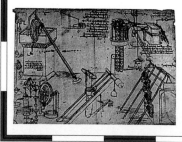

Pinacoteca Ambrosiana
This art gallery was founded by Cardinal Federico Borromeo in the 17th century to provide models for the students at the Fine Arts Academy. The collections include works by artists such as Caravaggio and Raphael (see pp56–9), while the Biblioteca Ambrosiana (library) contains the precious Codex Atlanticus *by Leonardo da Vinci.*

Museo Poldi Pezzoli
Together with the many works by Italian artists in this splendid residence-cum-museum (see p108) *is Lucas Cranach's* Portrait of Martin Luther.

Museo dell'Ottocento
Villa Belgiojoso Bonaparte (see p121) *houses 19th-century Italian art collections, the Museo Marini, the Vismara Collection and the Grassi Collection. Right,* Matilda Juva Branca *(1851) by Francesco Hayez.*

NORTHEAST
(see pp104–123)

Museo Bagatti Valsecchi
This marvellous example of a 19th-century private residence contains 16th-century handicrafts, furniture, arms, ivory pieces, paintings and ceramics (see p109).

Museo del Duomo
The Duomo Museum was founded in 1953 and holds fine sculptures and other objects representing the religious history of Milan. Right, the 16th-century Ambrosian Monstrance, *made of rock crystal and precious stones* (see p49).

HISTORIC CENTRE
(pp42–59)

SOUTHEAST
(see pp92–103)

Civico Museo d'Arte Contemporanea
On the second floor of Palazzo Reale, now under restoration (see p54), *this museum has a good Futurist collection and works by famous artists such as Picasso and Klee. The sculpture collection is also important, and includes this* Woman at the Mirror *by Lucio Fontana (1934).*

| 0 metres | 700 |
| 0 yards | 700 |

MILAN THROUGH THE YEAR

Milan offers a range of different events and attractions at different seasons of the year, from traditional to commercial. The city's citizens are still attached to traditional religious celebrations such as the Carnevale Ambrosiano (Milanese Carnival) and the festivities that take place around 7 December, the Festival of Sant'Ambrogio, the city's patron saint. This is also the date of opening night at La Scala, the world-famous opera house. Such traditional and characteristic festivities alternate with other events that are perhaps more in keeping with the image of a modern, industrial city. Among these are Fashion Week, one of the world's top fashion shows, held twice a year, and SMAU, an important international multimedia and communications technology trade show.

Private courtyards in Milan, open to the public in the spring

SPRING

After the long Milanese winter, local inhabitants welcome the arrival of spring with a sigh of relief. The pleasant spring breezes clear the air of the notorious Milanese smog and the city seems to take on different colours. On very clear days, if you look northwards you will see the peaks of the Alps, which are still covered with snow – one of the finest views the city affords at this time of year.

Towards the end of spring, the clear weather may very well give way to showers and even violent storms, which may blow up in the space of just a few hours, causing problems with city traffic.

This is the season when tourist activity resumes at the lakes. Boat services start up again and the water becomes a major weekend attraction for the Milanese once more.

MARCH

MODIT-Milanovendemoda *(beginning of month).* The autumn-winter collections of the leading international and Italian fashion designers go on show.

Milano-SanRemo *(third Sat).* Part of the city centre hosts the start of this prestigious international bicycle race.

Oggi Aperto *(third weekend).* Monuments and historic buildings usually closed to the public are now open.

BIT. The Fiera (Milan's Exhibition Centre) hosts an international tourist trade show.

APRIL

Fiera dei Fiori *(Mon after Easter).* In and around Via Moscova, near the Sant'Angelo Franciscan convent, is this fair devoted mainly to flower growing.

Bagutta-Pittori all'Aria Aperta *(third week).* The famous Via Bagutta plays host to a fascinating outdoor exhibition for artists' work.

Stramilano *(mid-Apr).* This celebrated marathon is for professionals and amateurs alike and attracts an average of 50,000 competitors every year.

MAY

Milano Cortili Aperti. The courtyards of the city's private residences are open to the public.

Pittori sul Naviglio. Outdoor art display along the Alzaia Naviglio Grande canal *(see p89).*

Estate all'Idroscalo. Near Linate airport, the Milan seaplane airport inaugurates its summer season with sports events, water entertainment and concerts.

The Fashion Week, held in March

Sagra del Carroccio. At Legnano, 30 km (19 miles) from Milan, there is a commemoration of the battle of 1176, when the Lombard League defeated Emperor Frederick Barba-rossa: parades in costume and folk festivities and events.

The March Milan-SanRemo race, opening the Italian cycling season

AVERAGE DAILY HOURS OF SUNSHINE

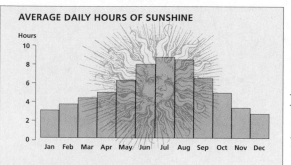

Hours: 10, 8, 6, 4, 2, 0

Jan Feb Mar Apr May Jun Jul Aug Sep Oct Nov Dec

Sunshine Hours
The hours of sunshine in Milan are in line with the Mediterranean average. However, in autumn and winter the weather can be very foggy, which is a typical feature of the climate in the Po river valley, exacerbated by city pollution. The lakes, surrounded by the Alps, are more shaded in the morning and evening.

Parco Sempione, a major venue for summer entertainment

SUMMER

June is one of the most pleasant months to visit Milan because the climate is mild and the programme of cultural and sports events is truly packed. In July the torrid, muggy summer heat (the temperature may be as high as 40° C/104° F), together with the heavy traffic, can make sightseeing quite uncomfortable.

In August, most of the factories and offices close for the summer holidays and the empty city is an unusual and, in some respects, quite pleasant sight. The same streets that were crowded a week earlier are now quiet, even restful.

Despite the exodus, many events, both cultural and recreational, are held in Milan during the summer.

This is the busiest season for visiting the lakes of Northern Italy, but also the sunniest. Even at the peak of the summer heat, the water can have a cooling effect.

JUNE

Festa del Naviglio *(first Sun)*. You can find everything under the sun at this festival, held in the atmospheric setting of the illuminated Navigli canals: street artists and performers, concerts, sports, an antiques market, handicrafts, regional cooking.

Milano d'Estate *(Jun–Aug)*. This marks the beginning of summer entertainment in the city (concerts, exhibits, various cultural events), which takes place in the Parco Sempione.

Sagra di San Cristoforo *(third Sun)*. The patron saint of travellers, St Christopher, is celebrated along the Naviglio, in the square facing the church. In the evening decorated barges glide along the canals.

Estate all'Umanitaria. The Humanitarian Association organizes a festival of cinema, dance, music, theatre and cartoons and shows for children.

Fotoshow. An interesting video, photography and optics show in the Fiera (Exhibition Centre) pavilions.

Orticola. Flower growing and garden furnishings show and market in the Porta Venezia public gardens *(see p120)*.

Sagra di San Giovanni. At Monza, a few miles north of Milan, the patron saint's feast day is celebrated with sports and cultural events, some of which are held at a splendid venue – the park at the Villa Reale.

JULY AND AUGUST

Festival Latino-Americano. The Forum di Assago hosts this lively festival of Latin-American music, handicrafts and cuisine.

Arianteo. At the Rotonda di Via Besana *(see p100)*, the Anteo motion-picture theatre organizes a series of outdoor showings, which includes all the most important films featured in Milan's cinemas and theatres during the year.

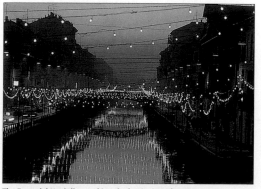

The Festa del Naviglio, marking the beginning of summer events

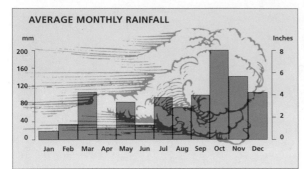

AVERAGE MONTHLY RAINFALL

mm | Inches

200 — 8
160 — 6
120 —
80 — 4
40 — 2
0 — 0

Jan Feb Mar Apr May Jun Jul Aug Sep Oct Nov Dec

Rainfall
The average monthly rainfall in the Milan area can vary quite considerably during the year. The wettest season is certainly autumn, when it may rain for several days without a break. In late spring and summer the average rainfall level may increase because of unexpected storms.

AUTUMN

September in Milan really gives you the impression of life beginning anew. In general, by the last week of August the Milanese have returned from holiday, but it is only in September that things get back into full swing.

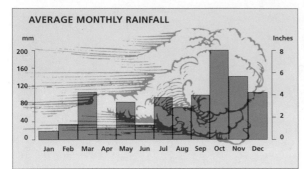

A Ferrari in action at Monza

As far as the weather is concerned, fog and rain alternate with lovely clear days with that typical "Lombard sky" which Alessandro Manzoni, in *The Betrothed*, described as being "so beautiful when it is beautiful, so blue, so serene".

SEPTEMBER

Premier League Football (soccer). By September the Italian football season is under way (the opening match takes place on the last Sunday in August). The football season is of great importance to the city, which is home to two of Italy's top teams, Inter and Milan. **Panoramica di Venezia** (*early Sep*). Milan cinemas show films from the Venice Film Festival while they are being screened there. **Gran Premio di Monza**. Held at one of the top motor racing circuits, the Grand Prix of Italy is often crucial to the outcome of the Formula One competition.

OCTOBER

Fiera Di Chiaravalle (*first Mon*). This famous fair is held in the shade of the *ciribiciaccola* (as the Milanese call the bell tower of the Chiaravalle Cistercian abbey, *see pp102–3*). The fair features music, dancing and an outdoor art exhibition. **SMAU** (*first week*). International multimedia show held in the Fiera

The Fiera, host to both SMAU and fashion shows

Exhibition Centre: IT, from computers for offices to CD-Roms and Virtual Reality. **MODIT-Milanovendemoda** (*beginning of month*). The second major fashion show for leading Italian and international fashion designers. The spring-summer collections in various show-rooms and the Fiera pavilions.

NOVEMBER

Premio Bagutta. Milan's most important literary prize is awarded.

PUBLIC HOLIDAYS
New Year's Day (1 Jan)
Epiphany (6 Jan)
Easter Sunday & Monday
Liberation Day (25 Apr)
Labour Day (1 May)
Festa della Repubblica (2 June)
Ferragosto (15 Aug)
All Saints' Day (1 Nov)
Sant'Ambrogio (7 Dec)
Immacolate Conception (8 Dec)
Christmas (25 Dec)
Santo Stefano (26 Dec)

San Siro stadium, packed with fans at the beginning of the season

AVERAGE MONTHLY TEMPERATURE

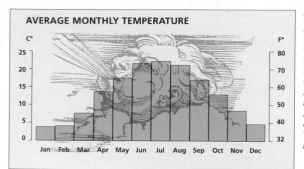

Temperature
Milan is inland and there are big differences in temperature between winter and summer. The winters can be very cold indeed, particularly in December and January, typical of continental Europe, while there may be torrid heat in summer. The climate is always very humid.

WINTER

Characterized by severe cold (heavy snowfall is not rare), the Milanese winter is "warmed up" by a rich and fascinating programme of cultural events, major holidays and special occasions. The city becomes especially lively around the feast day of Sant'Ambrogio (St Ambrose), the local patron saint, and then for Christmas, which is preceded by the usual shopping sprees in the city-centre shops. On the cultural side, the theatres of Milan present a high-quality theatre season, headed by the world-famous Piccolo Teatro.

Typical antiques stalls at the Oh bej Oh bej fair

Christmas decorations in the Galleria Vittorio Emanuele II

DECEMBER

Festa di Sant'Ambrogio
(*7 Dec*). This is the locals' favourite holiday, just before Immaculate Conception (*8 Dec*). Sant'Ambrogio is celebrated with many events: the jam-packed **Fiera degli Oh bej Oh bej**, a street fair featuring antiques as well as a

vast assortment of articles. It is held in the streets around the basilica of Sant'Ambrogio (*see pp84–7*).

La Scala. The season at the world famous opera house (*see pp52–3*) starts on 7 December. The opening night is a major cultural event, and an important occasion in the Milanese social calendar.

Teatro Grassi (ex Piccolo Teatro). Milan's other famous theatre, founded by Paolo Grassi and world-class director Giorgio Strehler, also inaugurates its programme of plays on 7 December.

JANUARY

Corteo dei Re Magi (*6 Jan*). A traditional procession with a *tableau vivant* of the Nativity goes from the Duomo to Sant'Eustorgio.

Fiera di Senigallia (*every Sat all year long*). Along the Darsena is a colourful market offering ethnic handicrafts, records and bicycles.

Mercato dell'Antiquariato di Brera (*third Sat of month, all year*). Stalls with antiques, books, postcards, jewellery.

FEBRUARY

Carnevale Ambrosiano.
The longest carnival in the world ends on the first Saturday of Lent. Floats and stock Milanese characters, such as Meneghin and Cecca, take part in a parade to Piazza del Duomo, which is filled with children throwing confetti everywhere.

Taking part in the Carnevale Ambrosiano in Piazza del Duomo

MILAN AREA BY AREA

HISTORIC CENTRE 42–59

NORTHWEST MILAN 60–75

SOUTHWEST MILAN 76–91

SOUTHEAST MILAN 92–103

NORTHEAST MILAN 104–123

TWO GUIDED WALKS 124–127

HISTORIC CENTRE

The area around the Duomo was the religious centre of Milan in the 4th century. Up to the 14th century it was the site of the basilicas of Santa Tecla and Santa Maria Maggiore and the Early Christian baptisteries, San Giovanni alle Fonti and Santo Stefano. These were all demolished to make room for the new cathedral. The political and administrative centre of the city was the nearby Palazzo della Ragione. At that time Milan was only slightly larger than the present-day historic centre; in fact, what is today Piazza della Scala was on the edge of town. Piazza del Duomo was the focus of small businesses until the 18th

Leonardo da Vinci, in Piazza della Scala

century, and a stage for the city's major religious and civic ceremonies. In the 19th century it became the nucleus from which avenues radiated. In the 1860s the decaying dwellings and the shops around the Duomo were demolished to make way for the construction of the then futuristic Galleria, the symbol of Milan after the unification of Italy. The damage caused by bombs in World War II created large empty areas later occupied by many modern buildings. The Historic Centre is always thronging with visitors, drawn by the world-famous churches, museums and galleries and also by the excellent shops.

SIGHTS AT A GLANCE

Streets, Squares and Historic Buildings
Casa degli Omenoni **6**
Casa Manzoni
　and Piazza Belgioioso **7**
Galleria Vittorio Emanuele II **2**
Palazzo Borromeo **14**
Palazzo Marino **4**
Palazzo Reale **10**

Piazza del Liberty and Corso
　Vittorio Emanuele II **8**
Piazza Mercanti **11**

Churches
Duomo pp46–9 **1**
San Fedele **5**
San Giorgio al Palazzo **15**
San Gottardo in Corte **9**

San Sepolcro **13**
Santa Maria presso San Satiro **16**

Galleries
Pinacoteca Ambrosiana
　pp56–9 **12**

Theatres
Teatro alla Scala pp52–3 **3**

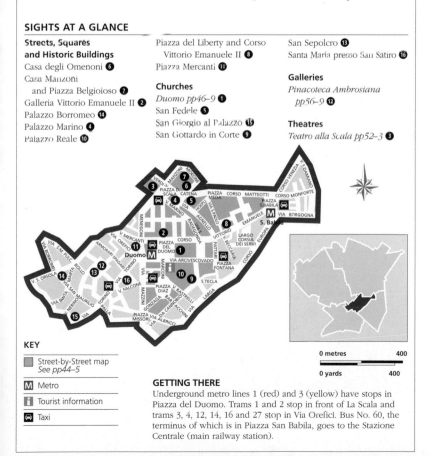

KEY

▣	Street-by-Street map See pp44–5
M	Metro
i	Tourist information
🚖	Taxi

0 metres　　　　400
0 yards　　　　400

GETTING THERE
Underground metro lines 1 (red) and 3 (yellow) have stops in Piazza del Duomo. Trams 1 and 2 stop in front of La Scala and trams 3, 4, 12, 14, 16 and 27 stop in Via Orefici. Bus No. 60, the terminus of which is in Piazza San Babila, goes to the Stazione Centrale (main railway station).

◁ **The Galleria Vittorio Emanuele II, Milan's elegant "drawing room" since 1867**

Street-by-Street: Piazza del Duomo

San Fedele
This church, a typical example of Counter-Reformation architecture, is popular with the old Milanese aristocracy ❺

Casa degli Omenoni

Piazza del Duomo, designed by Giuseppe Mengoni and opened in 1865 after protracted difficulties, is the ideal starting point for a visit to Milan's historic centre. The area is packed with visitors fascinated by the "great machine of the Duomo", as Alessandro Manzoni describes the cathedral in *The Betrothed*. There are numerous spots where the Milanese like to meet for an apéritif on Sunday morning. Young people prefer to go to Corso Vittorio Emanuele II, which has most of the cinemas as well as many shops and department stores.

Sculpture, Casa degli Omenoni

VIA MANZONI

PIAZZA SCALA

PIAZZA SAN FEDELE

VIA MENGONI

VIA GROSSI

★ **Teatro alla Scala**
This was the first monument in Milan to be rebuilt after the 1943 bombings ❸

Palazzo Marino

Piazza Mercanti

Zucca in Galleria is a popular café, decorated with mosaics and décor dating from 1921.

★ **Galleria Vittorio Emanuele II**
The Galleria was one of the first iron and glass constructions in Italy ❷

0 metres	100
0 yards	100

For hotels and restaurants in this area see p160 and pp172–3

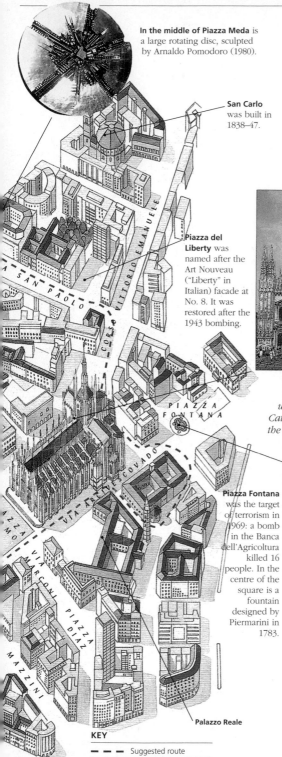

In the middle of Piazza Meda is a large rotating disc, sculpted by Arnaldo Pomodoro (1980).

San Carlo was built in 1838–47.

Piazza del Liberty was named after the Art Nouveau ("Liberty" in Italian) facade at No. 8. It was restored after the 1943 bombing.

LOCATOR MAP
See Street Finder, maps 3, 4, 7, 8, 10

★ **Duomo**
The third largest church in the world after St Peter's and Seville Cathedral, the Duomo towers over the large square named after it ❶

Piazza Fontana was the target of terrorism in 1969: a bomb in the Banca dell'Agricoltura killed 16 people. In the centre of the square is a fountain designed by Piermarini in 1783.

Palazzo Reale

KEY

- - - Suggested route

STAR SIGHTS

★ Duomo

★ Galleria Vittorio Emanuele II

★ Teatro alla Scala

Duomo ●

Statue in the interior

The construction of the Duomo began in 1386, with the city's bishop, Antonio da Saluzzo, as its patron. Duke Gian Galeazzo Visconti invited Lombard, German and French architects to supervise the works and insisted they use Candoglia marble, which was transported along the Navigli canals. The official seal AUF (*ad usum fabricae*), stamped on the slabs, exempted them from customs duty. The cathedral was consecrated in 1418, yet remained unfinished until the 19th century, when Napoleon, who was crowned King of Italy here, had the façade completed.

La Madonnina
The 4.16-m (14-ft) gilded statue of the Madonna was sculpted by Giuseppe Bini in 1774.

★ **Stained-Glass Windows**
Most of the windows depict scenes from the Bible, and date from the 19th century. The oldest one – the fifth in the right-hand aisle – dates back to 1470–75 and depicts the life of Christ, while the newest one (the seventh) dates from 1988.

Flying buttresses

★ **Trivulzio Candelabrum**
This masterpiece of medieval goldsmithery was donated in 1562 by Gian Battista Trivulzio. On the pedestal there are fantastic monsters and figures representing arts, crafts and the virtues.

Crypt

THE BUILDING OF MILAN CATHEDRAL

1386 The first stone of the Duomo is laid	**1567** Pellegrino Tibaldi ("il Pellegrini") redesigns the presbytery	**1656** Carlo Buzzi continues façade in Gothic style	**1774** The Madonnina is placed on the tallest spire		**1838–65** The Bertinis make the apse windows

1300	1400	1500	1600	1700	1800	1900

1418 Pope Martin V consecrates the high altar		**1500** Central spire inaugurated	**1617** Francesco Maria Richini begins work on the façade	**1813** façade completed with Gothic spires	**1981–4** Presbytery piers restored

Martin V

★ **Roof Terraces**
The view of the city from the roof terraces is simply unforgettable. You can also have a close-up look at the central spire. The roof bristles with spires, the oldest of which dates from 1404.

About 3,500 statues lend movement to the massive Duomo. They are typically medieval, representing saints, animals and monsters.

A plaque confirms that the Duomo is dedicated to Maria Nascente.

The Interior
The five aisles in the nave are separated by 52 piers, whose capitals are decorated with statues.

Main entrance

STAR FEATURES

★ Stained-Glass Windows

★ Trivulzio Candelabrum

★ Roof Terraces

The Doors
The five doors were made from 1840 to 1965. Right, The Flagellation by Ludovico Pogliaghi, a bronze relief in the central door.

Exploring the Duomo

So that the Duomo could be built, a great Jubilee was proclaimed in 1390 in order to urge the Milanese to contribute money and manual labour to carry out the work. The initial plan was to build it in fired bricks, as the excavations in the northern sacristy have revealed, but in 1387 Duke Gian Galeazzo Visconti, who wanted the cathedral to be seen as a great symbol of his power, demanded that marble should be used instead and that the architectural style should be International Gothic. Building continued over five centuries, resulting in the obvious mixture of styles that characterizes the cathedral.

Statue of Sant'Ambrogio

The presbytery, with the small ciborium dome in the foreground

THE FAÇADE

Up to the first level of windows the façade is Baroque. It was completed in the 19th century with Neo-Gothic ogival windows and spires, revealing the difficulties entailed in building the Duomo.

THE INTERIOR

Tall cross vaults cover the interior and the five aisles in the nave are separated by 52 piers (for the 52 weeks of the year). The capitals on the piers are decorated with statues of saints. Behind the façade, embedded in the floor, is a meridian ①, installed in 1786 by the Brera astronomers. It marked astronomical noon, thanks to a ray

of sunlight that enters from the first bay of the south aisle on the right-hand side.

This is a good starting point for a visit to the Duomo. To the right is the sarcophagus of Archbishop Ariberto d'Intimiano ②, bearing a copy of the crucifix that he donated to the San Dionigi monastery (the original is in the Museo del Duomo). Next to this, on the left, is a plaque with the date of the foundation of the cathedral. The corresponding stained-glass window, executed in the old mosaic technique, relates the *Life of St John the Evangelist* (1473–7). The stained-glass windows in the next three bays, showing episodes from the Old Testament, date from the 16th

Stained-glass window, detail

century. In the fifth bay there is a stained-glass window executed between 1470 and 1475 that illustrates the *Life of Christ* ③. Compare this with the other window in the seventh bay – it was made in 1988 and is dedicated to Cardinals Schuster and Ferrari ④. The presbytery ⑤ is constructed in the style imposed in 1567 by Pellegrini who, at the request of San Carlo Borromeo, made this part of the Duomo the Lombard model of a typical Counter-Reformation church. In the middle, under the ciborium behind the altar, is the Tabernacle ⑥, donated by Pius IV to his nephew San Carlo (St Charles). In front of them are two 16th-century gilded copper pulpits ⑦ with

FLOOR PLAN

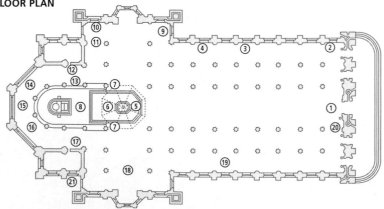

THE HOLY NAIL OF THE CROSS

Tabernacle of the Nail of the Cross

In the vault above the choir, a red light marks the location of the niche where a nail from Christ's Cross has been kept since 1461. The nail, which was once kept in the early medieval Santa Maria Maggiore, is in the shape of a horse-shoe and was found by St Helena and later given to her son, Emperor Constantine. It was later donated to Sant'-Ambrogio and carried by San Carlo in procession during the 1576 plague. It is shown to the public every 14 September, when the Bishop of Milan is raised up to the level of the niche which holds the nail in a kind of decorated balcony, drawn by invisible pulleys.

episodes from the Old and New Testaments, surmounted by the organs painted by Giovanni Ambrogio Figino, Camillo Procaccini and Giuseppe Meda.

Behind the altar is an extraordinary wooden choir with the *Life of Sant'Ambrogio* ⑧, carved in 1572–1620. In the right-hand transept is the funerary monument of Gian Giacomo Medici ⑨, the brother of Pope Pius IV, which was once attributed to Michelangelo but is in fact the work of Leone Leoni (1560–63). Past the chapel dedicated to St John the Good, Bishop of Milan in the 7th century, above the side entrance is the splendid stained-glass window of St Catherine of Alexandria ⑩, designed by the Arcimboldi brothers in 1556. A little further on is the strange statue of the flayed St Bartholomew ⑪, signed and dated 1562 by Marco d'Agrate.

At the beginning of the ambulatory there is a *Deposition* on the southern door of the sacristy ⑫ (1393), dedicated to the "Mysteries of the Virgin Mary". Steps ⑬ lead to the crypt (1606), where San Carlo Borromeo is buried, the Duomo Treasury, with its exceptional collection of church vestments and objects, and the Coro Jemale, a small 16th-century room decorated with fine stucco-work (check out the relief sculpture cycle of the *Life of the Virgin Mary*, a 17th-century masterpiece). The apse is illuminated by the

three huge 19th-century stained-glass windows by the Bertini brothers with episodes from the Old ⑯ and New ⑭ Testaments and the Apocalypse ⑮. The ambulatory ends at the northern portal of the sacristy ⑰, with *Christ the Lord and Judge* (1389). The left-hand transept is dominated by the 5-m (16-ft) bronze Trivulzio Candelabrum ⑱, a 12th-century masterpiece by the goldsmith Nicola da Verdun. The candelabrum carries scenes from the Old Testament and the Three Wise Men riding towards the enthroned Virgin. Going down the north aisle, you will

Chalice in the Duomo Treasury

see the Chapel of the Crucifix ⑲ carried by San Carlo in procession during the 1576 plague. Behind this is a window with a depiction of the *Discovery of the True Cross by St Helena* (1571–77). To the left of the entrance, steps lead down to the

remains of an Early Christian apse of Santa Tecla and an octagonal baptistery ⑳ where, according to tradition, Sant'Ambrogio (St Ambrose) baptized St Augustine in AD 387. From San Carlo's feast day to Epiphany, the *Quadroni di San Carlo* go on display in the nave. These paintings, the work of leading 17th-century Lombard artists, depict the story of the life and miracles of San Carlo.

ROOF TERRACES

On the way to the lift ㉑ which goes up to the roof, you should go to the apse to admire the central stained-glass window, designed by Filippino degli Organi in 1402. From the roof there is a magnificent view of the city and the mountains to the north, as well as the Duomo spires and statues and even the buttresses below.

MUSEO DEL DUOMO

The Cathedral museum, founded in 1953, is at No. 15 Via Arcivescovado. It houses paintings, sculptures, religious objects and stained-glass windows from the Duomo. Among the best works on display are the 15th-century *St Paul the Hermit*, Tintoretto's *Christ among the Doctors* (1530) and a wooden model of the Duomo, begun in 1519. Rooms 18 and 19 document the difficult restoration of the four central piers (1981–4).

One of the exhibition rooms in the Museo del Duomo

Palazzo Marino, the Town Hall since 1860, and the 1872 statue of Leonardo da Vinci on the right

Galleria Vittorio Emanuele II ❷

Piazza della Scala, Piazza del Duomo. **Map** 7 C1 (10 D2). Ⓜ *1, 3 Duomo.*

The Galleria is an elegant arcade lined with cafés, shops and a famous restaurant, Savini *(see p173)*. Work began in 1865, overseen by the architect Giuseppe Mengoni, and it was opened two years later by the king, Vittorio Emanuele II, after whom it was named. The gallery was designed to connect Piazza del Duomo and Piazza della Scala, and formed part of an ambitious urban renewal project. On the floor in the central octagonal area, directly under the 47-m (154-ft) high glass dome, is the heraldic symbol of the Savoy family, a white cross on a red ground. Around it are the arms of four major Italian cities: the bull of Turin, the wolf of Rome, the lily of Florence and the red cross on

a white ground (Milan). On the vault are mosaics of Asia, Africa, Europe and America.

Teatro alla Scala ❸

See pp52–3.

Palazzo Marino ❹

Piazza della Scala. **Map** 3 C5 (10 D2). Ⓜ *1, 3 Duomo.* ◐ *to the public.*

This palazzo was designed in 1558 by Galeazzo Alessi for the banker Tommaso Marino, but remained unfinished until 1892, when Luca Beltrami completed the façade. From Via Marino on the right you can see the richly decorated, porticoed courtyard of honour.

According to tradition the palazzo, home of Milan Town Hall since 1860, was the birthplace of Marianna de Leyva, the famous nun of Monza described by Alessandro Manzoni in *The Betrothed* as the "Signora".

San Fedele ❺

Piazza San Fedele. **Map** 3 C5 (10 D3). **Tel** *02-86 35 21.* Ⓜ *1, 3 Duomo.* ▦ *1, 2.* ▥ *61.* ◐ *7am–2:30pm, 4–7pm Mon–Fri.* ✝ *8, 11am, 12:45, 5:30pm Mon–Fri; 8, 11am, 6.30pm pre-hols; 9:30, 11am, 6:30, 8:30pm hols.*

This church is the Milanese seat of the Jesuit Order, commissioned by San Carlo Borromeo from Pellegrino Tibaldi in 1569. The work was continued by Martino Bassi and the dome, crypt and choir were designed by Francesco Maria Richini (1633–52). With its austere architecture and nave without aisles, this is a typical Counter-Reformation church. The façade is being restored, but the interior has three interesting paintings. By the first altar on the right is *St Ignatius's Vision* by Giovan Battista Crespi, known as "il Cerano" (c.1622). A *Transfiguration* by Bernardino Campi (1565) is in the atrium after the second altar on the left; Campi also painted the *Blessed Virgin and Child,* by the second altar (left). These last two works came from Santa Maria della Scala, which was demolished to make room for La Scala opera house *(see pp52–3).*

The wooden furniture is also worth a closer look: the confessionals (1596) have scenes from the life of Christ carved by Giovanni Taurini, and the cupboards in Richini's sacristy (1624–28) are by Daniele Ferrari (1639). A statue of the writer Alessandro Manzoni, whose death certificate is kept in San Fedele, stands in the square.

Galleria Vittorio Emanuele II, inaugurated in 1867

For hotels and restaurants in this area see p160 and pp172–3

Casa degli Omenoni ⑥

Via Omenoni 3. **Map** 3 C5 (10 D2).
Ⓜ 1, 3 Duomo. ⬜ to the public.

Eight telamones, which the
Milanese call *omenoni*,
are the most striking feature
of this house-cum-studio,
built by the sculptor Leone
Leoni in 1565. The artist
collected many works of art,
including paintings by Titian
and Correggio and Leonardo
da Vinci's famous *Codex
Atlanticus (see p59)*.
A reference to Leoni can be
seen in the relief under the
cornice, in which Calumny
is torn up by lions *(leoni)*.

**The entrance to the
Casa degli Omenoni**

Casa Manzoni and Piazza Belgioioso ⑦

Via Morone 1. **Map** 4 D5 (10 D2). **Tel**
02-86 46 04 03. Ⓜ 3 Montenapoleo-
ne. 🚊 1, 2. 🚌 61. ⬜ 9am–noon,
2–4pm Tue–Fri. ◑ public hols. ♿

This is the house where
Italian author Alessandro
Manzoni lived from 1814 until
his death in 1873 after a fall

Part of the façade of Palazzo Liberty, at No. 8 Piazza del Liberty

on the steps of San Fedele.
The perfectly preserved
interior includes Manzoni's
studio on the ground floor,
where he received Garibaldi
in 1862 and Verdi in 1868.
Next to this is the room where
poet and author Tommaso
Grossi had his notary office,
while on the first floor is
Manzoni's bedroom. The
house is now the seat of the
National Centre for Manzoni
Studies, which was founded
in 1937. It includes a library
with works by Manzoni and
critical studies of his oeu-
vre, as well as the
Lombard Historical
Society Library with
over 40,000 volumes.
The brick façade over-
looks Piazza
Belgioioso, named after
the palazzo at No. 2
(closed to the public).
This monumental
palazzo was designed
by Piermarini in
1777–81 for Prince
Alberico XII di Bel-   **The *Omm de preja***
gioioso d'Este. The   **statue**
façade bears heraldic
emblems. In the interior a
fresco by Martin Knoller
represents the apotheosis
of Prince Alberico.

Piazza del Liberty and Corso Vittorio Emanuele II ⑧

Map 8 D1 (10 D3). Ⓜ 1, 3 Duomo,
1 San Babila. 🚊 23. 🚌 61, 65, 73.

Once past the arch at the
end of Piazza Belgioioso,
go through Piazza Meda
(1926) and past Corso
Matteotti, which was built in
1934 to link Piazza della Scala
with Piazza San Babila, and
then go down Via San Paolo,
which will take you to
Piazza del Liberty. This
small square owes its
name to the Art Nou-
veau (Liberty) façade
on No. 8, restored by
Giovanni and Lorenzo
Muzio in 1963 with
architectural elements
from the Trianon café-
concert, a building
dating from 1905
which was moved
from Corso Vittorio
Emanuele II.
Go along Via San
Paolo to reach Corso
Vittorio Emanuele II. This is
Milan's main commercial
street, and was once called
"Corsia dei Servi" (Servants'
Lane). It follows the course
of an ancient Roman street
and in 1628 was the scene
of bread riots, described by
Manzoni in *The Betrothed*.
Near San Carlo al Corso, at
No. 13 is the *Omm de preja*
(local dialect for *uomo di
pietra* or "man of stone")
statue, a copy of an ancient
Roman work. It is also called
"Sciur Carera", a misspelling
of the first word of a Latin
inscription under the statue
*(carere debet omni vitio qui
in alterum dicere paratus est)*.

Casa Manzoni, now home to the National Centre for Manzoni Studies

Teatro alla Scala ❸

Poster for
Turandot

Built by Giuseppe Piermarini in 1776-8, this opera house owes its name to the fact that it stands on the site of Santa Maria della Scala, a church built in 1381 for Regina della Scala, Bernabò Visconti's wife. The theatre opened in 1778; it was bombed in 1943 and rebuilt three years later. After an extensive restoration programme that saw the addition of a new stage tower designed by Mario Botta, La Scala reopened in 2004. The opening night of the opera season is 7 December, the feast day of Sant'Ambrogio, Milan's patron saint.

Teatro alla Scala in 1852, by Angelo Inganni

The chandelier, made of Bohemian crystal (1923), holds 383 lightbulbs.

★ Foyer
This large, mirror-lined salon was renovated in 1936. There is a bust of the legendary conductor Arturo Toscanini.

The boxes were like small living rooms where romantic trysts and parlour games were arranged.

The façade was designed by Piermarini so that passers-by in Via Manzoni could catch a glimpse of it.

Entrance

★ Museo Teatrale
The theatre museum was founded in 1913 and boasts a fine collection of sculpture, original scores, paintings and ceramics related to the history of La Scala as well as of theatre in general.

STAR FEATURES

★ Auditorium

★ Foyer

★ Museo Teatrale

THE BALLET SCHOOL

Students at the Ballet School

La Scala's Ballet School was founded in 1813. Originally there were 48 students who studied dance, mime or specialist disciplines. At the end of an eight-year course, the best students were awarded merits of distinction and became part of the theatre's *corps de ballet* with an annual stipend of 3,000 lire. This rigorously disciplined school has produced such artists as Carla Fracci and Luciana Savignano.

VISITORS' CHECKLIST

Piazza della Scala. **Map** 3 C5 (10 D2). Ⓜ *1, 3 Duomo*. **Tel** 02-85 45 62 16. **Museo Teatrale alla Scala:** Largo Ghiringhelli 1 (Piazza Scala). **Tel** 02-88 79 24 73. ◻ *9am–noon, 1:30–5pm daily.* 🎫 *(a ticket to the museum includes a look at the theatre from a balcony, provided there are no rehearsals or shows).* ♿ 🖥 *www.teatroallascala.org*

A tank filled with water, placed over the wooden vault, was ready for use in case of fire.

Dressing rooms

The orchestra pit was introduced in 1907. Before then the orchestra played behind a balustrade on the same level as the stalls.

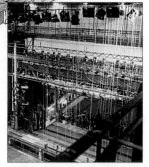

Stage
This is one of the largest stages in Italy, measuring 1,200 sq m (13,000 sq ft).

★ Auditorium
Made of wood covered with red velvet and decorated with gilded stuccowork, the interior boasts marvellous acoustics and has a seating capacity of 2,015.

The entrance to the church of San Gottardo in Corte

San Gottardo in Corte ❾

Via Pecorari 2. **Map** 8 D1 (10 D4).
Tel 02-86 46 45 00. Ⓜ 1, 3 Duomo.
🚋 12, 23, 27. 🚌 54, 60, 65.
⭘ 8am–noon, 2–6pm Mon–Fri (to 5:30 Fri), 2–4pm Sat, 8am–noon Sun.

Azzone Visconti, lord of Milan, ordered the construction of this church in 1336 as the ducal chapel in the Broletto Vecchio (Court-house) courtyard. The interior was rebuilt in Neo-Classical style by Piermarini. On the left-hand wall is a *Crucifixion* by the school of Giotto.

Azzone Visconti's funerary monument, by Giovanni di Balduccio, is in the apse: the reclining statue of Visconti is flanked by the figures of two women. The octagonal brick bell tower with small stone arches and columns is by Francesco Pecorari (c.1335).

Palazzo Reale ❿

Piazza del Duomo. **Map** 7 C1 (10 D3). **Tel** 02-860 16 52. Ⓜ 1, 3 Duomo. 🚋 15, 23, 27. 🚌 54, 60, 65. ⭘ 9:30am–8pm Tue–Sun. **CIMAC** 🔘 *for restoration.* **Palazzo della Permanente** Via Turati 34. **Map** 4 D3. **Tel** 02-659 98 03. ⭘ 10am–1pm, 2:30–6:30pm Tue–Fri, 10am–6:30pm Sat & Sun. 🔘 Mon. www.lapermanente-milano.it

The seat of the commune administration in the 11th century, this building was drastically rebuilt by Azzone Visconti in 1330–36. At the height of its importance it was the head-quarters of the lords of Milan. Galeazzo Maria Sforza's decision to move the palace began the decline of the Palazzo Reale. In 1598 it housed the first permanent theatre in Milan. Made of wood, it was rebuilt in 1737 and Mozart played here as a child. In 1776 it was destroyed by a fire.

The present Neo-Classical appearance dates from 1778, when Giuseppe Piermarini made it into a residence for Archduke Ferdinand of Austria. The interior once contained furniture by cabinet-maker Maggiolini and was frescoed by Martin Knoller and Giuliano

Unique Forms of Continuity in Space (1913) by Umberto Boccioni

Traballesi, becoming a model for aristocratic Milanese homes.

In 1920 Vittorio Emanuele III granted the place temporarily to the city of Milan, and in 1965 the city purchased it to use as offices and museums and for temporary shows. The **Civico Museo d'Arte Contemporanea (CIMAC)** is located on the second floor. There are two sections. The first begins with the famous Futurist sculpture *Unique Forms of Continuity in Space*, by Umberto Boccioni, and features 20th-century Italian art to the post-World War II period, including works by Balla, Morandi, Fontana, Modigliani, Carrà, and Arturo Martini. Metaphysical painting is represented mainly by De Chirico. A second section features Italian art from the 1950s to the 1980s, and includes works by Alberto Burri, Piero Manzoni, Vedova and Tancredi.

Although CIMAC is currently closed for restoration, the Futurist art collection is on show at the Palazzo della Permanente.

Piazza Mercanti ⓫

Map 7 C1 (9 C3). Ⓜ 1 Cairoli–Cordusio.

This corner of medieval Milan was the seat of public and civic activities and also housed the prison. Palazzo della Ragione was built in 1233 by the chief magistrate (and virtual ruler) Oldrado da Tresseno, who is portrayed in a relief by Antelami on the side facing the square. This courthouse is also known as "Broletto Nuovo" to distinguish it from the older Broletto Vecchio near Palazzo Reale. Markets were held under the porticoes, while the Salone dei Giudici on the first floor was used as the law court. In 1773 another storey was added to house the notarial archive.

Palazzo Reale, now used as a venue for temporary exhibitions

For hotels and restaurants in this area see p160 and pp172–3

The well in Piazza Mercanti and, on the left, Palazzo delle Scuole Palatine

On one side of the square is the Loggia degli Osii, built by Matteo Visconti in 1316. The façade is decorated with the arms of the districts of Milan and statues of the Virgin Mary and saints (1330). Next is the Palazzo delle Scuole Palatine (1645), the façade of which bears statues of St Augustine and the Latin poet Ausonius. The Palazzo dei Panigarola (to the right), which was rebuilt in the 15th century, was used to register public documents.

In the centre of the square is a 16th-century well. In Via Mercanti is the Palazzo dei Giureconsulti, dominated by the Torre del Comune, built by Napo Torriani in 1272. At the foot of this tower is a statue of Sant'Ambrogio.

Pinacoteca Ambrosiana ⑫

See pp56–9

San Sepolcro ⑬

Piazza San Sepolcro. **Map** 7 B1 (9 C4). **M** 1, 3 Duomo. 🚋 2, 3, 12, 14, 16, 19, 27. ○ noon–2pm Mon–Fri. 🕇 5pm pre-hols; noon (winter), 5pm hols. 📷

San Sepolcro was founded in 1030 in the area of the ancient Roman Forum and rebuilt in 1100 at the time of the second Crusade. The Neo-Romanesque façade was built in 1897, while the interior is basically Baroque. There are two terracotta groups by Agostino De Fondutis (16th century) depicting *Christ Washing His Disciples' Feet* and *The Flagellation of Christ with Caiaphas and St Peter*. The only remaining part of the 1030 church is the Romanesque crypt, with a sculpture group of the *Deposition* by the De Fondutis school in the apse.

Piazza Borromeo ⑭

Piazza Borromeo 7. **Map** 4 D4 (10 D1). **M** 1 Cordusio. 🚋 2, 3, 12, 14, 16, 19, 27 🚌 50, 54. ○ courtyard only.

This prestigious early 15th-century residence was badly damaged by the 1943 bombings and the only remaining original architectural element is the ogival portal, with leaf decoration and the coat of arms of the Borromeo family. The partly rebuilt second courtyard has porticoes on three sides and on the fourth, between the brick windows, is the original decoration with the family motto *Humilitas*. This courtyard leads to the 15th-century Sala dei Giochi, which is decorated with frescoes of the games played by the aristocracy of the time, including the *Game of Tarot* by a painter known as the Master of the Borromeo Games. The red background is the result of a chemical reaction which changed the original blue of the sky.

The Borromeo family coat of arms with the motto *Humilitas*

San Giorgio al Palazzo ⑮

Piazza San Giorgio 2. **Map** 7 B1 (9 B4). **Tel** 02-86 08 31. 🚋 2, 3, 14. ○ 7:30am–noon, 3:30–7pm daily. 🕇 6pm pre-hols, 11am, 6pm hols; 8am, 6pm Mon–Fri.

Founded in 750, this church was named after an ancient Roman *palatium* which stood here. It was radically changed in 1623 and 1800–21 by the architects Richini and Cagnola respectively, and little remains of the original or Romanesque (1129) structures. The third chapel in the right-hand aisle contains paintings by Bernardino Luini (1516) with scenes from the Passion. On the vault there is a fresco of the Crucifixion.

Santa Maria presso San Satiro ⑯

Via Speronari 3. **Map** 7 B1 (9 B3). **Tel** 02-87 46 83. **M** 1, 3 Duomo. 🚋 2, 3, 12, 14, 15, 16. ○ 7:30–11:30am, 3:30–5:30pm daily. 🕇 6pm pre-hols; 11am, 6pm hols; 7:45am, 6pm Mon–Fri.

The original nucleus of this church, founded by archbishop Ansperto da Biassono, dates from 876. The only remnant is the Sacello della Pietà (chapel of pity), which was altered by Bramante in the 15th century, and the Lombard Romanesque bell tower. In 1478 Bramante was asked to rebuild the church to salvage a 13th-century fresco on the façade, which was said to have miraculous powers. Bramante set it on the high altar, solving the problem of lack of space by creating a sort of *trompe l'oeil* apse of only 97 cm (38 in) with stuccowork and frescoes. The transept leads to the Chapel of San Satiro with a terracotta *Pietà* (c.1482). In the right-hand aisle is the octagonal baptismal font decorated by De Fondutis.

Pinacoteca Ambrosiana ⑫

The Ambrosiana art gallery was founded in 1618 by Cardinal Federico Borromeo, the cousin of San Carlo and his successor in charge of the archdiocese of Milan. A true art connoisseur, Borromeo planned the gallery as part of a vast cultural project which included the Ambrosiana Library, opened in 1609, and the Accademia del Disegno (1620) for the training of young Counter-Reformation artists. The gallery, founded to provide inspiration for emerging artists, held 172 paintings – some of which already belonged to Borromeo, while others were purchased later after painstaking research by the cardinal. The collection was then enlarged thanks to private donations.

★ **Portrait of a Musician**
This is the only Milanese wood panel painting by Leonardo da Vinci. The subject is Franchino Gaffurio, the Sforza court composer.

Adoration of the Magi
Cardinal Borromeo considered this painting by Titian (purchased in 1558) a treasure trove for painters "for the multitude of things therein".

STAR EXHIBITS

★ Portrait of a Musician

★ Cartoon for the School of Athens

★ Basket of Fruit

★ Madonna del Padiglione

The Library is on the ground floor.

★ **Madonna del Padiglione**
The recent restoration of this work by Botticelli has revealed its masterful and elegant brushwork.

GALLERY GUIDE

The most famous works are held in the Borromeo Collection, which was subsequently enriched with important 15th–16th-century paintings and sculptures. The Galbiati wing contains 16th–20th-century paintings, a collection of objects, the Sinigaglia Collection of miniature portraits and scientific instruments belonging to the Museo Settala.

VISITORS' CHECKLIST

Piazza Pio XI 2. **Map** 7 B1
(9 C3). **Tel** 02-80 69 21.
Ⓜ 1, 3 Duomo, 1 Cordusio.
🚊 2, 3, 4, 12, 14, 19, 24, 27.
🚌 50. ⬜ 10am–5:30pm
Tue–Sun. 🏷 ♿ partial.
📷 🔁 🚻
www.ambrosiana.it

Nicolò da Bologna Room

San Sepolcro was annexed to the gallery in 1932.

Centrepiece with Fishing Scene
This is part of the prestigious collection of Neo–Classical gilded bronze objects donated to the Ambrosiana by Edoardo De Pecis in 1827.

KEY

☐ Borromeo Collection and 15th–16th-century paintings

☐ Galbiati Wing

☐ De Pecis Collection & 19th century

☐ Sculpture

☐ Museo Settala

★ **Basket of Fruit**
Caravaggio painted this extraordinarily realistic work around 1594. The fruit alludes to the symbolism of the Passion of Christ.

★ **Cartoon for the School of Athens**
This was a preparation for the painting now in the Vatican. Raphael used the faces of contemporary artists - Leonardo, for instance, appears in the guise of Aristotle.

Exploring the Pinacoteca Ambrosiana

After seven years of painstaking restoration work, the Pinacoteca was reopened in October 1997. It is housed in a palazzo originally designed by Fabio Mangone in 1611. It was enlarged in the 19th century and again in 1932, when San Sepolcro was added. The new rooms were inaugurated on the third centenary of the death of Federico Borromeo, when about 700 paintings were exhibited, arranged in rows or set on easels. Today the Pinacoteca, whose collections are even larger thanks to donations, has 24 rooms and is one of Milan's finest museums.

18th-century silver stoup

Portrait of a Young Man, a copy of Giorgione's work

THE BORROMEO COLLECTION, 15TH–16TH-CENTURY PAINTINGS

Your visit begins in the atrium, which has plaster casts of Trajan's Column, narrating the emperor's victories against the Dacians; on the staircase there are other casts of the *Laocoön* and Michelangelo's *Pietà*. Rooms 1, 4, 5, 6 and 7 house the Borromeo Collection, which boasts many of the best-known works in the gallery. Room 1, which features Venetian and Leonardo-esque painting, opens with the *Holy Family with St Anne and the Young St John the Baptist* by Bernardino Luini (c.1520). Next to this is Titian's *Adoration of the Magi* (1559–60), which is

still in its original frame bearing the carved initials of Henry II of France and his wife, who commissioned the work. The main scene is at the far left, while animals and minor figures fill the right-hand half of this original composition. On the opposite wall is a series of portraits, including *Profile of a Lady* by Ambrogio De Predis, and those of *The Young St John the Baptist* and *Benedictory Christ* by Luini, ending with Titian's *Man in Armour*. Rooms 2 and 3 have works acquired after 1618. One is Leonardo da Vinci's *Portrait of a Musician* with its innovative three-quarter profile position and intense expression; it was probably painted in early 1485. Next to this masterpiece is Botticelli's *Madonna del Padiglione*, with its many symbols of the Virgin Mary, and *Sacred Conversation* by Bergognone (c.1485). Another unmissable work is *Adoration of the Child*, by the workshop of Domenico Ghirlandaio. Room 3 features 15th–16th-

Adoration of the Child, Domenico Ghirlandaio's workshop

century Leonardo-esque and Lombard paintings, among which is Salaino's *St John the Baptist*, whose finger pointing upwards alludes to the coming of Christ. Next to this are three works by Bartolomeo Suardi, better known as "il Bramantino". In his *Madonna of the Towers* (which may have had an anti-heretic function), next to the Virgin are an unrecognizable St Ambrose and St Michael Archangel kneeling and offering a soul to the Christ Child. Room 4 has copies from Titian and Giorgione and the *Rest on the Flight into Egypt* by Jacopo Bassano (c.1547). In room 5 is a Raphael masterpiece, a study for *The School of Athens*, the only great Renaissance cartoon that has come down to us. It was purchased by Cardinal Borromeo in 1626. Raphael executed the cartoon in 1510 as a study for the marvellous fresco in the Vatican. The architectonic setting and figure of Heraclitus (portrayed with Michelangelo's face), which were added after the fresco was completed, are not seen in the cartoon.

One of the most famous works in the museum, *Basket of Fruit*, is in room 6. Caravaggio painted it in the late

Holy Family with St Anne and the Young St John the Baptist by Bernardino Luini

1500s on a used canvas. The withered leaves represent the vanity of beauty.

The large body of Flemish paintings in the Borromeo Collection is on display in room 7, where you can compare the works of Paul Bril and Jan Brueghel. Interesting works by the latter are *The Mouse with Roses* and *Allegories of Water and Fire*, which Napoleon removed and took back to France. They were later returned.

THE GALBIATI WING

The Sala Della Medusa and the Sala delle Colonne feature Renaissance paintings and a collection of objects, the most curious of which are Lucrezia Borgia's blonde hair and Napoleon's gloves.

A short passageway leads to the Spiriti Magni courtyard, decorated with statues of illustrious artists. The three rooms that follow feature 16th-century Italian and Venetian paintings, including an *Annunciation* by Bedoli (room 10), the *Portrait of Michel de l'Hospital* by Giovan Battista Moroni (1554) and Moretto's altarpiece, *Martyrdom of St Peter of Verona* (c.1535, room 12). This latter room, known as the "exedra room", is decorated with a mosaic reproducing a miniature by Simone Martini from the volume of Virgil annotated by Petrarch in the Biblioteca Ambrosiana.

Lucrezia Borgia's hair

Italian and Flemish painting of the 16th and 17th centuries is on display in the Sala Nicolò da Bologna, on the upper floor, along with an unfinished *Penitent Magdalen* (1640–42) by Guido Reni. Seventeenth-century Lombard painting is on display in rooms 14, 15 and 16. Among the interesting works are *Still Life with Musical Instruments* by Evaristo Baschenis (room 14) and Morazzone's *Adoration of the Magi* (room 15), while the following room has

works by Francesco Cairo and Daniele Crespi, as well as *Magdalen* by Giulio Cesare Procaccini. Paintings by Magnasco, Magatti, Fra Galgario and Londonio represent 18th-century Italian art in room 17, but the jewels are two works by Tiepolo on the wall near the entrance.

DE PECIS COLLECTION AND 19TH CENTURY

Rooms 18 and 19 form the largest section of the Pinacoteca Ambrosiana, donated by Giovanni Edoardo De Pecis in 1827. This collection consists mostly of Italian and Flemish paintings and includes a series of small Neo-Classical bronze pieces and a *Self Portrait* by sculptor Antonio Canova, inspired by Roman portraiture. The exhibition in this wing ends with a selection of 19th- and early 20th-century canvases, including works by Andrea Appiani *(Portrait of Napoleon)*, Mosè Bianchi and Francesco Hayez. Emilio Longoni is represented with his masterpiece *Locked out of School* (1888). Room 21 has 15th–17th-century German and Flemish art as well as the

Dantesque Stain[e...] Giuseppe Bertini, t[...] master glassblower. [...] executed in 1865 and the author of the *Divine Comedy* surrounded by h[...] characters and with the Vir[...] Mary above him.

Funerary monument by il Bambaia

SCULPTURE

Room 22 is given over to sculpture. There are ancient Roman, Romanesque and Renaissance pieces as well as the highly elegant bas-reliefs by Agostino Busti – known as "il Bambaia" – sculpted for the tomb of Gaston de Foix around 1516.

MUSEO SETTALA

The final room contains the rich collection purchased by the Ambrosiana gallery in 1751. It had been collected a century earlier by Manfredo Settala, an eccentric lover of scientific instruments, exotic animals, semi-precious stones, fossils, furniture, paintings and books – forming a sort of "museum of wonders".

BIBLIOTECA AMBROSIANA

Virgil illuminated by Simone Martini

This was one of the first libraries open to the public. It boasts over 750,000 printed volumes, 2,500 of which are incunabula, and 35,000 manuscripts. Among them is the 5th-century *Ilias Picta*, a copy of Virgil's book annotated by Petrarch and illuminated by Simone Martini; a volume of Aristotle with annotations by Boccaccio; as well as Arab, Syrian, Greek and Latin texts. The Ambrosian Library also has over 1,000 pages of Leonardo da Vinci's *Codex Atlanticus*, purchased in 1637, removed by Napoleon in 1796 and only partly returned in 1815. The Library opened in 1609, already equipped with shelves and wooden footstools to protect readers from the cold floors.

NORTHWEST MILAN

In the 14th century, when the construction of the Castello Sforzesco began, this district stood outside the city walls and was covered in woods. After the demolition of the Spanish walls around the Castello in the early 19th century, a new plan for the area was drawn up (but only partly realized). The aim was to transform the zone into a monumental quarter by building the Arco della Pace and a number of

The personification of a river, part of the Arco della Pace (Arch of Peace)

elegant buildings, which were to be used as offices, luxury residences, markets and theatres. By the end of the century, Via Dante, which leads to the Castello and is lined with fine buildings, was complete, as was the Corso Magenta residential district around Santa Maria delle Grazie. Northwest Milan also hosts two historic theatres: Dal Verme (1872) and the Piccolo Teatro (now called Teatro Grassi), founded in 1947.

GETTING THERE

The Fiera (Amendola, Lotto) and Castello (Cairoli) are served by metro lines 1 and 2. A number of tramlines pass Piazza Cordusio (No. 16 goes to Santa Maria delle Grazie or San Siro stadium).

KEY

- Street-by-Street map *See pp62–3*
- **M** Metro
- **🚖** Taxi

0 metres 400
0 yards 400

SIGHTS AT A GLANCE

Parks and Gardens
Parco Sempione **2**

Streets, Squares and Historic Buildings
Arco della Pace **5**
Arena Civica **4**
Castello Sforzesco pp64–7 **1**
Certosa di Garegnano **10**
Corso Magenta **12**

Corso Sempione **7**
Palazzo Litta **13**
Piazza Affari **18**
Piazza Cordusio **17**
Via Brisa **16**

Public Buildings
Acquario Civico **3**
Fiera di Milano **8**
Meazza (San Siro) Stadium **9**

Churches
San Maurizio **15**
Santa Maria delle Grazie pp71–3 **11**

Museums
Civico Museo Archeologico **14**
Triennale di Milano **6**

◁ **The Salone degli Specchi in Palazzo Litta, a fine example of the 18th-century Lombard style**

Street-by-Street: Around the Castello Sforzesco

Visconti coat of arms

The Castello Sforzesco and Sempione park today are the result of late 19th-century landscaping and restoration. Architect Luca Beltrami managed to thwart attempts to demolish the castle by converting it into a museum centre. He restored many of its original elements. In the early 1800s, the Arco della Pace and the Arena were built in the Parco Sempione, which was landscaped as an "English" garden by Emilio Alemagna. To mark the 1906 opening of the Galleria del Sempione, an International Exposition was held, featuring new products which later became household names in Italy.

Arena Civica
This amphitheatre, built in 1806, was used for boating displays, when it was filled with water from the Naviglio canals ❹

★ **Parco Sempione**
The 47-hectare (116-acre) English-style garden was designed by Emilio Alemagna in 1893. It contains a number of historic buildings and monuments ❷

Corso Sempione
Napoleon built this avenue leading to the Castello, modelling it on the Champs-Elysées in Paris ❼

PIAZZALE SEMPIONE

VIALE BARI
VIALE ELE MALTA
VIALE BYRON
VIALE ALEMAGNA

★ **Arco della Pace**
Modelled on the triumphal arch of Septimius Severus, the Arch of Peace was built to celebrate Napoleon's victories. However, it was inaugurated by Francis I in memory of the peace declared in 1815 ❺

STAR SIGHTS
★ Castello Sforzesco
★ Parco Sempione
★ Arco della Pace

Acquario Civico
The Civic Aquarium was built in 1906 as an exhibition and educational centre. The building still has its original decoration of tiles and reliefs **3**

The Foro Buonaparte is a semicircular boulevard lined with imposing late 19th-century buildings.

LOCATOR MAP
See Street Finder, maps 2, 3, 9, 10

KEY

– – – Suggested route

Via Dante, one of the city's most elegant streets, is a pedestrian precinct, and one of the few in Milan where you can sit and have a drink outdoors.

★ Castello Sforzesco
The castle, a symbol of Milan, was initially the palace of the Visconti, who built it in 1368 and named it Castello di Porta Giovia, and then of the Sforza, who embellished it, turning it into a magnificent Renaissance residence **1**

Triennale di Milano
The Palazzo dell'Arte holds architecture and design shows. The Triennale show features decorative art, fashion and handicrafts **6**

0 metres 400
0 yards 400

Castello Sforzesco **❶**

Built in 1368 by Galeazzo II Visconti as a fortress, the Sforza castle was enlarged in the 14th century by Gian Galeazzo and then by Filippo Maria, who transformed it into a splendid ducal palace. It was partly demolished in 1447 during the Ambrosian Republic. Francesco Sforza, who became lord of Milan in 1450, and his son Lodovico il Moro made the castle

Umberto I, the Filarete Tower

the home of one of the most magnificent courts in Renaissance Italy, graced by Bramante and Leonardo da Vinci. Under Spanish and Austrian domination, the Castello went into gradual decline, as it resumed its original military function. It was saved from demolition by the architect Luca Beltrami, who from 1893 to 1904 restored it and converted it into an important museum centre.

★ Trivulzio Tapestries
The 12 tapestries designed by Bramantino, depicting the months and signs of the zodiac, are masterpieces of Italian textile art.

The Torre Castellana was where Lodovico il Moro kept his treasury. It was "guarded" by a figure of Argus, in a fresco by Bramante at the Sala del Tesoro entrance.

The Cortile della Rocchetta was the last refuge in the event of a siege. Its three porticoes, formerly frescoed, were designed by Filarete, Ferrini and Bramante. The oldest wing (1456–66), opposite the entrance to the Corte Ducale, was the apartment of Lodovico and his wife before he became duke.

The holes in the castle walls, now used by pigeons, were made to anchor the scaffolding used for maintenance work.

Porta Vercellina
Only ruins remain of the great fortified structure that once protected the gate of Santo Spirito.

Cappella Ducale
*The Ducal chapel still has
the original frescoes
painted in 1472 by
Stefano de Fedeli and
Bonifacio Bembo for
Galeazzo Maria
Sforza. On the vault
is a* Resurrection *and
on the wall to the left
of the entrance is an*
Annunciation *with saints
looking on.*

VISITORS' CHECKLIST

Piazza Castello. **Map** 3 B5
(9 B2). **Tel** 02-88 46 37 00.
 1 Cairoli– Cadorna, 2 Lanza–
Cadorna. 1, 3, 4, 12, 14, 27.
 43, 50, 57, 58, 61, 70, 94.
Castello 9am–5:30pm daily.
Musei Civici **Tel** 02-88 46 37 31
or 02-88 46 36 66. 9am–
5:30pm Tue–Sun (last adm 5pm).
 1 Jan, Easter, 1 May, 25 Dec.
 some rooms only.

Ducal
court

★ **Sala delle Asse**
*This pergola,
painted to look
like an open air
space, was the
work of Leonardo
(1498). The room
owes its name to
the planks (asse)
once thought to
cover the walls.*

★ **Rondanini Pietà**
*Michelangelo's final
work, held in the Civiche
Raccolte, was altered
several times and never
completed. Christ's arm
on the left and a different
angle for Mary's face,
visible from the right, are
part of the first version.*

STAR FEATURES

★ Rondanini Pietà

★ Sala delle Asse

★ Trivulzio Tapestries

The Filarete Tower collapsed
in 1521 when the gunpowder
kept there exploded. It was
rebuilt in 1905 by Luca
Beltrami, who worked from
Filarete's original design for
the central castle tower.

Exploring the Civic Museums in the Castello Sforzesco

Since 1896, the Castello Sforzesco has housed the Civic Museums with one of the largest collections of art in Milan. The Corte Ducale houses the Raccolte di Arte Antica and the art and sculpture gallery as well as the furniture collection, while the Rocchetta holds decorative arts (ceramics, musical instruments and gold) and the Trivulzio Tapestries. The archaeological museum, the stamp collections and the Achille Berta-relli Collection, with about 700,000 prints and books, are also here. Major institutions are also housed here such as the Art Library, Trivulziana Library, Drawing Collection and School of Applied Industrial Art.

Relief of the Three Magi, School of Antelami (12th century)

CIVICHE RACCOLTE d'ARTE ANTICA

The displays making up the collections of Ancient Art are arranged in chronological order (except for Room 6) in rooms facing the Corte Ducale, where the 14th-century Pusterla dei Fabbri postern, rebuilt after being demolished in 1900, has 4th-6th-century sculpture. In room 1 ① is the Sarcophagus of Lambrate (late 4th century) and a bust of the Empress Theodora (6th century). Room 2 ② features Romanesque and Campionese sculpture, with a fine early 12th-century tela-mon. The relief of the Three Magi is by the school of Benedetto Antelami, the great 12th-century sculptor and architect. The main attraction, however, is the *Mausoleum of Bernabò Visconti*, sculpted by Bonino da Campione in 1363 for the lord of Milan. He is portrayed on horse-back between Wisdom and Fortitude, while on the sarcophagus are *Scenes from the Passion.* Room 3 ③ has a window with a 14th-century Tuscan *Benedictory Christ.* Room 4 ④ is given over to Giovanni di Balduccio, with fragments from the façade of Santa Maria di Brera (14th century). A passage leads to the Cappel-letta ⑤, dominated by a 14th-century wooden Crucifix.

Room 6 ⑥ features reliefs from the Porta Romana (1171) narrating the *Return of the Milanese after Being Driven out of Town by Barbarossa* and *St Ambrose Expelling the Arians.* In room 7 ⑦ is the *Gonfalone* (Standard) of Milan designed by Giuseppe Meda in 1566, with scenes from Sant'Ambrogio's life. On the walls are 17th-century Flemish tapestries. The Sala delle Asse ⑧ is known for its fine fresco decoration on the vault, designed by Leonardo in 1498, which, despite its poor condition, is a good example of Sforza decoration. From here you go to the bridge over the moat ⑨ ⑩, with important small sculptures by Agostino Busti (La Bambaia). Next is the Sala dei Ducali ⑪, named after the arms of Galeazzo Maria Sforza, with Lodovico's set above. Here the early 15th-century sculpture is dominated by Agostino di Duccio's relief of *St Sigismund on a Journey* from the Malatesta Temple in

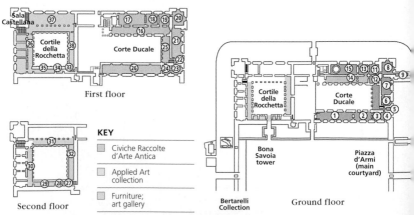

The Mausoleum of Bernabò Visconti

PLAN OF THE CASTELLO SFORZESCO

Sala Castellana ③⑦

③⑥ Cortile della Rocchetta ③⑧

③⑤ ③④ ③③

⑰ ⑱ ⑲ ⑳

⑯

Corte Ducale ㉕

㉑

㉒

㉖ ㉔ ㉓

First floor

㉛

㉜

㉚

㉙ ㉘ ㉗

Second floor

KEY

■ Civiche Raccolte d'Arte Antica

■ Applied Art collection

■ Furniture; art gallery

Bona Savoia tower

Cortile della Rocchetta

Corte Ducale

⑮ ⑬ ⑪ ⑧
⑫ ⑨
⑦
⑥
⑤
① ② ③ ④

Bertarelli Collection

Piazza d'Armi (main courtyard)

Ground floor

The armour collection in the Sala Verde

Rimini. Left, is the door to the Cappella Ducale ⑫, with a braided Virgin, *Madonna del Coazzone*, a 15th-century work attributed to Pietro Antonio Solari. On the vault is a *Resurrection* painted around 1472 by Bonifacio Bembo and Stefano de' Fedeli. Late 15th-century sculpture is featured in the Sala delle Colombine ⑬, with the Visconti coat of arms and motto, *A Bon Droit*. One of the finest works here is Antonio Mantegazza's *Kneeling Apostles*. The 1463 portal displayed in the Sala Verde ⑭ is attributed to Michelozzo. This room also has some fine armour.

The last room, the Sala degli Scarlioni ⑮, boasts two world-famous sculptures: Gaston de Foix's funerary monument with marvellous reliefs, and Michelangelo's *Rondanini Pietà*. The former is by Agostino Busti, known as "il Bambaia", and commemorates the death on the battlefield of the young captain of the French troops in 1512. Behind a partition is Michelangelo's unfinished masterpiece, which he was working on until a few days before his death in 1564 (he had begun it in 1552–3): the standing Mother of Christ supporting the heavy body of her Son. The exit route goes through the Cortile della Fontana, where the only original window left in the castle can be seen. It was used by Beltrami as a model in his restoration of the Castello.

FURNITURE COLLECTION AND PINACOTECA

Four rooms on the first floor house 15th–18th-century furniture. Of particular interest are the Torrechiara Choir (15th century) ⑯, the Passalacqua casket ⑱ (1613) and a chest of drawers by Giuseppe Maggiolini ⑲. Room 17 ⑰ has a reconstruction of an interior with frescoes from the Castello di Roccabianca with the *Stories of Griselda* (1460), inspired by a story by Boccaccio. The Belgioioso collection of 17th-century Flemish paintings is on display in room 18.

The art gallery begins at the Sala Nuziale ⑳, with 14th- and 15th-century Italian paintings, including Mantegna's *Madonna in Glory and Saints*

Madonna in Glory and Saints, by Andrea Mantegna

(1497), which you can compare with a *Madonna and Child*, an early work by Giovanni Bellini. Also on show are the two *Saints* by Carlo Crivelli (c.1479).

Fifteenth-century Lombard painting ㉑ is perhaps best represented by Bramantino's *Deposition* (1513). There are also many works by Leonardo-esque painters (Marco d'Oggiono, Cesare da Sesto), together with Correggio *(see pp32–3)* and Romanino.

A room of Mannerist art ㉒ leads to room 23 ㉓, with episodes from the history of the Milanese church by Procaccini, Morazzone, Ambrogio Figino and Cerano. Room 24 ㉔ features 17th-century Lombard art (Giovanni Battista Trotti, Bernardino Campi and Fede Galizia). The permanent collection of portraits (Room 25 ㉕) boasts masterpieces such as *Poet Laureate* (c.1475) attributed to Giovanni Bellini, *Portrait of Giulio Zandemaria* by Correggio (1521), *Young Man* by Lotto and canvases by Titian and Fra Galgario. Room 26 ㉖ has some 17th- and 18th-century works by artists such as Canaletto and Bellotto.

APPLIED ART COLLECTION

Return to the entrance for access to the first floor to see the collection of old musical instruments ㊱ ㊳, which includes a Flemish double virginal with ottavino. Between these two rooms is the large Sala della Balla (ballroom) ㊲, with Bramantino's splendid Trivulzio Tapestries of the months (1503–09). On the second floor (rooms 28–32) is a large collection of fine Italian and European glass, ceramics, majolica and porcelain, and collections of costumes, ivory works, gold jewellery and scientific instruments. Lastly, in the basement, is the Archaeological Museum: the *Ritrovare Milano* section features Roman objects, a Prehistoric section, and an Egyptian section with funerary cult objects, including a tomb dating from c.640 BC.

arco Sempione ❷

Piazza Castello–Piazza Sempione
(Eight entrances around perimeter).
Map 2 F3–4, 3 A3–4 (9 A1). Ⓜ 1
Cadorna, Cairoli, 2 Lanza, Cadorna. Ⓠ
Ferrovie Nord, Cadorna. 🚃 1, 3, 4,
12, 14, 27, 29, 30. 🚌 43, 57, 61,
70, 94. ◯ Mar–Apr: 6:30am–9pm;
May: 6:30am–10pm; Jun–Sep:
6:30am–11:30pm; Oct: 6:30am–9pm;
Nov–Feb: 6:30am–8pm.

Although it covers an area of
about 47 ha (116 acres), this
park occupies only a part of
the old Visconti ducal garden,
enlarged by the Sforza in the
15th century to make a 300-ha
(740-acre) hunting reserve. The
area was partly abandoned
during Spanish rule, and in the
early 1800s part of it was used
to create a parade ground
extending as far as the Arco
della Pace. The present-day
layout was the work of Emilio
Alemagna, who in 1890–93
designed it along the lines of
an English garden. In World
War II the park was used to
cultivate wheat but after the
reconstruction period it
returned to its former
splendour as a locals' haunt,
especially in spring and
summer, when it plays host to
many entertainment events.
Walking through the park
after dark is not advisable.

Standing among the trees
are the monuments to
Napoleon III (designed by
Francesco Barzaghi), De

Chirico's Metaphysical construction *Mysterious Baths*,
the sulphur water fountain
near the Arena and the Torre
del Parco, a tower made of
steel tubes in 1932 after a
design by Gio Ponti.

Acquario Civico ❸

Via Gadio 2. **Map** 3 B4 (9 B1).
Tel 02-88 46 57 50. Ⓜ 2 Lanza.
🚃 3, 4, 12, 14. 🚌 43, 57, 70.
◯ 9:30am–5:30pm Tue–Sun.
📷 by appt (02-89 01 07 95).

The Civic Aquarium was built
by Sebastiano Locati for the
1906 National Exposition, and
it is the only remaining
building. Its 36 tanks
house about 100
species (fish,
crustaceans,
molluscs and
echinoderms)
typical of the
Mediterranean
sea and Italian
freshwater
fauna. There are
also rare kinds
of tropical fish
on display.

**Sea creature decorating the
facade of the Aquarium**

The aquarium
museum is also home to the
Hydrobiological Station,
which has a library
specializing in the subject.
The aquarium building itself
(1906) is a fine example of
Art Nouveau architecture and
is decorated with Richard-

Ginori ceramic tiles and
statues of aquatic animals,
dominated by Oreste Labò's
statue of Neptune.

Arena Civica ❹

Via Legnano, Viale Elvezia. **Map** 3
A-B3. Ⓜ 2 Lanza. 🚃 3, 4, 12, 14.
🚌 43, 57, 70. ◯ for exhibitions
and events only.

This impressive Neo-Classical
amphitheatre, designed in
1806 by Luigi Canonica, was –
together with the Arco della
Pace, Caselli Daziari and Foro
Buonaparte – part of the
project to transform the
Castello Sforzesco area into a
monumental civic
centre. Napoleon
was present at the
Arena inaugura-
tion, and it was
the venue for
various cultural
and sports
events, from
horse and mock
Roman chariot races
to hot-air balloon
launchings, mock
naval battles and
festivities. With a
seating capacity of 30,000, it
has also been a football
stadium, but San Siro (see
p70) is now the more
important ground. The Arena
is mainly a venue for athletics
(it has a 500-m, 1,640-ft track),
concerts and civil weddings.

View of the Parco Sempione: in the foreground, the artificial lake and in the background, the Arco della Pace

For hotels and restaurants in this area see pp160–61 and p173

Arco della Pace ❺

Piazza Sempione. **Map** 2 F3. 🚋 *1, 29, 30.* 🚌 *61.* ⭕ *ascent to the top (Associazione Amici Arco della Pace).*

Work on Milan's major Neo-Classical monument was begun by Luigi Cagnola in 1807 to celebrate Napoleon's victories. It was originally called the Arch of Victories, but building was interrupted and not resumed until 1826 by Francis I of Austria, who had the subjects of the bas-reliefs changed to commemorate the peace of 1815 instead. The Arch of Peace was inaugurated on 10 September 1838 on the occasion of Ferdinand I's coronation as ruler of the Lombardy–Veneto kingdom. The arch is dressed in Crevola marble and decorated with bas-reliefs depicting episodes of the restoration after Napoleon's fall. On the upper level are personifications of the rivers in the Lombardy–Veneto kingdom: the Po, Ticino, Adda and Tagliamento.

From the top of the monument there is a magnificent view of the Castello and Corso Sempione and a close view of the huge bronze Chariot of Peace, by Abbondio Sangiorgio, surrounded by four Victories on horseback. The chariot originally faced France, but when Milan was ceded to Austria, it was turned to face the centre of the city.

Tree-lined Corso Sempione

Triennale di Milano ❻

Viale Alemagna 6. **Map** 3 A4. **Tel** *02-72 43 41.* Ⓜ *1–2 Cadorna.* 🚌 *43, 61, 94.* 🚆 *Ferrovie Nord, Cadorna.* ⭕ *10:30am–8:30pm Tue–Sun.* 🔴 *1 Jan, Easter, 1 May, 15 Aug, 25 Dec.* 📷 🎟 *(depending on event).* ♿ 🏠 🏪 🖼 **www.** triennale.it

The Triennale Decorative Arts Show is housed in the Palazzo dell'Arte, on the southwestern side of the Parco Sempione. The Palazzo was built by Giovanni Muzio in 1932–3 as a permanent site for the International Exhibition of Decorative Arts. The Triennale show was founded in 1923 to foster the development of Italian arts and handicrafts against a background of their international counterparts. In addition, the Milan Triennale has always played a primary role in promoting architectural development.

Obelisk in front of the Palzzo dell'Arte

Art exhibitions, conferences and occasional lectures on the themes of art and architecture are held in the building. Alongside the exhibition space stands the Teatro dell'Arte, which was redesigned in 1960.

Corso Sempione ❼

Map 2 D1, E2, F3. 🚋 *1, 19, 29, 30, 33.* 🚌 *57, 61, 94.*

Modelled on the grand boulevards of Paris, Corso Sempione was the first stage of a road built by Napoleon to link the city with Lake Maggiore, Switzerland and France via the Simplon Pass. The first section, starting at the Arco della Pace, is pedestrianized. The Corso is lined with late 19th-century and early 20th-century houses and is now the main thoroughfare in a vast quarter. The initial stretch (towards the park) is considered an elegant area, with good shops, bars and restaurants, the headquarters of Milanese banks and Italian State Radio and TV, RAI (at No. 27). Opposite, at No. 36, is a residence designed by Giuseppe Terragni and Pietro Lingeri in 1935, one of the first examples of Rationalist architecture in Milan.

The semicircular Via Canova and Via Melzi d'Eril cross the Corso, every angle of which offers a different view of the Arco della Pace.

he horses on the Arco della Pace, each cast in one piece

Fiera di Milano ➑

Largo Domodossola 1. **Map** 1 C3.
Tel 02-499 71. **Fax** 02-49 97 76 05.
Ⓜ *1 Amendola Fiera, Lotto.* 🚋 *19,
27.* 🚌 *48, 68, 78. Shuttle from
Linate airport. ATM circle line buses
(free).* ◯ *for exhibitions only.*
🈸 ♿ 🕐 🖼 **www.fieramilano.it**

The Fiera Campionaria, or
Trade Fair, was founded in
1920 to stimulate the domestic
market in postwar Italy. It was
originally located near Porta
Venezia and in 1923 was
moved to the ground behind
the Castello Sforzesco. It was
fitted out with permanent
pavilions and buildings, many
of which were damaged or
destroyed in World War II.
Some original Art Nouveau
buildings have survived
at the entrance in Via
Domodossola and the
Palazzo dello Sport
(sports arena). The
old main entrance to
the Fiera is in Piazza
Giulio Cesare, which
is dominated by a
Four Seasons
fountain, placed there in 1927.

**Fiera di
Milano logo**

One of the leading exhibition centres in Europe, the
Fiera di Milano has become a
symbol of Milanese industri-
ousness. It hosts 78 specialist
international shows attracting
2.5 million visitors and 31,000
exhibitors every year.

The Largo Domodossola
site is now known as Fiera
Città to avoid confusion with
the new Fiera Milano, an
innovative trade fair centre
that recently opened in Rho,
northwest of Milan.

San Siro Stadium, now named after footballer Giuseppe Meazza

Meazza (San Siro) Stadium ➒

Via Piccolomini 5. **Tel** 02-404 24 32
or 02-48 70 71 23. Ⓜ *1 Lotto*
(Map 1 A2); *shuttle bus.* 🚋 *16.*
San Siro Museum Entrance gate
21. ◯ *10am–5pm Mon–Sat.*
🈸 🕐 **www.**sansirotour.com

Named after Giuseppe
Meazza, the famous
footballer who played
for the local teams,
Inter and Milan,
Italy's top stadium is
commonly known as
San Siro, after the
surrounding district.
It was built in 1926,
rebuilt in the 1950s
with a capacity of 85,000,
and then renovated in 1990,
when another ring of tiers
and a roof were added (*see
Entertainment pp202–3*).
The stadium and changing
rooms can be visited on the
museum tour.

Certosa di Garegnano ➓

Via Garegnano 28. **Tel** 02-38 00 63
01. 🚋 *14.* ◯ *7am–noon, 3–7pm
daily.* ✝ *6pm pre-hols; 8:30, 10 &
11:15am, & 6pm.*

The church that
forms the heart
of this important
Carthusian
monastery, dedicated
to Our Lady of the
Assump-tion, was
founded in 1349 by
Archbishop Giovanni
Visconti. Sadly, the
Certosa is well-
known because the
main cloister was
ruined by the con-
struction of the A4
motorway. The
courtyard is of

impressive size, with the
monks' houses, each with a
kitchen garden, around the
sides. The rules imposed by
the semi-closed order
required each monk to live
independently. The complex
was rebuilt in late
Renaissance style in 1562;
the façade, completed in
1608, was decorated with
obelisks and statues, crowned
by a statue of Our Lady.
A porticoed atrium with an
exedra-shaped vestibule
provides a harmonious
introduction to the complex.

Vincenzo Seregni designed
the interior in the 1500s. The
aisleless nave is crowned by a
barrel vault flanked by blind
arcades. The church is famous
for the frescoes by Daniele
Crespi, a leading 17th-century
Lombard artist. He reputedly
painted the entire cycle (*The
Legend of the Foundation of
the Order*) to thank the
Carthusian monks for offering
refuge after he had been
charged with murder. The
cycle begins by the first arch
on the right, continues on
the wall behind the façade,
designed by Simone Peter-
zano, and is resumed on the
vault, where there are four
medallions. In the first bay on
the left Crespi included a self-
portrait of himself as a servant
blowing a horn and added
the date (1629) and his
signature in a scroll.

Simone Peterzano painted
the frescoes in the presbytery
and apse (1578), with scenes
from the life of Mary. The
chapel on the right has two
macabre 17th-century
paintings informing novices of
the various forms of torture
they might encounter while
spreading Christianity. On
leaving, look at the 14th-
century cloister on the right,
the only surviving part of the
original monastery.

Façade of the Certosa di Garegnano (1608)

Santa Maria delle Grazie ⓫

Piazza Santa Maria delle Grazie.
Map 2 F5. **Tel** 02-48 01 42 48.
Ⓜ 1, 2 Cadorna, 1 Conciliazione.
🚋 16. ⏰ 7:30am–noon, 3–7pm
daily. ✝ 6:30pm pre-hols; 8, 9:30,
10:30 & 11:30am, 6:30pm hols.

Construction of this famous church was begun in 1463. Designed by Guiniforte Solari, it was completed in 1490. Two years later Lodovico il Moro asked Bramante to change the church into the family mausoleum: Solari's apse section was demolished and then replaced by a Renaissance apse. After il Moro lost power in 1500, the Dominicans continued to decorate the church, later assisted by the court of Inquisition, which had moved here in 1558. Restoration was undertaken only in the late 19th century. In 1943 a bomb destroyed the main cloister, but the apse and the room containing Leonardo's *Last Supper* were miraculously left intact, and restoration work has continued

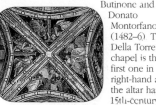

Frescoed cross vaulting in Santa Maria delle Grazie

since then. On the exterior, Solari's wide brick façade is worthy of note. The doorway was designed by Bramante; it is preceded by a porch supported by Corinthian columns and the lunette has a painting by Leonardo da Vinci with the Madonna between Lodovico and his wife, Beatrice d'Este. The sides and poly-

gonal apse are also of interest. As you enter the church you notice the difference between Solari's nave, which echoes Lombard Gothic architecture – entirely covered with frescoes and with ogival arches – and Bramante's design for the apse, which is larger, better lit and is almost bare of decoration. The two parts of the church reflect Bramante's impact on Milanese culture; he introduced the Renaissance style that dominated Tuscany and Umbria in the early 15th century. The all-pervasive painting decoration of the aisle walls is by Bernardino Butinone and Donato Montorfano (1482–6). The Della Torre chapel is the first one in the right-hand aisle: the altar has a 15th-century fresco and to the left is the tomb of Giacomo Della Torre, with bas-relief sculpture by the Cazzaniga brothers (1483). The fourth chapel, dedicated to Santa Corona, has frescoes by Gaudenzio Ferrari. In the next chapel is a *Crucifixion* by Giovanni Demìo (1542).

The apse, decorated only with graffiti to maintain the purity of the architectural

The nave of Santa Maria delle Grazie

volumes, is a perfect cube crowned by a hemisphere. It was built to house the tomb of Lodovico il Moro and Beatrice d'Este, sculpted by Cristoforo Solari, but the work never reached Santa Maria delle Grazie (it is now in the Charterhouse of Pavia). The decoration of the dome is rich in Marian symbols, while the Doctors of the Church appear in the roundels in the pendentives. The carved and inlaid wooden stalls of the choir are lovely; above them on the walls are figures of Dominican saints.

A door on the right leads to the small cloister known as Chiostrino delle Rane because of the frogs *(rane)* in the central basin. The cloister leads to the old sacristy, with its painted wardrobes, one of which conceals a secret underground passageway, used by Lodovico to come from the Castello on horseback. Back in the church, the chapels in the north aisle begin with the Madonna delle Grazie chapel, with Cerano's *Madonna Freeing Milan of the Plague* (1631) on the entrance archway. The altarpiece, *Madonna delle Grazie*, dates from the 15th century. The sixth chapel has a *Holy Family with St Catherine* by Paris Bordone, and the first chapel contains the cloak of St Catherine of Siena.

The façade of Santa Maria delle Grazie, designed by Guiniforte Solari

Leonardo da Vinci's *Last Supper*

Lodovico
il Moro

This masterpiece was painted for Lodovico il Moro in the refectory of Santa Maria delle Grazie in 1495–7. Leonardo depicts the moment just after Christ has uttered the words, "One of you will betray me". The artist captures their amazement in facial expressions and body language in a remarkably realistic and vivid *Last Supper*. It is not a true fresco, but was painted in tempera, allowing Leonardo more time to achieve the subtle nuances typical of his work. The room was used as a stable in the Napoleonic era and was badly damaged by bombs in 1943. Fortunately, the work was saved because it was protected by sandbags.

Jesus Christ
The isolated, serene figure of Christ contrasts with the agitated Apostles. Half-closed lips show he has just spoken.

The Last Supper
is famous for the gesturing hands of the Apostles, which are so harmonious and expressive that critics have said they "speak".

Judas
Unable to find a truly evil face for Judas, Leonardo drew inspiration from that of the prior in the convent, who kept on asking when the work would be finished.

The Apostle Andrew, with his arms upraised, expresses his horror at Christ's words.

The Crucifixion by Montorfano
The Dominicans asked Donato Montorfano to paint a fresco of the Crucifixion on the opposite wall to depict Christ's sacrifice. In this dense composition the despairing Magdalen hugs the cross while the soldiers on the right throw dice for Christ's robe. On either side of the work, under the cross, Leonardo added the portraits – now almost invisible – of Lodovico il Moro, his wife Beatrice and their children, signed and dated (1495).

THE RESTORATION

It was not the humidity but the method used by Leonardo, *tempera forte*, that caused the immediate deterioration of the *Last Supper*. As early as 1550 the art historian Vasari called it "a dazzling blotch" and regarded it as a lost work. There have been many attempts to restore the *Last Supper*, beginning in 1726, but in retouching the picture further damage was done. The seventh and most recent restoration ended in spring 1999: although it lacks the splendour of the original, it is at least authentic.

Material used for restoration

The tablecloth, plates and bowls were probably copied from those in the convent to give the impression that Christ was at table with monks.

Sketches of the Apostles

Leonardo used to wander around Milan in search of faces to use for the Apostles. Of his many sketches, this one for St James is now in the Royal Library in Windsor.

CHRIST AND THE APOSTLES

13 12 11 10 9 8 1 2 3 4 5 6 7

1 Christ
2 Thomas
3 James the Greater
4 Philip
5 Matthew
6 Thaddaeus
7 Simon

8 John
9 Peter
10 Judas
11 Andrew
12 James the Lesser
13 Bartholomew

Corso Magenta

Map 3 A5 (9 A3). **M** *1 Conciliazione, 1, 2 Cadorna.* **▦** *18, 19, 24.*

This street is fascinating, with its elegant shops and historic buildings making it one of the loveliest and most elegant quarters in Milan. At No. 65, just past Santa Maria delle Grazie, is a building incorporating the remains of the Atellani residence, decorated by Luini, where Leonardo da Vinci stayed while working on the *Last Supper*. Piero Portaluppi carried out the work on No. 65 in 1919. In the garden at the back there are some vines, said to be the remains of the vineyard that Lodovico il Moro gave to the great artist. The next building (No. 61), Palazzo delle Stelline, originally a girls' orphanage, is now a convention centre. At the corner of Via Carducci, which was constructed over the original course of the Naviglio canal, stands Bar Magenta *(see p186)*. The medieval city gate, the Porta Vercellina, once stood at this junction. At No. 71 is Museo Teatrale, which relates the history of La Scala *(see p52)*.

Pastry shop sign in Corso Magenta

The Sala Rossa in Palazzo Litta, with mementos of Napoleon's visit here

Palazzo Litta

Corso Magenta 24. **Map** 3 A5 (9 A3). **M** *1, 2 Cadorna.* **▦** *18, 19, 24, 27.* **▭** *50, 58.* ◯ *during cultural events only.*

Considered one of the most beautiful examples of 18th-century Lombard architecture, this palazzo was first built in 1648 for Count Bartolomeo Arese by Francesco Maria Richini. At the end of the century the interior was embellished and in 1763 the pink façade was built at the request of the heirs, the Litta Visconti Arese. The façade, by Bartolomeo Bolli, is late Baroque, the door flanked by large telamones. Since 1905 the building has housed the State Railway offices.

Inside is a number of sumptuous rooms looking onto a 17th-century courtyard. The broad staircase, designed by Carlo Giuseppe Merlo in 1740 and decorated with precious marble and the family coat of arms (a black and white check), has a double central flight. It leads up to the *piano nobile*, where one of the rooms is named the Sala Rossa (Red Room) after the colour of its wallpaper (a copy of the original). Set in the floor is a pearl, there to commemorate a tear said to have been shed during a meeting between the Duchess Litta and Napoleon.

The next room is the Salone degli Specchi, which seems to be enlarged to infinity by the large mirrors *(specchi)* on the walls. The vault decoration is by Martin Knoller. The Salotto della Duchessa is the only room in the palazzo which still has its original 18th-century wallpaper. The Teatro Litta stands to the left of the palazzo, the oldest theatre in the city.

Civico Museo Archeologico

Corso Magenta 15. **Map** 3 A5 (9 A3). **Tel** *02-86 45 00 11.* **M** *1, 2 Cadorna.* **▦** *18, 19, 24, 27.* **▭** *50, 54, 58.* ◯ *9am–5:30pm Tue–Sun.* **⅃** *(phone ahead).* **Ⓟ**

The Archaeological Museum is well worth a visit for the finds and to see the only remaining part of the city's Roman walls. At the entrance visitors are greeted by a huge stone from the Val Camonica *(see p155)* with Bronze Age engravings. Further on is a model of Milan in Roman times. The visit begins in a hall on the right, with clay objects, including a collection of oil lamps. This is followed by Roman sculpture. One of the most interesting pieces in the series of portraits dating from Caesar's era to late antiquity (1st–4th century AD), is the *Portrait of Maximin* (mid-3rd century AD).

Roman sarcophagus of a lawyer, on display in the Civico Museo Archeologico

At the end of this room is a huge fragment of a torso of Hercules from the Milanese thermae, dating from the first half of the 2nd century AD. Behind these are some 3rd-century AD floor mosaics found in Milanese houses.

By the window are two of the most important works in the museum: the Parabiago Patera and the Diatreta Cup. The Patera is a gilded silver plate with a relief of the triumph of the goddess Cybele, mother of the gods, on a chariot pulled by lions and surrounded by the Sun and Moon and sea and Zodiac divinities (mid-4th century AD). The marvellous Diatreta Cup, also dating from the 4th century AD, comes from Novara and consists of a single piece of coloured glass, with finely wrought, intricate decoration. Winding around the cup is the inscription *Bibe vivas multis annis* ("Drink and you will live many years"). To the left of the entrance are 6th-century Lombard finds. The entrance hall leads to a second courtyard, where you will see the Torre di Ansperto, a Roman tower from the ancient Maximinian walls. The basement contains a collection of Attic red- and black-figure vases and the museum display ends with a fine collection of Etruscan pieces.

Stela with portraits, Museo Archeologico

San Maurizio ⑮

Corso Magenta. **Map** 3 A5 (9 A3). *Tel* 02-86 66 60 (Santa Maria alla Porta). Ⓜ 1, 2 Cadorna. 🚋 16, 18, 19, 27. 🚌 50, 54, 58. ◯ 9am–noon, 2–5pm Tue–Sun. ✝ 6pm Mon–Fri, 10:15 am (Greek–Albanian) Sun.

In 1503 Gian Giacomo Dolcebuono began construction of this church, which was intended for the most powerful closed order of Benedictine nuns in Milan, with one hall for the public and another for the nuns. In the first hall, to the right of the altar, is the opening through which the nuns receive the Body of Christ. Most of the decoration was done by Bernardino Luini. He painted the frescoes in the first hall, including the *Life of St Catherine* (third chapel to the right) and those on the middle wall. The second chapel on the right was decorated by Callisto Piazza, the chapels to the left by pupils of Luini. On the altar is an *Adoration of the Magi* by Antonio Campi. The middle wall of the second hall, occupied by the choir, has frescoes by Foppa, Piazza, an *Annunciation* attributed to Bramantino and *Episodes of the Passion*. Concerts are held here in the winter.

The Roman ruins in Via Brisa

Via Brisa ⑯

Map 7 B1 (9 B3). Ⓜ 1, 2 Cadorna. 🚋 16, 18, 19, 27. 🚌 50, 58.

Excavations carried out after the 1943 bombing of this street revealed Roman ruins which were probably part of Maximin's imperial palace: the foundation of a round hall surrounded by apsidal halls and preceded by a narthex. Note the columns that raised the pavement to allow warm air to pass into the palace.

Piazza Cordusio ⑰

Map 7 C1 (9 C3). Ⓜ 1 Cordusio. 🚋 16, 18, 19, 27. 🚌 50, 58, 60.

This oval-shaped piazza was named after the *Curtis Ducis*, the main seat of the Lombard duchy. The area, Milan's financial district, was laid out from 1889 to 1901. Buildings include Luca Beltrami's Assicurazioni Generali building, Casa Dario, and the main offices of Credito Italiano, designed by Luigi Broggi.

Piazza Affari ⑱

Map 7 B1 (9 B3). Ⓜ 1 Cordusio. 🚋 16, 18, 19, 27. 🚌 50, 58, 60.

The heart of the financial district, this square was laid out in 1928–40 to house the city's markets (especially farm produce). The Borsa Valori, Italy's most important Stock Exchange, stands here. Founded in 1808, it is housed in a building designed by Paolo Mezzanotte in 1931. Ruins of a 1st-century BC Roman theatre were found in the basement area.

The Milan Stock Exchange in Piazza Affari, built in 1931

SOUTHWEST MILAN

eligious complexes once covered this district, preventing further building until the early 19th century. The suppression of the monasteries in the late 18th century paved the way for the urbanization of the area between the medieval and Spanish walls, crossed by two large avenues, Corso Italia and Corso di Porta Ticinese. Beyond Porta Ticinese, which leads to the southern part of Milan, is Corso San Gottardo. The area is bordered by the inner ring

Vault mosaic, Sant'Ambrogio

road, which follows the course of the medieval walls, and the outer ring road, which replaced the Spanish walls. Further on is the Naviglio canals quarter, with the Naviglio Grande and the Pavese, the last vestiges of what was once a major network for communications and commerce. Barges used the Naviglio Grande to transport the Candoglia marble used to build the Duomo and, in the 1950s, the material for postwar reconstruction.

SIGHTS AT A GLANCE

Churches

San Bernardino alle
   Monache ❺
*San Lorenzo alle Colonne
   pp80–81* ❶
San Paolo Converso ⓬
San Vittore al Corpo ❽
Sant'Alessandro ⓭
Sant'Ambrogio pp84–7 ❻
Sant'Eustorgio ❿
Santa Maria presso
   San Celso ⓫

Streets, Squares and Historic Buildings

Largo Carrobbio and Via Torino ❸
Piazza della Vetra and medieval
   Porta Ticinese ❷
Via Circo ❹

Museums and Galleries

Museo Diocesano ❾
Museo Nazionale della Scienza
   e della Tecnica ❼

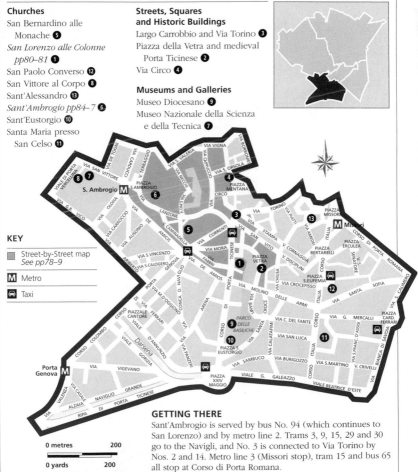

KEY

▦	Street-by-Street map *See pp78–9*
Ⓜ	Metro
🚕	Taxi

GETTING THERE

Sant'Ambrogio is served by bus No. 94 (which continues to San Lorenzo) and by metro line 2. Trams 3, 9, 15, 29 and 30 go to the Navigli, and No. 3 is connected to Via Torino by Nos. 2 and 14. Metro line 3 (Missori stop), tram 15 and bus 65 all stop at Corso di Porta Romana.

0 metres 200

0 yards 200

◁ **The antiques market, held on the towpath of the Naviglio Grande on the last Sunday of every month**

Street-by-Street: From Sant'Ambrogio to San Lorenzo

Situated just outside the Roman walls, this area was occupied by Early Christian cemeteries and Imperial Age buildings such as the Arena and Circus. Though little remains of this ancient heritage, it is however significant, particularly the columns of the triumphal entrance to the basilica of San Lorenzo. Nine kings of Italy were crowned in Sant'Ambrogio in the 9th–15th centuries and four were buried here. Napoleon came here in 1805, and Ferdinand of Austria in 1838, after their respective coronations in the Duomo. On the feast day of Sant' Ambrogio, 7 December, the *Oh bej Oh bej* fair is held in the streets.

Statue, Università Cattolica

Via Circo
The remains of an ancient Roman circus, used for public spectacles, were found in this street ❻

Cloister of Santa Maria Maddalena al Cerchio

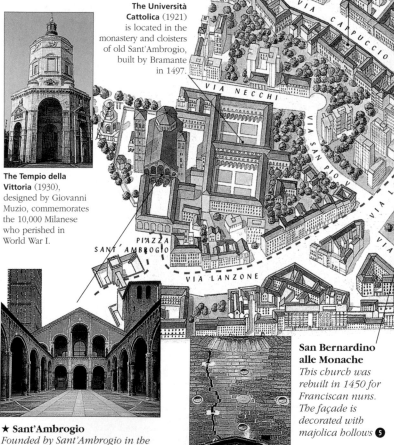

The Università Cattolica (1921) is located in the monastery and cloisters of old Sant'Ambrogio, built by Bramante in 1497.

The Tempio della Vittoria (1930), designed by Giovanni Muzio, commemorates the 10,000 Milanese who perished in World War I.

VIA CAPPUCCIO

VIA NECCHI

VIA SAN PIO

VIA LANZ

VIA OR

PIAZZA SANT' AMBROGIO

VIA LANZONE

★ Sant'Ambrogio
Founded by Sant'Ambrogio in the 4th century, this church contains masterpieces such as the San Vittore mosaics and the Golden Altar ❻

San Bernardino alle Monache
This church was rebuilt in 1450 for Franciscan nuns. The façade is decorated with majolica hollows ❺

0 metres	100
0 yards	100

For hotels and restaurants in this area see pp161–2 and pp173–5

Largo Carrobbio
The name of the crossroads at the end of Via Torino may derive from Quadrivium. meaning a place where four streets converge ③

LOCATOR MAP
See Street Finder, map 7, 8

A tower from the Roman Porta Ticinese is hidden in the courtyard of a building between Via del Torchio and Via Medici.

In Largo Carrobbio the small deconsecrated church of San Sisto houses the Museo Messina.

Piazza della Vetra
From this square there are spectacular views of the apses of San Lorenzo and Sant'Eustorgio. Until 1840 the piazza was the scene of executions ②

VIA TORINO

LARGO CARROBBIO

VIA SAN VITO

VIA CESARE CORRENTI

PORTA TICINESE

VIA PIO IV

VIA MORA

VIA DE AMICIS

VIA MOLINO DELLE ARMI

KEY

— — — Suggested route

STAR SIGHTS

★ San Lorenzo alle Colonne

★ Sant'Ambrogio

The 16 Corinthian columns may have come from a 2nd–3rd-century AD pagan temple.

Medieval Porta Ticinese

★ **San Lorenzo alle Colonne**
This superb 4th-century basilica consists of a main domed section linked to a series of minor buildings, dating from different periods ①

San Lorenzo alle Colonne ●

Dating from the 4th century, San Lorenzo is
one of the oldest round churches in Western
Christendom and may have been the ancient
Imperial palatine chapel. The church was built
utilizing materials from a nearby Roman
amphitheatre. The plan, with exedrae and women's
galleries, is unlike Lombard architecture and reveals
the hand of Roman architects and masons. Some
art historians also see the influence of Byzantine art
in the unusual plan. After several fires the church
was reconstructed in the 11th and 12th centuries
and was again rebuilt after the dome collapsed
in 1573, but the original quatrefoil plan has been
preserved. The chapel of Sant'Aquilino contains
some of the best mosaics in Northern Italy.

Cappella di San Sisto
*This chapel was frescoed by
Gian Cristoforo Storer in the
17th century.*

A bas-relief above the entrance depicts San
Lorenzo, who was burnt over live coals in the
3rd century (a recurring symbol in the church).

Main entrance

★ Roman Columns
*The 16 Corinthian columns, from
the 2nd–3rd century, were part
of an unidentified temple and
were placed in their present
location in the 4th century.*

**Statue of
Constantine**
*This bronze work is
a copy of a Roman
statue of the emperor
who issued the Edict of
Milan in AD 313,
bringing persecution of
Christians to an end.*

The dome, the largest in Milan, is supported by an octagonal tambour lit by eight large windows. It was rebuilt by Martino Bassi after it collapsed in 1573.

An upside-down column symbolizes Christianity rising from the ruins of paganism.

VISITORS' CHECKLIST

Corso di Porta Ticinese 39.
Map 7 B2. **Tel** 02-89 40 41 29.
M 3 Missori. 3. 94.
8:30am–12:30pm, 2:30–6:30pm
daily. 6pm Mon–Fri; 6pm
pre-hols; 9:30, 11:30am, 4pm
(in Philippine language), 6pm hols.
Cappella di Sant'Aquilino
9am–6:30pm daily.
www.sanlorenzomaggiore.com

★ **Cappella di Sant'Aquilino**
This 5th-century chapel has mosaics from the same period: Elijah on the Chariot of Fire and Christ with the Apostles. The entire chapel was once decorated with mosaics.

Byzantine sarcophagus

Behind the altar, steps lead to the crypt, which has stones taken from the amphitheatre and used for compacting the earth.

The 17th-century presbyteries, designed by Trezzi and Richini, were originally designed to join up with the columns so as to revive the pattern of the ancient quadriporticus.

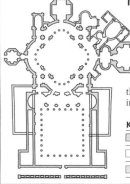

THE STRUCTURE

Most of the walls, towers and three chapels date from the late 4th century. The upper parts of the towers are Romanesque. The dome was built in the late 1500s and the façade in 1894 by Cesare Nava.

KEY

☐	Early Christian
☐	Medieval and modern
☐	Romanesque

STAR FEATURES

★ Roman Columns

★ Cappella di Sant'Aquilino

Piazza della Vetra, linking San Lorenzo to Sant'Eustorgio

Piazza della Vetra and medieval Porta Ticinese ❷

Map 7 B2 (9 B5). 🚋 2, 3, 14. 🚌 94.

The vast area of greenery dominated by a column bearing the statue of San Lazzaro (1728) is also called Parco delle Basiliche, because it lies between the basilicas of San Lorenzo and Sant'Eustorgio. The name "Vetra" seems to derive from the Latin *castra vetera*, which probably alluded to the Roman military camps positioned here to defend the nearby imperial palace. The name was also given to a canal that was once on the northern side of the square and was lined with tanners' work-shops (the tanners were

Detail of the tabernacle of Porta Ticinese:
Madonna and Child with St Ambrose
by Giovanni di Balduccio's workshop

called *vetraschi*). Until 1840 the square was used for the public hangings of condemned commoners, while nobles were decapitated in front of the law court, the Broletto (*see p54*).

During the Roman era there was a small port here, at the point where the Seveso and Nirone rivers converged in the navigable Vettabbia canal.

This square is worth visiting just for the magnificent view of the apses of the basilicas. In the 12th century, when the city walls were enlarged to include San Lorenzo, the Roman gate at present-day Largo Carrobbio was replaced by the "new" medieval Porta Ticinese. A moat ran around the new walls and along present-day Via Molino delle Armi, which was named after the water mills *(molini)* used mostly to forge weapons.

Porta Ticinese was remodelled after 1329 by Azzone Visconti and decorated with a tabernacle of the *Madonna and Child with St Ambrose Proffering the Model of the City* by the workshop of Giovanni di Balduccio (14th century). This city gate – the only one, along with Porta Nuova on Via Manzoni, still standing – was fortified with two towers in 1865.

Largo Carrobbio and Via Torino ❸

Map 7 B2 (9 B4). 🚋 2, 3, 14.
Museo Messina *Via San Sisto 4.*
Tel *02-88 46 36 51.* ⭕ *Opening hours vary. Call for up-to-date information.* ⬤ *1 Jan, Easter, 1 May, 15 Aug, 25 Dec.* 🚫 ♿

The vast Carrobbio square, which connects Via Torino and Corso di Porta Ticinese, was either named after the *quadrivium*, a crossroads of four streets, or after *carrubium*, a road reserved for carts. One of the towers flanking the Roman Porta Ticinese still stands at the corner of Via Medici and Via del Torchio. The name of the gate derived from the fact that it opened onto the road for Pavia, which in ancient times was called *Ticinum*. At the junction with Via San Sisto is the deconsecrated 17th-century church of San Sisto. In 1976 it became the museum-studio of sculptor Francesco Messina (who died in 1990) and now houses a collection of his bronze and

Female nude by Francesco Messina (1967)

coloured plaster sculpture pieces and graphic art.

Largo Carrobbio is at one end of Via Torino, a major commercial street that developed after the merger of the old city districts, which were filled with the workshops of oil merchants, silk weavers, hatters and famous armourers – as can be seen by the names of some streets.

The 16th-century Palazzo Stampa, built by Massimiliano Stampa, stands in Via Soncino. When the Sforza dynasty died out in 1535, Stampa introduced Spanish dominion to the city by hoisting the flag of Charles V on the Castello Sforzesco in exchange for land and privileges. The imperial eagle still stands on the palazzo tower, over the bronze globe representing the dominions of Charles V.

The cloister at Santa Maria Maddalena al Cerchio

Via Circo ❹

Map 7 B1 (9 B4). 🚊 *2, 3, 14.*

The area extending from Largo Carrobbio to Corso Magenta is very rich in 3rd- and 4th-century ruins, particularly mosaics and masonry, much of it now part of private homes. This was the period when the Roman emperor Maximian lived in Milan: his splendid palace was near Via Brisa. In order to create a proper imperial capital, he built many civic edifices to gain the favour of the Milanese: the Arena, the thermae and the huge Circus used for two-horse chariot races. The Circus, 505 m

(1,656 ft) long, was one of the largest constructions in the Roman Empire. The only remaining parts are the end curve, visible at the junction of Via Cappuccio and Via Circo, and one of the entrance towers, which became the bell tower of San Maurizio in Corso Magenta.

The Circus, active long after the fall of the Roman Empire, was the venue of the coronation of the Lombard king Adaloaldo in 615, while in the Carolingian period it became a vineyard, as the place name of nearby Via Vigna indicates. At No. 7 Via Cappuccio, the 18th-century Palazzo Litta Biumi has incorporated, to the left of the central courtyard, the delightful 15th-century nuns' convent Santa Maria Maddalena al Cerchio, which has been partly rebuilt. Its name, a corruption of the Latin *ad circulum*, refers to the Circus over which it was built. The hood of the nuns' habit *(cappuccio)* is probably the origin of the name of the street where the convent is located. Further along, at No. 13, is Palazzo Radice Fossati (a private house), of medieval origin, with a 13th-century portal and 18th-century frescoes inside.

On Via Sant'Orsola you come to Via Morigi, named after a famous Milanese family who once lived here; all that remains of their residence is a 14th-century tower with a small loggia. The nearby square is dominated by the 14th-century Torre dei Gorani, another tower crowned by a loggia with small stone columns.

Fifteenth-century frescoes by the school of Vincenzo Foppa

San Bernardino alle Monache ❺

Via Lanzone 13. **Map** 7 A1 (9 A4). *Tel 02-86 45 19 48 (Amici di San Bernardino cultural association).* 🚊 *2, 3, 14.* 🏛 *for restoration.*

The church is the only remaining building in a Franciscan nuns' convent dating from the mid-15th century and attributed to the Lombard architect Pietro Antonio Solari. The church was named after the preacher Bernardino da Siena, whose relics are kept here. It was partly rebuilt in 1922. The narrow, elegant brick façade is decorated with majolica bowls and a fine elaborate cornice with small arches.

The interior houses fine 15th-century frescoes painted by the school of Vincenzo Foppa, and others dating from the early 16th century. The church is under restoration and will be re-opened to the public in the future.

Part of the curve of the Circus built by the Roman emperor Maximian in the late 3rd century AD

Sant'Ambrogio

Detail of the apse mosaic

The basilica was built by Bishop Ambrogio (Ambrose) in AD 379–86 on an Early Christian burial ground as part of a programme to reorganize the Christian face of Milan. The church was dedicated to Ambrogio, a defender of Christianity against Arianism, after his burial here. The Benedictines began to enlarge it in the 8th century, then in the following century Archbishop Anspert built the atrium, which was rebuilt in the 12th century. In the 11th century, reconstruction of the entire church began. The dome collapsed in 1196, and the vaults and pulpit were rebuilt. In 1492 the Sforza family asked Bramante to restructure the rectory and the Benedictine monastery. Sadly, the basilica was badly damaged by bombs in 1943.

The Canons' bell tower was erected in 1124 to surpass in height and beauty the campanile of the nearby Benedictines.

The Capitals
The columns are enlivened by Bible stories and fantastic animals symbolizing the struggle between Good and Evil. Some date from the 11th century.

Anspert's Atrium (11th century) was used by local people as a refuge from danger before the city walls were built.

The Interior
The solemn proportions typical of Lombard Romanesque characterize the interior. The nave is covered by ribbed cross vaulting supported by massive piers.

Apse Mosaic
The mosaic dates from the 4th–8th centuries and was partially restored after the 1943 bombings. It depicts the enthroned Christ and scenes from Sant'Ambrogio's life.

Apse

VISITORS' CHECKLIST

Piazza Sant'Ambrogio 15. **Map** 7 A1 (9 A3). **Tel** 02-86 45 08 95. Ⓜ 2 Sant'Ambrogio. ▣ 50, 54, 58, 94. ▢ 7am–noon, 3–7 pm daily. ✝ 6:30pm pre-hols; 8 & 10am (in Latin), 12:15, 6 & 7pm hols; 7:30, 8 & 9am, 6:30pm Mon–Fri. ▢ ▢ **Museo della Basilica Tel** 02-86 45 08 95. Access through presbytery or rear of church. ▢ 10am–noon, 3–5pm Tue–Sun. ● am pre-hols and hols. ▣ ▢ **Chapel of San Vittore in Ciel d'Oro** ▣

★ **Chapel of San Vittore in Ciel d'Oro**
The chapel was named after the gold (oro) mosaics on the vault. Sant'Ambrogio is depicted in one of the 5th-century panels.

Museum entrance

★ **Golden Altar**
This golden altar was made by Volvinius (9th century) for the remains of Sant'-Ambrogio. The reliefs depict the lives of Christ (front) and Ambrogio (to the rear).

The ciborium is the small 10th-century baldachin that protects the Golden Altar. It is supported by four Roman porphyry columns and decorated with stuccowork.

★ **Sarcophagus of Stilicho**
Situated under the pulpit, this 4th-century master-piece has a wealth of relief figures with religious significance. It is tradition-ally referred to as the tomb of the Roman general Stilicho, but probably contained the remains of the emperor Gratian.

STAR FEATURES

★ Golden Altar

★ Chapel of San Vittore in Cie l d'Oro

★ Sarcophagus of Stilicho

Exploring Sant'Ambrogio

The fact that the church of Sant'Ambrogio houses the remains of the city's patron saint, the church's founder, makes it a special place for the Milanese. Most of its present-day appearance is the result of rebuilding in the 10th and 12th centuries by the Benedictines from the nearby monastery, who made it a model of Lombard Romanesque religious architecture. All that remains of the 4th-century basilica are the triumphal arch and its columns, which became part of the apse. In 1937–40 and in the postwar period the Romanesque structure and delicate colours were restored. From the Pusterla (gate) there is a marvellous view of the church, with its two bell towers and atrium, flanked by the rectory and museum.

Papal statue

PUSTERLA DI SANT'AMBROGIO

The Pusterla di Sant' Ambrogio, one of the minor gates on the medieval walls, is a good starting point for a visit to the church. Rebuilt in 1939, it houses a museum with old weapons and instruments of torture.

A decorated capital in the atrium

ANSPERT'S ATRIUM

Just before the atrium, to the left, is the isolated Roman Colonna del Diavolo (Devil's Column), with two holes halfway up which, according to tradition, were made by the Devil's horns while he was tempting Sant'Ambrogio. The present-day atrium, with its blind arches, dates from the 12th century and replaced one built by Archbishop Anspert in the 9th century.

This large courtyard acts as an entrance foyer for the church proper and sets off the façade. A row of piers

(some Roman) with sculpted capitals continues into the basilica.

The rhythmic pattern of the arches, half-columns and small suspended arches, as well as the proportions, match those in the church, creating a harmonious continuity between exterior and interior. The atrium houses finds and tombstones from this area, which was once an Early Christian cemetery.

The fourth side of the atrium, or narthex, has five bays and is part of the façade, which has an upper loggia with five arches. In the narthex is the main portal (8th–10th centuries), with small columns with figures of animals and the Mystic Lamb, while its wooden wings (1750) have reliefs of the *Life of David*.

The atrium, with finds and tombstones from the surrounding area

THE INTERIOR

The nave provides the best view of the interior, revealing the basilica in all its splendour. The nave has two side aisles divided by arcades supporting the women's galleries with piers with carved capitals. At the beginning of the nave is the Serpent's Column, said to have been erected by Moses in the desert. Beside it, to the left, excavations show the level of the original 4th-century floor.

The pulpit (or ambo) is made of pieces saved when the dome collapsed in 1196. This magnificent monument is decorated with an eagle and a seated man, symbols of the evangelists John and Matthew. Underneath is the sarcophagus of Stilicho (4th century) with reliefs representing (going clockwise) *Christ Giving the Law to St Peter*, four scenes from the Old Testament, *Christ among the Apostles* and the *Sacrifice of Isaac*. Under the octagonal cupola is the ciborium (10th century), the heart of the basilica, supported by columns taken from the 4th-century ciborium. Its painted stucco sides depict various episodes: on the front is *Christ Giving the Keys to St Peter and the Law to St Paul*. The ciborium acts as a baldachin for the Golden Altar, an embossed work that Archbishop Angilberto commissioned from Volvinius in the 9th century. On the back, a silver relief narrates the *Life of Sant'Ambrogio* and has the artist's signature. On the same side, two small doors allowed the faithful to worship the body of St Ambrose, once kept under the altar. The front is made of gold and jewels, and narrates the *Life of Christ*. Behind the ciborium is the wooden choir with the *Life of Sant' Ambrogio* (15th century) and, in the middle, the bishop's throne (4th and 9th centuries), also used by

The Serpent's Column, at the beginning of the nave

the kings of Italy crowned here. Part of the large mosaic in the apse dates from the 6th and 8th centuries. The scene on the left, a *Benedictory Christ*, is of the same period, while the one on the right is the result of 18th-century and postwar reconstruction. Next to the presbytery is the stairway to the crypt, decorated with stucco (c.1740). Under the Golden Altar, an urn (1897) has the remains of Saints Ambrogio, Gervasio and Protasio. Back upstairs, at the end of the south aisle is the stunning San Vittore in Ciel d'Oro Sacellum,

The Risen Christ by Bergognone (c.1491)

the 4th-century funerary chapel of the martyr, which was later incorporated into the basilica. The 5th-century mosaics on the walls show various saints, including Saints Ambrogio, Gervasio and Protasio.

THE SOUTH AISLE

Returning to the entrance in the south aisle, you will see the monks' chapels, built in different eras. St George's chapel – sixth from the entrance – houses an altarpiece of the *Madonna and Child with the Infant St*

John the Baptist by Bernardo Lanino, who frescoed the *Legend of St George* on the sides (1546). The Baroque chapel of the Holy Sacrament, the fifth, contains the frescoes *The Death of St Benedict* by Carlo Preda and *St Bernard* by Filippo Abbiati (17th and 18th century respectively). In St Bartholomew's chapel (the second) are the *Legends of Saints Vittore and Satiro* (1737) by Tiepolo, detached from the San Vittore Sacellum; they demonstrate the cultural openness of the Cistercians, who commissioned the work. The altarpiece in the second chapel, *The Virgin Mary with St Bartholomew and St John the Baptist*, is attributed to Gaudenzio Ferrari, as is the 1545 *Deposition* in the next chapel, which also has frescoes by Luini on the pillars.

THE NORTH AISLE

Go up this aisle from the baptistery (first chapel), which has a porphyry font by Franco Lombardi with the *Conversion of St Augustine* (1940), the saint baptized by Sant'Ambrogio in Milan. It is dominated symbolically

by Bergognone's *The Risen Christ* (c.1491).

In the third chapel is an interesting painting by Luini, a *Madonna with Saints Jerome and Rocco*.

MUSEO DELLA BASILICA

At the end of the north aisle you come out into the Portico della Canonica, the presbytery portico, which was left unfinished by Bramante (1492–4) and rebuilt after World War II. The columns of the central arch, sculpted to resemble tree trunks, are unusual. The entrance to the Basilica Museum, with six rooms featuring objects and works of art from the church, is here. Among the most interesting pieces are a 12th-century multicoloured tondo of St Ambrose; a cast of Stilicho's sarcophagus; St Ambrose's bed; fragments of the apse mosaics and four wooden panels from the 4th-century portal. The museum also has a *Triptych* by Bernardo Zenale (15th century) and *Christ among the Doctors* by Bergognone. In the garden opposite is St Sigismund's oratory, already famous by 1096, with 15th-century frescoes and Roman columns.

Plaque of the Università Cattolica del Sacro Cuore

UNIVERSITÀ CATTOLICA DEL SACRO CUORE

On the right-hand side of the church (entrance at No. 1 Largo Gemelli), in the former Benedictine monastery, is the university founded by padre Agostino Gemelli in 1921. Its two cloisters, with Ionic and Doric columns, were two of the four Bramante had designed in 1497. In the refectory is *The Marriage at Cana* by Callisto Piazza (1545).

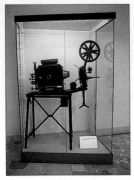

Old motion picture camera, the Science and Technology Museum

Museo Nazionale della Scienza e della Tecnica ❼

Via San Vittore 21. **Map** 6 F1. *Tel 02-48 55 51.* Ⓜ *2 Sant'Ambrogio.* 🚌 *50, 54, 58, 94.* ⏱ *9:30am–4:50pm Tue–Fri; 9.30am– 6:20pm Sat, hols.* 📷 ♿ 🛗 🍴 🎁 💳 *(book at Ufficio Didattico). Library, lecture rooms.* **www**.museoscienza.org

The Science and Technology Museum is housed in the former Olivetan monastery of San Vittore (16th century) – partly designed by Vincenzo Seregni – which became a military hospital and then a barracks after monasteries were suppressed in 1804. It was badly damaged in World War II, was restored, and in 1947 became the home of the museum. In the two court-yards surrounded by the old section of the museum, you can see part of the foundation of the San Vittore fortress and that of the octagonal mauso-leum of Emperor Valentinian II, both ancient Roman.

The museum boasts one of the world's leading science and technology collections. The vast exhibition space is housed in different buildings. The former monastery con-tains the technological sec-tions on metallurgy, casting and transport, as well as science sections featuring physics, optics, acoustics and astronomy. Another section shows the development of calculation, from the first mechanical calculating machine, invented by Pascal

in 1642, to IBM computers. There is also a section on time measurement, with a reconstruction of a 1750 watchmaker's workshop. The printing section is also worth a visit: it shows the 1810 automatic inking method by which 800 sheets an hour could be printed, and also has the father of the modern typewriter (1855).

The cinema photography section shows how the claw device, used to make motion-picture film move, grew out of a sewing machine needle conceived by Singer in 1851. In the rooms given over to telephones and television, there is a reconstruction of the 1856 pantelegraph, the ancestor of the fax machine.

The history of trains begins with the first locomotive used in Italy, used for the Naples-Portici line in 1839, and ends with 1970s models. A pavilion in Via Olona houses the air and sea transport section, featuring two historic pieces: the bridge of the transatlantic liner *Conte Biancamano* and a naval training ship.

The Leo-nardo da Vinci Gallery has fascinating wooden models of the machines and apparatus invented by the genius, shown together with his drawings. Some, like the rotating crane and the helical airscrew, which demonstrate principles of physics and applied mechanics, can be operated by the public.

Façade detail, San Vittore al Corpo

San Vittore al Corpo ❽

Via San Vittore 25. **Map** 6 F1. *Tel 02-48 00 53 51.* Ⓜ *2 Sant'Ambrogio.* 🚌 *50, 54, 58, 94.* ⏱ *7:30am–noon, 3:30–7pm daily.* 🕆 *6pm pre-hols; 8:30, 10 & 11:15am; 12:15, 6 & 9 pm hols.* 📷 *(no flash).* 🎁 *available for groups (book in advance).*

The original basilica on this site was founded in the 4th century, next to the mausoleum of Emperor Valentinian II, who died in 392. The church was rebuilt in the 11th and 12th centuries by Benedictine monks, and again altered in 1560 by the Olivetans, who replaced the monks. The architect (either Alessi or Seregni) reversed the orientation and made it one of Milan's most sumptuous churches, with splendid late 16th-century paintings. The Baroque Arese Chapel (1668), designed by Gerolamo Quad-rio, and the right-hand apse, with scenes from the life of St Gregory by Camillo Procac-cini (1602), are of particular interest. Moncalvo frescoed the angel musicians on the cupola in 1619. The wooden choir stalls, with carvings of episodes from St Benedict's life, date from 1583; above them are three canvases on the same subject by Gio-vanni Ambrogio Figino. Last, the chapel of Sant'Antonio Abate was entirely frescoed in 1619 by Daniele Crespi.

The façade of San Vittore al Corpo

Along the Naviglio Grande

Now one of the liveliest quarters in Milan, the Navigli formed the city's port district until the 19th century. Work on the Naviglio Grande canal began in 1177, followed by the Pavia, Bereguardo, Martesana and Paderno canals. A system of locks allowed boats to travel along the canals on different levels (Candoglia marble was taken to the Duomo in the 14th century in this way). Lodovico il Moro

One of the 12 locks

improved this network with the help of Leonardo da Vinci in the 15th century. Barges arrived laden with coal and salt and departed with handmade goods and textiles. Some sections of the canals, which once extended for 150 km (93 miles), were filled in during the 1930s and navigation ceased altogether in 1979. Thanks to the Navigli canals, in 1953 landlocked Milan was ranked the 13th port in Italy.

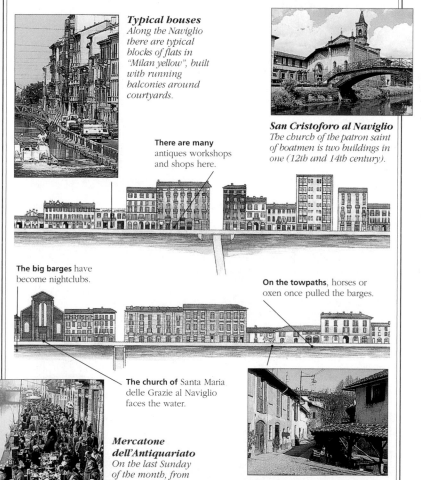

Typical houses
Along the Naviglio there are typical blocks of flats in "Milan yellow", built with running balconies around courtyards.

San Cristoforo al Naviglio
The church of the patron saint of boatmen is two buildings in one (12th and 14th century).

There are many antiques workshops and shops here.

The big barges have become nightclubs.

On the towpaths, horses or oxen once pulled the barges.

The church of Santa Maria delle Grazie al Naviglio faces the water.

Mercatone dell'Antiquariato
On the last Sunday of the month, from September to June, 400 antique dealers take part in this lively market on the Naviglio Grande.

Vicolo dei Lavandai
On the towpath you can still see the old washing troughs, sheltered by wooden roofs, where women washed clothes in the canal water.

Museo Diocesano ⑨

Corso di Porta Ticinese 95.
Map 7 B3. *Tel* 02-89 40 47 14.
🚃 9, 15, 29, 30. 🚋 94.
🕐 10am–6pm Tue–Sun. 🎫 📷 (to book, call 02-89 42 00 19).

A stucco of Sant'Ambrogio kept at the Museo Diocesano

The mission of the Museo Diocesano is to recover and highlight the artistic heritage of the Milan diocese, which extends as far north as the towns of Varese and Lecco.

This museum of religious art is housed in the cloisters of Sant'Eustorgio, next to the basilica. It features about 320 works of art dating from the 6th to the 19th centuries, from paintings from the private collections of past Milanese archbishops to items rescued from tiny village churches. Two of the highlights are the frescoes of the Stations of the Cross by late 19th-century artist Gaetano Previati and the section devoted to Milan's patron saint, Sant'Ambrogio.

THE RELICS OF THE MAGI

Emperor Costante donated the relics in around 315 and they were taken to Milan by Bishop Eustorgius. Legend has it that the sarcophagus was so heavy the cart had to stop at the city gates, where the original Sant'Eustorgio basilica was founded and the Apostle Barnabas baptised the first Milanese Christians. Barbarossa transferred the relics to Cologne in 1164. Some were returned in 1903, an event still celebrated at Epiphany with a procession.

Tabernacle with the relics of the Magi

Sant'Eustorgio ⑩

Piazza Sant'Eustorgio 1. **Map** 7 B3.
Tel 02-58 10 15 83. 🚃 3, 9, 15, 29, 30. 🚋 59. 🕐 7:30am–noon, 3:30–6:30pm. ✝ 5pm pre-hols; 9:30, 11am, 12:30, 5pm hols; 5pm Jul, Aug. **Portinari Chapel** *Tel* 02-89 40 26 71. 🕐 10am–6pm daily.

In the 11th century work began on building a basilica over one founded by St Eustorgius in the 4th century, to house the relics of the Magi. The main body of the present-day church was built in the 1300s. On the right-hand side of the façade, which was rebuilt in 1865, there are several chapels dating from the 13th–15th centuries. The Brivio chapel houses Tommaso

Sculpture on the façade of Sant'Eustorgio

Cazzaniga's tomb of Giovanni Stefano Brivio (1486). The middle bas-relief depicts the *Adoration of the Magi*, and

the altarpiece is a triptych by Bergognone. In the Baroque Crotta-Caimi chapel is a fine sarcophagus by 15th-century sculptor Protaso Caimi, and a *St Ambrose on Horseback*. The Visconti chapel has beautiful 14th-century frescoes: on the vault are the Evangelists; below left, a *St George and the Dragon*; and right, the *Triumph of St Thomas*. The Torriani chapel is frescoed with symbols of the Evangelists. In the south transept is the large late-Roman sarcophagus that once housed the relics of the Magi, and on the altar is a Campionese school marble triptych of the journey of the Magi (1347). The Magi are also the subject of the fresco on the left, attributed to Luini. The high altar houses the remains of St Eustorgius and bears a marble altar-front depicting an unfinished Passion of Christ by various artists.

Behind the altar, a passageway leads to the Portinari chapel, commissioned by banker Pigello Portinari as his tomb, and to house the body of St Peter Martyr. The first example of a 15th-century central-plan church in Milan, it exemplifies the clarity of Bramante's vision and features typical Lombard decoration attributed to Vincenzo Foppa. Under the dome is the tomb of St Peter Martyr (1339) by Giovanni di Balduccio, held up by the eight Virtues and showing scenes of his ministry. The small chapel on the left has an urn containing the saint's skull.

The Neo-Romanesque façade of Sant'Eustorgio, built in 1865

The Sanctuary of Santa Maria dei Miracoli and San Celso

Santa Maria presso San Celso ⓫

Corso Italia 37. **Map** 7 C3 (9 C5).
Tel 02-58 31 31 87. 15. 65, 94. 7am–noon, 4–6:30pm daily. 6pm pre-hols; 9 & 11am, 12, 5:30 & 7pm hols. **San Celso** ask sacristan.

San Celso was founded in the 11th century over a church built by St Ambrose in the 4th century to mark the spot where he had found the remains of the martyrs Celso and Nazaro. In 1493 construction began on a sanctuary dedicated to Santa Maria dei Miracoli, designed by Gian Giacomo Dolcebuono and subsequently by Vincenzo Seregni and Alessi. The late 16th-century façade is enlivened by sculptures by Stoldo Lorenzi and Annibale Fontana. The late Renaissance interior has a pavement by Martino Bassi and was frescoed by Cerano and Procaccini. There are major works of art in the various chapels: a painting (1606) by Procaccini; the *Holy Family with St Jerome* altarpiece (1548) by Paris Bordone; Antonio Campi's *Resurrection* (1560); *Baptism of Jesus* by Gaudenzio Ferrari; Moretto da Brescia's *Conversion of St Paul* (1539–40); *Martyrdom of St Catherine* by Cerano (1603); an altarpiece by Bergognone.

Under the cupola with terracotta Evangelists by De Fondutis and paintings by Appiani (1795) is the high altar (16th century) in semi precious stones. The wooden choir is from 1570. Statues by Fontana and Lorenzi adorn the pillars.

On the Altar of the Madonna is Fontana's *Our Lady of the Assumption*. Below, a 4th-century fresco lies under two embossed silver doors. By the right-hand transept is the entrance to **San Celso**, with 11th–15th-century frescoes and columns with carved capitals.

San Paolo Converso ⓬

Piazza Sant'Eufemia. **Map** 7 C2 (9 C5). 15. 65, 94. for exhibitions only. **Fondazione Metropolitan Tel** 02-86 30 50.

This church was founded in 1549 for the Angeliche di San Paolo convent and is attributed to Domenico Giunti, while the façade was designed by Cerano in 1611. Now deconsecrated, the church has a front section for the public and another one to the rear, facing the opposite direction, reserved for the nuns. The interior was frescoed in the late 1500s by Giulio and Antonio Campi: in the presbytery are episodes from the life of St Paul, the Ascension of Christ and the Assumption of Mary, framed in an architectural setting with bold foreshortening.

At the end of Corso di Porta Romana is Piazza Missori, with the remains of San Giovanni in Conca (11th cen-

tury), once a Visconti mausoleum. The façade was remade for the Waldensian church in Via Francesco Sforza.

Sant'Alessandro ⓭

Piazza Sant'Alessandro. **Map** 7 C2 (9 C4). **Tel** 02-86 45 30 65. M 3 Missori. 4, 12, 15, 24. 65. 7:30am–noon, 4–7pm daily. 6:30pm pre-hols; 8am (winter), 10:30am (winter), noon, 6:30pm hols.

Lorenzo Binago built this church in 1601 for the Barnabiti family. The interior has lavish Baroque furnishings and decoration; the frescoes were painted by Moncalvo and by Daniele Crespi. In the presbytery is the *Life of St Alexander* by Filippo Abbiati and Federico Bianchi. The high altar (1741) is decorated with semi-precious stones.

Next to the church are the Scuole Arcimbolde, schools for the poor founded in 1609 by the Barnabiti family, where the poet Giuseppe Parini studied. Opposite is Palazzo Trivulzio, rebuilt by Ruggeri in 1713, with the family coat of arms on the middle window. This family founded the Biblioteca Trivulziana, the library now in the Castello Sforzesco. Nearby Via Palla leads to the Tempio Civico di San Sebastiano, begun by Pellegrino Tibaldi in 1577 and completed in the 1700s. Its round interior has works by Legnanino, Montalto and Federico Bianchi.

The cupola and bell tower of Sant'Alessandro, seen from Corso di Porta Romana

SOUTHEAST MILAN

The area between Corso Monforte and Corso di Porta Romana was a typical suburb up to the early 19th century, characterized by aristocratic residences, monasteries and more modest houses typical of the artisans' and commercial districts of Milan. Development of the area began in the 17th century with the construction of Palazzo Durini, one of the most important civic buildings of its time. At the end of the 18th century Corso di Porta Romana and the adjacent streets were changed in keeping with the vast street

A statue in the Guastalla gardens

network renewal plans encouraged by Maria Theresa of Austria. When the empress ordered the suppression of many monasteries, the land where they had stood was purchased by rich nobles. Other areas became available when the Spanish ramparts were demolished. The old atmosphere of Southeast Milan survives above all around the Ca' Granda (now the University), which for almost 500 years was the city hospital, and in the first stretch of Corso di Porta Romana. However, the only vestige of the Verziere, the old vegetable market in Largo Augusto, is the place-name.

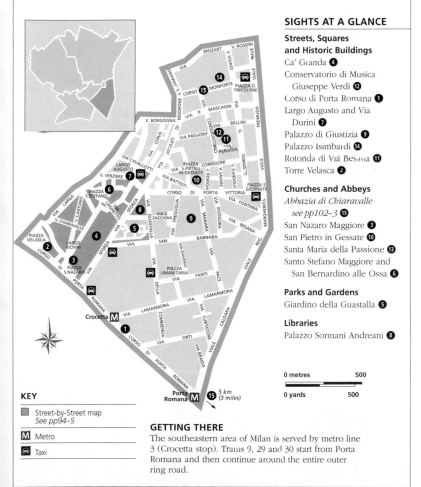

SIGHTS AT A GLANCE

Streets, Squares and Historic Buildings
Ca' Granda **4**
Conservatorio di Musica Giuseppe Verdi **12**
Corso di Porta Romana **1**
Largo Augusto and Via Durini **7**
Palazzo di Giustizia **9**
Palazzo Isimbardi **14**
Rotonda di Via Besana **11**
Torre Velasca **2**

Churches and Abbeys
Abbazia di Chiaravalle see pp102–3 **15**
San Nazaro Maggiore **3**
San Pietro in Gessate **10**
Santa Maria della Passione **13**
Santo Stefano Maggiore and San Bernardino alle Ossa **6**

Parks and Gardens
Giardino della Guastalla **5**

Libraries
Palazzo Sormani Andreani **8**

0 metres	500
0 yards	500

KEY

- Street-by-Street map See pp94–5
- **M** Metro
- Taxi

GETTING THERE

The southeastern area of Milan is served by metro line 3 (Crocetta stop). Trams 9, 29 and 30 start from Porta Romana and then continue around the entire outer ring road.

◁ Detail of *The Legend of St Anthony Abbot*, in San Pietro in Gessate

Street-by-Street: San Nazaro to Largo Augusto

There are many interesting old buildings in this area, which includes the university quarter, with cafés and specialist bookshops, as well as crafts shops on Via Festa del Perdono. Architectural styles range from the 4th-century San Nazaro, founded by St Ambrose, to the Ca' Granda, the old hospital, a marvellous sight when viewed from Largo Richini because of its sheer size and the beauty of its 15th-century arcade. More changes of style come with the palazzi in Corso di Porta Romana and Via Sant'Antonio, and the modern Torre Velasca. The quarter's hospital tradition can be seen in the votive columns at the crossroads, where mass for the sick was celebrated, and the San Bernardino alle Ossa chapel, decorated with the bones of those who died in the hospital.

Sant'Antonio Abat was rebuilt in 158? It houses paintings by Bernardino Campi, Moncalvo and Ludovico Carracci and is a kind of gallery of early 17th-century painting in Milan.

Torre Velasca
The symbol of modern Milan was built in 1956–8. The tower, 106 m (348 ft) high, houses both offices and flats and is often compared to medieval towers because of the shape of the upper section ❷

Duomo

VIA LARGA

PIAZZA VELASCA

VIA PANTA...

Corso di Porta Romana
Palazzi with magnificent gardens line this avenue. It follows the route of the ancient Roman road which led from Porta Romana all the way to Rome ❶

CORSO DI PORTA ROMANA

KEY

– – – Suggested route

★ San Nazaro Maggiore
One of four basilicas founded by Sant'Ambrogio, this church still has some of the original 4th-century masonry. It is preceded by the Trivulzio Chapel, the only Milanese architectural work by Bramantino (1512–50). The view of the back of the church is very striking ❸

STAR SIGHTS

★ San Nazaro Maggiore

★ Ca' Granda

Santo Stefano Maggiore and San Bernardino alle Ossa

The San Bernardino ossuary chapel, rebuilt in the 17th century, is entirely covered with human bones and skulls from the cemeteries that were abolished in the 1600s **6**

Colonna del Verziere

Santo Stefano

LOCATOR MAP
See Street Finder, maps 7, 8, 9, 10

PIAZZA SANTO STEFANO

Palazzo Sormani Andreani

The Biblioteca Civica di Milano, housed here, is the largest library in Milan. It includes the private library of the French novelist Stendhal **8**

Largo Augusto

The Colonna del Verziere here commemorates the end of the 1576 plague **7**

Giardino della Guastalla

Milan's oldest public garden was laid out in 1555. There are several monuments, including a small Neo-Classical temple designed by Luigi Cagnola **5**

★ Ca' Granda

This was the old city hospital, also known as Ospedale Maggiore. It was built in 1456 to bring all the small hospitals of the city together on a single site. It was in use until 1939. Today it is home to Milan's state university **4**

0 metres   300
0 yards   300

Entrance to the Teatro Carcano, in Corso di Porta Romana

Corso di Porta Romana ❶

Map 7 C2 (9 D4). Ⓜ *3 Missori.* 🚊 *4, 12, 15, 16, 27.* 🚌 *65, 94.*

This avenue was laid out over a porticoed stretch of the ancient Roman road outside the city walls (2nd–3rd century AD) that led to Rome. It ran from Porta Romana – then just beyond present-day Piazza Missori – to a triumphal arch (near the widening in the road known as Crocetta), transformed by Barbarossa into a fortified gate in the walls in 1162. The new gate (1171), further back, was demolished in 1793.

The Corso is lined with many noble palazzi. The 17th-century Palazzo Acerbi at No.3; Palazzo Annoni at No. 6, designed by Francesco Maria Richini (1631), famous for its art collection which includes works by Rubens and Van Dyck; Palazzo Mellerio at No.13 and Casa Bettoni (1865) at No.20, with statues of Bersaglieri flanking the door. Via Santa Sofia crosses the Corso, and over the Naviglio canal close to the Crocetta, whose name derives from a votive cross set there during the 1576 plague.

Opposite is the Teatro Carcano (1803), where the great Italian actress Eleonora Duse performed. The Corso ends at the Porta Romana (in Piazzale Medaglie d'Oro), built in 1598. To the right you can see a fragment of the Spanish walls built by Ferrante Gonzaga (1545); they ran for 11,216 m (37,000 ft) and were demolished in 1889.

Torre Velasca ❷

Piazza Velasca 5. **Map** 7 C2 (10 D4). Ⓜ *3 Missori.* 🚊 *4, 12, 15, 16, 27.* 🚌 *65, 94.*

This tower, built in the late 1950s by architects Belgioioso, Nathan Rogers and Peressutti, is one of the best-known monuments in modern-day Milan. The overhang of the upper part of the building and its red colour are reminiscent of Italian medieval towers, but the shape actually grew out of the need to create more office space in a limited area.

Cappella Trivulzio, in San Nazaro Maggiore (16th century)

San Nazaro Maggiore ❸

Piazza San Nazaro. **Map** 8 D2 (10 D5). **Tel** 02-58 30 77 19. Ⓜ *3 Missori.* 🚊 *4, 12, 15, 16, 27.* 🚌 *65, 94.* ⏰ *7:30am–12:30pm, 3–7pm.* ✝ *6pm pre-hols; 8:30, 10, 11:30am, 6pm hols.* 📷 ♿

The original basilica was built by Sant'Ambrogio in AD 382–6 to house the remains of the Apostles Andrew, John and Thomas, which is why it was known as the *Basilica Apostolorum*. It was dedicated to San Nazaro when his remains – found by Sant'Ambrogio near the basilica – were buried here in 396. The church was built outside the walls in an Early Christian burial ground – as can be seen by the sarcophagi outside and the epitaph in the right-hand transept – and looked onto an ancient Roman porticoed street. It was rebuilt after a fire in 1075 reusing much original material.

The church is preceded by the octagonal Trivulzio Chapel, begun in Renaissance style in 1512 by Bramantino and continued by Cristoforo Lombardo. It houses the tomb of Gian Giacomo Trivulzio and his family.

The nave of the church has a cross vault. Either side of the entrance you will see the remains of the Romanesque doorway covered by the Trivulzio Chapel. On the walls, among fresco fragments, are parts of the original masonry. In the crossing, the dome is supported by the 4th-century piers; two altars in the choir contain the remains of the Apostles and San Nazaro. Left of the altar is the small cruciform chapel of San Lino, with traces of 10th – 15th-century frescoes. In the transepts are a fine *Last Supper* by Bernardino Lanino (right) and *Passion of Jesus* by Luini (left). The Chapel of St Catherine (1540) has Lanino's *Martyrdom of St Catherine* and a 16th-century stained-glass window depicting the *Life of St Catherine*.

The remains of San Nazaro, found by Sant'Ambrogio in AD 396

Ca' Granda ❹

17th-century window

The "Casa Grande", or Ospedale Maggiore, was built for Francesco Sforza from 1456 on with the aim of uniting the city's 30 hospitals. The "large house" was designed by Filarete, who built only part of it, and was finished in stages in the 17th and 18th centuries. In 1939 the hospital moved to a new site, and since 1952 the Ca' Granda has housed the liberal arts faculties of the Università Statale, Milan's university. The hospital was modern for its time: there were separate wings for men and women – each with a central infirmary – and a large courtyard between them.

VISITORS' CHECKLIST

Via Festa del Perdono 5. **Map** 8 D2 (10 D4). **Tel** 02-503 11. Ⓜ 1, 3 Duomo, 3 Missori. 🚌 12, 23, 27. 🚌 54, 60. ⬤ 7:30am–7:30pm Mon–Fri; 8am–noon Sat (first 3 weeks of Aug: 7:30am–3:30pm Mon–Fri). ● Sun & hols (open in morning pre-hols). ♿ 🏛 **Chiesa dell'Annunciata Tel** 02-58 30 77 19. ⬤ 8am–7pm (when University is open).

The church of the Annunciata (17th-century) contains a 1639 canvas by Guercino.

The Neo-Classical Macchio Wing, seat of the Faculty of Letters, Philosophy and Jurisprudence, housed the benefactors' art gallery, with portraits by leading artists.

★ **Fifteenth-century Façade**
The brick façade has round arches and is richly decorated. There were workshops and warehouses at ground level.

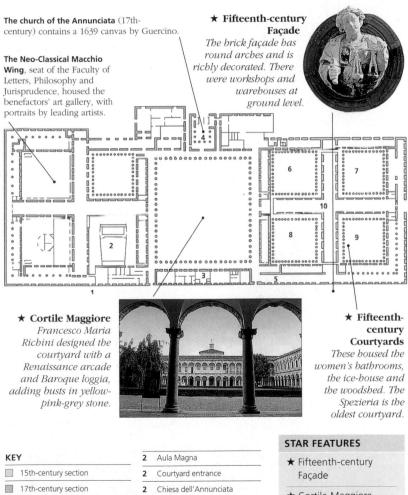

★ **Cortile Maggiore**
Francesco Maria Richini designed the courtyard with a Renaissance arcade and Baroque loggia, adding busts in yellow-pink-grey stone.

★ **Fifteenth-century Courtyards**
These housed the women's bathrooms, the ice-house and the woodshed. The Spezieria is the oldest courtyard.

KEY		2	Aula Magna
▢	15th-century section	2	Courtyard entrance
▢	17th-century section	2	Chiesa dell'Annunciata
▢	18th–19th-century section	2	Porticoes, 15th-century wing
1	Entrance to the Faculties of Liberal Arts, Philosophy and Jurisprudence	6-9	Courtyards, 15th-century wing
		10	Crociera, formerly the infirmary

STAR FEATURES

★ Fifteenth-century Façade

★ Cortile Maggiore

★ Fifteenth-century Courtyards

The fish pond in the Giardino della Guastalla, near Via Sforza

Giardino della Guastalla ❺

Via Francesco Sforza, Via S Barnaba, Via Guastalla. **Map** 8 D2 (10 E5). 🚊 12, 23, 27. 🚌 37, 60, 73, 77, 84, 94. ⏰ daily. Mar: 7am–8pm; Apr & Oct: 7am–9pm; May–Sept: 7am–10pm; Nov–Feb: 7am–7pm.

This garden – Milan's oldest – was laid out in 1555 by Countess Ludovica Torelli della Guastalla, next to the college of the same name for the daughters of impoverished aristocrats. In the early 1600s it was transformed into an Italian-style garden, and a goldfish pond on two communicating terraces was added. There is also a 17th-century shrine representing Mary Magdalen attended by angels and a Neo-Classical temple by Luigi Cagnola. In 1939 the garden was separated from the adjacent Sormani park and opened to the public. At the Via Guastalla exit (No. 19) you can visit the Synagogue, designed by Luca Beltrami (1890–92) and, at the corner of Via San Barnaba, the church of Santi Barnaba e Paolo, which is part of the nearby Chierici Regolari di San Paolo college. It is a prototype of 16th-century Lombard churches, founded in 1558 and then modified by Galeazzo Alessi. Inside are paintings by Aurelio Luini, son of Bernardino, Camillo Procaccini and Moncalvo.

Santo Stefano Maggiore and San Bernardino alle Ossa ❻

Piazza Santo Stefano. **Map** 8 D1 (10 E4). 🇲 1, 3 Duomo. 🚊 12, 23, 27. 🚌 54, 60, 65. **Archivio Storico Diocesano (Historic Archive)** Via San Calimero 13. **Map** 8 D2. **Tel** 02-58 49 98 01. ⏰ 9:15am–12:15pm Mon–Fri. ● Aug. **San Bernardino alle Ossa**. **Tel** 02-76 02 37 35. ⏰ 7:30am–noon, 1–6pm daily. ⛪ 8:30am Mon–Sat; 11am hols. 🚫 ♿

Statue on the façade of San Bernardino alle Ossa

Santo Stefano dates back to the 5th century. It was rebuilt in 1075 after being destroyed by a fire and was again rebuilt in its present form in 1584 by Giuseppe Meda. The Baroque bell tower was built in 1643–74 by Carlo Buzzi: the pilaster at the base is all that remains of the quadriporticus that once faced the medieval basilica. The church was used as the Diocesan Archive, which has now moved. Next door are San Bernardino alle Ossa, originally medieval but since rebuilt many times, and the ossuary chapel (with a concave façade) built in 1210 and altered in 1695. The latter is small and covered with human bones and skulls. The dim light and dark walls contrast with the bright colours of the fresco on the vault by Sebastiano Ricci (1695): *The Triumph of Souls among Angels.*

Largo Augusto and Via Durini ❼

Map 8 D1 (10 E3). 🇲 1, 3 Duomo. 🚊 12, 23, 27, 37. 🚌 54, 60, 65, 73, 84, 94.

The Verziere Column, commissioned by San Carlo Borromeo to celebrate the end of the 1576 plague, has stood in the middle of Largo Augusto since 1580. It is one of the few votive columns to survive the late 18th century. Many were lost after the suppression of the monastic orders that owned them, or sacrificed to make room for new buildings. This square marks the beginning of Via Durini, which is dominated by the concave façade of Santa Maria della Sanità (1708). No. 20 is Casa Toscanini, the great conductor's house, and No. 24 is Palazzo Durini, built in 1648 by Francesco Maria Richini. On nearby Corso Europa is 16th-century Palazzo Litta Modignani, where a Roman mosaic was found. Palazzo Litta was altered in the 1700s.

Palazzo Sormani Andreani ❽

Corso di Porta Vittoria 6. **Map** 8 E1 (10 F4). **Tel** 02-884 63 51. **Fax** 02-76 00 65 88. 🚊 12, 23, 27. 🚌 54, 60, 65, 73, 84, 94. ⏰ 9am–7:30pm Mon–Sat. ● public hols, Aug.

The palazzo, constructed in the 18th century, was enlarged in 1736 by Francesco Croce, who made it into one of the most lavish residences

Façade of Palazzo Sormani, the Municipal Library since 1956

of the time. Croce also designed the characteristic late Baroque curved façade. Reconstructed after World War II, the palazzo became the home of the Municipal (or Sormani Andreani) Library, the largest in Milan. It has over 580,000 works, including Stendhal's private library, a newspaper library with about 19,500 Italian and foreign publications, and a record and CD collection. A catalogue of all the Milan libraries is also here, as is the regional periodicals catalogue.

The Neo-Classical back opens onto a garden, part of the larger original one, which is used for small exhibitions. Nearby, at No. 2 Via Visconti di Modrone, is one of Milan's excellent traditional *pasticcerie*, the Taveggia pastry shop *(see p187)*.

Palazzo di Giustizia ❾

Corso di Porta Vittoria. **Map** 8 E1 (10 F4). 🚋 12, 23, 27. 🚌 37, 60, 73, 77, 84.

The centre of attention in the early 1990s because of the Mani Pulite (clean hands) corruption inquests and trials that changed much of the face of Italian politics, the Milan Law Courts were designed in typical Fascist style (1932–40) by Marcello Piacentini. The building also houses the Notarial Acts Archive, formerly in the Palazzo della Ragione *(see p54)*. The Palazzo has 1,200 rooms and 65 law courts with works by contemporary artists, including Mario Sironi's fresco in the Assize Court.

The Palazzo di Giustizia (1932–40), a typical example of Fascist architecture

Detail from *The Legend of the Virgin*, San Pietro in Gessate

San Pietro in Gessate ❿

Piazza San Pietro in Gessate. **Map** 8 E1 (10 F3). **Tel** 02-545 01 45. 🚋 12, 23, 27. 🚌 37, 60, 77, 84. ⭕ 7:30am–6pm daily. ✝ 8am Mon–Fri; 7pm pre-hols; 9am, 12:15 & 7pm hols.

This church was built in 1447–75 by the Solari school and financed by the Florentine banker Pigello Portinari, whose emblem is on the outer wall of the apse. In the middle of the façade, rebuilt in 1912, is a portal with an effigy of St Peter, which was added in the 1600s. The Gothic interior has a three-aisle nave with ribbed vaulting and pointed arches and has preserved some original painting. The church was damaged during World War II, in particular the right-hand chapels, where there are traces of

frescoes by Antonio Campi, Moncalvo and Bergognone (whose *Funeral of St Martin* is in the fifth chapel). The third and fifth chapels on the left have fine frescoes by Montorfano: *Life of St John the Baptist* (1484) and *The Legend of St Anthony Abbot*. The eight choir stalls were rebuilt with the remains of the 1640 ones by Carlo Garavaglia, damaged in 1943 and partly used as firewood during the war. The left-hand transept (or Cappella Grifi) has frescoes of the *Life of Sant'Ambrogio* (1490) commissioned by the Sforza senator Ambrogio Grifi from Bernardino Butinone and Bernardino Zenale. In the lunettes under the vault, next to *Sant'Ambrogio on Horseback*, you can see the figure of a hanged man whose rope "drops" into the scene below, down to the hangman. These recently restored frescoes were discovered in 1862 under the plaster put on the walls during the plague to disinfect the church.

The arcade in the Rotonda di Via Besana

Rotonda di Via Besana ⓫

Via San Barnaba, corner of Via Besana. **Map** 8 F2 (10 F4). 🚊 *9, 29, 30.* 🚌 *77, 84.* ⬭ *for exhibitions and summer cultural events only.*

The Rotonda was the cemetery of the nearby Ca' Granda Hospital designed in 1695 by Francesco Raffagno on present-day Viale Regina Margherita. About 150,000 dead were buried in the crypts under the arcades. When it was closed in 1783, viceroy Eugène de Beauharnais tried to change it into the Pantheon of the Regno Italico (1809), but the project fell through and the round brick building first housed patients with infectious diseases and then, up to 1940, was the hospital laundry. It is now used for temporary exhibitions and as an outdoor cinema in summer.

In the middle is the deconsecrated San Michele ai Nuovi Sepolcri, built in 1713. It has a Greek cross plan with a central altar, visible from all sides. The small skulls sculpted on the capitals are a reminder of the original function of this complex.

On Via San Barnaba is Santa Maria della Pace, designed by Pietro Antonio Solari in 1466, the property of the Order of Knights of the Holy Sepulchre. In 1805 the church was suppressed and the paintings removed (some are now in the Brera), but some 17th-century frescoes by Tanzio da Varallo remain.

The nearby monastery is the home of the Società Umanitaria, founded in 1893 to educate and aid the poor. It has a library devoted to labour problems. The only remaining part of the monastery is the refectory, with a *Crucifixion* by Marco d'Oggiono. Returning to Corso di Porta Vittoria, you come to Piazza Cinque Giornate, with a monument by Giuseppe Grandi (1895) commemorating the anti-Austrian insurrection of 1848 *(see p24)*. The female figures symbolize the Five Days, whose dead are buried in the crypt below.

Conservatorio di Musica Giuseppe Verdi ⓬

Via Conservatorio 12. **Map** 8 E1 (10 F3). **Tel** *02-762 11 01.* 🚌 *54, 61, 77.* ⬭ *for concerts only.* **Library Tel** *02-762 110 219.* ⬭ *2–7:30pm Mon–Wed, 8am–2pm Thu–Fri, 8am–1pm Sat.*

Milan's Conservatory was founded by viceroy Eugène de Beauharnais in 1808. Important musicians and composers have studied here – but the young Verdi was refused admission. There is a chamber music hall and a large auditorium for symphonic music. The library boasts over 35,000 books and 460,000 pieces of written music, scores, etc, including works by Mozart, Rossini, Donizetti, Bellini and Verdi, as well as a small museum of precious stringed instruments.

Santa Maria della Passione ⓭

Via Bellini 2. **Map** 8 E-F4. **Tel** *02-76 02 13 70.* 🚊 *54, 61, 77.* 🚌 *94.* ⬭ *7am–noon, 3:30–6:15 pm daily.* ✝ *7:15, 8:15 am, 5:30pm Mon–Fri; 5:30pm pre-hols; 10, 11:15am, 3, 5:30pm hols.* 🅿 **Museum** ⬭ *for restoration.*

The second largest church in Milan, after the Duomo, was built under the patronage of the prelate Daniele Birago, who had donated the land to the Lateran Canons. Work began in 1486 to a design by Giovanni Battagio. Originally the church had a Greek cross plan but it was lengthened with a nave and six semi-circular chapels on each side in 1573 by Martino Bassi. The façade of the church – and the nearby convent, now the home of the Conservatory – was added in 1692 by Giuseppe Rusnati, who kept it low so that visitors could appreciate the majestic octagonal covering of the dome designed by Cristoforo Lombardo (1530). To enhance this view and link the church with the Naviglio, Abbot Gadio had the Via della Passione laid out in front of the entrance in 1540. The interior, with a frescoed barrel vault, is very atmospheric. Fourteen early 17th-century portraits of the saints of the Lateran Order, attributed to Daniele Crespi and his school, are on the piers. In the right-hand chapels, two works worth seeing are *Christ at the Pillar*

The Giuseppe Verdi Conservatory, housed in a former monastery

The octagonal dome of Santa Maria della Passione (17th century)

by Giulio Cesare Procaccini, on the altar of the third chapel, and the *Madonna di Caravaggio*, a fresco attributed to Braman-tino, in the sixth chapel. The presbytery still has its original Greek cross structure. The paintings hanging from the piers, mostly the work of Crespi, narrate the Passion and include *Christ Nailed to the Cross*. Behind the Baroque high altar is a wooden choir (16th century) with mother of pearl inlay. Either side of the choir are two 16th–17th-century organs, still used for concerts. The doors of the left one have scenes from the Passion painted by Crespi.

There are remarkable Cinquecento paintings in the transepts: the right-hand one has a *Deposition* altarpiece by Bernardino Luini (1510–15) with the *Legend of the Cross* in the predella; and on the altar of the left-hand one is Gaudenzio Ferrari's *Last Supper* (1543), with a *Crucifixion* by Giulio Campi (1560) alongside.

The chapels on the left-hand side of the nave contain fine works by Camillo Procaccini and Duchino and the first chapel is noteworthy because of the impressive realism of Crespi's *St Charles Fasting*. The organ recess to the right leads to the Museum, founded in the old

Santa Maria della Passione: one of the saints of the Lateran Order

monastery in 1972. It consists of four sections. The Old Sacristy has 17th-century Lombard paintings and ten 18th-century wooden panels with scenes from the Bible. The 15th-century Chapter House was designed and painted by Bergognone; saints and doctors are in a false peristyle. On the right-hand wall is Christ with the Apostles. The Gallery has works by Crespi, Procaccini and Nuvolone; the Sala degli Arredi has 17th-century furniture and a vault frescoed by Giulio Campi (1558). In Via Bellini you can see the left side of the church and the dome. At No. 11 is the Art Nouveau Casa Campanini (1904), with wrought iron work by Alessandro Mazzucotelli.

Palazzo Isimbardi ⓮

Corso Monforte 35. **Map** 4 E5 (10 F2). **Tel** 02-77 40 29 73 or 02-77 40 24 16 (Lombardy Province PR Office). Ⓜ 1 San Babila. 🚊 9, 23, 29, 30. 🚌 54, 61, 94. ◯ apply to IAT (see p209).

The seat of the Milan provincial government since 1935, this palazzo dates from the 15th century but was enlarged by the noble families who lived in it, among whom were the Isimbardi, who purchased it in 1775. The 18th-century façade on Corso

Monforte leads to the porticoed court of honour (16th century), which still has its original herringbone pattern paving. The garden behind this boasts an admirable Neo-Classical façade designed by Giacomo Tazzini (1826).

The palazzo was recently opened to the public and features many interestingly decorated rooms and fine works of art, such as the wooden 17th-century globe by Giovanni Jacopo de Rossi. The most important room is the Giunta (Council Chamber), which in 1954 became the home of Tiepolo's masterful *Triumph of Doge Morosini*, which came from Palazzo Morosini in Venice. The Sala dell'Antegiunta has a lovely 18th-century Murano glass chandelier, while the Sala degli Affreschi boasts 17th-century frescoes taken from the villa of Cardinal Monti at Vaprio d'Adda. The Studio del Presidente is decorated with a Neo-Classical ceiling, partly in fine gold. In 1940 the Province of Milan enlarged the palazzo. The new façade on Via Vivaio was decorated with bas-reliefs sculpted by Salvatore Saponaro depicting the activities of the Milanese. At No. 31 Corso Monforte is the Palazzo della Prefettura, rebuilt in its present state in 1782. It has frescoes by Andrea Appiani. It is not open to the public.

The 18th-century façade of Palazzo Isimbardi, in Corso Monforte

Abbazia di Chiaravalle ⑮

French Cistercian monks began constructing this church in 1150–60 and it was dedicated to the Virgin Mary in 1221. The complex is a combination of French Gothic and Lombard Romanesque, resulting in a delightful example of Cistercian architecture. The bell tower was added in 1349. The entrance is in the 16th-century tower flanked by two small churches. In 1798 Napoleon suppressed the monastic order, the monks were forced to leave and the abbey deteriorated so much that in 1858 Bramante's 15th-century cloister was demolished to make room for a railway line. Restored and given back to the monks, the abbey has regained its former splendour and is again an oasis of peace.

★ Frescoes
The 14th-century frescoes on the dome narrate The Legend of the Virgin. *Those in the transept (above), represent among other things the genealogical tree of the Benedictine monks.*

★ Wooden Choir
The 44 stalls have carvings of the Life of St Bernard *by Carlo Garavaglia (1645), who according to legend took refuge in the abbey to expiate the murder of his brother.*

The interior had no paintings because this would have distracted the monks from their prayers. The 17th-century frescoes tell the story of the order.

Entrance

The top of the façade, made of brick is what remains of the original. The porch was added in 1625.
The 16th-century main portal has figures of Cistercian saints, including St Bernard holding the church in his hand.

THE MONKS' LAND RECLAMATION

The Cistercian monasteries were based on the rule of *ora et labora* – prayer and labour – and played a crucial role in reclaiming the marshy Milanese terrain, which thanks to the monks became extremely fertile. They used the new water meadow technique, which consisted in flooding the meadows with water from an adjoining stream (kept at a constant temperature of 12° C/54° F) so that the grass would grow quickly and could be harvested even in winter.

A Cistercian monk at work in the garden

★ **Bell Tower** (*ciribiciaccola*)
Eighty small marble columns adorn the bell tower designed by Francesco Pecorari in 1349. Called ciribiciaccola *(clever contraption) by the Milanese, its bells accompanied the farmers' and monks' working day. The tower bell rope still hangs in the church.*

The many windows (double, triple and quadruple lancet) lend movement to the tower structure.

Madonna della Buonanotte
Painted in 1512 by Bernardino Luini at the top of the steps leading to the dormitory, this picture is known as the Madonna della Buonanotte *because she "said goodnight" to the monks going to bed.*

VISITORS' CHECKLIST

Via Sant'Arialdo 102, Chiaravalle Milanese. **Tel** 02-57 40 34 04. **M** 3 Corvetto. 🚌 77. ◯ 9–11:30am, 3–6:30pm Tue–Sun. ✝ 8, 9:15 (Gregorian chant), 11:30am, 6pm hols; 8am Mon–Sat. ♿ 🚻 📷 (no flash). 🖥

The chapter house, designed in the late 15th century by Bramante, has three graffiti from that period depicting Santa Maria delle Grazie, the Duomo and Castello Sforzesco.

Refectory

★ **Cloister**
Rebuilt in 1952 by using the one surviving side as a model, the cloister has a plaque commemorating the founding of the church, next to which is a stork, the symbol of Chiaravalle.

STAR FEATURES

★ Wooden Choir

★ Cloister

★ Bell Tower (*ciribiciaccola*)

★ Frescoes

NORTHEAST MILAN

Elegant Via Manzoni is the heart of a vast area stretching from the Brera quarter to Via Montenapoleone and Corso Venezia. Brera is known for its characteristic winding streets, some of which still have their 18th-century paving. The fashion district around Via Montenapoleone is the domain of the designer shops. Starting from Piazza San Babila and continuing through

Logo of the Museo
Bagatti Valsecchi

Corso Venezia, with its many aristocratic palazzi, you will come to the Giardini Pubblici and the Villa Reale, home of the Modern Art Gallery. The area extending beyond the ramparts, which was undeveloped up to the early 19th century, includes the Cimitero Monumentale, the Stazione Centrale (main railway station) and the Pirelli building, Milan's tallest.

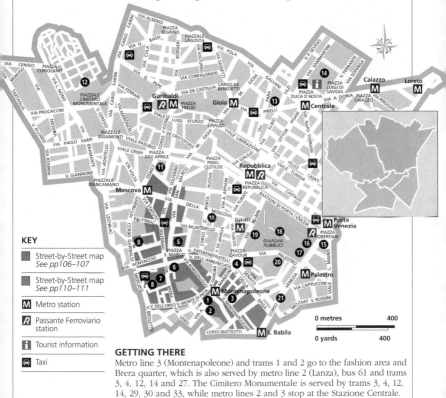

KEY

■	Street-by-Street map See pp106–107
■	Street-by-Street map See pp110–111
M	Metro station
R	Passante Ferroviario station
i	Tourist information
🚖	Taxi

0 metres 400
0 yards 400

GETTING THERE
Metro line 3 (Montenapoleone) and trams 1 and 2 go to the fashion area and Brera quarter, which is also served by metro line 2 (Lanza), bus 61 and trams 3, 4, 12, 14 and 27. The Cimitero Monumentale is served by trams 3, 4, 12, 14, 29, 30 and 33, while metro lines 2 and 3 stop at the Stazione Centrale.

SIGHTS AT A GLANCE

Streets and Squares
Archi di Porta Nuova ④
Bastioni di Porta Venezia ⑮
Corso Venezia, see pp122–3 ㉑
Via Manzoni ①

Historic Buildings
Palazzo Cusani ⑦
Palazzo Dugnani ⑲
Pirelli Building ⑬
Stazione Centrale ⑭

Museums and Galleries
Museo Bagatti Valsecchi ③
Museo di Storia Naturale ⑰
Museo Poldi Pezzoli ②
Pinacoteca di Brera see pp114–17 ⑥
Planetarium ⑯
Villa Belgiojoso Bonaparte – Museo dell'Ottocento ⑳

Gardens and Cemeteries
Cimitero Monumentale ⑫
Giardini Pubblici ⑱

Churches
San Marco ⑤
San Simpliciano ⑨
Sant'Angelo ⑩
Santa Maria del Carmine ⑧

◁ Statue of Napoleon by Canova (1809), in the middle of the Brera art gallery courtyard

Street-by-Street: the Fashion District

Versace logo

Via Montenapoleone represents the elegant heart of Milan and is one of the four sides of the so-called *quadrilatero* or fashion district (the other three sides are Via Manzoni, Via Sant'Andrea and Via della Spiga). When strolling through this district, besides the shops of some of the top Italian and international fashion designers, you will see grand Neo-Classical aristocratic residences such as Palazzo Melzi di Cusano, at No. 18 Via Montenapoleone, built in 1830. Via Bigli, on the other hand, is lined with 16th- and 17th-century palazzi with porticoed courtyards.

Archi di Porta Nuova
This city gate, once part of the medieval walls, is decorated with copies of 1st-century AD Roman tombstones. Left, a stele representing a family ❹

VALENTINO

GIORGIO ARMANI

Via Manzoni
This broad street is lined with aristocratic palazzi ❶

Grand Hotel et de Milan

Under the Portico del Lattèe (milkman's arcade) is the wall of the demolished church of San Donnino alla Mazza.

Museo Poldi Pezzoli
The Portrait of a Young Lady (15th century), attributed to Antonio Pollaiolo, is the symbol of this museum created by Gian Giacomo Poldi Pezzoli. Besides paintings by Mantegna, Piero della Francesca and Bellini, it has rugs, armour and precious ceramics ❷

STAR SIGHTS

★ Museo Poldi Pezzoli

★ Museo Bagatti Valsecchi

| 0 metres | 50 |
| 0 yards | 50 |

For hotels and restaurants in this area see pp162–4 and pp176–8

★ Museo Bagatti Valsecchi

This Neo-Renaissance palazzo was built as the family residence by the Bagatti Valsecchi brothers. It still has 16 rooms with their original 19th-century furnishings and many works of art belonging to the owners, who were art collectors ③

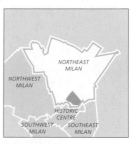

LOCATOR MAP
See Street Finder, map 4, 10

DOLCE & GABBANA

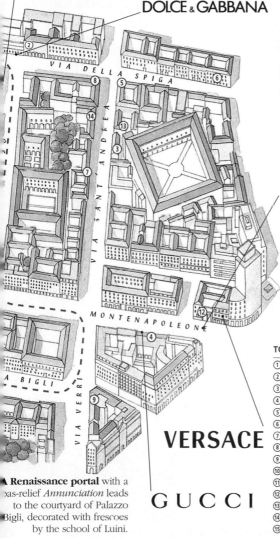

VIA DELLA SPIGA

VIA SANT'ANDREA

MONTENAPOLEONE

A BIGLI

VIA VERRI

VERSACE

GUCCI

A Renaissance portal with a bas-relief *Annunciation* leads to the courtyard of Palazzo Bigli, decorated with frescoes by the school of Luini.

Via Montenapoleone follows the course of the ancient Roman walls. It gets its name from a bank that once stood here called "Monte Napoleone". Designer shops line the street.

KEY

--- Suggested route

TOP FASHION DESIGNERS

① **Byblos** Via della Spiga 42.
② **Cerruti 1881** Via della Spiga 20.
③ **Chanel** Via Sant'Andrea 10a.
④ **Etro** Via Montenapoleone 5.
⑤ **Fendi** Via Sant'Andrea 16.
⑥ **Genny** Via della Spiga 4.
⑦ **Gianfranco Ferrè** Via Sant'Andrea 15.
⑧ **Hermès** Via Sant'Andrea 21.
⑨ **Jil Sander** Via P Verri 6.
⑩ **Krizia** Via della Spiga 23.
⑪ **Laura Biagiotti** Via Borgospesso 19.
⑫ **Mila Schön** Via Montenapoleone 2.
⑬ **Moschino** Via Sant'Andrea 12.
⑭ **Prada** Via Sant'Andrea 21.
⑮ **Romeo Gigli** Via della Spiga 30.

The inner garden of a palazzo in Via Manzoni

Via Manzoni ❶

Map 4 D4 (10 D2). **M** *1 Duomo, 3 Montenapoleone.* 🚊 *1, 2.* 🚌 *61, 94. Palazzi not open for visitors.*

Once known as "Corsia del Giardino" (Garden Lane) because of its many parks, this street acquired its present name in 1865, when the great Italian novelist Manzoni died. Its aristocratic appearance is created by the patrician palazzi and Teatro alla Scala *(see pp52–3)*, which stimulated the opening of chic cafés attracting a smart clientele. At No. 6 is 19th-century Palazzo Brentani, decorated with medallions with busts of illustrious persons, and No. 10 is Palazzo Anguissola (1775–8), which now houses the historic archive of the Banca Commerciale Italiana. No. 12, another 19th-century building, is the home of the famous Museo Poldi Pezzoli, and No. 29 is the Grand Hotel et de Milan (1865), where Giuseppe Verdi died in 1901.

Near the end of Via Monte-napoleone stands Aldo Rossi's monument to former Italian President Sandro Pertini (1990) and, next to this, Palazzo Gallarati Scotti (No. 30), built in the early 1700s. Opposite, Via Pisoni takes you to the remains of the 15th-century cloister of the Umiliate di Sant'Erasmo monastery, now part of a modern building. In the last stretch is 18th-century Palazzo Borromeo d'Adda, which was a haunt for literati and artists, including Stendhal.

Museo Poldi Pezzoli ❷

Via Manzoni 12. **Map** 4 D5 (10 D2). **Tel** 02-79 48 89. **M** *3 Montenapoleone.* 🚊 *1, 2.* 🚌 *61, 94.* ⏰ *10am–6pm Tue–Sun.* ● *1 Jan, Easter, 1 May, 15 Aug, 25 Dec.* 🚫📷 *(no flash).* ♿ *ground floor only.* 🎧 *Lecture hall, Library.* **www**.museopoldipezzoli.it

This private museum was established by nobleman Gian Giacomo Poldi Pezzoli and opened to the public in 1881. The building, a singular example of a late 19th-century aristocratic Milanese residence, contains Poldi Pezzoli's fine collection of paintings, sculpture, rugs, armour, glass, watches and textiles. The ground floor houses arms and armour from ancient Roman times to the 18th century. The Salone dell'Affresco, named after *The Apotheosis of Bartolomeo Colleoni* frescoed by Carlo Innocenzo Carloni, boasts a Tabriz carpet with hunting scenes (Persia, 1522–3), made of wool and silver on silk. In the adjoining room is the museum's collection of textiles, including a 15th-century cope with Florentine embroidery representing *The Coronation of the Virgin,* after a drawing by Botticelli.

Poldi Pezzoli Museum logo

The staircase, decorated with landscapes by Magnasco, leads to the first floor. In the Salette dei Lombardi is 15th–16th-century Lombard painting, with canvases by Bergognone, Luini, the Leonardo-esque painters, a *Polyptych* by Cristoforo Moretti, and Vincenzo Foppa's *Portrait of Giovanni Francesco Brivio.* The portraits of Martin Luther and his wife by Lucas Cranach

(1529) are in the Sala degli Stranieri. A display case with precious porcelain separates the next room from the Salone Dorato. Designed by Poldi Pezzoli and destroyed by bombs in 1943, this hall was restored in 1974 by Luigi Caccia Dominioni. On display are fine works such as *St Nicholas of Tolentino* by Piero della Francesca, Botticelli's *Madonna and Child* and Pietà, a *Madonna and Child* by Andrea Mantegna, Giovanni Bellini's *Pietà* and a *Portrait of a Young Woman* attributed to Antonio Pollaiolo. Three small rooms house the Visconti Venosta collection of portraits by Fra Galgario, including *Gentleman with Tricorn,* and interesting 16th–18th-century clocks. The Saletta dei Vetri Antichi di Murano has fine specimens of glass-work, and the Gabinetto Dantesco features two stained-glass windows narrating episodes from Dante's life. The last rooms house a collection of small bronzes, paintings by Tiepolo, a *Sacred Conversation* by Lotto, and Giovanni Bellini's *Crucifixion.* Lastly, the Gabinetto degli Ori has a collection of precious ancient jewellery and goldsmithery.

Botticelli's *Pietà* **(1495), Museo Poldi Pezzoli**

A cradle from the Camera Rossa in the Museo Bagatti Valsecchi

Museo Bagatti Valsecchi ❸

Via Gesù 5. **Map** 4 D5 (10 E2). **Tel** 02-76 00 61 32. Ⓜ 3 Montenapoleone. 🚋 1, 2. ◯ 1–6pm Tue–Sun. ⬤ 1 Jan, Easter, 1 May, 15 Aug, 25 Dec. ♿ ground floor only. 📷 by appt. 🅿 **www.**museobagattivalsecchi.org

Opened in 1994 in the prestigious late 19th-century residence of the two Bagatti Valsecchi brothers, Fausto and Giuseppe, this fascinating museum is an important record of art collectors' taste in that period. The building was designed in Neo-Renaissance style, with an elegant façade and two well proportioned courtyards, and was furnished with works of art and imitation Renaissance furniture. It was seen as a private house and not a museum, and was furnished with every possible comfort. The rooms feature tapestries, ivory work, ceramics and arms, as well as important paintings such as the elegant *Santa*

Giustina by Giovanni Bellini (c.1475; kept in what was Giuseppe Bagatti Valsecchi's bedroom), Bernardo Zenale's panels and a *Polyptych* by Giampietrino. The library, with its valuable 15th-century parchments and a series of 16th–17th-century porcelain pharmacy vases, is also worth a look.

The intriguing Valtellinese bedroom has a magnificent 16th-century bed with Christ ascending Calvary and scenes from the Old Testament carved in the bedstead. The Sala della Stufa Valtellinese is also interesting, with its marvellous 16th-century wood panelling with an elegant sculpted frieze and a piece of furniture ingeniously concealing a piano. The Camera Rossa contains a delightful small collection of 15th–17th-century furniture for children that includes a high chair, a baby walker and a cradle. The dining room has a collection of kitchenware, tapestries and sideboards.

Archi di Porta Nuova ❹

Map 4 D4 (10 E1). Ⓜ 3 Montenapoleone. 🚋 1, 2. 🚌 61, 94.

This city gate, restored in 1861, is one of two surviving ones forming part of the medieval wall system. Construction began in 1171, and the gate was probably modelled on the corresponding Porta Romana, some of whose building materials it used. The inner side on Via Manzoni is decorated with copies of 1st-century AD Roman tombstones, while the outside facing Piazza Cavour bears a tabernacle decorated with a *Madonna and Child with Saints Ambrose, Gervase and Protasius* (1330–39).

Facing the piazza is Palazzo dei Giornali (No. 2), built in 1942 as the main office of the newspaper *Il Popolo d'Italia* and decorated with bas-reliefs by Mario Sironi. The square is framed by the Giardini Pubblici, in front of which is a monument to Cavour by Odoardo Tabacchi (1865).

The Porta Nuova arches seen from Via Manzoni

MUSEUMS DEVOTED TO THE HISTORY OF MILAN

Several museums, collectively the Civiche Raccolte Storiche, are devoted to the history of Milan. Palazzo Morando Attendolo Bolognini (No. 6 Via Sant'Andrea) houses the Museo di Milano and the Museo di Storia Contemporanea. The former features documents and paintings about old Milan and its illustrious citizens, and the latter has mementoes from the period of the two world wars. The palazzo is also home to the Civico Museo Marinaro Ugo Mursia, a nautical museum. The Museo del Risorgimento in Palazzo Moriggia (No. 23 Via Borgonuovo) covers the history of the Italian unification movement, from the late 1700s to the annexation of Rome (1870).

Sign for the entrance to a chocolate factory, now in the Museo di Milano

Street-by-Street: the Brera Quarter

The name of Milan's traditional Bohemian quarter derives from the Germanic word *braida,* which denoted a grassy area. The presence of art students at the Accademia di Belle Arti and the world-famous Brera art gallery has contributed to the lively feel of this quarter, which is reinforced by the many cafés, restaurants, galleries, antique shops and night-clubs established here. In summer the narrow streets are enlivened even more by street stalls and fortune tellers. An antiques market is held on the third Saturday of each month in Via Brera.

The Indian Café is one of the most popular spots in the area.

The Museo Minguzzi has 100 pieces by the Bolognese sculptor.

The Naviglio della Martesana canal flowed from the Adda river and along present-day Via San Marco. It was used for transporting foodstuffs and building materials. At the end of the street is the Tombone di San Marco, a wooden canal lock that regulated the water flow.

★ **San Simpliciano**
This church was one of the four basilicas founded by Sant'Ambrogio and has preserved most of its original Early Christian architecture ⑨

CAFE LIFE IN THE BRERA

Inside the Jamaica café, in Via Brera

The cafés and bars of the Brera quarter are lively and atmospheric. The Tombon de San Marc (Via San Marco) was once the haunt of the stevedores from the nearby Naviglio and now welcomes customers of all kinds. The famous Jamaica café (Via Brera) has jazz sessions on Mondays. Other atmospheric spots are the Louisiana Bistò (Via Fiori Chiari), Sans Égal, in the pedestrian precinct of Via Fiori Chiari, the Indian Café (Corso Garibaldi) and the ethnic Soul to Soul (Via San Marco) (*see pp186–7, pp198–9*).

0 metres   100

0 yards   100

STAR SIGHTS

★ Pinacoteca di Brera

★ San Simpliciano

★ San Marco

★ **San Marco**
The façade of this church, founded in 1254, was rebuilt in 1871 in Neo-Gothic style. The only remaining part of the original is the stone doorway, which has a relief of Christ between two saints and among symbols of the Evangelists ❺

LOCATOR MAP
See Street Finder, maps 3, 4, 9, 10

The Civico Museo del Risorgimento, opened in 1896, is in Neo-Classical Palazzo Moriggia.

★ **Pinacoteca di Brera**
The nucleus of one of Italy's top art galleries consists of works taken from churches that were suppressed in the late 1700s. The Brera boasts masterpieces by great artists such as Piero della Francesca, Mantegna, Raphael and Caravaggio ❻

VIA FATEBENEFRATELLI

VIA BORGONUOVO

VIA BRERA

VIA MADONNINA

VIA PONTE VETERO

VIA DELL'ORSO

Palazzo Cusani
This building with a late Baroque façade (1719) is the headquarters of the Third Army Corps. On the first floor is the Officers' Club ❼

Santa Maria del Carmine
The 15th-century church was built with material taken from the nearby Castello Sforzesco when it was partly demolished ❽

- - - Suggested route

The lunette over the entrance to San Marco

San Marco ❺

Piazza San Marco 2. **Map** 3 C4
(9 C1). **Tel** 02-29 00 25 98. 🚌 41,
43, 61. ◯ 7am–noon, 4–7pm
daily. ✝ 7:45, 9:30am, 6:30pm
Mon–Fri; 6:30pm pre-hols; 9:30,
11am, 12:15, 6:30pm hols.

This church was begun in
1254 by the Augustine monk
Lanfranco Settala. It was built
on the site of an older church,
dedicated by the Milanese to St
Mark, patron saint of Venice,
to thank the Venetians for help
in the struggle against Emperor Frederick Barbarossa. In
1871 Carlo Maciachini built a
new, Neo-Gothic façade
around the Camionese school
ogival portal and tabernacle.

The church has a Latin
cross plan and nine patrician
chapels, which were added
to the right-hand aisle in the
14th–19th century. They contain 16th–17th-century paintings, including some by Paolo
Lomazzo. In the right-hand
transept is the *Foundation of
the Augustine Order* by the
Fiammenghino brothers, Settala's sarcophagus by Giovanni Balduccio (1317–49),
and fragments of late Gothic
frescoes found during the
1956 restoration. The presbytery is decorated with large
canvases by Camillo Procaccini and Cerano depicting the
Legend of St Augustine, and
the *Genealogical Tree of the
Order* by Genovesino (17th
century), who also painted the
Angels' Backs on the cupola.
The left-hand transept leads to
the Chapel of the Pietà, with
The Ascent to Calvary by
Ercole Procaccini. The left-
hand aisle has canvases by
Camillo and Giulio Cesare
Procaccini and Palma il
Giovane, and a Leonardo-

esque fresco found in 1975.
From outside the Roman-
esque transept the 13th-
century bell tower is visible.

Pinacoteca di Brera ❻

See pp114–7.

Palazzo Cusani ❼

Via Brera 15. **Map** 3 C4 (9 C1).
Ⓜ 2 Lanza. 🚋 3, 4, 12, 14.
🚌 61. ◐ to the public.

Originally built in the
1500s, this palazzo was
rebuilt in 1719 by Giovanni
Ruggeri, who designed the
late Baroque façade with its
ornate windows and balco-
nies, while the Neo-Classical
façade facing the garden
was designed by Piermarini.
Tradition has it that the
Cusani brothers ordered twin
entrances so that each could
have independent yet equal
access. In the drawing room
is an allegorical Tiepolo-like
fresco (1740). The palazzo
was the seat of the Ministry
of War in the 19th century.

Santa Maria del Carmine ❽

Piazza del Carmine 2. **Map** 3 B4
(9 C1). **Tel** 02-86 46 33 65. 🚋 1,
3, 4, 12, 14, 27. 🚌 61. ◯ 7:15–
11:30am, 3:30–7pm daily. ✝
7:55, 9:45am, 6:30pm Mon– Sat;
9:45, 10:45 (English) & 11:45am,
4:45 (English) & 6:30pm hols.

Santa Maria del Carmine was
built in Gothic style in 1447
over a Romanesque church
and was then rebuilt in the

Baroque period, while the
present-day façade was
designed by Carlo Maciachini
in 1880. The spacious interior
has a three-aisle nave
covered by cross vaulting.
The inclination of the first
piers is due to the absence
of a façade for a long period
and the subsequent gradual
settling of the building.

The right-hand transept
contains part of the tomb of
the Ducal Councillor Angelo
Simonetta, above which are
two paintings by Carlo
Francesco Nuvolone and
Fiammenghino;
the opposite transept
is decorated with
a painting
by Camillo
Landriani.

The statues
in the wooden
choir (1579–85)
are the original
plaster models
created for the
spires of the
Duomo by 19th-
century artists. The
Cappella del
Rosario, built on
the right of the
choir (1673) by
Gerolamo Quadrio, has
marble dressing and is
decorated with canvases by
Camillo Procaccini depicting
The Legend of Mary.

**A statue in
the choir**

On the left-hand side of
the church is the monastery
cloister, with remains of
noble tombs and ancient
tombstones, and a Baroque
sacristy, with furniture made
by Quadrio in 1692.

**Part of the Baroque sacristy, Santa
Maria del Carmine**

Angel Musicians by Aurelio Luini (16th century), in the church of San Simpliciano

San Simpliciano ❾

Piazza San Simpliciano 7. **Map** 3 B4.
Tel 02-86 22 74. Ⓜ 2 Lanza.
🚋 3, 4, 12, 14. 🚌 43, 57, 70.
🕐 winter: 7:15am–noon, 3–7pm
daily; summer: 8am–noon, 4–7pm
daily. ✝ 6pm Mon–Fri; 6pm pre-
hols; 10 & 11:30am, 6pm hols.

The church was founded by
Sant'Ambrogio in the 4th
century as the *Basilica Virginum* and completed in 401. It is
preceded by a porch and once
had open galleries on either
side where penitents and new
converts could take part in
Mass. The façade, decorated
with glazed plates, was added
in 1870 by Maciachini, who
retained the main portal. The
capitals have 12th-century
carvings of the processions of
the Wise and Foolish Virgins.
Fourteenthcentury frescoes
have been discovered in the
first chapel on the right, and in
the fourth is Enea Salmeggia's
Miracle of St Benedict (1619).
The apse is frescoed with the
Coronation of the Virgin by
Bergognone (1508). The Neo-
Classical altar covers the
wooden choir
(1588),

and on either side are two
organ pedestals frescoed by
Aurelio Luini in the 1500s.
The transept leads to the Early
Christian Sacellum of San
Simpliciano (closed), built
to house the remains of San
Simpliciano and of martyrs.

Sant'Angelo ❿

Piazza Sant'Angelo 2. **Map** 4 D3.
Tel 02-63 24 81. 🚋 41, 43.
🚌 94. 🕐 6:30am–8pm daily.
✝ 7pm Mon–Fri; 7pm pre-hols;
9, 10 & 11 am, 12.15 & 7pm hols.

Built in 1552 by Domenico
Giunti to replace the older
Franciscan church outside the
Porta Nuova gate, which had
been demolished to make
room for the Spanish ramparts,
Sant'Angelo is an important
example of 16th-century
Milanese architecture. The
nave is separated from the
presbytery by a triumphal arch
with the *Assumption of Mary*
by Legnanino (17th century).
There are many 16th and
17th-century paintings in the
chapels. The first one on the
right has canvases by Antonio
Campi (1584) and a copy of
the *Martyrdom of St Catherine*

of Alexandria by Gaudenzio
Ferrari (the original is in the
Brera); the second has
Morazzone's *St Charles in
Glory* and in the apse is Pro-
caccini's *Legend of the Virgin*.

Santa Maria Incoronata ⓫

Corso Garibaldi 116. **Map** 3 C2.
Tel 02-65 48 55. Ⓜ 2 Garibaldi.
🚌 94. 🕐 7:15am–1:30pm,
4–7pm Mon–Fri, 8am–12.30pm,
4–7:30pm Sat–Sun. ✝ 7:30 &
9:30am, 4:30pm Mon–Sat; 8:30,
10 & 11:30am, 6:30pm hols.

This church consists of two
buildings designed by
Guiniforte Solari, which were
merged in 1468. The left one
was built for Francesco Sforza
in 1451 and the other was
built soon afterwards for his
wife. The brick façade is
double, as is the nave, which
has two apses with 15th and
17th-century frescoes. In the
right-hand chapels are plaques
in memory of Sforzesco court
personages. The chapels
opposite have frescoes by
Montalto and Bernardino
Zenale (the fresco in the first
chapel is attributed to Zenale).

**Lunette over one of the doors
of San Simpliciano**

SAN SIMPLICIANO, THE THREE MARTYRS AND THE CARROCCIO

St Ambrose asked the young Sisinius, Martirius and
Alexander to go to Anaunia (today Val di Non) in
northern Italy to spread Christianity. In 397 they were
martyred and the bodies were given to Bishop Simpliciano, who buried them in the *Basilica Virginum*.
According to legend, the martyrs were decisive in leading the Milanese to victory in the
battle of Legnano against Barbarossa (1176). On that occasion three white doves flew out of
the basilica and landed on the Carroccio (cart), the symbol of Milan, waiting to be blessed
before the battle. On 29 May the city commemorates this event with a solemn ceremony.

Pinacoteca di Brera ❻

The Brera art gallery holds one of Italy's most important art collections, featuring masterpieces by leading Italian artists from the 13th to the 20th centuries, including Raphael, Mantegna, Piero della Francesca and Caravaggio. The Pinacoteca is housed in the late 16th–early 17th-century palazzo built for the Jesuits in place of the Santa Maria di Brera Humiliati monastery. The Jesuits made this into a cultural centre by establishing a prestigious school, a library and the astronomical observatory – all activities supported by Empress Maria Theresa of Austria, who founded the Accademia di Belle Arti after the Jesuit order was suppressed (1773).

Portrait of Moisè Kisling
Amedeo Modigliani painted this work in 1915, reflecting his interest in African sculpture. (Room 1)

Finding the Body of St Mark
The bold perspective and almost super-natural light in the room where the saint's body is found make this canvas (1562–6) one of Tintoretto's masterpieces. (Room 9)

Mocchirolo Chapel

KEY

☐	Jesi Collection (20th-century art)
☐	13th–15th-century Italian painting
☐	15th–16th-century Venetian painting
☐	15th–16th-century Lombard painting
☐	15th–16th-century Central Italian painting
☐	17th–18th-century Italian, Flemish and Dutch painting
☐	18th–19th-century Italian painting

Twin staircases
lead to the entrance to the gallery on the first floor.

The Kiss
This canvas by Francesco Hayez (1859) is one of the most reproduced 19th-century Italian paintings – a patriotic and sentimental work epitomizing the optimism that prevailed after Italy's unification. (Room 37)

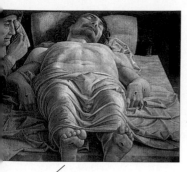

★ Dead Christ
This masterpiece by Mantegna (c.1480) is striking for its intense light and bold foreshortening. The work was among the artist's possessions at the time of his death. (Room 6)

VISITORS' CHECKLIST

Via Brera 28.
Map 3 C4 (9 C1). **Tel** 02-72 26 31. Info 02-89 42 11 46. **M** 1, 3 Duomo, 2 Lanza. 1, 8, 12, 14. 61.
8:30am–7:30pm Tue–Sun (last adm: 1 hour before closing). Mon, 1 Jan, 1 May, 25 Dec.
www.brera.beniculturali.it

Room 15 has works by painters active in Lombardy from the late 15th to the mid-16th century, including Bergognone, Luini, Bramantino and Vincenzo Foppa.

★ Montefeltro Altarpiece
Piero della Francesca painted this great work in 1475 for Federico da Montefeltro, the Duke of Urbino, who is portrayed dressed in a Milanese suit of armour. (Room 24)

The courtyard with twin columns is the work of Richini (17th century).

GALLERY GUIDE
The Brera Gallery has 38 rooms, with works arranged in chronological order. The only exception is Room 10, where the Jesi and Vitali collections are on display It includes 20th-century works which will be exhibited elsewhere in future. The paintings are also grouped together by schools of painting (Venetian, Tuscan, Lombard, etc.). The Sala della Passione on the ground floor is used for temporary exhibitions.

STAR PAINTINGS

★ Dead Christ

★ The Marriage of the Virgin

★ Montefeltro Altarpiece

Entrance

★ The Marriage of the Virgin
Raphael signed and dated (1504) his masterful altarpiece on the temple in the background. Some scholars say the young man breaking the staff is a self-portrait of the artist. (Room 24)

Exploring the Pinacoteca di Brera

The original nucleus of the Brera Gallery consisted mainly of plaster casts and drawings used as models for the art students of the Accademia di Belle Arti (founded in 1776). This collection was augmented with works from suppressed churches in Northern Italy and was officially opened in 1809, the paintings being arranged in rows on the wall, from floor to ceiling. The Pinacoteca became independent from the Accademia in 1882, and its fine collection further expanded through 19th- and 20th-century donations. The gallery has always suffered from lack of space, but there are plans to use the adjacent Palazzo Citterio.

The City Rises (c.1910) by Umberto Boccioni

JESI COLLECTION

The 72 works donated by Emilio and Maria Jesi in 1976 and 1984 are on show in room 10. The collection, mostly by Italian artists, covers the 1910–40 period. Key works include *Portrait of Moisè Kisling* by Modigliani, Umberto Boccioni's *Brawl in the Galleria* (1911) and *The City Rises* (a study for the canvas now in the New York MOMA), Carlo Carrà's *The Metaphysical Muse* (1917) and still lifes by Giorgio Morandi, as well as sculpture by Medardo Rosso, Arturo Martini and Marino Marini.

13TH–15TH-CENTURY ITALIAN PAINTING

The section given over to 13th–15th-century Italian art (rooms 2–4) includes frescoes from the Oratory at Mocchirolo, painted by an unknown Lombard master in around 1365–70. Among the gold-background works are the *Santa Maria della Celestia Polyptych* by Lorenzo Veneziano (14th century), Ambrogio Lorenzetti's *Madonna and Child* and *Christ the Judge* by Giovanni da Milano. A fine example of the International Gothic style is the *Valle Romita Polyptych* by Gentile da Fabriano, flanked by Stefano da Verona's *Adoration of the Magi* (1435), in which the viola and carnation at the feet of Jesus symbolize his humility and the Passion.

15TH–16TH-CENTURY VENETIAN PAINTING

Rooms 5 and 6 feature works by 15th–16th-century artists active in the Veneto such as Giovanni d'Alemagna and Antonio Vivarini, who painted the *Praglia Polyptych* (1448). Room 6 also has

Mantegna's masterpieces *Dead Christ* and *St Luke Altarpiece* (1453–4). Giovanni Bellini is represented by two Madonnas with Child and a *Pietà* (c.1470), and Carpaccio by *Legend of the Virgin*. There are portraits by Titian, Lotto and Tintoretto in room 7. *St Mark Preaching in Alexandria* (room 8) was painted for the Scuola Grande in St Mark's in Venice by Giovanni and Gentile Bellini.

The following room has works by Titian and Paolo Veronese, as well as the *Finding of the Body of St Mark*, which Tintoretto painted for Tommaso Rangone, who is portrayed as the kneeling man in the middle of the scene.

15TH–16TH-CENTURY LOMBARD PAINTING

A large collection of 15th–16th-century Lombard paintings is exhibited in rooms 15, 18 and 19. The leading figure, Vincenzo Foppa, is represented by the *Politico delle Grazie* (c.1483). An unknown master contributed the *Sforzesca Altarpiece* (1494), showing Lodovico il Moro and his family worshipping the Madonna. This room also has works by Bergognone, Gaudenzio Ferrari – an artist with a marked narrative vein, as can be seen in *Martyrdom of St Catherine* – and Bramantino's *Crucifixion*. Works influenced by Leonardo

Gentile da Fabriano's *Valle Romita Polyptych*

Supper at Emmaus, painted by Caravaggio in 1606

da Vinci include the small paintings for private chapels by De Predis and Luini (*Madonna del Roseto*), while the Cremona area is represented by names such as Boccaccino, Campi and Piazza.

15TH–16TH-CENTURY CENTRAL ITALIAN PAINTING

Rooms 20–23 illustrate artistic movements in the regions of Emilia and Le Marche. The Ferrara school is represented by its leading artists, Cosmè Tura, Francesco del Cossa and Ercole de' Roberti (whose *Madonna and Child among Saints* was painted around 1480). Correggio's *Nativity* is a major Emilian school work, while painting in Le Marche is documented by the works of Carlo Crivelli, including his *Madonna della Candeletta* (1490–91), rich in symbols.

Room 24 houses the two best-known masterpieces in the Brera. Piero della Francesca's *Montefeltro Altarpiece* (c.1475), was commissioned by Federico da Montefeltro. The egg suspended from its shell is a symbol of the Creation and of the Immaculate Conception. Next is Raphael's splendid *Marriage of the Virgin (see p115)*.

Christ at the Pillar is a rare painting by Bramante, while works by Bronzino and Genga represent Mannerism.

17TH–18TH-CENTURY ITALIAN AND FLEMISH PAINTING

Room 28 features works by the Bolognese school, founded by the Carracci, including Guido Reni and Guercino. The next room boasts a masterpiece by Caravaggio, *Supper at Emmaus* (1606), in which the appearance of Christ occurs in a setting illuminated only by the light emanating from Jesus's face. Lombard artists shown here are Cerano, Morazzone and Giulio Cesare Procaccini, who painted the *Martyrdom of Saints Rufina and Seconda* together. Baroque painting is represented by Pietro da Cortona and the still lifes of Baschenis. Among the non-Italian artists are Rubens (*Last Supper,* 1631–32), Van Dyck, Rembrandt (*Portrait of the Artist's Sister,* 1632), El Greco and Brueghel the Elder (*The Village*).

18TH–19TH-CENTURY ITALIAN PAINTING

The following rooms cover various genres in 18th-century Italian art. Large-scale religious paintings are in room 34 with works by the Neapolitan Luca Giordano and two Venetians: Giovan Battista Tiepolo's *Madonna del Carmelo* (1721–7), intended to be viewed from the side, and Piazzetta's *Rebecca at the Well.*

Giacomo Ceruti (Il Pitocchetto) represents "genre painting", which was popular in the 18th century. This is followed by Venetian *vedutismo*, views by Bernardo Bellotto, Guardi and Canaletto. The works of Bellotto and Canaletto are characterized by their bright light and precision of detail (the latter even used a camera obscura to help him render this "photographic" effect).

Portraiture is best exemplified by Fra Galgario (*Portrait of a Gentleman*). A representative 19th-century painting is Andrea Appian's Neo-Classical *Olympus*, while the Macchiaioli movement is on display with works by Silvestro Lega and Giovanni Fattori, among others. The Brera also has paintings by the leading exponent of Lombard Romanticism, Francesco Hayez: his famous *The Kiss* and several portraits. The gallery closes with Divisionist Giuseppe Pelizza da Volpedo's *The Flood* (1895–97), a hymn to the struggle of the working class, and an early version of his *Fourth Estate*, now on display at the Villa Belgiojoso Bonaparte (*see p121*).

Madonna della Candeletta by Crivelli

Cimitero Monumentale ⓬

Piazzale Cimitero Monumentale.
Map 3 A1. *Tel* 02-88 46 56 00.
🚋 3, 4, 11, 12, 14, 29, 30, 33.
🚌 41, 51, 70, 94. ⬜
8:30am–5:15pm Tue–Sun;
8:30am–1pm hols. Free
map of the cemetery
available at the entrance.

Sculpture by Fontana, Cimitero Monumentale

Extending over an area of 250,000 sq m (300,000 sq yds), the Cimitero Monumentale was begun by Carlo Maciachini in 1866. The eclectic taste of the time dictated the use of various styles for the cemetery, from mock-Lombard Romanesque to Neo-Gothic, with touches of Tuscan thrown in. The linchpin of the structure is the Famedio *(Famae Aedes)*, or House of Fame, a sort of pantheon of illustrious Milanese and non-Milanese buried here. Author Alessandro Manzoni, Luca Beltrami, the architect who oversaw restoration of the Castello Sforzesco, the patriot Carlo Cattaneo and the Nobel Prize-winning poet Salvatore Quasimodo all have tombs in this cemetery. There are also busts of Garibaldi, Verdi and Cavour. The Romantic painter Hayez lies in the crypt. A visit

to the Cimitero Monumentale, which is a kind of open-air museum of art from the late 19th century to the present, begins at the large square inside, which contains the tombs of important Milanese figures. Around the square are monumental shrines and the Civico Mausoleo Palanti, an enormous mausoleum with a crypt, used as an air raid shelter in 1943. Among its tombs are those of comic actor Walter Chiari and Hermann Einstein, Albert's father. On the terraces, to the left are the Elisi (sculpted by Francesco Penna, 1916) and Morgagni tombs, and an epigraph by Mussolini commemorating a disastrous aeroplane crash. In the central avenue are two tombs designed and sculpted by Enrico Butti: that of Isabella Casati, *Young Woman Enraptured by a Dream,* a typical Lombard realist work (1890), and the Besenzanica shrine with *Work* (1912). On your right, you will come to the monumental Toscanini tomb (Bistolfi, 1909–11), built for the conductor's son.

Among other monumental tombs for major figures in Milanese life are those of Carlo Erba, Bocconi, Campari and Falck. Many famous sculptors made pieces for this place: Leonardo Bistolfi, Giacomo Manzù, Odoardo Tabacchi, Adolfo Wildt and Lucio Fontana. The two enclosures beside the Famedio are for Jews and Catholics, with the remains of sculptor Medardo Rosso, publishers Arnoldo Mondadori and Ulrico Hoepli and Jules Richard, founder of the Richard-Ginori ceramics industry.

The Cimitero Monumentale, with tombs and shrines produced by famous sculptors

The Pirelli Building, symbol of Milan's postwar reconstruction

Pirelli Building ⓭

Piazzale Duca d'Aosta-Via Pirelli.
Map 4 E1. Ⓜ 2, 3 Centrale.
🚋 2, 5, 9, 33. 🚌 42, 60, 82.
● to the public.

The symbol of postwar reconstruction in Milan, the Pirelli Building, affectionately called "Pirellone" (big Pirelli) by the Milanese, was built in 1955–60. It was designed by a group of leading architects and engineers: Gio Ponti, Antonio Fornaroli, Alberto Rosselli, Giuseppe Valtolina, Egidio Dell'Orto, Pier Luigi Nervi and Arturo Danusso. At 127.10 m (417 ft) high, it was the largest reinforced concrete skyscraper in the world until the 1960s. The slender, elegant edifice occupies only 1,000 sq m (1,200 sq yds) and stands on the site where, in 1872, Giovan Battista Pirelli built his first tyre factory. The skyscraper was constructed as the Pirelli company's main offices. Among the many records established by the "Pirellone" was that it was the first building in Milan taller than the Madonnina on the Duomo (108.50 m, 356 ft). As a token of respect, a small statue of the Virgin Mary was placed on the Pirelli roof. Since 1979 the building has been the headquarters of the regional government of Lombardy. Next door is the luxurious Excelsior Hotel Gallia, opened in the 1930s.

For hotels and restaurants in this area see pp162–4 and pp176–8

The Stazione Centrale, with its spectacular iron and glass roof

Stazione Centrale ⑭

Piazzale Duca d'Aosta. **Map** 4 E1.
Ⓜ *2, 3 Centrale.* 🚋 *2, 5, 9, 33.*
🚌 *42, 53, 60, 82, 90, 91, 92.*

Milan's main railway station is one of the largest and perhaps the most monumental in Europe. Ulisse Stacchini's project design was approved and ready in 1912, but construction work proved so slow that the building was not opened until 1931. The new railway station replaced one located in present-day Piazza della Repubblica.

The building is dressed in Annisina stone, and was clearly inspired by the late Art Nouveau style in vogue in the early 20th century, in marked contrast with the austere 1930s architecture of the surrounding buildings.

The façade is 207 m (679 ft) wide and 36 m (118 ft) tall and is crowned by two winged horses. The large arcades link up with the Galleria dei Transiti, a gallery decorated with four medallions by Giannino Castiglioni representing Labour, Commerce, Science and Agriculture. In the large ticket office hall, flights of steps lead up to the huge departures and arrivals lobby, with tile panels representing the cities of Milan, Rome, Turin and Florence.

The massive building is a landmark in Milan and second only to the cathedral in size. There are numerous shops inside, and some are open 24 hours a day.

Bastioni di Porta Venezia ⑮

Map 4 E3. Ⓜ *1 Porta Venezia, 3 Repubblica.* 🚋 *1, 2, 9, 11, 29, 30.*

What is today a major road was once part of the walls built to defend the city in 1549–61 by the Spanish governor Ferrante Gonzaga. In 1789 the walls became a tree-lined avenue for walking and coach parking. The Porta Venezia ramparts, flanked by the Giardini Pubblici, link Piazza della Repubblica and Piazza Oberdan. The former was laid out in 1931 when the 19th-century railway station was demolished and rebuilt 800 m (2,624 ft) away and greatly

enlarged to cope with increasing traffic resulting from the opening of the St Gotthard (1882) and Simplon (1906) passes through the Alps.

Not far from the piazza, in Via Turati, is the Palazzo della Permanente, designed by Luca Beltrami in 1885 as the home of the Permanent Fine Arts Exhibition and now used for temporary exhibitions.

Piazza Oberdan is dominated by Porta Venezia, the city gate rebuilt in 1828 on the site of the Spanish gate of the same name and used as a customs toll station. The two buildings are decorated with statues and reliefs concerning the history of Milan. Porta Venezia separates Corso Venezia and Corso Buenos Aires, a major commercial thoroughfare.

In 1488–1513, Lazzaro Palazzi chose a site beyond the gate to build the *luzzaretto*, a hospital for plague victims commissioned by Lodovico il Moro. The few remains from the 1880 demolition can be seen in Via San Gregorio. A slight detour from Piazza Oberdan towards Viale Piave will take you past some interesting Art Nouveau style buildings: Casa Galimberti, designed by Giovan Battista Bossi in 1903–4, decorated with wrought iron and panels of ceramic tiles, and the Hotel Diana Majestic.

Plaque commemorating the *lazzaretto*

Casa Galimberti, decorated with wrought iron and tile panels

Planetarium ⑯

Corso Venezia 57. **Map** 4 E4 (10 F2). **Tel** 02–29 53 11 81. Ⓜ 1 Porta Venezia-Palestro. 🚋 9, 29, 30. ◯ 3 & 4:30pm Sat & Sun. 📷 ✂ ♿ **www**.comunemilano.it/planetario

Donated to the city by the publisher Ulrico Hoepli, the Planetarium was built in 1930 in Classical style by Piero Portaluppi. The projection hall has a large hemispherical dome and 600 swivelling seats to enable you to gaze at the movements of the stars in comfort.

The Planetarium offers guided tours (including tours for students of the subject) and scientific or popular-level lectures on astronomy.

Museo di Storia Naturale ⑰

Corso Venezia 55. **Map** 4 E4 (10 F2). **Tel** 02–88 46 32 80. Ⓜ 1 Porta Venezia-Palestro. 🚋 9, 29, 30. ◯ 9am–6pm Tue–Fri, 9:30am–6:30pm Sat–Sun. ● 1 Jan, Easter, 1 May, 15 Aug, 25 Dec. 📷 ✂ (tel. 02-78 35 28). ✂ ♿ Lecture hall, library.

The museum of Natural History was founded in 1838 with the donation of the Giuseppe de Cristoforis and Giorgio Jan collections. The building was constructed in Neo-Romanesque style and with terracotta decoration in 1893 by Giovanni Ceruti. The museum has a specialist library holding over 30,000 volumes, including sections on mineralogy and zoology. On the ground floor are the mineralogy and entomology

The Giardini Pubblici, a rare area of greenery in Milan

collections, and part of the Museo Settala, which was created by a canon named Manfredo. It features scientific instruments and natural history specimens of varied provenance. In the palae-ontology halls there are reconstructions of dinosaurs such as the Triceratops and a large Allosaurus skeleton. The ground floor also has displays of molluscs and insects. The upper floor is reserved for reptiles, ceta-ceans and mammals. There are also several reconstruc-tions of animal habitats.

Giardini Pubblici ⑱

Corso Venezia, Via Palestro, Via Manin, Bastioni di Porta Venezia. **Map** 4 E4 (10 F1). Ⓜ 1 Porta Venezia-Palestro, 3 Repubblica-Turati. 🚋 1, 9, 11, 29, 30. 🚌 94. ◯ 6:30am–sunset daily.

The public gardens extend for about 160,000 sq m (192,000 sq yds) and form the largest city park in Milan. They were designed by Piermarini

in 1786 and enlarged in 1857 by Giuseppe Balzaretto, who annexed Palazzo Dugnani and its garden. Further changes were made by Emilio Alemagna after the international exhibitions held in the 1871–81 period.

The park is also home to the Padiglione del Caffè (1863), now a nursery school, and the Museo di Storia Naturale.

Palazzo Dugnani ⑲

Via Manin 2. **Map** 4 D3 (10 E1). Ⓜ 3 Turati. 🚋 1, 2. 🚌 61, 94 ◯ Tiepolo rooms only. **Museo del Cinema Tel** 02–655 49 77. ◯ 3–6:30pm Fri–Sun. 📷 ♿

Palazzo Dugnani was built in the late 1600s and reno-vated a century later. Since 1846 it has belonged to Milan city council. A monumental staircase leads up to a magni-ficent two-storey salon with a gallery for musicians. Here, in 1731, the great Giambattista Tiepolo painted the frescoes *The Allegory of the Dugnani Family and The Legends of Scipio and Massinissa.* Both were damaged by the 1943 bombings and by the terrorist bomb that exploded in Via Palestro in 1993.

The palazzo houses the Museo del Cinema which documents the evolution of motion-picture cameras from the 18th-century magic lan-terns to those used by the Lumière brothers, as well as apparatus that became obsolete when talking pictures were invented. There are also movie posters from 1905 to 1930.

Reconstruction of a dinosaur skeleton, Museo di Storia Naturale

For hotels and restaurants in this area see pp162–4 and pp176–8

Villa Belgiojoso Bonaparte – Museo dell'Ottocento ⑳

Milan's 19th-century art gallery is housed in a Neo-Classical villa built by Leopold Pollack in 1790 for Count Ludovico Barbiano di Belgioioso. It was lived in by Napoleon in 1802 and later by Marshal Radetzky. The gallery is devoted to 19th-century art movements in Italy, from Hayez to Piccio, the Scapigliatura, Divisionism and the Macchiaioli artists Fattori and Lega. The villa also houses the Grassi and Vismara collections of 19th- and 20th-century Italian and foreign artists (including Impressionists, Matisse, Picasso, Morandi) as well as the Marino Marini Museum.

VISITORS' CHECKLIST

Via Palestro 16. **Map** 4 E4 (10 E1). **Tel** 02-76 34 08 09. Ⓜ 1 Palestro. 🚃 1, 2. 🚌 61, 94. 🕐 phone for times. 🚫 1 Jan, Easter, 1 May, 15 Aug, 25 Dec. 🖼️ ♿ 📷 many rooms closed for restoration. **www.**villabelgiojoso bonaparte.it **Giardini di Villa Belgiojoso Bonaparte** 🚪 only to adults accompanying children. 9am–noon, 2–7pm daily (Mar, Oct: to 6pm, Nov–Feb: to 4pm).

KEY

- ☐ Vismara Collection
- ☐ Modern Art Gallery
- ☐ Marino Marini Museum
- ☐ Grassi Collection

Grassi Collection

In 1956 Nedda Grassi donated this fine collection to the city in memory of her son Gino. It comprises rugs, Oriental objects d'art and 135 paintings, including foreign and Italian 19th- and 20th-century artists such as Van Gogh, Cézanne, Corot and Gauguin, Fattori, Lega, Balla, Boccioni and Morandi.

Antonio Canova's bronze of Napoleon and plaster sculpture of Hebe are displayed here.

Furnishings and frescoes decorate the main floor; the top attraction is the dining room, with a *Parnassus* by Appiani.

STAR EXHIBIT

★ Fourth Estate

★ Fourth Estate

In this fine 1901 canvas, Quarto Stato, Giuseppe Pelizza da Volpedo expresses solidarity with the struggles and suffering of the lower classes.

Marino Marini Museum

This section opened in 1973. It holds paintings and sculptures donated by Marini himself, including portraits of people he admired, such as Arp, De Pisis, Carrà, Chagall and Stravinsky.

Corso Venezia ㉑

Formerly called Corso di Porta Orientale, this famous and popular street was named after the gate in the medieval walls corresponding to present-day Via Senato. The same name was given to the quarter, whose emblem is the lion on the column in front of the church of San Babila. Corso Venezia was lined with relatively few buildings and bordered by kitchen gardens and orchards until the mid-18th century, when the reforms carried out by Maria Theresa of Austria led to the construction of the numerous patrician palazzi that make this one of Milan's most elegant streets.

LOCATOR MAP
See Street Finder, map 4, 10

Three inner courtyards lead to the garden.

On the balustrade are statues of the *Dei Consenti* (the 12 chief Roman gods) by Pompeo Marchesi and Grazioso Rusca.

Palazzo Rocca-Saporiti ①

Giovanni Perego designed this building in 1812 and it reflects the taste of the Napoleonic period. On the façade is a frieze with scenes of Milanese history.

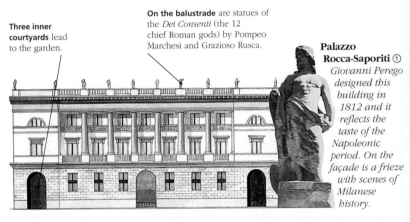

Palazzo Castiglioni ②

This palazzo was built by Giuseppe Somma-ruga in 1904. There were once two female nudes on the façade (later removed), hence its name Ca' di Ciapp *(House of Buttocks).*

On the first floor is a lovely three-flight staircase and the Sala dei Pavoni.

A loggia with Ionic columns emphasizes the central section.

The side facing Via San Damiano has retained its original 17th-century features.

Palazzo Serbelloni ③

Completed in 1793 by Simone Cantoni, this palazzo played host to Napoleon and Vittorio Emanuele.

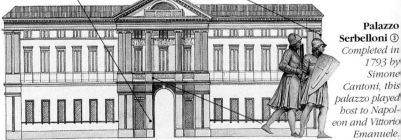

VISITORS' CHECKLIST

Map 4 E4. **M** 1 Porta Venezia–Palestro–San Babila. 9,29,30. 54, 61, 65, 73, 94. Palazzi not open to public. **San Babila** Piazza San Babila. **Tel** 02-76 00 28 77. ◯ 7:30am–noon, 3:30–7pm daily. 8:30, 10:30am, 6:30pm Mon–Fri; 3:30pm pre-hols; 8, 10, 11:30 am, 12:30 & 6:30pm hols.

★ Casa Fontana-Silvestri ④
This rare example of a Renaissance residence in Milan was built in the late 15th century by Angelo Fontana. The windows on the façade are framed in brick and the portal by candelabrum columns.

Bramante is thought by a number of scholars to have worked on the decoration of the façade.

Above the portal is San Carlo's motto, *Humilitas*.

Seminario Arcivescovile ⑤
This seminary was begun in 1565 by Seregni for San Carlo Borromeo. The portal was added in 1652 by Francesco Maria Richini.

The campanile was built in 1820, after the original collapsed.

The present-day Neo-Romanesque façade was designed in 1906 by Paolo Cesa Bianchi, who also built the high altar.

★ San Babila ⑥
The church was built in the 11th century over a 4th-century basilica and rebuilt in the 1500s. The rather heavy-handed restoration of the Romanesque original began in 1853.

STAR SIGHTS

★ San Babila

★ Casa Fontana-Silvestri

TWO GUIDED WALKS IN MILAN

Most visitors travel around by Metro and come away with the impression that Milan offers little more than the Gothic-spired Duomo, the famed *Last Supper* and some chillingly expensive fashion boutiques. But by strolling around at a slower pace, you can find a Milan of great art, deep history and glorious monuments. The first walk investigates the hidden heart of Milan's historic centre, from church gems to fantastical façades tucked just off busy modern thoroughfares, and from designer boutiques to the elegant townhouses of Milan's 19th-century

A painting of La Scala

elite. The second walk examines the ages of Milan, from its Roman roots to Palaeochristian basilicas rich in mosaics and frescoes, and from the medieval Castello Sforzesco to Renaissance masterpieces by the likes of Bellini, Mantegna and Leonardo da Vinci. In fact, Leonardo pops up frequently on this walk in all his guises, from artist to inventor to engineer. The walk ends at the Navigli, a thriving restaurant and nightlife district based around the remnants of a canal system that the multi-talented Leonardo helped design.

CHOOSING A WALK

The Two Walks
This map shows the location of the two guided walks in relation to the main sightseeing areas of Milan.

Milan's Hidden Glories
(p125)

Northeast Milan

Northwest Milan

Historic Centre

Southeast Milan

Southwest Milan

Cova, a historic café in the heart of the fashion district *(p125)*

0 metres   800

0 yards   800

KEY

・・・・・ Walk route

Milan's Historic Past
(pp126–7)

The main nave of the Sant'Ambrogio basilica *(p126)*

A 90-Minute Walk Around Milan's Hidden Glor

Milan's beauty is not immediately obvious. With a few exceptions, such as the Duomo and the Galleria, the city's glories are hidden. This walk takes in stunning Baroque façades lost amid bland buildings, and tours the fashion boutiques in the "Golden Rectangle".

Around the Duomo

Begin at the jewel-box church of Santa Maria presso San Satiro ① (see p55), which is encased by modern buildings making it hard to find (it is down a short alley off Via Torino). A right down Via Speronari leads to its 10th-century bell tower. Leave the church, turn left up Via Mazzini into Piazza del Duomo ② (see pp44–5) and ascend to the cathedral's roof ③ (see pp46–9) for panoramic views. Descend and stop for a drink at the renowned Caffè Zucca ④ (see p187), which lies near the entrance to the Galleria Vittorio Emanuele II ⑤ (see p50), an imposing 19th-century shopping arcade. Stroll through its glass-roofed atrium, ensuring good luck by stomping on the testicles of the mosaic bull near the centre. Emerge at Piazza della Scala ⑥, for the splendid Teatro alla Scala opera house ⑦ (see pp52–3) and pay your respects to Verdi in the attached Museo Teatrale.

Cross the square and walk behind Palazzo Marino ⑧ (see p50) to the Counter-Reformation church of San Fedele ⑨ (see p50). Head northeast along its left flank past the surreal Casa degli Omenoni ⑩ (see p51). Turn left on Via Morone at the 18th-century Palazzo Belgioioso ⑪ and turn right onto Via Manzoni ⑫ (see p108), lined with grand palazzi.

The shopping district

Admire the magnificent Grand Hotel et de Milan ⑬, where Giuseppe Verdi died in 1901,

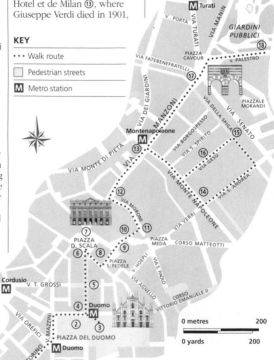

The Theatre Museum, part of the La Scala opera house ⑦

KEY

- ••• Walk route
- ☐ Pedestrian streets
- Ⓜ Metro station

then turn right onto Via Montenapoleone, the heart of the fashion district. Versace, Gucci and Prada all have boutiques here. Continue along the road until you reach Cova ⑭ (see p187), an elegant café famous for its *panettone*.

Turn left and left again onto Via della Spiga, home to chic Dolce & Gabbana ⑮. Turn left onto Via Gesù and half way down is Museo Bagatti Valsecchi ⑯ (see p109), a refined town-house filled with 15th- to 17th- century furnishings. At the end of the road turn right and right again onto Via Manzoni. Walk through Archi di Porta Nuova ⑰ (see p109), a medieval gate with Roman funerary reliefs, and head to Giardini Pubblici ⑱ (see p120), a welcome respite from the urban streetscape.

...va, a Milanese must for an ...ant coffee break since 1817 ⑭

TIPS FOR WALKERS

Starting point: Santa Maria presso San Satiro, off Via Torino.
Length: 2.8 km (1.7 miles)
Getting there: Duomo station.
Best time for walk: Morning.
Stopping-off points: Historic cafés such as Zucca and Cova.

wo-Hour Walk around Milan's Historic Past

n is a city that tends to keep its history largely
ied under a modern, business-oriented veneer.
he following walk seeks out the remnants of Roman,
medieval and Renaissance Milan while paying homage
to the city's most famous adopted son, Leonardo da
Vinci. The Renaissance master has left a distinctive
stamp on the city. Examples of his genius are scattered
all around town, from the *Last Supper* fresco to models
of his inventions in the Museo della Scienza e della
Tecnica, not to mention the surviving canals that were
once part of a vast and intricate waterway system
Leonardo helped plan.

Santa Maria delle Grazie, home to
Leonardo's famous *Last Supper* ④

From the Castello Sforzesco to Leonardo's *Last Supper*

Begin at Milan's splendid 15th-
century castle ① *(see pp64–7)*,
which houses archaeological
artifacts, paintings by Bellini
and Mantegna, and sculptures
from the medieval to ones by
Michelangelo. From the front
gate head towards Largo Cairoli
and then turn right into Via San
Giovanni sul Muro. At the
junction with Via Meravigli
turn right into Corso Magenta.

The cloistered entrance to the
basilica of Sant'Ambrogio ⑦

TIPS FOR WALKERS

Starting point: Castello
Sforzesco.
Length: 4.9 km (3 miles).
Getting there: Cairoli metro
station.
Best time for walk: Morning.
Stopping-off points: Not far
from the Castello Sforzesco is
the genteel Marchesi pastry
shop (see p178), or you can stop
at the Art Nouveau Bar Magenta
in Via Carducci (see p178). The
walk ends in Milan's best district
for wine bars and eateries.

Follow it west, and across
from the Rococo Palazzo Litta
② *(see p74)*, you will see the
Museo Archeologico ③ *(see
p74)* – its cloisters preserve a
bit of the city's Roman-era
walls. Keep moving west on
Corso Magenta to the
church of Santa
Maria delle Grazie
④ *(see p71)*,
where you will
find Leonardo's *Last
Supper (see pp72–3)*.
(Tickets to see this
fresco should be
booked at least two
weeks in advance.)

**Leonardo-designed
wooden model**

Roman and medieval Milan

Trace your steps back along
Corso Magenta and turn right
at Via Carducci. At the bottom
of this street is the Pusterla di
Sant'Ambrogio ⑤ *(see p86)*, a
remnant of the medieval city
gates. Turn right into Via San
Vittore for the Museo della
Scienza e della Tecnica ⑥ *(see
p88)*, which contains models
of Leonardo's inventions built
to the master's sketches.

Double back along Via San
Vittore to visit Sant'Ambrogio
⑦ *(see pp84–7)*, a 4th-century
basilica with Palaeochristian
mosaics, medieval
carvings, and
Renaissance
frescoes. Head
down Via de'
Amicis, angling
left at Piazza
Resistenza
Partigiana to
continue along Via GG
Mora ⑧. This street curves
slightly since it follows the
track of the interred Olona
River. In ancient times this
stream joined with the

Nirone, Seveso and Vetra
rivers at Corso di Porta
Ticinese. The Vetra used to
run south through what is now
Piazza della Vetra and the
Parco delle Basiliche ⑨. Head
up Via Poi IV and turn left on
Corso di Porta Ticinese for
the church of San
Lorenzo alle
Colonne ⑩ *(see
pp80–1)*. This
magnificent 4th-
century church is
preceded by a set
of free-standing
Roman columns ⑪,
probably the portico
to a 2nd-century
pagan temple, dismantled
and moved here when the
church was built.

Continue south along Corso
di Porta Ticinese and go
through the medieval Porta
Ticinese ⑫ *(see p82)*, built as
part of the city's 12th-century
walls and modified in the
1860s. Keep
following the
road until you

reach Sant'Eustorgio ⑬ *(see p90)*, a 4th-century church hiding behind an insipid 19th-century façade. Beyond the main church and behind the altar lies the Cappella Portinari, a masterpiece of early Renaissance architecture gorgeously frescoed with the story of St Peter Martyr by Vincenzo Foppa. The church houses a vast marble arch carved in the 1330s.

Along the Navigli

One more road south, past the confusingly named Porta Ticinese ⑭ *(see p82)* (unlike its medieval

The façade of Sant'Eustorgio hides a 4th-century church ⑬

namesake up the street, this Neo-Classical pile dates from 1801–14), and you are in the Piazza XXIV Maggio. This marks the intersection of the last

1603 Darsena ⑮, an artificial basin at the confluence of the underground Olona River and two canals.

The canal closest to the square is the Naviglio Pavese ⑯, running 33 km (20.5 miles) south to the Ticino River, near Pavia. Once the busiest canal in the entire system, since 1978 it has served as a very long irrigation ditch.

To the southwest of the Darsena is the Naviglio Grande ⑰ *(see p89)*, a 50-km (31-mile) waterway connecting Milan to the Ticino since 1177. Like the Naviglio Pavese, this also

KEY

• • • Walk route

▢ Pedestrian streets

Ⓜ Metro station

significant remnant of Milan's once-vast system of *navigli* (canals). The system was begun in the 12th century and expanded under Lodovico il Moro, who turned to Leonardo for help with the plans. At its late 19th-century peak, the system included 150 km (93 miles) of canals along which 8,300 boats hauled 350,000 tons of merchandise a year, making Milan the 13th-busiest port in Italy – impressive for a land-locked city. The canals' importance faded with the rise of the railways, and from the 1930s they were slowly filled in. West of Piazza XXIV Marzo stretches the main "port", the

The pretty Vicolo dei Lavandai ⑱

now serves merely to irrigate fields south of the city. Walk along its far embankment (Alzaia Naviglio Grande) to the blind alley of Vicolo dei Lavandai ⑱, down which is a pretty miniature canal of stone washbasins covered by a tiled roof.

The Navigli has blossomed into Milan's trendiest bar and restaurant zone, packed with wine bars, trattorias, pizzerias and jazz clubs and is the pefect place for a post-walk drink or lunch. Porta Genova metro station is a short stroll from here.

0 metres   200

0 yards   200

THE LAKES OF NORTHERN ITALY

INTRODUCING THE LAKES 130–131

EXPLORING THE LAKES 132–133

LAKE MAGGIORE 134–139

LAKE COMO 140–145

LAKE GARDA 146–153

THE SMALLER LAKES 154–155

THE LAKES OF NORTHERN ITALY

*A*ppreciated by the ancient romans for their beautiful location and mild climate, the lakes of Northern Italy – most of which are in Lombardy – are deservedly renowned for the fascinating and unique combination of magnificent scenery and historic and artistic heritage that characterizes the lakeside towns.

Besides Lake Maggiore, Lake Como and Lake Garda, there are smaller and less well-known bodies of water such as the lakes of Orta, Varese, Iseo and Idro. All these lovely lakes are the result of glaciation in the Pleistocene era, which enlarged clefts already in the terrain. The lake shores were inhabited during the prehistoric period – traces of ancient civilizations have been found almost everywhere – and for the most part were colonized by the Romans, as can be seen in the grid street plans of many towns and in the villas at Lake Garda. Churches, sanctuaries and castles were built here in the Middle Ages. In the winter the shores of the lakes can be battered by winds from Central Europe, but the climate remains quite mild thanks to the water. Typical Mediterranean vegetation can be seen everywhere: vineyards, olive trees, oleanders and palm trees. The many splendid villa gardens along the lakes' shores enhance the environment, and nature reserves have been established to protect some stretches.

In the 18th century a visit to the lake region was one of the accepted stages on the Grand Tour, the trip to Europe considered essential for the education of young people of good birth. These shores were also favourites with writers, musicians and artists such as Goethe, Hesse, Klee, Toscanini, Hemingway, Stendhal, Byron and Nietzsche. The numerous vantage points, connected to the shore by funiculars, narrow-gauge trains and cable cars, offer truly spectacular views over the landscape.

The peaceful shores of Lake Como, southwest of Bellagio

Torre di San Marco at Gardone Riviera, on the western shore of Lake Garda

Exploring the Lakes

The larger lakes offer the best facilities for visitors, with hotels, restaurants and cafés lining the lake front. The lake shores are dotted with pretty villages, castles (Sirmione sul Garda), villas and gardens such as Villa Taranto or the Vittoriale, the residence of the poet D'Annunzio at Lake Garda, as well as a number of small local museums. In summer, you may be able to participate in cultural events such as the famous Settimane Musicali di Stresa music festival at Lake Maggiore. Although the smaller lakes offer fewer facilities, they are very peaceful, unspoilt places.

Cannobio, Lake Maggiore

0 kilometres   10

0 miles   10

GETTING THERE

The lakes of Northern Italy can be reached via Malpensa and Linate airports in Milan and Catullo airport in Verona. There are also good connections by motorway from Milan: the A8 autostrada goes to lakes Maggiore and Varese, the A9 to Lake Como, and the A4 to Iseo and Garda. Traffic on the major and minor roads is often heavy, so make allowances when planning. Boat services on the three major lakes are quite efficient; they go to the islands and are an enjoyable way of getting about.

KEY

═══	Motorway	────	Minor railway
═══	Major road	▬▬▬	International border
───	Secondary road	─ ─ ─	Regional border
───	Minor road	△	Summit
───	Main railway		

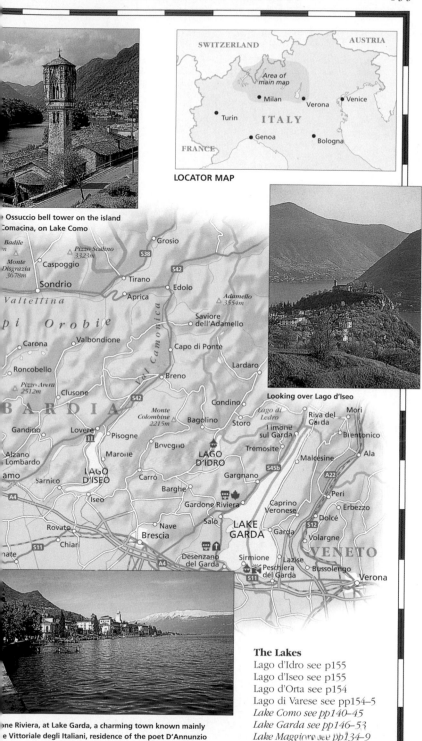

LOCATOR MAP

Ossuccio bell tower on the island Comacina, on Lake Como

Looking over Lago d'Iseo

...one Riviera, at Lake Garda, a charming town known mainly ...e Vittoriale degli Italiani, residence of the poet D'Annunzio

The Lakes

Lago d'Idro see p155
Lago d'Iseo see p155
Lago d'Orta see p154
Lago di Varese see pp154–5
Lake Como see pp140–45
Lake Garda see pp146–53
Lake Maggiore see pp134–9

Lake Maggiore

With borders in Piedmont, Lombardy and the Ticino canton in Switzerland, Lake Maggiore, or Verbano, is the second largest lake in Italy (212 sq km, 82 sq miles) and has a maximum depth of 372 m (1,220 ft). For the most part it is fed and drained by the Ticino river, and is also fed by the Toce. The towns were embellished with churches and paintings from 1449 on, thanks to the wealthy Borromeo family, and with villas and gardens in the 18th–19th centuries. The opening of the Simplon pass and the introduction of ferry services (1826) helped trade to develop in the area.

Villa statue, Isola Madre

★ Isole Borromee
Of the three islands, the best known is Isola Bella, named after Isabella d'Adda, wife of Charles III Borromeo ❺

The two castles of Malpaga, built in the 13th–14th century on two islets at the foot of Mount Carza, belonged to the Mazzardites, the pirates who raided the lake.

Stresa
This old fishermen's village began to become a tourist attraction thanks to the descriptions of famous writers such as Stendhal, Byron and Dickens ❹

Magaduno

Vira

Locarno

San Nazzaro

Gerra-Gambarogno

Ascona

Sant' Abbondio

Porto Ronco

Isola di Brissago

Brissago

Maccagno

Luin

Cannobio ❽

Gannero Riviera

Veltra

Pieggio

Ghiffa

Intra

Verbania

Isola Madre

★ Villa Taranto
One of Italy's best-known botanic gardens was founded here in 1931 by an Englishman called McEacharn in an area of about 16 ha (40 acres). Many examples of species of plants from all over the world, including Victoria amazonica, *are grown here (see p138).*

★ Santa Caterina del Sasso Ballaro

Perched on a rocky spur near Laveno, this monastery is one of the most enchanting sights on Lake Maggiore. It was built by a local merchant in the 12th century to fulfil a vow made when he was saved from a storm ⑪

VISITORS' CHECKLIST

🛈 *Local tourist bureau.* 🚆 *FS Milan–Domodossola or Milan–Bellinzona line (89 20 21); Ferrovie Nord Milano, to Laveno (02-202 22).* 🚌 *to Sesto Calende and Angera, Autolinea Zani (02-86 46 48 54) or Autolinee Varesine (0332-73 11 10); to Luino (0332 53 02 71).* ⛴ *Navigazione Lago Maggiore (800-55 18 01).* **www**.navigazionelaghi.it

SIGHTS AT A GLANCE

Arona ②
Baveno ⑥
Cannobio ⑧
Isole Borromee ⑤
Laveno ⑩
Lesa and Belgirate ③
Luino ⑨
Rocca di Angera ⑫
Santa Caterina
    del Sasso Ballaro ⑪
Sesto Calende ①
Stresa ④
Verbania ⑦

★ Rocca di Angera

The imposing medieval fortress of the Borromeo family has 14th- and 15th-century frescoes. It now houses the Doll Museum ⑫

Arona

The huge 17th-century statue of San Carlo Borromeo was placed in Arona in honour of its illustrious citizen. A 35-m (115-ft) stairway leads to the top, from where there is a fine panoramic view ②

Sesto Calende
The town museum in Piazza Mazzini contains objects found in nearby Bronze Age sites.

Laveno

⑪ Santa Caterina del Sasso Ballaro

la Bella

④ Stresa

omee

Belgirate ③

Lesa

Mèina

Angera ⑫

② Arona ①

KEY

-- Ferry routes

⛴ Ferry service

🔆 Viewpoint

0 kilometres   2

0 miles   2

STAR SIGHTS

★ Santa Caterina
   del Sasso Ballaro

★ Rocca di Angera

★ Villa Taranto

★ Isole Borromee

Sesto Calende ①

Varese. 🏠 9,500. 🚇 IAT, Viale Italia 3 (0331-92 33 29). 🏺 antiques, 3rd Sat of month. **www**.prolocosesto calende.it

The town at the southern tip of Lake Maggiore marks the end of two motorways leading to the Verbano region. The road to Arona goes to **San Donato**, known as "La Badia" or abbey, a 9th-century basilica rebuilt in the 11th–12th century. The capitals have sculpted figures of animals and humans. There are frescoes from the 15th and 16th centuries in the nave and from the 18th century in the crypt. South of Sesto, near Golasecca, are Iron Age tombs (9th–5th century BC), part of the civilization named after the place. State road 33 to Arona will take you to the **Lagoni di Mercurago Regional Park**, with varied bird species and the remains of ancient villages.

🏛 **Abbazia San Donato**
Via Sandonato 6. **Tel** 0331-92 46 92. ◷ noon–noon, 4–7pm daily.

🏕 **Lagoni di Mercurago Regional Park**
Via Gattico 6, Mercurago.
Tel 0322-24 02 39.
www.parchilagomaggiore.it

Arona ②

Novara. 🏠 16,000. 🚇 Piazzale Duca d'Aosta (0322-24 36 01). 🏺 antiques, 3rd Sun of month.

Arona once occupied an important trading position between Milan and the lake and mountain regions of Northern Italy. Because of its strategic location, a Rocca or fortress (the twin of the one at Angera; see p139), was built here; it was enlarged by the Borromeo and dismantled by Napoleon. Corso Marconi has a view of the Rocca at Angera, and leads to Piazza del Popolo. Here are the 15th-century Casa del Podestà, with an arched portico, and the 16th-century Madonna di Piazza church. Santi Martiri has 15th-century paintings by Bergognone, and Santa Maria Nascente has an altarpiece by Gaudenzio Ferrari (1511).

Just north of the centre is a massive **statue of San Carlo**. It was designed by Cerano in 1614 and finished in 1697. In the church of San Carlo there is a reconstruction of the room where San Carlo was born.

Villa Ponti is a mid-17th-century villa with Baroque and Art Deco decoration. It stands in a garden with a nympheum and a fountain.

🏛 **Statue of San Carlo**
Piazza San Carlo. **Tel** 0322-24 96 69. ◷ mid-Mar–Oct: 9am–noon, 2–6:30pm daily; Jan, Feb, Nov, Dec: 9:15am–12:30pm, 2–4:45pm Sun; 1–14 Mar: 9:15am–12:30pm, 2–5pm Sat & Sun. Children under eight are not allowed inside the statue. 🖼
San Carlo and Birthplace of San Carlo. Collegio De Filippi: 🏛 Piazzale San Carlo (0322-24 24 88).

🏯 **Villa Ponti**
Via San Carlo 57. **Tel** 0322-444 22. ◉ to the public

The square in Arona with the huge statue of San Carlo Borromeo

Lesa and Belgirate ③

Lesa (Novara). 🏠 2,400. Belgirate (Verbania). 🏠 500. 🚇 IAT, Via Portici, Lesa (0322-77 20 78).

Lesa lies on a particularly charming stretch of the lake between Arona and Stresa, and has been a resort for noble Lombard families since the 18th century. The **Museo Manzoniano di Villa Stampa** has mementos of author Alessandro Manzoni, who was a guest here. The hamlet of Villa boasts the Romanesque church of San Sebastiano.

Once past Lesa, continue to Belgirate and its charming historic centre, whose houses have porticoes and porches. This village also commands a panoramic view of the lake. It was a haunt of philosopher Antonio Rosmini and poet Guido Gozzano.

On the hills 4 km (2 miles) from Belgirate is the 13th-century **Castello Visconti di San Vito**, decorated with frescoes of the period. Nearby is the Romanesque church of San Michele, with a leaning bell tower.

🏛 **Museo Manzoniano di Villa Stampa**
Via alla Fontana, Lesa.
Tel 0322-764 21. ◷ on request.

🏯 **Castello Visconti di San Vito**
Via Visconti 1, Massino Visconti.
Tel 0322-21 97 13. ◉ to the public.

Looking over the lakeside town of Arona

For hotels and restaurants in this region see pp164–5 and pp178–80

Stresa ④

Verbania. 🏠 *4,800.*
🛈 *IAT, Piazza Marconi 16*
(0323-301 50 or 0323-31 300).

The origins of medieval Strixia, dating from before 1000, are partially hidden by the palazzi and villas built for the aristocracy in the late 19th–early 20th century, partly because of the opening of an electric rack-railway (the first in Italy), which goes to the top of Mount Mottarone. The town is now a centre for conferences and tour groups, attracted by the easy access to the Borromean islands. On the lakefront are 19th-century villas, Sant'Ambrogio (18th century) and the **Villa Ducale** (1770), with mementos of 19th-century philosopher Antonio Rosmini, who died here (the villa is now the Rosmini Study Centre). Mount Mottarone (1,491 m, 4,890 ft), a ski resort, has a view from the Alps to the plain.

🏛 Villa Ducale
Centro di Studi Rosminiani
Corso Umberto I 15.
Tel 0323-300 91.
🕒 *10am–noon, 3–6pm Mon–Fri.*

ENVIRONS
🌳 Parco di Villa Pallavicino
State road 33.
Tel 0323-324 07. 🕒 *Mar–Oct: 9am–6pm daily.* ♿ 🅿
🖼 🍴 www.parcopallavicino.it

This villa near Stresa is famous for its gardens. The luxuriant English garden has centuries-old plants as well as exotic creatures such as llamas and pelicans.

The garden of the 18th-century palazzo on Isola Madre

Isole Borromee ⑤

Verbania. 🚢 *from Arona, Laveno, Stresa, Baveno, Pallanza. To Isola Madre: tel. 0323-312 61; to Isola Bella: tel. 0323-305 56 Apr–Oct.*
🕒 *27 Mar–31 Oct: 9am–5pm daily.*
⚫ *Nov–Mar.* 🖼 🎫 *by appt.* 🍴
www.borromeoturismo.it

These three islands, which can be reached easily from Stresa, became famous thanks to the Borromeo family, who built elegant palazzi and magnificent gardens there. The loveliest is **Isola Bella**, an old fishing village transformed from 1632 to 1671 by the Borromeo family into a lovely complex consisting of a Baroque palazzo and a terraced Italian-style garden with rare plants. Inside are a music room (where Mussolini met British and French officials in 1935),

A fountain at Villa Pallavicino

the Sala di Napoleone (where Napoleon stayed in 1797), a ballroom, throne room and bedroom with 17th-century decoration and furnishings and paintings by Carracci, Cerano and Tiepolo. The six grottoes are decorated with shells and pebbles.

Isola Madre, the largest island, boasts an 18th-century villa with a garden where white peacocks roam freely; it has rare plants as well as azaleas, rhododendrons and camellias. The villa has period furnishings and a collection of 18th- and 19th-century puppet theatres.

Tiny **Isola dei Pescatori**, once the leading fishing village, has retained its quaint atmosphere and architecture.

Baveno ⑥

Verbania. 🏠 *4,500.* 🛈 *IAT, Piazza Dante Alighieri 14 (0323-92 46 32).*

Made famous by its pink granite quarries, which among other things supplied the stone for the Galleria in Milan *(see p50)*, Baveno became a fashionable resort in the mid-19th century, entertaining guests such as Queen Victoria, who stayed in the Villa Clara (now Villa Branca) in 1879. A major attraction is Santi Gervasio e Protasio, with its 12th-century facade and 15th-century octagonal baptistery with Renaissance frescoes. Going towards Verbania, take the turn-off for San Giovanni at Montorfano, one of the loveliest churches in the area.

The garden at Villa Pallavicino, the home of many species of animals

Verbania ❼

🏛 *31,000.* ▮ IAT, Corso Zanitello 6-8 *(0323-50 32 49)*; Pro Loco, Viale delle Magnolie 1 *(0323-55 76 76)*. 🔲 *antiques, summer: from 7pm Fri.*

Pallanza and Intra were merged in 1939 to create the town of Verbania (capital of the Verbano-Cusio-Ossola province established in 1992). The former, facing the Borromeo gulf, is the seat of the municipal government and has retained its medieval aspect and atmosphere. The latter dominates the promontory of Castagnola and has a decidedly Baroque and Neo-Classical flavour. Intra, the main port of call on the lake and one of its major industrial centres, was the regional leader in textile manufacturing in the 18th century. Pallanza was the only town in Lake Maggiore not under Borromeo dominion, and it has some of the most important monuments. These include Romanesque Santo Stefano, the parish church of San Leonardo and 18th-century Palazzo Dugnani, home to the **Museo del Paesaggio**, which has on exhibit 16th–20th-century landscape paintings, sculpture by Arturo Martini and Giulio Branca and a plaster cast gallery. Isolino di San Giovanni was a favourite refuge of Arturo Toscanini. In the environs is 16th-century Madonna di Campagna,

with a small Romanesque campanile and frescoes by Gerolamo Lanino and Camillo Procaccini (16th–17th centuries).

🏛 **Museo del Paesaggio**
Via Ruga 44. *Tel 0323-50 24 18.* 🔲 *Apr–Oct: 10am–noon, 3:30–6:30pm Tue–Sun.*

ENVIRONS
🌿 **Giardini di Villa Taranto**
Via Rossano 22, Pallanza. *Tel 0323-55 66 67.* 🔲 *Apr–Oct: 8:30am–7:30pm daily (last adm 6:30pm).*
🅿 🖼 ♿ 🚻

In 1931 a British captain named McEacharn created one of the outstanding botanic gardens in Europe on the Castagnola promontory, using the lake water for irrigation. He is buried in the small park church. McEacharn exploited the valley terrain, creating terraced gardens, a winter garden and a marsh garden among small falls and water lily ponds. He donated the Villa Taranto garden to the Italian state and it was opened to the public in 1952. It has a range of exotic plants, including *Victoria amazonica* in the glasshouses. Azaleas, dahlias and rhododendrons (over 300 varieties) look wonderful in full flower.

Effigy of McEacharn, who created the Villa Taranto gardens

The Orrido di Sant'Anna, in Val Cannobina

In nearby Val Cannobina, the Orrido di Sant'Anna is worth a visit. This deep gorge was carved out of the rock by the Cannobino river.

Cannobio ❽

Verbania. 🏛 *5,300.* ▮ IAT, Viale Vittorio Veneto 4 *(0323-712 12).* **www**.cannobio.net

This pleasant tourist resort is the last Italian town on the Piedmontese side of the lake. It still retains its old medieval character, exemplified in the Palazzo della Ragione or Palazzo Parrasio, the town hall with a 12th-century Commune Tower. The Santuario della Pietà, which was rebuilt by San Carlo Borromeo in 1583, contains a fine altarpiece by Gaudenzio Ferrari.

Luino ❾

Varese. 🏛 *15,300.* ▮ APT, Via Chiara 1 *(0332-53 00 19).*

Luino, which occupies a cove on the eastern side of the lake, is a town dating from ancient Roman times. Its name may have derived from the Luina torrent or perhaps from the local term *luina* (landslide). In the Middle Ages it was contested by the leading Como and Milanese families and became famous when Garibaldi landed here in 1848 with a group of volunteers and routed an entire Austrian detachment.

The large railway station (1882) shows how important the town was when it linked Italy with Central Europe, a position that declined when railway traffic shifted to Chiasso. Luino's market was founded by an edict of Charles V in 1541 and is still a tourist attraction. San Pietro in Campagna has frescoes by Bernardino Luini and a lovely Romanesque bell tower; the oratory of the Chiesa del Carmine dates back to 1477. A must is a visit to the town's symbol, the 17th-century oratory of San Giuseppe.

Laveno ❿

Varese. 🏠 8,800.
ℹ️ IAT, Piazza Italia 2
(0332-66 66 66).

The natural harbour of Laveno, once an Austrian naval base

The name of this town goes back to Titus Labienus, the Roman general who was Caesar's legate in Cisalpine Gaul. Laveno was important strategically because of its port, the only natural harbour on Lake Maggiore. During their period of rule, the Austrians moored the gunboats controlling the lake here. Today the town is the main ferry point to the Piedmontese shores. The Ferrovie Nord railway linked Laveno to Varese and Milan, fostering commercial development, especially in the field of ceramics with the founding of well-known Società Ceramica Italiana Richard-Ginori, in 1856. In the town centre, the garden in the Villa Frua (18th century) is worth visiting.

A cable car goes up to Sasso del Ferro, at 1,062 m (3,483 ft), behind Laveno with fine views of the lake, Monte Mottarone and Monte Rosa.

Santa Caterina del Sasso Ballaro ⓫

Via Santa Caterina 5, Leggiuno.
Tel 0332-64 71 72. ⏰ Apr–Oct: 8:30am–noon, 2:30–6pm daily; Nov–Mar: 9am–noon, 2–5pm Sat & Sun (except Mar & 23 Dec–6 Jan: daily). 🕓 4:30pm hols. 📷

To get to this small monastery perched on a steep rock 18 m (59 ft) above the lake, you can either climb the steps near Leggiuno or take the boat and enjoy the lovely views. The place was founded in the mid-12th century by a local merchant. The Dominicans arrived in 1230 and after numerous changes in fortune have since returned. Over the centuries the original building was enlarged and rebuilt, as can be seen by the different architectural styles. The chapter at the entrance has important 14th–15th-century frescoes, including a *Crucifixion with Armigers*. In the second portico the 17th-century fresco, only partly preserved, represents a *Dance of Death*. The frescoes inside the church were executed in the 16th century, and the *Madonna and Child with Saints* on the high altar dates from 1612. By the entrance porticoes there is a large wine press made in 1759.

14th–15th-century frescoes, Rocca di Angera

Rocca di Angera ⓬

Fortress and museum Via Rocca, Angera. **Tel** 0331-93 13 00.
⏰ Apr–Oct: 9am–5pm daily.
🎫 ♿ 📷 📚

A majestic fortress, probably built over the ruins of an ancient Roman fortification, the Rocca once belonged to the archbishops of Milan. In the 13th century it was taken over by the Visconti family and in 1449 was granted as a fief to the Borromeo family, who still own it. The Visconti building has single and double lancet windows and partly lies against the earlier castle tower. The frescoes in the halls are well worth a look, especially those in the Salone Gotico, with a cycle of the *Battles of Ottone Visconti against the Torriani* (14th century). The vaults in this hall are decorated with the Visconti coat of arms, while those in the other rooms have geometric patterns and signs of the Zodiac. The Borromeo wing has frescoes removed from Palazzo Borromeo in Milan in 1946, with *Aesop's Fables* by the school of Michelino da Besozzo (15th century). The Rocca is used for art shows and is also home to the **Museo della Bambola** (Doll Museum) in the Visconti wing, one of the best of its kind in Europe, created with the collection of Princess Bona Borromeo. Besides dolls and doll's houses, it contains books, games and children's clothing.

Santa Caterina del Sasso Ballaro, built on a cliff overlooking the lake

ↄ

...his lake, which is also known as Lario, is the third largest in Italy and the deepest (410 m, 1,345 ft). It is shaped like a sprawling upside-down Y, with the arms of Como, Lecco and Colico. The Como shore is the most developed, with numerous restaurants and hotels, as well as a scenic road that follows the ancient Strada Regina, lined with elegant villas and aristocratic gardens. The Lecco area has more stark scenery and small coves. You may spot the typical "Lucia" boats, named after the heroine in Manzoni's *The Betrothed*, which was partly set here.

Decoration in Villa d'Este, at Cernobbio

★ Bellagio
Its position at the junction of the arms of the lake and the spectacular view from the Spartivento point make this one of the most popular spots on Lake Como ⑫

The bell tower on Santa Maria Maddalena at Ossuccio is one of the symbols of the lake.

★ Como
Construction of Como's Duomo began in 1396 and ended in 1740 with the huge dome. Next to it is the elegant 13th-century Broletto, the old town hall ①

Menaggio
Sala Comacina
Lenno Tremezzo Cader
Isola Comacina ③
④   ⑤
Argegno
Lake Como
Lezzeno

STAR SIGHTS

★ Bellagio

★ Como

★ Tremezzo

Nesso
Careno
Torriggia
Urio
Pognana Lario
Moltrasio
②
⑬ Torno
Belvio
Travernola
Como ① Brunate

KEY

− − − Ferry routes

🚢 Ferry service

🔆 Viewpoint

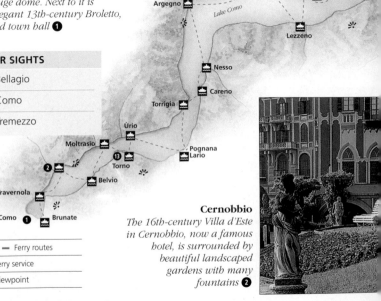

Cernobbio
The 16th-century Villa d'Este in Cernobbio, now a famous hotel, is surrounded by beautiful landscaped gardens with many fountains ②

Gravedona
Santa Maria del Tiglio in Gravedona is the most famous Lombard Romanesque construction in the Alto Lario region. Its main features are the layers of black and white stone and the unusual octagonal bell tower set into the façade **7**

VISITORS' C

ℹ️ Local informatie
🚉 FS: Milan–Chiasse
20 21); Ferrovie Nord f
(031-30 48 00 or 02-202
🚌 SPT: Como-Colico line
(031-24 72 47). ⛴ Navigazi
Lago di Como (800-55 18 01
(freefone) or 031-57 92 11).
www.navigazionelaghi.it

Stazzona •
Gravedona **7** 🚉⛴
Domase ⛴
Dongo 🚉⛴
Musso 🚉⛴
Abbazia di Piona 🚉⛴ **8**
Colico ⛴
Pianello del Lario 🚉⛴
Lake Como
Siro
Dervio ⛴

Lake Mezzola, separated from the Lario region by silt from the Adda river, is a natural reserve inhabited by grey herons.

The "crotti" are typical mountain caves in the upper Lario region, used as wine cellars since the 19th century.

🚉 **9** Bellano

The medieval Vezio castle, built on the site of a Roman tower, is a 20-minute walk from Varenna and offers a stunning panoramic view.

🚉 **10** Varenna
io

Varenna
Some of the paths in this village, one of the best preserved on the lake, consist of steps and raised boardwalks perched over the water **10**

🚉 Lierna
onta
Lake Lecco
ala ena 🚉
Onno 🚉
Mandello del Lario 🚉
Abbadia Lariana 🚉

🚉 **11** Lecco

★ Tremezzo
The Villa Carlotta in Tremezzo was a wedding gift for Carlotta of Prussia (1843). Inside there is a copy of Canova's Cupid and Psyche **5**

SIGHTS AT A GLANCE

Abbazia di Piona **8**
Bellagio **12**
Bellano **9**
Cernobbio **2**
Como **1**
Gravedona **7**
Isola Comacina **3**
Lecco **11**
Lenno **4**
Menaggio **6**
Torno **13**
Tremezzo **5**
Varenna **10**

was founded by
nans in 196 BC and
12th century fought
nst Milan as an ally of
rbarossa, who built the
nedieval walls. In 1335 Como
came under Visconti rule and
in 1451 under Sforza rule.
The town shared Milan's fate
under Spanish and Austrian
domination, becoming part of
the Kingdom of Italy in 1859.

Como's many Romanesque
churches include the 12th-
century San Fedele and the
jewel of the Comacine masters, 11th-century Lombard–
Romanesque Sant' Abbondio.

The **Duomo**, begun in
1396, is dominated by Filippo
Juvarra's Baroque dome. The
sculpture on the Gothic façade
and the Porta della Rana door
were executed by Tommaso
and Jacopo Rodari (c.1500).
The nave and side altars are
decorated with 16th-century
tapestries and canvases by
Ferrari and Luini. Next to the
Duomo is the Romanesque-
Gothic Broletto (1215).

The **Tempio Voltiano**
(1927) contains relics of
Alessandro Volta, the great
physicist from Como, who
gave his name to "voltage".
The Casa del Fascio (1936)
exemplifies Italian Rationalist
architecture. **Villa Olmo**,

Piazza del Duomo in Como, the birthplace of Pliny the Elder

designed by Simone Cantoni in
1797, has frescoed rooms and
a park, open to the public. A
funicular goes up to Brunate.

🏛 **Duomo**
Piazza Duomo. **Tel** 031-26 52 44.
🕐 7am–noon, 3–7pm daily.

🏛 **Tempio Voltiano**
Viale Marconi. **Tel** 031-57 47 05.
🕐 Apr–Oct: 10am–noon, 3–6pm
Tue–Sun; Nov–Mar: 10am–noon,
2–4pm Tue–Sun. 🎫

🏛 **Villa Olmo**
Via Cantoni 1. **Tel** 031-25 24 43.
🕐 9am–noon, 3–6pm Mon–Sat.
● hols. 🎫 🎫

Cernobbio ❷

Como. 🚶 7,200. 🛈 Via Regina
33b (031-51 01 98) (open Apr–Sep);
Piazza Cavour 17, Como (031-330
01 11).

Cernobbio marks
the beginning of a
series of splendid
villas that have
made the western
side of the lake
famous. **Villa d'Este**,
built by Pellegrino
Tibaldi in 1570 for
the Gallio family,
became a luxury
hotel in 1873, fre-
quented by princes
and actors. The
rooms have period
furnishings and are
used for conferen-
ces. The villa stands
in an Italianate
garden with a
nympheum. 18th-
century **Villa Erba**
(now a conference

centre) is known for its interior (visits by request): the
Salone da Ballo, chapel and
Sala delle Nozze, decorated by
architect and designer Giocondo Albertolli, are lovely.

🏨 **Hotel Villa d'Este**
Via Regina 40. **Tel** 031-34 81.
● Nov–Mar.

🏨 **Villa Erba**
Largo Visconti 4. **Tel** 031-34 91. ●
to the public. The Luchino Visconti
rooms can be booked for group visits.

Lenno ❸

Como. 🚶 1,600. 🛈 IAT, Piazza
Cavour 17, Como (031-330 01 11).

This town is famous for the
Villa del Balbianello, built by
Cardinal Durini in the 17th
century onto a 16th-century

FROM MULBERRY TO SILK

Como produces
about 80 per cent
of Europe's silk.
Silk worms were
imported in the
14th century and
production thrived
in the 17th century   Cocoons
with the large-scale
cultivation of mulberries,
the worms' food. Silk
thread was woven and
sent on the "silk route"
in Austria and Bavaria.
Competition from Chinese
silk now forces Como to
concentrate on quality
silk, as shown in the
Museo della Seta (Silk
Museum) in Como.

The Villa d'Este in Cernobbio, once host to the
Duke of Windsor and Mrs Simpson

building attributed to Pellegrini. The magnificent garden has a loggia with a view of Isola Comacina on one side and the Tremezzina bay on the other. Access to the villa is by boat from Sala Comacina.

Also worth a visit are the octagonal baptistery and church of Santo Stefano, built in the 11th century over a Roman building and decorated with frescoes by Luini. Above the town is the Cistercian abbey of Acquafredda, rebuilt in the 17th century, with frescoes by Fiammenghino. At nearby Giulino di Mezzegra, the Fascist dictator Benito Mussolini and his mistress Claretta Petacci were executed on 28 April 1945, after their capture on the previous day.

🏛 **Villa del Balbianello**
Balbianello. **Tel** 0344-561 10 (FAI).
Garden ☐ Apr–Oct: 10am–1pm,
2–6pm Tue, Thu, Fri; 10am–6pm Sat,
Sun & hols. **Villa** ☐ by appt only.

Isola Comacina ❹

Como. 🛈 IAT, Piazza Cavour 17,
Como (031-330 01 11). 🚢 (as far
as Sala Comacina, then by boat).

The only island on Lake Como has been inhabited since Roman times. It was fortified by the Byzantines and enjoyed a period of splendour in the Middle Ages. The people of Como conquered the fortress in 1169 and destroyed the seven churches on the island. The ruins, along with those of a mosaic-decorated baptistery, were found after World War

Villa Carlotta, built in the 18th century by Marchese Giorgio Clerici

II and are now being studied. Sala Comacina, where boats depart for the island, has an 18th-century church with a fresco by Carlo Carloni, and the villa of Cesare Beccaria, where Manzoni was a guest.

Tremezzo ❺

Como. 🏘 1,300. 🛈 IAT, Via Regina 3
(0344-404 93) (open Apr–Sep); Piazza
Cavour 17, Como (031-330 01 11).

This lakeside town is a major tourist resort and its main claim to fame is the 18th-century **Villa Carlotta**. The residence, surrounded by a terraced garden with landscaped staircases, was converted in the 1800s into a Neo-Classical villa. It houses paintings by Hayez, furniture by Maggiolini and sculpture pieces by Canova, including a copy of *Cupid and Psyche* and *Terpsichore*. Among the

rooms decorated with stuccowork is one with Appiani's frescoes taken from the Palazzo Reale in Milan. The villa is famous for its garden.

🏛 **Villa Carlotta**
Via Regina 2b. **Tel** 0344 404 05.
☐ 15 Mar–31 Oct: 9–11:30am,
2–4:30pm daily; Apr–Sep: 9am–6pm
daily. **www.**villacarlotta.it

Menaggio ❻

Como. 🏘 3,200.
🛈 IAT, Piazza Garibaldi 3 (0344-
329 24) **www.**menaggio.com

The name Menaggio supposedly derives from two Indo-European words: *men* (mountain) and *uigg* (water), referring to the mouth of the Sanagra river on which the town lies. Menaggio is the leading commercial centre in the upper Lario region and a popular tourist resort. It is dominated by the ruins of a castle and has preserved some of its medieval layout. Sights worth visiting are the parish church of Santo Stefano–& whose Baroque architecture conceals its Romanesque origin–& and 17th-century San Carlo, with a good painting by Giuseppe Vermiglio (1625). The lakeside promenade, with arcaded houses and villas, is a must. Past Menaggio, at Loveno, is the Neo-Classical Milyus-Vigoni villa with family portraits by Francesco Hayez. Around it is a lovely park, designed by Balzaretto in 1840.

Menaggio, a lakeside town especially popular with British visitors

Gravedona ➐

Como. 🏛 *2,800.* ℹ️ *Pro Loco, Piazza Cavour 7 (0344-896 37); IAT, Piazza Cavour 17, Como (031-330 01 11).*

A fortified town of some importance in Roman times, Gravedona was destroyed by the people of Como in the 13th century because it was allied with Milan. It later became capital of the small Tre Pievi republic. The town then declined and was ceded to Cardinal Tolomeo Gallio, who in 1583 asked Tibaldi to build Palazzo Gallio. Gravedona is known for the church of **Santa Maria del Tiglio** (12th century). The aisled nave with tall galleries houses a 12th-century wooden Crucifix, a floor mosaic dating from the 6th century and various 12th–14th-century frescoes. Santi Gusmeo e Matteo was frescoed by Fiammenghino, while Santa Maria delle Grazie (1467) contains 16th-century frescoes. Nearby Dongo is an ancient village known for the Falck steelworks, which was responsible for building the metal parts of the *Italia* and *Norge* airships. Above Gravedona, at Peglio, is the Sant' Eusebio complex, with fine 17th-century frescoes in the church. The Spanish fort in the outskirts was built in 1604 to guard the Adda river plain.

🏠 **Santa Maria del Tiglio**
Piazza XI Febbraio. **Tel** *0344-852 61.* ⬜ *9am–6pm daily.*

Palazzo Gallio, designed by architect Pellegrino Tibaldi in 1583

The Cluniac Piona abbey, founded in the 11th century

Abbazia di Piona ➑

Via Santa Maria di Piona 1, Colico. **Tel** *0341-94 03 31.* ⬜ *summer: 8:30–11:45am, 2:30–5:30pm daily; winter: 9:30–noon, 2:30–5pm daily.* 🅿️

A promontory on the north–eastern shore of the lake conceals this extraordinary abbey built by Cluniac monks in the 11th century. The exterior of Romanesque San Nicolao is adorned with small arches and pilasters. The bell tower dates from 1700 and the cloister (1252–7) has sculpted capitals with fantastic figures. There are 13th-century frescoes here as well as in the apse.

Bellano ➒

Lecco 🏛 *3,400.* ℹ️ *IAT, Via Nazario Sauro 6, Lecco (0341-36 93 90).*

In the middle ages Bellano was the summer residence of Milanese bishops and it has preserved its medieval character. Among houses with wrought-iron coats of arms is the church of Santi Nazaro, Celso e Giorgio, the work of Campionese masters (14th century). Santa Marta houses a *Pietà* executed in 1518. However, the main appeal of Bellano is the Orrido, a deep gorge created by the Pioverna torrent.

🦌 **Orrido**
Tel *0341-82 11 24.* ⬜ *Apr–Sep: 10am–1pm, 2–10pm daily; Oct–Mar: 10am–noon, 2–7pm Sat & Sun.* 🖼

Varenna ➓

Lecco. 🏛 *800.* ℹ️ *Pro Loco, Via IV Novembre 3 (0341-83 03 67).*

This splendid village of ancient Roman origin, with a perfectly intact medieval layout, was a haven for the inhabitants of Isola Comacina when the citizens of Como burned the island (1169). In the town centre, 14th-century San Giorgio has an altarpiece by Pietro Brentani (1467), while Santa Marta houses the parish art gallery. Varenna is famous for **Villa Cipressi**, with its terraced garden, and **Villa Monastero**, built over a Cistercian monastery. Now a conference centre, the villa has preserved some of its original furnishings and has an elegant garden. All around the town were quarries for black Varenna marble – used for the flooring in the Milan Duomo. Since 1921 Mandello del Lario has been the home of the **Moto Guzzi factory**, with a Motorcycle Museum.

🏛 **Villa Cipressi**
Via IV Novembre 18. **Tel** *0341-83 01 13.* ⬜ *(garden) Mar–Oct: 9am–7pm (6pm Mar–Jun) daily.* ⚫ *Nov–Feb.* 🖼

🏛 **Villa Monastero**
Via Polvani 2. **Tel** *0341-83 01 29.* ⬜ *(garden) Mar–Oct: 9am–7pm (6pm Mar–Jun) daily.* ⚫ *Nov–Feb.* 🖼

ⓜ Museo Moto Guzzi della Motocicletta
Via Parodi 57, Mandello del Lario. *Tel 0341-70 91 11.* ◯ *3–4pm Mon–Fri.* ◉ *hols.*

Lecco ⑪

⚇ *46,000.* ▮ *IAT, Via Nazario Sauro 6 (0341-36 23 60).* **www**.aptlecco.com

Lecco lies on the southern tip of the arm of the lake of the same name. It was inhabited in prehistoric times and fortified in the 6th century AD. In the 1300s it was taken over by Azzone Visconti, who built the Ponte Vecchio.

Manzoni set his novel *I Promessi Sposi (The Betrothed)* here. Mementos of his life can be found in his childhood home, the **Casa Natale di Manzoni** at Caleotto, which also houses the Galleria Comunale d'Arte. In the centre are the Teatro della Società (1844) and San Nicolò, whose baptistery chapel has 14th–15th-century frescoes. The **Museo di Storia Naturale** in the 18th-century **Palazzo Belgioioso** is also of interest. Sites described by Manzoni in his novel have been identified, including the castle of the Unnamed at Vercurago, and Lucia's home at Olate. Near Civate is Romanesque **San Pietro al Monte** (12th century), with frescoes and reliefs with scenes from the Passion. A turn-off on the road to Bellagio leads to the Madonna del Ghisallo sanctuary.

The Italian writer Manzoni, author of *The Betrothed*

A drawing room in Villa Serbelloni overlooking the lake

⊞ Casa Natale di Manzoni
Via Guanella 1. *Tel 0341-48 12 47.* ◯ *9:30am–5:30pm Tue–Sun.* 📷 ♿

⊞ Palazzo Belgioioso and Museo di Storia Naturale
Corso Matteotti 32. *Tel 0341-48 12 48.* ◯ *9:30am–2pm Tue–Sun.* ◉ *1 Jan, Easter, 15 Aug, 1 May, 25 Dec.* 📷 ♿

⛪ San Pietro al Monte
Civate. *Tel 0341-31 91 501.* ◯ *summer: 9am–4pm daily; winter: 9am–noon, 2–3pm daily (booking necessary Mon–Fri).*

Bellagio ⑫

Como. ⚇ *3,050.* ▮ Piazza G Mazzini 12 *(031-95 02 04).* **www**.bellagiolakecomo.com

One of the statues at Villa Melzi d'Eril

Known since antiquity for its fine climate and scenery, Bellagio still has its medieval layout, with stepped alleyways. It became the site of splendid noble villas in the 1700s and then became a famous resort town in the 19th century. Among the attractive residences, the loveliest are **Villa Serbelloni** and **Villa Melzi d'Eril**. In 1870 the former, set in the middle of a park, became a hotel that numbered Winston Churchill and JF Kennedy among its guests. The Neo-Classical Villa Melzi was built in 1810 by Giocondo Albertolli. The interior is not open to the public, but the Museo Archeologico, the chapel and the gardens are.

Near the town are the 18th-century Trivulzio and Trotti villas. Do not miss the 12th-century San Giacomo, with its pulpit decorated with symbols of the Evangelists.

⊞ Villa Serbelloni
Piazza Garibaldi (book at IAT). *Tel 031-95 19 55.* ◯ *11am–4pm Tue–Sun Apr–Oct.* 📷 📷 *for groups of up to six people (book in advance).*

⊞ Villa Melzi d'Eril
Lungolario Marconi. *Tel 031-95 02 04.* ◯ *9am–6:30pm Apr–Oct.* 📷

Torno ⑬

Como. ⚇ *1,100.* ▮ *IAT, Piazza Cavour 17, Como (031-33 00 111).*

The village of Torno boasts the churches of Santa Tecla, which has a beautiful marble portal dating from 1480, and the 14th-century San Giovanni, with its remarkable Renaissance door. However, Torno is best known for the Villa Pliniana, built in 1573 (and attributed to Tibaldi) for Count Anguissola, the governor of Como. The villa is surrounded by a park and stands right by the lake. The writers Foscolo, Stendhal and Byron, and composer Rossini were all guests here.

Lake Garda

Remains of mosaics in the Roman villa at Desenzano del Garda

Italy's largest lake was created by glaciation. The scenery is varied, with steep, rugged cliffs at the northern end and softer hills southwards, where the basin widens and Mediterranean flora prevails. Over the centuries the praises of Lake Garda have been sung by such greats as Catullus, Dante and Goethe, and today it caters for luxury holidays and tour groups alike. Garda is an ideal spot for windsurfing and sailing, and it hosts famous regattas such as the Centomiglia.

★ **Desenzano del Garda**
This is one of the liveliest and most popular towns on Lake Garda. Above, one of the mosaics in the Roman villa, built in the 4th century and discovered in 1921 ❷

Villa Bettoni in Bogliaco (1756) has elegant frescoed rooms with masterpieces by Reni and Canaletto, as well as a garden with a nympheum.

★ **Gardone Riviera**
In this pleasant tourist resort is the Vittoriale degli Italiani, where the writer Gabriele D'Annunzio lived from 1921 to 1938. It embodies the decadence of which this poet and novelist was the last exponent ❺

Toscolano Maderno ❻

Gardone Riviera ❺   Fasano

Salò ❹

The Valténesi and San Felica del Benaco ❸   Isola di Garda

Manerba

Moniga del Garda

Sirmione ❶

San Peitro in Mavino

Desenzano ❷

★ **Sirmione**
This Roman villa, which extends over a large area and was once thought to be the residence of the Latin poet Catullus, is one of the most impressive examples of an ancient Roman dwelling in Northern Italy ❶

KEY

– – – Ferry routes

🛥 Ferry service

☼ Viewpoint

🚉 Railway station

0 kilometres   5

0 miles

VISITORS' CHECKLIST

ℹ️ Local information bureaus. 🚆
FS Milan–Venice line (89-2021).
🚌 Azienda Provinciale Trasporti
di Verona (045-805 78 11) or
Società Italiana Autoservizi (840-
62 00 01). 🚢 Navigazione Lago
di Garda (freefone 800-55 18
01). **www**.navigazionelaghi.it

Limone sul Garda

*The abundance of citrus trees grown
here is supposedly the reason why
the locals have the longest life
expectancy in Italy* ❼

❽ Riva del Garda

Torbole

Limone sul Garda ❼

Campione del Garda

❾ Malcésine

Isola di Trimelone

Porta di Brenzone

Castelletto de Brenzone

nano

Pai

At Torbole, now a surfers'
paradise, Venetian ships –
which defeated the Visconti
in 1440 – were reassembled
after being transported along
the Val d'Adige.

Punta San Vigilio was named after
the bishop from Trent who brought
Christianity to the area
in the 4th century.

❿ Torri del Benàco

The Camaldolite Hermitage
(16th century), which only recently
allowed women visitors, has a
splendid panoramic view.

⓫ Garda

Bardolino ⓬

Lazise

SIGHTS AT A GLANCE

Bardolino and Lazise ⓬
Desenzano del Garda ❷
Garda ⓫
Gardaland ⓮
Gardone Riviera ❺
Limone sul Garda ❼
Malcesine ❾
Peschiera del Garda ⓭
Riva del Garda ❽
Salò ❹
Sirmione ❶
Torri del Benaco ❿
Toscolano Maderno ❻
The Valtènesi and San Felice del Benaco ❸

STAR SIGHTS

★ Sirmione

★ Gardone Riviera

★ Desenzano del Garda

⓮ Gardaland

❸ Peschiera del Garda

Torri del Benaco
*The economy of this small town, which thanks
to its strategic position controls access to the
upper lake region, is based on tourism and
fishing. The townspeople have enjoyed special
fishing privileges since the 1400s* ❿

Sirmione ❶

Brescia. 🏛 5,100.
ℹ Viale Marconi 8 (030-91 61 14).
www.comune.sirmione.bs.it

Roman Sirmio lay in the hinterland and only the villa quarter faced the lake. In the 13th century the Scaligeri lords of Verona turned it into a fortress to defend Lake Garda. In 1405 Sirmione was taken over by Venice, which then ruled until the 18th century. The main focus of the town is the **Rocca Scaligera**, a castle built by Mastino I della Scala (13th century), the inner basin of which served as shelter for the Veronese boats. Roman and medieval plaques are in the entrance arcade.

Fifteenth-century Santa Maria Maggiore, built over a pagan temple, has a Roman column in its porch, while the campanile was a Scaligera tower. The interior has 15th- and 16th-century frescoes and a 15th-century Madonna.

The **spas** use the water from the Boiola spring, known since 1546. San Pietro in Mavino, re built in 1320, boasts fine 13th–16th-century frescoes. Sirmione is also famous for the so-called **Grotte di Catullo**, a huge Roman residence built in the 1st centuries BC–AD. The most evocative rooms are the Grotta del Cavallo, the Cryptoporticus and the pool. The Sala della Trifora del Paradiso and Sala dei Giganti overlook the lake. The Antiquarium has finds from the villa, including a mosaic of a seascape and a portrait of Catullus (1st century BC).

⚓ Rocca Scaligera
Piazza Castello
Tel 030-91 64 68. ⬤ 8:30am–7pm Tue–Sun. ⬤ hols. 🖼

Terme Catullo (Spa)
Piazza Castello 12.
Tel 030-990 49 33.

✣ Grotte di Catullo
Via Catullo **Tel** 030-91 61 57. ⬤ Mar–14 Oct: 8:30am–7pm Tue–Sun; 15 Oct–Feb: 8:30am–4:30pm Tue–Sun. ⬤ Mon (Tue if Mon is hol). 🖼

Christ Enthroned with Angels and Saints, San Pietro in Mavino

Desenzano del Garda ❷

Brescia 🏛 21,000. ℹ Via Porto Vecchio 34 (030-914 15 10). ⬤ (antiques, 1st Sun of month (except for Jan & Aug).

Probably founded by the Romans on a site inhabited since prehistoric times, Desenzano was taken over by Venice in the 15th century, when it became the leading lakeside town. Since the 19th century it has been a tourist resort. The heart of the town centre is Piazza Malvezzi, home to an antiques market known for its silverware and prints. The 16th-century town hall and Provveditore Veneto buildings are also here. In the **Duomo** (16th century) is a fine *Last Supper* by Tiepolo. The **Museo Civico Archeologico**, in the cloister of Santa Maria de Senioribus, contains displays of Bronze Age finds and the oldest known wooden plough (2000 BC).

The **Villa Romana** was built in the 4th century AD and rediscovered in 1921. It had been covered by a landslide, which preserved some lovely mosaics with geometric motifs such as the *Good Shepherd* and *Psyche and Cupids*. Finds from the villa are in the Antiquarium.

⛪ Duomo
Piazza Duomo. **Tel** 030-914 18 49. ⬤ 8–11:30am, 4–6:30pm daily.

🏛 Museo Civico Archeologico
Via Santa Maria. **Tel** 030-914 45 29 or 030-999 42 75. ⬤ 3–7pm Tue, Fri–Sun, hols. ⬤ Mon, Wed, Thu.

🏛 Villa Romana
Via Crocifisso 2. **Tel** 030-914 35 47. ⬤ Mar–14 Oct: 9am–7pm Tue–Sun; 15 Oct–Feb: 9am–5pm Tue–Sun. ⬤ Mon (Tue if Mon is hol). 🖼

The Valtènesi and San Felice del Benaco ❸

Brescia 🏛 2,500.
ℹ Via Portovecchio 34, Desenzano del Garda (030-914 15 10)

The area between Desenzano and Salò, called Valtènesi, is rich in medieval churches and castles. At Padenghe, the Rocca (9th–10th century) is reached by a drawbridge. Nearby is 12th-century Sant'Emiliano. The houses in Moniga del Garda are protected by a 10th-century wall with turrets. Here stands Santa Maria della Neve, built in the 14th century. The Rocca di Manerba del Garda (8th century) lies on a headland over the lake where a

The Rocca Scaligera at Sirmione, with its tower and battlements

Cappella del Santissimo Sacramento, Salò Duomo (18th century)

castle once stood. The ruins have become part of a regional park. At Solarolo, the 15th-century Santissima Trinità has a fresco cycle with the *Last Judgment*, while prehistoric finds from this area are in the **Museo Archeologico della Valtènesi** at Montinelle. The bay between the Punta Belvedere and Punta San Fermo headlands is dominated by San Felice del Benaco. To the south is the Madonna del Carmine sanctuary (1452). In the town centre the parish church has a *Madonna and Saints* by Romanino. Opposite Punta San Fermo is Isola di Garda. Tradition has it that the Franciscans in the 13th-century monastery introduced citrus fruit cultivation to Lake Garda.

🏛 **Museo Archeologico della Valtènesi**
Piazzale Simonati, Montinelle.
Tel 030-914 15 10. ◯ *summer: 7:30–9pm Tue–Sat, 10am–noon Sun; winter: 2–4pm Sat; 10am–noon Sun.* ◉ Mon.

Salò ❹

Brescia. 🏚 10,200 🛈 *Lungolago Zanardelli, Palazzo Municipale (0365-214 23).*

A former Roman town, in 1337 Salò became the seat of the Consiglio della Magnifica Patria, the governing body of 42 towns which met in the palazzo built by Sansovino in 1524 (now the Museo Archeologico). The late Gothic cathedral has a *Madonna and Saints* by Romanino (1529) and an altarpiece from 1476. Palazzo Fantoni is home to the Biblioteca dell'Ateneo di Salò and **Museo del Nastro Azzurro**, a military museum with items from 1796 to 1945. Palazzo Terzi-Martinengo at Barbarano was the seat of Mussolini's Salò puppet government.

🏛 **Museo del Nastro Azzurro**
Via Fantoni 49. **Tel** 0365-29 68 27.
◯ *2:30–5:30pm Thu–Fri; 10am–noon, 2:30–5:30pm Sat & Sun.*

Gardone Riviera ❺

Brescia. 🏚 2,500. 🛈 *Corso Repubblica 8 (0365-203 47).*

Boasting the highest winter temperatures in Northern Italy, Gardone Riviera became a fashionable tourist resort in the late 19th century because of its mild dry climate, which is beneficial for those suffering from lung ailments. Two celebrated villas are Villa Alba and Villa Fiordaliso.

Gardone is also famous for the **Vittoriale degli Italiani**, Gabriele D'Annunzio's residence, where the poet collected over 10,000 objects including works of art, books and mementos, which he later donated to the state. In the garden are the Prioria, his residence, the Schifamondo with mementos, the Auditorium and the Mausoleum. On display are objects related to his exploits during and after World War I, such as his motor boat and aeroplane.

Another attraction is the **Giardino Botanico Hruska**, a fine botanic garden with over 2,000 Alpine, Mediterranean and subtropical species of plants,

D'Annunzio, who lived out his days at the Vittoriale degli Italiani

🎪 **Vittoriale degli Italiani**
Gardone. **Tel** 0365-29 65 11.
◯ *Apr–Sep: 8:30am–8pm daily; Oct–Mar: 9am–5pm daily.* 📷
House ◯ *Apr–Sep: 8:30am–8pm Tue–Sun; Oct–Mar: 9am–5pm Tue–Sun.* ◉ *Mon.* 📷📷📷
www.vittoriale.it

🌿 **Giardino Botanico Hruska**
Via Motta 2 **Tel** 0365-203 47 (IAT Gardone). ◯*15 Mar–15 Oct: 9am–6pm daily.* 📷

The medieval church of San Pietro in Lucone

VINES, CHURCHES AND CASTLES

The Valtènesi area is known for its vineyards, where the rosé wine Chiaretto della Riviera del Garda is produced. A visit to the wineries here offers a chance to visit the inland region of this side of Lake Garda and also see the medieval fortresses of Soiano del Lago, Puegnago sul Garda and Polpenazze del Garda. In the cemetery of this last-mentioned village is the Romanesque church of San Pietro in Lucone, with its 15th-century frescoes depicting the lives of St Peter and the Apostles.

Canvas by Celesti in the Santi Pietro e Paolo parish church, Toscolano

Toscolano Maderno ⑥

Brescia. 🏠 6,700. 🅸 Piazza San Marco 1, Maderno (0365-641 330).

This town is made up of the two villages of Toscolano and Maderno. Sights of interest at Maderno are the Romanesque church of Sant'Andrea, with a panel by Paolo Veneziano, and the parish church of Sant'Ercolano, with paintings by Veronese and Andrea Celesti. Here the Gonzaga family built the Palazzina del Serraglio (17th century) for Vincenzo I's amorous assignations. Toscolano, ancient Benacum, was the largest town on Lake Garda in Roman times. At Santa Maria del Benaco, with 16th-century frescoes, archaeologists found Roman and Etruscan objects and the ruins of a mosaic-decorated villa (1st century AD). The parish church of Santi Pietro e Paolo has 22 canvases by Andrea Celesti. Gargnano boasts San Giacomo di Calino (11th–12th century) and San Francesco (1289), whose cloister has Venetian arches. Other sights are Villa Feltrinelli, Mussolini's residence during the Republic of Salò.

Limone sul Garda ⑦

Brescia. 🏠 990. 🅸 Lungolago Zanardelli 18, Maderno (0365-641 330).

Known for its mild climate, Limone may have been named after the lemon tree terraces (no longer used) typical of this area. Or the name may derive from *Limen* (border), since the Austrian frontier was here until 1918. In the town centre are the 15th-century church of San Rocco and a parish church (1685), with canvases by Celesti. Near Tignale is the **Montecastello Sanctuary** (13th–14th century) with a *Coronation of the Virgin* (14th century) and medallions by the school of Palma il Giovane. Towards Tremosine is the Brasa river gorge, in a panoramic setting.

🅰 **Montecastello Sanctuary**
Via Chiesa, Tignale. ⭘ 9am–6pm daily mid-Mar–Oct. **Tel** 0365-730 20.

Riva del Garda ⑧

Trento. 🏠 13,500. 🅸 Largo Medaglie d'Oro (0464-55 44 44). **www**.gardatrentino.it

Situated at a strategic point on the northern tip of the lake, in the Trentino region, Riva was under Austrian rule until 1918. The Rocca and Torre Apponale (13th century) were built to defend the town; an angel, the town symbol, stands on top of the tower. In the square opposite are Palazzo Pretorio (1370) and Palazzo del Provveditore (1482). The 12th-century Rocca is the home of the **Museo Civico**, with 14th–20th-century paintings. Santa Maria Assunta has two canvases by

Piazzetta, while the octagonal, richly frescoed Inviolata (1603) has works by Palma il Giovane. The impressive waterfalls of the Varone river, above Riva, are 80 m (262 ft) high.
    Nearby Torbole was described by Goethe in *Italian Journey* and is a popular spot for sailing.

🏛 **Museo Civico**
Piazza Battisti 3. **Tel** 0464-57 38 69. ⭘ Mar–Oct: 10am–6pm Tue–Sun. ⬤ Nov–Feb.

Malcesine ⑨

Verona. 🏠 3,500. 🅸 Seasonal office: Via del Capitanato 6–8 (045-740 00 44).

One of the most fascinating towns along the lake shore, Malcesine stands on a stretch of impervious rock, hence the name *mala silex*, inaccessible rock. The 12th-century **Castello** was rebuilt by the Scaligeri of Verona in 1277. It houses the Museo di Storia Naturale del Garda e del Monte Baldo, the lake's natural history museum, which among other things shows how the Venetians transported ships to Torbole (1438–40). The parish church contains a 16th-century Deposition. Towering above Malcesine is Monte Baldo (2,218 m, 7,275 ft), accessible by cable car, with nature trails and stunning views.

Deposition (15th century), Malcesine parish church

The Legend of Maria (c.1614–20) by Martino Teofilo Polacco, in the Inviolata at Riva del Garda

For hotels and restaurants in this region see pp166–7 and pp181–3

The castle at Torri del Benaco, built in 1393

⛴ **Castello Scaligero**
Via Castello. *Tel 045-657 03 33.*
⏰ Apr–Oct: 9:30am–6:30pm daily;
Dec–Mar: 10am–4pm Sat & Sun.
⚫ 3, 4 Jan; Nov; 25, 28, 29 Dec.

Torri del Benaco ❿

Verona. 🏘 2,500.
ℹ Lungolago Regina Adelaide,
Garda (045-627 03 84).

Roman Castrum Turrium was a major stop between Riva and Garda and has preserved the typical grid plan. Due to its strategic position, Torri was fortified and a castle was built; it is now a **museum**, with old farm tools and prehistoric finds. Santissima Trinità has some 15th-century frescoes.

🏛 **Museo del Castello**
Via Fratelli Lavanda. *Tel 045-629 61 11.* ⏰ Jun–Sep: 9:30am–1pm, 4:30–7:30pm daily; Oct: 9:30am–12:30pm, 2:30–6pm daily; Nov–May: 9am–2:30pm Sat & Sun.

Garda ⓫

Verona. 🏘 3,500. ℹ Lungolago Regina Adelaide (045-627 03 84).

Built around a small bay, Garda was one of the major towns along the lake, controlling the southern basin. Its name, then given to the lake as well, comes from the German *Warten* (fortress), referring to the wall around the historic centre with its small port, accessible through the Torre dell'Orologio tower and gate. Among the historic buildings are the 15th-century Palazzo del Capitano, the Iosa, the dock of Palazzo Carlotti

designed by Sanmicheli, and **Santa Maria Maggiore** (18th century) with a painting by Palma il Giovane and a 15th-century cloister. At the new port is Villa Albertini, with an English-style park, while at Punta San Vigilio is Villa Guarienti (1542), designed by Sanmicheli, where the WWF offers a tour of the Bronze Age rock engravings.

🔒 **Santa Maria Maggiore**
Piazzale Roma. *Tel 045-725 68 25*

Bardolino and Lazise ⓬

Verona. 🏘 5,900. ℹ Piazzale Aldo Moro (045-721 00 78).
🛍 antiques, 3rd Sun of month.

The Cornicello and Mirabello headlands enclosing Bardolino made it a natural harbour. Originally it was a prehistoric settlement and then became a Roman camp. The historic centre has two early medieval churches, San Zeno and San Severo. The first still has its 9th-century Carolingian cruciform structure. Romanesque San Severo was founded in the 9th century but rebuilt in the 12th. It has 12th–13th-century frescoes with battle scenes and biblical episodes, and a 10th-century crypt. Among the civic buildings is the Loggia Rambaldi,

in the Rambaldi family palazzo. Bardolino is also famous for its wine.

Lazise also boasted a prehistoric civilization. A castle was built in the 11th century and the lords of Verona erected the walls in the 1300s. The 16th-century Venetian Customs House is all that remains of the old harbour. Next to it is San Nicolò (12th century), with Giotto school frescoes. Near Colà a spa was recently opened.

🌿 **Terme di Villa Cedri**
Piazza di Sopra 4, Località Colà di Lazise. *Tel 045-759 09 88.*
⏰ 9am–9pm Mon–Thu, 9–2:00am Fri & Sat. 🖾

Peschiera del Garda ⓭

Verona. 🏘 8,700. ℹ Piazzale Betteloni 15 (045-755 16 73). www.tourism.verona.it

Peschiera has retained its military image more than any other town on Lake Garda. The old town lies on an island surrounded by a star-shaped wall – "a fortress beautiful and strong", says Dante. The walls were reinforced by the Scaligeri of Verona, rebuilt for the new Venetian rulers by Sanmicheli in 1556, and completed with two forts by the Austrians two centuries later. Besides the frescoed 18th-century San Martino, there is the 16th-century Madonna del Frassino sanctuary, with a beautiful frescoed cloister.

San Zeno in Bardolino, crowned by a tower, containing traces of its original frescoes

Gardaland ⓮

This theme park was opened in 1975 and is one of the largest in Italy (500,000 sq m, 600,000 sq yds). The 38 attractions range from the rollercoaster to reconstructions of the pyramids and a jungle, the PalaBlú dolphin pool and the Village of the Elves, all ideal for families with children. The fun park facilities are good, including a wide range of refreshments, theme shops and souvenir photos. At busy times queues are kept informed about the length of the wait.

The canoe safari, one of the many attractions

PalaBlù
Italy's largest dolphin pool: four dolphins perform acrobatic tricks in front of the crowd.

Space Vertigo
There's a bacteriological alarm in the space station – everyone must escape! The only hope is to jump into space at top speed from a 40-m (131-ft) high tower. Thrills galore for everyone.

Arab Souk

Top Spin

Dinosaur Island
On a remote island – and without human interference – dinosaurs have continued to exist. You can join an expedition to study and help save them.

Monorail station

The floating tree trunks of the Colorado Boat confront the canyon rapids.

Magic Mountain
This super-fast rollercoaster is one of the most famous rides of all, with two hairpin bends and two death-defying spins. Only for the most intrepid of visitors.

The Valley of the Kings
Lovers of ancient Egypt can go into the temple of Abu Simbel, and discover the pharaohs' secrets among hieroglyphs, archaeologists and a mysterious green ray.

VISITOR'S CHECKLIST

Peschiera del Garda.
Tel 045-644 97 77. ☐ last
week Mar–mid-Jun & second
week Sep–Oct: 9:30am–6pm
daily; mid-Jun–first week Sep:
9am–midnight daily; Dec–first
week Jan: 10am–6:30pm daily.
◯ Nov–Mar. ♿ (free for ♿
and children under 1m tall).
Cameras for hire. 🍷 🍴 🐕
www.gardaland.it

★ **Blue Tornado**
*Even more exciting than the
rollercoaster, this attraction
offers you the chance to
experience first-hand
the thrills of piloting
an American
fighter plane.*

Jungle Rapids
*Here you climb aboard
a rubber dinghy and
are taken over the
rapids of a canyon, past
a volcano, into the heart
of mysterious and
magical Southeast Asia
with its temples.*

★ **Fantasy Kingdom**
*Children will love this! The
talking trees, singing animals
and puppet show will keep
them entertained for hours.*

Prezzemolo
*Gardaland's mascot, Prezzemolo
(Parsley) the dragon, is always
at the park entrance to welcome
all new visitors.*

0 metres	100
0 yards	100

STAR FEATURES

★ Blue Tornado

★ Fantasy Kingdom

The stepped Motta ascent, the setting for the Ortafiori festivities in April and May

Lago d'Orta

🏛 APTL, Via Panoramica, Orta–San Giulio *(0322-90 56 14)*. 🚉 FS Novara-Domodossola line *(848-88 80 88)*. 🚢 Nav. Lago d'Orta *(0322-84 48 62)*.

Lake Orta, or Cusio, is the westernmost lake in the lower Alps region, characterized by soft hills and scenery. Villages are dotted around the lake, along the shore or perched among green terracing. The Mottarone, a ski resort, and the other mountains surrounding the lake offer attractive hiking trails.

As far back as the 1700s, Orta was a tourist attraction and many villas were built in large parks. The chief town is Orta San Giulio, on a promontory in the middle of the lake. The village alleyways wind around Piazza Motta, on which lies the Palazzetto della Comunità (1582) and where the stepped Motta ascent begins. Opposite the square is the island of San Giulio, converted to Christianity by the Greek deacon Julius, who built the 4th-century **basilica**. The church was restored in the 11th–12th centuries and has a 12th-century Romanesque marble pulpit and

Figure on the pulpit, San Giulio

15th-century frescoes. Next door is the Palazzo del Vescovo (16th–18th century). Another sight is the **Sacro Monte**, a sanctuary built in 1591 on the rise above Orta. Dedicated to St Francis, it consists of 20 chapels with 17th–18th-century terracotta statues and frescoes. Opposite, perched over a steep quarry, is the Madonna del Sasso sanctuary (1748).

On the northern tip of the lake is Omegna, whose medieval quarter boasts the late Romanesque collegiate church of Sant'Ambrogio.

At Quarna there is the **Museo Etnografico e dello Strumento a Fiato**, with displays of wind instruments, made in this village for centuries. Other interesting villages are Vacciago di Ameno, with the Calderara Collection of contemporary art, featuring 327 international avant-garde works of the 1950s and 1960s; Gozzano, with the church of San Giuliano (18th century), Palazzo Vescovile and the seminary; and, lastly, Torre di Buccione. San Maurizio d'Opaglio has a curious attraction: a museum devoted to the production of taps.

🏛 **Basilica di San Giulio**
Isola di San Giulio.
APTL, ring road, Orta San Giulio *(0322-90 56 14)*.
🕐 11am–12:15pm Mon; 9:30am–12:15pm, 2–6:45pm Tue–Sun (5:45pm solar time).

🏛 **Sacro Monte**
Via Sacro Monte. **Tel** 0322-91 19 60. **Chapels** 🕐 summer: 8:30am–6:30pm daily; winter: 9am–4:30pm daily (5pm hols).
🚫 1 & 6 Jan, 25, 26 & 31 Dec.

🏛 **Museo Etnografico e dello Strumento Musicale a Fiato**
Quarna Sotto. 🕐 Jul–mid-Sep: 10am–noon, 2–6pm Tue–Sun.
🚫 Mon.

Lago di Varese

🏛 IAT, Via Carrobbio 2, Varese *(0332-28 36 04)*. 🚉 Ferrovie Nord Milano, Milan-Laveno line to Gavirate *(02-202 22)*. 🚌 Autolinee Zani *(0332-73 11 10)*.

This lake basin was created by glacial movement during the Quaternary era. It offers pleasant scenery, with rolling hills and the Campo dei Fiori massif. In prehistoric times it was inhabited by a prehistoric civilization, the important remains of which were found on the island of Isolino Virginia (which can be reached from Biandronno), where they are on display at the **Museo Preistorico**.

Part of the lake shore is now protected as the Brabbia marsh nature reserve. Not far away, at Cazzago Brabbia, are ice-houses used to conserve fish in the 18th century. On the northern tip of the lake,

Fishing boats along the shores of the Lago di Varese

at Voltorre di Gavirate, the church of **San Michele** is worth a visit. It was part of a 12th-century Cluniac monastery and is now used for exhibitions. On the slopes of Campo dei Fiori you can see the lake of the **Sacro Monte** di Varese, a sanctuary made up of 14 17th-century chapels with frescoes and life-size statues narrating the Mysteries of the Rosary.

🏛 Museo Preistorico
Isolino Virginia. **Tel** 0332-28 15 90 (Musei Civici di Varese). ◯ Apr–Nov: 2–6pm Sat & Sun (Oct: 2–6pm Sun). 📷 📋 (book in advance).

🔒 San Michele
Voltorre di Gavirate. **Tel** 0332-74 39 14. ◯ 10am–6pm Tue–Sun. **www**.museoartemoderna.it

🔒 Sacro Monte
Varese. **Tel** 0332-83 03 73. ◯ daily.

Lago d'Iseo

ℹ IAT, Lungolago Marconi 26, Iseo (030-98 02 09). 🚉 FS to Brescia, then Ferrovie Nord Milano (02-20 222). 🚌 SAB (035-28 9 0 11). ⛴ Navigazione Lago d'Iseo (035-97 14 83). **www**.lagodiseo.org

Lake Iseo, also known as Sebino, extends between the provinces of Bergamo and Brescia. It is the seventh-largest lake in Italy and the fourth in Lombardy, created by a glacier descending from the Val Camonica. The chief towns here are Iseo, Sarnico, Lovere and Pisogne. The historic centre of Iseo has kept its medieval character, with

the church of Sant'Andrea (1150), the Neo-Classical interior of which contains a painting by Hayez. Next to this is the tomb of the feudal landowner Giacomo Oldofredi and, on a hill at the entrance to the town, the Castello degli Oldofredi (both built in the 14th century), which in 1585 became a Capuchin monastery. At Provaglio d'Iseo there is the San Pietro in Lamosa Cluniac monastery, founded in 1030. Its 11th–12th-century Romanesque church has frescoes by the school of Romanino. Sarnico, at the southern end of the lake, was an important commercial and industrial town. Among the Art Nouveau houses built here by Giuseppe Sommaruga is Villa Faccanoni (1912), one of the best examples of this style.

The road that follows the western side of the lake rounds the Corno headland, which has a fine views of Monte Isola, the largest lake island in Europe, with its typical villages, dominated by the Madonna della Ceriola sanctuary and the 15th-century Rocca Oldofredi. At the northern end of the lake is Lovere, which has medieval tower-houses.

On the lakeside is the **Galleria dell'Accademia Tadini**, featuring fine works of art ranging from the 14th to the 20th century, including Jacopo Bellini, Strozzi, Tiepolo, Hayez and Canova. The church of Santa Maria in Valvendra (1483) has paintings by Floriano Ferramola and

The Piramidi di Zone pinnacles, some reaching 30 m (98 ft)

Moretto and a 16th-century wooden altarpiece on the high altar. At Pisogne is Santa Maria della Neve (15th century), with scenes of the Passion frescoed by Romanino (1534). From here you can go to the Val Camonica rock engravings park. The lake is also famous for its lovely scenery, including the Piramidi di Zone, pinnacles protected from erosion by the rock massif above them, and the Torbiere d'Iseo, a marshy area with peat bogs which is now a nature reserve.

🏛 Galleria dell'Accademia Tadini
Via Tadini, Lovere. **Tel** 035-96 27 80. ◯ mid-Apr–mid-Oct: 3–7pm Tue–Sat; 10am–noon, 3–6pm Sun & hols. ● Mon. 📷

Lago d'Idro

ℹ Pro Loco, Via Trento 15, Idro (0365-832 24). 🚌 SIA (02-63 79 01).

The highest large lake in Lombardy (368 m, 1,207 ft above sea level) was turned into an artificial basin in 1932 to provide irrigation and hydroelectricity. It is dominated by the Rocca di Anfo, a fortress with a splendid panoramic view that was built over older fortifications by the Venetians in 1450, and then rebuilt many times. From here you can reach Bagolino, with its charming stone houses and San Rocco (1478), which contains a fresco cycle by Giovan Pietro da Cemmo.

..ca Oldofredi, Monte Isola, the Martinengo residence since the 1500s

TRAVELLERS' NEEDS

WHERE TO STAY 158–167

WHERE TO EAT 168–183

BARS AND CAFES 184–187

SHOPS AND MARKETS 188–195

ENTERTAINMENT 196–205

WHERE TO STAY

It is not easy to find atmospheric hotels or charming guesthouses in Milan because the city caters mostly to businessmen and women and the majority of hotels are therefore geared to their needs, with working facilities in the rooms and public areas. This type of accommodation comes in the medium–high price range and usually offers either private parking or nearby garage facilities. The four-star hotels not only have prestigious restaurants that are among the best in the city, but may also have lovely inner gardens not seen from the street. It is best to book

Porter, Westin Palace, Milan *(see p164)*

accommodation well in advance, especially during the international fashion shows (held in March and October) and the many top trade fairs. At the lakes, on the other hand, the choice ranges from guesthouses to fascinating historic hotels, which have drawn visitors and celebrities from all over the world since the 19th century. The most luxurious are in charming 17th- and 18th-century villas, with flower-filled terraces, health clubs and heated pools. For more detailed information regarding accommodation in Milan and at the lakes, *see pages 160–167.*

CHOOSING A HOTEL

The Italian for hotel is *albergo*. A *pensione* or *locanda* theoretically indicates a more modest guesthouse, but in practice the distinctions are quite blurred.

Most of the hotels in Milan are concentrated in the Buenos Aires-Stazione Centrale area, near the Fiera and in the Città Studi district. The first group is situated for the most part in Piazza della Repubblica and near the main railway station, which is practical for visitors on a short stay. Some of the more interesting hotels are the five-star **Westin Palace** *(see p164)*, the **Sanpi** *(see p163)*,

Entrance to the Hotel Regency *(see p161)* in Milan

which features a charming inner courtyard filled with flowers – and the **Principe di Savoia** *(see p163)*, in 1930s style. Around the Fiera, large hotels cater for business visitors. The **Regency** *(see p161)* is smaller, with a warm atmosphere. At Città Studi you can find clean, inexpensive two-star hotels: an example is the **San Francisco** *(see p162)*.

In the historic centre a few charming, small hotels remain. The **Antica Locanda Solferino** *(see p162)* has a family atmosphere. The **Grand Hotel et de Milan** *(see p163)* and the **Four Seasons** *(see p163)* are both elegant, historic hotels.

At the lakes, hotels are more geared to holiday-makers and families. Some

The elegant Four Seasons Hotel in Milan *(see p163)*

of Italy's most famous luxury hotels are sited around the lake shores. The **Des Iles Borromées** *(see p165)* at Lake Maggiore was once a royal residence. Lake Como boasts famous luxury hotels such as the **Grand Hotel Villa d'Este** *(see p165)* at Cernobbio, and the **Grand Hotel Villa Serbelloni** *(see p165)* at Bellagio.

BOOKING

Accommodation can be booked by phoning or sending a fax. The hotel will probably ask for a credit card number in advance. Almost all Milanese hotels have e-mail facilities and some, usually the luxury ones, have websites where you can book directly online.

The Grand Hotel Villa Serbelloni *(see p165)* at Lake Como

Milan is a busy commercial city so it is best to book well in advance.

GRADING

Along with the rest of Italy, hotels in Milan and at the lakes are classified by a star system, from one (the lowest) to five stars. It is best to avoid one-star hotels in Milan (unlike the rest of Italy).

Two-star hotels usually offer bed and breakfast, and rooms may not have private bathrooms. Three-star hotels offer en-suite bathrooms, TV and sometimes a mini-bar; room service is usually available.

Four-star hotels, besides the above facilities, usually provide a laundry service, services for business travellers and (in Milan) a shuttle service to and from the airports. Five-star hotels are luxurious and offer exclusive restaurants and facilities for conferences.

At the lakes, accommodation ranges from luxury hotels to family-run guesthouses. There are also inexpensive youth hostels and campsites with tents and caravans (RVs). Some have self-catering (efficiency) apartments.

PRICES

Accommodation in Milan is generally expensive. Because Milan is primarily a business destination, there is little seasonal variation in pricing; in fact, tariffs usually increase when the fashion shows are held and when there are major trade shows at the Fiera, which is quite often. Some of the larger hotels may also require you to take half-board (MAP) during your stay. For a hotel bargain, visit Milan in August. This is when most Italians leave the city to go on holiday – so, as well as cheaper accommodation, you will have Milan to yourself.

At the lakes, prices vary according to the season: in spring and summer, the peak tourist seasons, prices are higher. August is the busiest time. Many hotels expect you to take full board, especially in the summer months. Some hotels close for part of the year, usually in winter.

By law, prices have to be displayed in every hotel bedroom. Beware of extras: mini-bar drinks will be expensive. A view and air conditioning will add to costs, and hotel phone charges are higher

than stand.
the hotel mu
a receipt whe.
the receipt shou
until you leave It.

CHILDREN

In general, children are
comed everywhere in Ital,
but hotels may not go out o
their way to provide special
facilities. Some of the cheaper
hotels may not be able to
provide cots. However, most
hotels, from the simplest to
the most grand, will put a
small bed or two into a double
room for families travelling
together. The price is usually
an additional 30–40 per cent
of the double room rate per
bed. Hotels around the lakes
tend to be better equipped for
children than the business
hotels of Milan. Babysitting
services are offered by some
large hotels at the lakes.

PETS

For those travelling with their
dog or other pet, some hotels
actively welcome animals and
provide special facilities for
them, especially at the lakes
In Milan it is more difficult to
find hotels and guesthouses
that accept pets, but some of
the larger hotels have rooms
specially furnished for clients
and can even offer dog-sitting
services. However, if you
mean to travel with pets it is
always a good idea to check
these details when booking.

Four-poster bed in a room at the Villa Crespi *(see p167)*, Lake Orta

a Hotel

...his guide have been selected across a
...nge for the quality of service, decor and
...tels within the same price category are listed
...ally. All the hotels listed accept credit cards
...herwise stated. For Milan map references, see
224–37 and the inside back cover.

PRICE CATEGORIES
The price ranges are for a standard
double room and taxes per night
during the high season. Breakfast
is not included, unless specified.

€ under €120
€€ €120–€160
€€€ €160–€210
€€€€ €210–€275
€€€€€ over €275

MILAN

CITY CENTRE Gran Duca di York
€€€
Via Moneta 1, 20123 **Tel** *02 87 48 63* **Fax** *02 869 03 44* **Rooms** *33*　　**Map** *7 B1, 9 C3*

This recently renovated 18th-century palazzo is close to Piazza del Duomo and the best designer shops. It has retro bathrooms and cheerful ochre-coloured rooms that are quite compact in size. A small bar adjacent to the lobby serves hot and cold drinks. Parking is available for a daily fee at a nearby garage. **www.ducadiyork.com**

CITY CENTRE Spadari al Duomo
€€€€
Via Spadari 11, 20123 **Tel** *02 72 00 23 71* **Fax** *02 86 11 84* **Rooms** *40*　　**Map** *7 C1, 9 C3*

A cosy hotel just steps from the Duomo, the famous Peck delicatessen and restaurant, and some of Milan's great shops. The blue-themed rooms are decorated with art and designer furniture; the best ones have balconies and even views from the bathroom. There is a small bar with Internet access. Friendly staff. **www.spadarihotel.com**

CITY CENTRE The Gray
€€€€€
Via San Raffaele 6, 20121 **Tel** *02 720 89 51* **Fax** *02 86 65 26* **Rooms** *21*　　**Map** *7 C1, 10 D3*

Each room at The Gray has completely different decor, layout and focus, such as split levels, fitness facilities or a steam room. It is Milan's ultimate upmarket design hotel, with a fabulous restaurant and a central location just a stone's throw from the Duomo, La Scala and the shops in the Galleria. **www.sinahotels.com**

CITY CENTRE Hotel de la Ville
€€€€€
Via Hoepli 6, 20121 **Tel** *02 87 91 31* **Fax** *02 86 66 09* **Rooms** *109*　　**Map** *4 D5, 10 D3*

This hotel is located within walking distance of the Duomo and fashionable Via Montenapoleone. The decor is reminiscent of an English country house and features a stunning wood-panelled hall. The bedrooms have silk tapestries and marble bathrooms. The in-house bar Il Visconteo is popular for pre-dinner drinks. **www.delavillemilano.com**

CITY CENTRE Park Hyatt Milano
€€€€€
Via Tommaso Grossi 1, 20121 **Tel** *02 88 21 12 34* **Fax** *02 88 21 12 35* **Rooms** *117*　　**Map** *7 C1, 9 C3*

An elegantly designed hotel occupying a former bank. The luxurious modern decor in muted tones and the high level of service are synonymous with the global Hyatt group. Some of the best fashion shops are on the doorstep. The hotel's restaurant is excellent and the bathrooms are very spacious. **www.milan.park.hyatt.com**

CITY CENTRE Straf
€€€€€
Via San Raffaele 3, 20121 **Tel** *02 80 50 81* **Fax** *02 89 09 52 94* **Rooms** *64*　　**Map** *7 C1, 10 D3*

Behind the 1883 Neo-Classic façade, the Straf has an ultra-modern interior. Luxurious natural materials set the minimal design tone. It boasts five unique chromatherapy and aromatherapy rooms. Straf's cosy lounge bar next door is very popular with the fashion and design set. An excellent central location. **www.straf.it**

NORTHWEST MILAN Hotel Fiera
€
Via Spinola 9, 20149 **Tel** *02 48 00 54 95* **Fax** *02 48 00 84 94* **Rooms** *29*　　**Map** *1 C3*

This hotel is located right at the Fiera, ideal for business guests. It is also near the famous San Siro stadium for football and concerts, and Corso Vercelli for shops. Simple and conventional in style, it has clean, spacious rooms, mostly overlooking the garden. Non-smoking rooms are available. **www.milan-hotels.hotelfiera.it**

NORTHWEST MILAN Johnny
€€
Via Prati 6, 20145 **Tel** *02 34 18 12* **Fax** *02 33 61 05 21* **Rooms** *31*　　**Map** *2 D3*

This recently renovated hotel is close to the Fiera in a quiet side street. The colourful decor is understated, with a brick-vaulted breakfast room and a lounge like a winter garden. The metro is nearby and will take you to the Duomo and shops in ten minutes. A small, friendly, family-run hotel. **www.hoteljohnny.com**

NORTHWEST MILAN Antica Locanda dei Mercanti
€€€
Via San Tomaso 6, 20121 **Tel** *02 805 40 80* **Fax** *02 805 40 90* **Rooms** *14*　　**Map** *3 B5, 9 C2*

A peaceful and pleasant inn in a pedestrian area near La Scala, Piazza del Duomo, the Castello Sforzesco and the shops. There is no sign outside, just a number. Four rooms have a terrace and relaxed, Mediterranean-style decor, but some are rather compact. Wi-Fi and broadband access are available throughout the hotel. **www.locanda.it**

Key to Symbols *see back cover flap*

NORTHWEST MILAN Antica Locanda Leonardo €

Corso Magenta 78, 20123 **Tel** *02 46 33 17* **Fax** *02 48 01 90 12* **Rooms** *20*   **Map** *3 A5, 9*

This hotel is short walk from the church housing Leonardo da Vinci's *Last Supper*. Period furniture, brocade, bows and lace feature in the cosy rooms. There is also a leafy garden with cobblestones and wrought-iron furniture. A brief tram ride takes you directly to the city centre. **www.anticalocandaleonardo.com**

NORTHWEST MILAN Europeo €€€

Via Luigi Canonica 38, 20154 **Tel** *02 331 47 51* **Fax** *02 33 10 54 10* **Rooms** *45*   **Map** *3 A3*

Handy for visitors to the Fiera, the Europeo is also close to Parco Sempione. The restaurants in the Chinese quarter are also within easy access. The bedrooms are comfortable and elegant and the hotel also has a swimming pool. Garage parking available for a fee.

NORTHWEST MILAN King €€€

Corso Magenta 19, 20123 **Tel** *02 87 44 32* **Fax** *02 89 01 07 98* **Rooms** *48*   **Map** *3 A5, 9 A3*

This hotel is within walking distance from the Castello Sforzesco and close to Cadorna station for the Malpensa Express train. The style is chintzy, with reproduction tapestries, Regency furniture and a grand old façade. Some rooms have views over the rooftops and castle towers. Bikes available for hire. **www.hotelkingmilano.com**

NORTHWEST MILAN Montebianco €€€

Via Monterosa 90, 20149 **Tel** *02 48 01 21 30* **Fax** *02 48 00 06 58* **Rooms** *44*   **Map** *1 B3*

Montebianco is located in an Art Nouveau building near the Fiera. It offers a bar and lounge, parking, bike hire and Internet facilities (pay per hour), and there are restaurants nearby. The entrance is rather grand, with plush seating and chandeliers. Rooms are bright and elegant, though some are compact. **www.hotelmontebianco.com**

NORTHWEST MILAN Palazzo delle Stelline €€€

Corso Magenta 61, 20123 **Tel** *02 481 84 31* **Fax** *02 49 51 90 97* **Rooms** *105*   **Map** *6 F1*

The Palazzo delle Stelline is a former 15th-century monastery, restored to house a hotel and conference centre. Windows in the corridors overlook the cloister garden, giving it a certain feeling of privacy and tranquillity. With simple understated decor, a café-bar, terrace and garden access in summer. **www.hotelpalazzostelline.it**

NORTHWEST MILAN Ariosto €€€€

Via Ariosto 22, 20145 **Tel** *02 481 78 44* **Fax** *02 498 05 16* **Rooms** *49*   **Map** *2 E5*

Close to Conciliazione metro station, near the shops on Corso Vercelli and not far from Leonardo's famous *Last Supper*, this Art Nouveau building has a grand staircase, a detailed façade and wrought-iron railings. The bathrooms have modern frosted-glass doors and there are contemporary mosaics in the courtyard. **www.brerahotels.com**

NORTHWEST MILAN Enterprise €€€€

Corso Sempione 91, 20154 **Tel** *02 31 81 81* **Fax** *02 31 81 88 11* **Rooms** *120*   **Map** *2 D1*

This contemporary hotel built in a former radio factory is within walking distance from the Fiera. It is also close to some popular nightspots. It features modern design throughout and a first-class restaurant, Sophia's, with a red dining room. All rooms have a sophisticated digital multimedia system and soundproofing. **www.enterprisehotel.com**

NORTHWEST MILAN Regency €€€€

Via G Arimondi 12, 20155 **Tel** *02 39 21 60 21* **Fax** *02 39 21 77 34* **Rooms** *71*

The Regency is rich in character, style and refined taste. It is housed in the renovated 19th-century home of a famous nobleman, with a spectacular façade, open fire, marble bathrooms, stained-glass details and an inner courtyard. The elaborate rooms are floral in design, while the lounge has chequered walls. **www.regency-milano.com**

SOUTHWEST MILAN Hotel dei Fiori €€

Via Renzo e Lucia 14, 20142 **Tel** *02 843 64 41* **Fax** *02 89 50 10 96* **Rooms** *53*   **Map** *7 A5*

Hotel dei Fiori is easily accessible from the motorway and close to the Navigli area, which is great for nightlife. The nearby road is busy, but the clean and comfortable rooms all have soundproofing. They are basic in design, with wooden furnishings. The hotel also offers an Internet point and laundry service. **www.hoteldeifiori.com**

SOUTHWEST MILAN Liberty €€€

Viale Bligny 56, 20136 **Tel** *02 58 31 85 62* **Fax** *02 58 31 90 61* **Rooms** *52*   **Map** *8 D4*

A classic, elegant hotel with a nice courtyard close to the Bocconi university. Tastefully decorated with spacious comfy rooms and Art Nouveau touches, it is spread over six floors. The lobby is filled with light from the stained-glass roof, while the marble bathrooms have a Jacuzzi. Close to a leafy park. **www.hotelliberty-milano.com**

SOUTHWEST MILAN Carrobbio €€€€

Via Medici 3, 20123 **Tel** *02 89 01 07 40* **Fax** *02 805 33 34* **Rooms** *56*   **Map** *7 B2, 9 B4*

This original 30s-style hotel has pleasant rooms, decorated in a simple style favouring muted colours and plaids or stripes. Rooms look on to the street or an internal garden courtyard. Suites have a private garden, and some rooms feature large terraces. There is a small communal room with Internet access. **www.hotelcarrobbiomilano.com**

SOUTHWEST MILAN Corte del Naviglio €€€€

Via Lodovico il Moro 117, 20143 **Tel** *02 89 18 12 92* **Fax** *02 89 15 55 16* **Rooms** *51*   **Map** *5 A5*

in a fabulous old house on the canal, this hotel is full of charm and character, with balconies, terracotta-tiled ring and a lovely garden with fountains and statues. The hotel's restaurant serves a selection of Milanese cuisine as occasional live entertainment.

SOUTHWEST MILAN Regina
€€€€

Correnti 13, 20123 **Tel** *02 58 10 69 13* **Fax** *02 58 10 70 33* **Rooms** *43*   **Map** *7 B2, 9 B4*

...nort tram ride away from Piazza del Duomo, near Cordusio metro station, is this cosy, pleasant hotel in a ...nverted 18th-century residence. The colonial-style lobby has palms, pillars and a domed glass roof. Some rooms ...ave small balconies. In summer you can breakfast outdoors on the cobblestoned terrace. **www.hotelregina.it**

SOUTHWEST MILAN Zurigo
€€€€

Corso Italia 11/a, 20122 **Tel** *02 72 02 22 60* **Fax** *02 72 00 00 13* **Rooms** *41*   **Map** *7 C2, 9 C5*

Facilities at the Zurigo, located a ten-minute walk from Piazza del Duomo, include a Wi-Fi zone, as well as a free Internet point. It is the perfect choice for lovers of everything organic – this simple and basic hotel features an organic breakfast buffet. Snacks are available from the bar. Bike hire is free. **www.brerahotels.com**

SOUTHWEST MILAN Pierre
€€€€€

Via de Amicis 32, 20123 **Tel** *02 72 00 05 81* **Fax** *02 805 21 57* **Rooms** *51*   **Map** *7 A2, 9 A5*

Pierre is set back from a busy road in a lively area with good restaurants and shops. This quiet and luxurious hotel has classic five-star service and decor, ancient tapestries, Baroque wallpapers and lots of light. Staff are attentive but discreet. Rooms have Wi-Fi and soundproofing. There is also a sophisticated piano bar. **www.hotelpierremilano.it**

SOUTHEAST MILAN Hotel del Sud
€

Corso Lodi 74, 20139 **Tel** *02 57 40 99 18* **Fax** *02 569 34 57* **Rooms** *30*   **Map** *8 F4*

Hotel del Sud is a small, homely one-star hotel on Corso Lodi, a busy street with easy access to Porta Romana train station. There are a few bars and pizzerias nearby. The metro station Brenta is opposite the hotel, so access to the city centre is quick and easy. Rooms are small and simple, all with bathroom and TV. **www.hoteldelsud.it**

SOUTHEAST MILAN Vittoria
€

Via Pietro Calvi 32, 20129 **Tel** *02 545 65 20* **Fax** *02 55 19 02 46* **Rooms** *25*   **Map** *8 F1*

This fairly central hotel has a modern façade. The compact rooms are decorated in a light, classic style, and the staff are welcoming and friendly. It is a family-owned hotel on a residential street, not far from the Duomo and the Galleria Vittorio Emanuele. In summer, breakfast can be taken in the little garden at the back. **www.hotelvittoriamilano.it**

SOUTHEAST MILAN Piacenza
€€

Via Piacenza 4, 20135 **Tel** *02 545 50 41* **Fax** *02 546 52 69* **Rooms** *24*   **Map** *8 F4*

Located in the Porta Romana area, the Piacenza has friendly staff and good amenities. Rooms are a little spartan, with cherrywood furnishings and parquet flooring, as well as double glazing and Wi-Fi access. Bars and restaurants are in the vicinity, and a local market takes place on Fridays in nearby Via Crema. **www.hotelpiacenza.com**

SOUTHEAST MILAN Townhouse 31
€€€€

Via Goldoni 31, 20129 **Tel** *02 701 56* **Fax** *02 71 31 67* **Rooms** *20*   **Map** *4 F5*

With only 20 rooms, this hotel feels very cosy, with a warm, relaxing, friendly atmosphere. The emphasis is on well-being, with tasteful decor, artifacts from the owners' travels, a large communal breakfast table and a cosy lobby. In summer the garden bar is very popular for apéritifs and cocktails. **www.townhouse.it**

NORTHEAST MILAN San Francisco
€

Viale Lombardia 55, 20131 **Tel** *02 236 03 02* **Fax** *02 26 68 03 77* **Rooms** *31*   **Map** *4 F3*

Located in the academic area of town, this family-run hotel is small, affordable and only six metro stops from the Duomo and three from Central Station. Rooms are adequate, if sparse. Ask for one overlooking the pretty little garden with its pergola, roses, lawn and paved terrace. Internet point for guests' use. **www.hotel-sanfrancisco.it**

NORTHEAST MILAN Alle Meraviglie
€€€

Via San Tomaso 8, 20121 **Tel** *02 805 10 23* **Fax** *02 805 40 90* **Rooms** *6*   **Map** *3 B5, 9 C2*

Tucked away in a side street between the Duomo and the castle is Le Meraviglie, one of Milan's best-kept secrets. Set in a recently renovated 18th-century listed building, it is close to shops, museums and restaurants. Discreet and chic, it has only six rooms, which all differ in size and decor. Breakfast is served in the room. **www.allemeraviglie.it**

NORTHEAST MILAN Antica Locanda Solferino
€€€

Via Castelfidardo 2, 20121 **Tel** *02 657 01 29* **Fax** *02 657 13 61* **Rooms** *11*   **Map** *3 C3*

Old-world charm reigns at this upmarket B&B, which is more stylish and affordable than most conventional hotels. Located in the heart of bohemian Brera, it features antique and retro details such as tiny wrought-iron balconies, traditional floorboards and narrow corridors. **www.anticalocandasolferino.it**

NORTHEAST MILAN Baviera
€€€

Via Panfilo Castaldi 7, 20124 **Tel** *02 659 05 51* **Fax** *02 29 00 32 81* **Rooms** *50*   **Map** *4 E3*

This hotel has a traditional feel, with a spacious lobby and a design mix of stripes and chintz. It is situated a couple of streets behind Piazza della Repubblica, where there is a metro station. There are restaurants nearby, secure parking and a shuttle to and from the main train station. Bike hire is available, as is Internet access. **www.hotelbaviera.com**

NORTHEAST MILAN Cavour
€€€

Via Fatebenefratelli 21, 20121 **Tel** *02 62 00 01* **Fax** *02 659 22 63* **Rooms** *113*   **Map** *3 C4, 10 D1*

Close to Villa Reale and Milan's wonderful public gardens of La Palestra, the Cavour is also near Brera, the lively quarter with art galleries and bars. The impressive lobby has an elegant villa style, with columns and staircases, and the rooms are clean and contemporary. The hotel restaurant Conte Camillo is excellent. **www.hotelcavour.it**

Key to Price Guide *see p160* **Key to Symbols** *see back cover flap*

NORTHEAST MILAN Hermitage

Via Messina 10, 20154 **Tel** *02 31 81 70* **Fax** *02 33 10 73 99* **Rooms** *131*

Situated between Garibaldi station and Corso Sempione, next to the Cimitero Monument, and bright hotel offers good amenities, such as a garden, spa, steam room and fitness facil. Il Sambuco is renowned for great fish and seafood. There is also a sun terrace and garage. W

NORTHEAST MILAN Lombardia

Viale Lombardia 74–76, 20131 **Tel** *02 289 25 15* **Fax** *02 289 34 30* **Rooms** *78*

Housed in a decorative old palazzo with a lovely façade, the Lombardia has a warm, welcoming feel wi. marble and oriental rugs in the lobby. Some of the clean and pleasant rooms look on to a small courtyard. Apartments with kitchenette are also available. **www.hotellombardia.com**

NORTHEAST MILAN Marriott

  €€€

Via Washington 66, 20146 **Tel** *02 485 21* **Fax** *02 481 89 25* **Rooms** *323*

Map 5 C

Milan's Marriott hotel is corporate in style, suitable for conferences or weddings, with reliably high standards of service. Located slightly out of the centre, it offers good facilities, including a fitness centre, a restaurant and a large lobby with complimentary coffees and papers. Decor is a mix of stripes, florals and chintz. **www.marriott.com**

NORTHEAST MILAN Ritter

€€€€

Corso Garibaldi 68, 20121 **Tel** *02 29 00 68 60* **Fax** *02 657 15 12* **Rooms** *89*

Map 3 B3

Ritter is located in Brera, the bohemian quarter of the city. The decor is rather old, but the hotel offers comfort and a good base from which to explore Milan, being close to Parco Sempione and the Castello Sforzesco. There is a garden terrace, solarium and Internet access for a fee. **www.ritter-hotel.com**

NORTHEAST MILAN Bulgari

€€€€€

Via Privata Fratelli Gabba 7b, 20122 **Tel** *02 805 80 51* **Fax** *02 805 80 52 22* **Rooms** *58*

Map 3 C4

The luxury and superior taste you would expect from Bulgari, one of Italy's high-class designers. In a peaceful setting, a few minutes' walk from the best shops and next to the Botanical Gardens. Rooms are decorated with the finest natural materials. Exclusive spa and treatment room and an innovative restaurant. **www.bulgarihotels.com**

NORTHEAST MILAN Carlton Baglioni

€€€€€

Via Senato 5, 20121 **Tel** *02 770 77* **Fax** *02 78 33 00* **Rooms** *92*

Map 4 D4, 10 E1

This hotel is in an ideal location for the shops, just off the boutique-laden Via della Spiga. The excellent restaurant, Il Baretto, a bar in summer on the roof terrace, a cosy library with an open fireplace and spacious rooms are just some of its charms. Three rooms have a modern, sleek design. **www.baglionihotels.com**

NORTHEAST MILAN Excelsior Hotel Gallia

€€€€€

Piazza Duca d'Aosta 9, 20124 **Tel** *02 678 51* **Fax** *02 66 71 32 39* **Rooms** *238*

Map 4 E1

This luxurious hotel dominates the square next to Central Station. It retains an Art Nouveau feel, with elegant rooms, antique furniture and the popular Baboon Bar, with stained-glass windows. Facilities include a beauty centre and gym and 24-hour room service. Ristorante Gallia serves excellent food. **www.lemeridien.excelsiorgallia.com**

NORTHEAST MILAN Four Seasons

€€€€€

Via Gesu 8, 20121 **Tel** *02 770 88* **Fax** *02 77 08 50 00* **Rooms** *118*

Map 4 D5, 10 E2

The tranquil setting of the Four Seasons is a former monastery with rooms overlooking the 15th-century cloistered garden. Service is faultless (there is 24-hour room service), the food refined, and the spacious rooms exude luxury through rich fabrics, handcrafted lampshades and extremely comfortable beds. **www.fourseasons.com/milan**

NORTHEAST MILAN Grand Hotel et de Milan

€€€€€

Via Manzoni 29, 20121 **Tel** *02 72 31 41* **Fax** *02 86 46 08 61* **Rooms** *95*

Map 4 D4, 10 D1

Dating back to 1863, the Grand is steeped in history. Hemingway and Callas stayed here, and Giuseppe Verdi called it his home for 27 years. It offers luxury and elegance in a Renaissance setting, with 19th-century furniture throughout and Art Nouveau skylights in the bar. The rooms have large marble bathrooms. **www.grandhoteletdemilan.it**

NORTHEAST MILAN Manin

€€€€€

Via Manin 7, 20121 **Tel** *02 659 65 11* **Fax** *02 655 21 60* **Rooms** *118*

Map 4 D4

The Manin sits in a quiet side street, facing the public gardens of Via Palestro, which offer plenty of greenery, ponds and space. Part of the Tulip group, it features all the amenities we would expect of such a chain. It has a restaurant, American bar and pretty garden with pergola. Large painted scenes decorate the bedheads. **www.hotelmanin.it**

NORTHEAST MILAN Principe di Savoia

€€€€€

Piazza della Repubblica 17, 20124 **Tel** *02 623 01* **Fax** *02 659 58 38* **Rooms** *404*

Map 4 D2

A Milanese landmark, this hotel set in a charming 19th-century building is known for its elegance and high level of service (24-hour room service is available). The VIP atmosphere is compounded by modern facilities. The top-floor fitness and spa club with beauty centre offers sauna, Jacuzzi and indoor pool. **www.principedisavoia.com**

NORTHEAST MILAN Sanpi

€€€€€

Via Lazzaro Palazzi 18, 20124 **Tel** *02 29 51 33 41* **Fax** *02 29 40 24 51* **Rooms** *79*

Map 4 E3

With a modern façade and simple, sophisticated decor, Sanpi offers easy access to the shops on Corso Buenos Aires, the public gardens and a metro station. Pick a room overlooking the pretty little garden. Some rooms have balconies, suites have Jacuzzis, the hotel is Wi-Fi, and there is also a restaurant. **www.hotelsanpimilano.it**

...on Diana Majestic
...05 81 **Fax** 02 20 58 20 58 **Rooms** 107   **Map** 4 F4

...g one of the loveliest gardens in the city (ask for a room overlooking it). Built in 1908 on the ...aths, the Diana is close to some great design and fashion shops, art galleries and restaurants. ...ers at the hotel bar to socialise at happy hour. **www.sheraton.com/dianamajestic**

...LAN Westin Palace
...oblica 20, 20124 **Tel** 02 633 61 **Fax** 02 65 44 85 **Rooms** 228   **Map** 4 E3

...ace is minutes away from the Duomo, La Scala and the designer shopping streets. Palatial touches ...ole pillars, wood panelling and chandeliers. The extra-comfortable beds guarantee a great sleep. Enjoy ...n the lounge bar or work out in the state-of-the-art gym. **www.westin.com**

LAKE MAGGIORE

BELGIRATE Villa Carlotta €€
Via Sempione 121–125, 28832 **Tel** *0322 764 61; 800 82 00 80 (within Italy)* **Fax** *0322 767 05* **Rooms** *129*

Set in private parkland on the lush banks of Lake Maggiore, Villa Carlotta is a splendid three-storey villa. The classic decor is slightly outdated and the compact rooms have an old-fashioned charm. As well as extensive grounds, the hotel offers bike hire, horse riding, tennis and golf facilities nearby. **www.bestwestern.it/villacarlotta_vb**

CANNOBIO Hotel Cannobio €€
Piazza Vittorio Emanuele III 6, 28822 **Tel** *0323 73 96 39* **Fax** *0323 73 95 96* **Rooms** *18*

A lovely hotel in a grand romantic building facing the lake. The rooms are clean and pleasant, with elegant decor in rich colours. The painted antique bedheads add a striking touch. Modern facilities, friendly staff and a lovely restaurant with a summer terrace over the lake complete the experience. **www.hotelcannobio.com**

CANNOBIO Hotel Pironi €€
Via Marconi 35, 28822 **Tel** *0323 706 24; 0323 70 87* **Fax** *0323 721 84* **Rooms** *12*

This hotel is housed in a former Franciscan monastery and original touches include frescoes, antiques and vaulted ceilings. Decor is tasteful and intimate. Some rooms have views, others small balconies. There is an open fire in the first-floor lobby and a tavern in the cellar. Closed Nov–Mar. **www.pironihotel.it**

GHIFFA Castello di Frino €
Via C Colombo 8, 28823 **Tel** *0323 591 81* **Fax** *0323 597 83* **Rooms** *14*

The former residence of Cardinal Morigia (1623–1701) has been architecturally restored to its former glory. It boasts ornamental details and wonderful parkland with a formal garden, pool and lake. The dark period furniture and simplicity of decor set a sober, quasi-religious tone. Good restaurant with terrace. **www.castellodifrino.com**

GHIFFA Hotel Ghiffa €
Corso Belvedere 88, 28823 **Tel** *0323 592 85* **Fax** *0323 595 85* **Rooms** *39*

Ghiffa offers its guests lots of sporting opportunities, plus a large pool, sun terrace with loungers, private beach and landing stage for boats. The elegant villa-like hotel has simple decor and the rooms with lake views have floor-to-ceiling windows. Ask for one with a balcony or terrace. **www.hotelghiffa.com**

GHIFFA Park Hotel Paradiso €
Via Marconi 20, 28823 **Tel** *0323 595 48* **Fax** *0323 598 78* **Rooms** *15*

This early 20th-century villa is now a family-run hotel in a beautiful setting. Peaceful, charming and welcoming, it sits on a steep road above the lake amid exotic botanical gardens with palms, banana plants and hydrangeas. Well kept and neat, it has plenty of Art Nouveau decorative details, as well as an outdoor pool and tennis court.

ISOLA DEI PESCATORI, STRESA Verbano 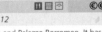 €€€
Via Ugo Ara 2, 28838 **Tel** *0323 304 08; 0323 325 34* **Fax** *0323 331 29* **Rooms** *12*

Hotel Verbano has an idyllic setting on an island in the lake, overlooking Isola Bella and Palazzo Borromeo. It has charming rooms named after flowers, such as Camelia and Daisy. Enjoy breakfast on the terrace, listen to the waves lapping on the shore and take in the lake views. There is a shuttle boat service from Stresa. **www.hotelverbano.it**

RANCO Il Sole di Ranco €€€€
Piazza Venezia 5, 20120 **Tel** *0331 97 65 07* **Fax** *0331 97 66 20* **Rooms** *14*

Located amid verdant parkland leading to the shores of Lake Maggiore, this hotel boasts a private garden, views from the excellent restaurant where you can dine alfreso in the summer and even a helicopter landing area. It has undergone recent extensions and improved facilities include a pool, sauna and *hammam*. **www.ilsolediranco.it**

STRESA Villa Aminta  €€€€
Via Sempione Nord 123, 28838 **Tel** *0323 93 38 18* **Fax** *0323 93 39 55* **Rooms** *66*

North of Stresa, this beautiful villa is set in its own flower-filled park, with great views of the islands on the lake. The five-star hotel has elegant decor throughout, including chandeliers, trompe-l'oeil paintings and ornate gilt. There is a piano lounge, refined restaurant, pool and tennis court. Closed Nov–Feb. **www.villa-aminta.it**

STRESA Grand Hotel Iles de Borromées

Corso Umberto I 67, 28838 **Tel** *0323 938 938* **Fax** *0323 324 05* **Rooms** *172*

This imposing *belle époque* hotel was once a favourite with royalty. It features palatial decor as well as lake and alpine views. The facilities are excellent, ranging from sports amenities to beauty and fitness, piano bar, extensive lush gardens, pools, tennis courts and a great restaurant. Stunning setting and great service. **www.borromees.it**

LAKE COMO

BELLAGIO Florence

Piazza Mazzini 46, 22021 **Tel** *031 95 03 42* **Fax** *031 95 17 22* **Rooms** *30*

In a great location on the shores of Lake Como, this stylish hotel has elegant modern decor, with canopy beds, roll-top baths, a charming bar and a gourmet restaurant. A shady terrace offers guests wonderful views of the lake. Extra facilities include a spa with sauna, Turkish bath and Jacuzzi. **www.hotelflorencebellagio.it**

BELLAGIO La Pergola

Piazza del Porto 4, 22021 **Tel** *031 95 02 63* **Fax** *031 95 02 53* **Rooms** *11*

This former convent dating back to 1500 has a peaceful lakeside location in a tiny fishing hamlet. Interesting features include vaulted ceilings, frescoes and antique furniture. Enjoy the views from the terrace restaurant, which serves regional cuisine. Credit cards are not accepted. Closed Dec–Feb. **www.lapergolabellagio.it**

BELLAGIO Grand Hotel Villa Serbelloni

Via Roma 1, 22021 **Tel** *031 95 02 16* **Fax** *031 95 15 29* **Rooms** *81*

Set in a breathtaking position on a headland between two branches of the lake, Villa Serbelloni was once the holiday home of Milanese aristocracy. Frescoes, Italianate gardens full of plants, period wall coverings, marble staircases and crystal echo the prestige of this Neo-Classical villa. Ask for a large room with a lake view. **www.villaserbelloni.com**

COMO Hotel Firenze

Piazza Volta 16, 22100 **Tel** *031 30 03 33* **Fax** *031 30 01 01* **Rooms** *44*

This recently renovated Neo-Classic hotel sits in a pedestrianised square in the town centre, a short walk from the lakeside, with a terrace on which to enjoy an apéritif. The rooms have a basic contemporary design, though some retain original beams or parquet flooring. Ask for one looking onto the inner courtyard. **www.albergofirenze.it**

COMO Le Due Corti

Piaza Vittoria 12/3, 22100 **Tel** *031 32 81 11* **Fax** *031 32 88 00* **Rooms** *60*

This antique palazzo, a monastery in the 18th century, is close to the old city walls and features nice rooms with original brick walls and ceilings, as well as several courtyards, one of them now housing the pool. The excellent restaurant is located in the old stable wing. Dine alfresco in summer. Self-catering apartments are also available.

COMO Metropole Suisse

Piazza Cavour 19, 22100 **Tel** *031 26 94 44* **Fax** *031 30 08 08* **Rooms** *71*

Located in the heart of Como, this hotel commands great views over the lake. The façade by famous architect Comasco Terragni dates back to 1892 and incorporates wrought-iron balconies for most rooms. Boat trips leave from the pier in front of the hotel. Choose between formal or informal dining. **www.hotelmetropolesuisse.com**

COMO Terminus

Lungo Lario Trieste 14, 22100 **Tel** *031 32 91 11* **Fax** *031 30 25 50* **Rooms** *40*

Before being converted into a hotel, this was the 19th-century home to Lombard aristocracy. It is full of atmosphere, with Art Nouveau details, beautiful frescoes and tapestries. The decor is colourful, with precious fabrics and floral bedspreads. There are also formal gardens, a lovely terrace and a small restaurant. **www.hotelterminus-como.it**

COMO Grand Hotel Villa d'Este

Via Regina 40, 22012 **Tel** *031 34 81* **Fax** *031 34 88 44* **Rooms** *154*

A sumptuous, luxurious *grande dame* of a hotel, with elegantly appointed rooms. Period furniture, fine paintings, chandeliers, marble fireplaces and the finest silk add to the old-world charm and feeling of a private palatial villa. The hotel is steeped in history but not lacking in modern services and facilities. **www.villadeste.it**

LENNO San Giorgio

Via Regina 81, 22016 **Tel** *0344 404 15* **Fax** *0344 415 91* **Rooms** *26*

A calm hotel with large gardens facing Lake Como and wonderful panoramic views. The 1920s building has period-style rooms with modern facilities and bathrooms. A lovely terrace, tennis courts and a good restaurant serving fish fresh from the lake add to its charm. Ask for a room with lake views. Closed mid-Oct–Easter.

TORNO Villa Flora

Via Torrazza 10, 22020 **Tel** *031 41 92 22* **Fax** *031 41 83 18* **Rooms** *20*

An old villa with spacious rooms, lovely gardens and a terrace bar facing the lake. The best corner rooms face Como, located 7 km (4.3 miles) away. Guests come here to enjoy the unique peaceful setting, not the villa's interior, which is spartan and somewhat dated. Pool and beach with landing stage. **www.vademecumturistico.com/villaflora.htm**

TREMEZZO Grand Hotel Tremezzo

Via Regina 8, 22019 **Tel** *0344 424 91* **Fax** *0344 402 01* **Rooms** *98*

This prestigious and recently renovated lakeside hotel built in Art Nouveau style in 1910 is surrounded by gardens and terraces with lake views. The grand hotel feel is echoed in the ornate gilt and splendid antiques. There is also a floating pool on the lake. Sauna, gym, tennis courts and golf facilities are available. **www.grandhoteltremezzo.com**

VARENNA Hotel du Lac

Via del Prestino 4, 23829 **Tel** *0341 83 02 38* **Fax** *0341 83 10 81* **Rooms** *17*

A smallish hotel at the water's edge with enchanting views from the lake-facing rooms. Enjoy the terrace restaurant under vines at the side of hotel, looking out over the lapping water. Charming features include marble columns, wrought-iron balustrades and the floral names given to every room. Tranquil and relaxing. **www.albergodulac.com**

LAKE GARDA

DESENZANO DEL GARDA Piroscafo

Via Porto Vecchio 11, 25015 **Tel** *030 914 11 28* **Fax** *030 991 25 86* **Rooms** *32*

Located at the old dock of the town in a tranquil, historic building. The terrace on the ground floor is housed in an arched portico. Pick a room looking out on to the dock or watch the boats from the terrace restaurant, which serves a simple menu of fish and international dishes. Parking is available nearby. **www.hotelpiroscafo.it**

DESENZANO DEL GARDA Tripoli

Piazza Matteotti 18, 25015 **Tel** *030 914 13 05* **Fax** *030 914 43 33* **Rooms** *24*

This pleasant and relatively quiet hotel overlooking the harbour in Desenzano sits on the pretty pedestrianised promenade overlooking the lake. The basic bedrooms are comfortable and pleasant; be aware that you need to book well ahead for a room with a balcony and lake view. **www.gardalake.it/hotel-tripoli**

FASANO, GARDONE RIVIERA Grand Hotel Fasano

Corso Zandarelli 190, 25083 **Tel** *0365 29 02 20* **Fax** *0365 29 02 21* **Rooms** *87*

This former Austrian imperial hunting lodge set in private parkland with semi-tropical vegetation is now a luxurious and romantic hotel. The rooms are fairly small, but some have four-poster beds, classic Italian-style decor and balconies. The Fasano also boasts the fine restaurant, Il Fagiano and an Aveda spa. **www.grand-hotel-fasano.it**

GARDONE Villa Capri

Via Zandarelli 172, 25083 **Tel** *0365 215 37* **Fax** *0365 227 20* **Rooms** *55*

Located between Fasano and Gardone, Villa Capri has an air of old worldliness. This family-run hotel has great views and setting; the grounds are breathtaking, with lawns, ancient trees, a pool and a bathing jetty in the lake. Rooms are standard, simply furnished and compact. Closed Nov–Mar. **www.hotelvillacapri.com**

GARDONE RIVIERA Hotel du Lac

Via Repubblica 58, 25083 **Tel** *0365 215 58* **Fax** *0365 219 66* **Rooms** *44*

Located on the water's edge, in front of the ferry landing stage, this hotel boasts a panoramic outdoor terrace, snack bar, lounge bar and restaurant. Rooms are simply but tastefully decorated and half of them have lake views. The hotel can organise boat trips, golf and transfers to the Gardaland fun park. **www.gardalake.it/hotel-dulac**

GARDONE RIVIERA Villa Fiordaliso

Corso Zandarelli 132, 25083 **Tel** *0365 201 58* **Fax** *0365 29 00 11* **Rooms** *7*

This beautiful four-story villa overlooking Lake Garda is situated ten minutes from the centre of Gardone. All rooms are named after flowers and the eclectic decor reflects the name. The hotel also boasts a lovely garden. Try the regional specials in the restaurant, especially the fresh catch of lake fish. **www.villafiordaliso.it**

GARDONE RIVIERA Villa del Sogno

Via Zandarelli 107, 25083 **Tel** *0365 29 01 81* **Fax** *0365 29 02 30* **Rooms** *30*

This splendid Neo-Classical villa boasts a peaceful panoramic position. It is set in a large park not far from the town centre. Enjoy facilities such as tennis and a great pool, or hire a car to explore the surrounding countryside and towns before dining on the creative Italian cuisine in the villa's restaurant. **www.villadelsogno.it**

GARDONE SOPRA Locanda Agli Angeli

Piazza Garibaldi 2, 25083 **Tel** *0365 208 32* **Fax** *0365 207 46* **Rooms** *16*

This little hotel is a short walk from the lake, between the Botanical Gardens and the Vittoriale. The rooms are located in two houses above the popular eponymous trattoria. Rooms are spacious and stylish, and both the hotel and restaurant are decorated with furniture from Bali. There is also a lovely sun veranda. **www.agliangeli.com**

LIMONE SUL GARDA Capo Reamol

Via IV Novembre 92, 25010 **Tel** *0365 95 40 40* **Fax** *0365 95 42 62* **Rooms** *58*

The hotel sits on the lakeside in a verdant area 3 km (1.8 miles) from Limone – take the bus or use the hotel's bikes. Boasting a private beach, pool, and balconies with lake views for all the rooms, plus an excellent surf school, it is ideal for families keen on sport. Closed mid-Oct–mid-Apr. **www.hotelcaporeamol.com**

Key to Price Guide *see p160* **Key to Symbols** *see back cover flap*

RIVA DEL GARDA Feeling Hotel Luise

Viale Rovereto 9, 38066 **Tel** *0464 55 08 58* **Fax** *0464 55 42 50* **Rooms** *68*

This recently renovated hotel is close to the centre of Riva del Garda and the lakeside. It h.
swimming pool, and welcomes cyclists and mountain-bike enthusiasts. A good family hotel
miniclub for children in high summer. **www.feelinghotelluise.com**

RIVA DEL GARDA Du Lac et du Parc

Viale Rovereto 44, 38066 **Tel** *0464 56 66 00* **Fax** *0464 56 65 66* **Rooms** *164*

Du Lac et du Parc is a large modern building with wooden decking on the north shore of Lake Garda. S.
grounds with ancient trees and exotic plants, it offers a good range of sports, a well-reputed sailing club
school plus spa and pools, making it a good choice for active families. **www.dulacetduparc.com**

RIVA DI SOLTO Albergo Ristorante Miranda

Via Cornello 8, 24060 **Tel** *035 98 60 21* **Fax** *035 98 00 55* **Rooms** *25*

A peaceful panoramic setting on a hillside overlooking Lago d'Iseo. This simple family-run *pensione* offers comfortable
rooms, all with balconies. There is an outdoor pool in an olive grove and a play area for kids. Good fresh fish dishes are
offered in the terrace restaurant by the lake. **www.albergomiranda.it**

SALÒ Laurin

€€€€

Viale Landi 9, 25087 **Tel** *0365 220 22* **Fax** *0365 223 82* **Rooms** *30*

A romantic lakeside villa on a hillside overlooking Lake Garda. It features sweeping gardens, spacious bedrooms, a
beach, outdoor pool and tennis courts. Dine under frescoes in the elegant restaurant or alfresco on the terrace under
the stars. A warm and welcoming atmosphere. Minimum stay is three nights. **www.laurinsalo.com**

SIRMIONE Villa Cortine

€€€€€

Via Grotte 6, 25019 **Tel** *030 990 58 90* **Fax** *030 91 63 90* **Rooms** *54*

A huge, luxurious Neo-Classical villa in a tranquil setting of lush, immaculate gardens. Enjoy the splendid meandering
paths through parkland, ponds, mythological fountains, a cypress grove by the lake, statues and a jetty with loungers.
The lakeside terrace offers summer lunches of barbecued meat and fish. **www.hotelvillacortine.com**

LAGO D'ISEO

ERBUSCO L'Albereta

 €€€€€

Via Vittorio Emanuele 23, 25030 **Tel** *030 776 05 50* **Fax** *030 776 05 73* **Rooms** *57*

This old country mansion was converted to a luxurious hotel and restaurant run by chef Gualtiero Marchesi. The
wonderful setting of the hotel is inland from Lago d'Iseo, surrounded by vineyards and beautiful countryside.
Excellent food and wines, and a wellness beauty spa. High-quality design and fine furnishings. **www.albereta.it**

ISEO I Due Roccoli

 €€

Via Silvio Bonomelli, 25049 **Tel** *030 982 29 77* **Fax** *030 982 29 80* **Rooms** *19*

Housed in a charming patrician home, this fine rustic residence has a country setting but still offers panoramic views
over the lake from its rooms and terrace. The converted farmhouse has a good restaurant with regional cuisine, and
the hotel also offers a swimming pool and tennis. Impressive parkland all around. **www.idueroccoli.com**

LAGO D'ORTA

ORTA SAN GIULIO Hotel Orta

€

Piazza Motta 1, 28016 **Tel** *0322 902 53* **Fax** *0322 90 56 46* **Rooms** *25*

Charming Hotel Orta has a romantic feel. Dating back to 1864, it is situated in an old square full of noble houses,
porticoes and chestnut trees. Some rooms have lake views and little balconies. There is also a lakeside terrace and a
landing stage for boats. The restaurant has a veranda and a panoramic view of the lake. **www.hotelorta.it**

ORTA SAN GIULIO Hotel San Rocco

€€€€

Via Gippini 11, 28016 **Tel** *0322 91 19 77* **Fax** *0322 91 19 64* **Rooms** *85*

A splendid hotel overlooking Lago d'Orta, with stunning terraces to lounge in and soak up the views. Converted
from a 17th-century convent, it still retains the tranquillity of former days. Facilities include a spa with sauna and
massage, and a private boat for tours round the lake. **www.hotelsanrocco.it**

ORTA SAN GIULIO Villa Crespi

 €€€€

Via Fava 18, 28016 **Tel** *0322 91 19 02* **Fax** *0322 91 19 19* **Rooms** *14*

Surrounded by woodland, this unique fairytale hotel is located within an Islamic villa with murals, minarets and
precious fabrics, reminiscent of *Arabian Nights*. Luxurious marble and mosaics are everywhere. It has a first-class
restaurant and a fitness centre with sauna. Its elaborate design makes it unique. **www.hotelvillacrespi.it**

WHERE TO EAT

...osmopolitan city ...rs a wide range of ...rants in all price ... As well as Milanese ...n cooking (the latter ...ome a real speciality of ...ty), ethnic cuisine has ...ntly come to the fore – from ...orth African to Oriental and ...ven South American, reflecting the city's multicultural character. The fish restaurants are excellent, offering skilfully prepared fish and seafood.

The Barchetta chef, Bellagio *(see p180)*

Restaurants are at their most crowded at the weekend, and it is often best to book in advance. Sunday brunch has become part and parcel of the Milanese life style, and a number of cafés offer this late morning meal. At the lakes there are restaurants with terraces overlooking the water, and cafés with tables outside. Menus are dominated by fish dishes and local specialities. For more detailed information, see the chart on pages 172–83, with a selection of 122 restaurants.

CHOOSING A RESTAURANT

In Milan the Brera and Navigli districts are filled with both trendy restaurants and inexpensive eateries. Around the Brera quarter, the fashion crowd congregate at the hip **La Briciola** *(see p178)*, while vegetarians head for **Joia** *(see p178)*, which also serves some fish dishes. Those on a budget will find many options around the Navigli, such as the Neapolitan-inspired **Pizzeria Tradizionale con Cucina di Pesce** *(see p173)* and **Premiata Pizzeria** *(see p174)*. Near Porta Genova is **Osteria del Binario** *(see p174)*, serving Lombard and Piedmontese dishes. The **Centro Ittico** *(see p177)* and **Malavoglia** *(see p177)*, near the fish market, have excellent fresh fish.

Classic restaurants in the city centre include **Boeucc**

The Premiata Pizzeria sign, Milan *(see p174)*

(see p172) and the historic **Savini** *(see p173)*, both of which specialize in traditional Milanese cuisine. Also popular are **Aimo e Nadia** *(see p174)*, in the Bande Nere district, and **Il Pesce d'Oro** *(see p178)*, near the Città Studi.

Some of Italy's best restaurants are in beautiful locations near the lakes. At Lake Maggiore, **Il Sole di Ranco** *(see p179)* is one of Italy's finest, while at Lake Como good places include **Barchetta** *(see p180)* at Bellagio and **Raimondi del Villa Flori** *(see p180)*, a hotel/restaurant near Como. Lake Garda also boasts excellent restaurants, such as **Villa Fiordaliso** *(see p182)*, at Gardone. At Erbusco (Lake Iseo), is **Gualtiero Marchesi** *(see p183)*, the restaurant of Italy's most famous chef.

To prevent disappointment, book a table ahead if there is a restaurant you are particularly keen on trying.

The counter at La Briciola, in the Brera quarter of Milan *(see p178)*

ETIQUETTE

Not surprisingly, the Milanese are very dress-conscious: they like to dress up for dinner, and indeed looking smart will also ensure better (and speedier) service.

In 2005 new regulations came into force in Italy, and now restaurants and bars must provide separate no-smoking areas or face a fine. Smokers who light up in no-smoking areas are also liable to a fine. At cafés and restaurants that do not provide sealed-off areas, smoking is limited to outside tables.

EATING HOURS

Lunch is generally served between 1 and 2:30pm. Dinner is usually at about 8pm and goes on until about 11pm (or later in summer). Most restaurants close during the month of August.

TYPES OF RESTAURANTS

Milan offers an unusually wide range of types of cuisine for an Italian city. Alongside traditional Italian cooking you can also find Asian, North African and Mexican food of all kinds. Classic Milanese cooking survives in the traditional

The refined interior of Boeucc, in the centre of Milan *(see p172)*

restaurants of the centre. International cuisine is found in places frequented by business people. Italian regional cooking, from Tuscan to Piedmontese, Neapolitan and Sicilian, is increasingly popular in Milan.

There are several different types of restaurant. Traditionally, a *ristorante* is smarter and more expensive than an *osteria* or a *trattoria*, but the divisions are increasingly blurred. A pizzeria is usually an inexpensive place to eat and many serve pasta, meat and fish dishes as well as pizza. Those with wood-fired ovens *(forno a legna)* are the most highly rated. Milan's pizzerias tend to be more expensive than in the rest of Italy but the quality is excellent thanks to the many Neapolitan pizza chefs in the city. An *enoteca* or *vineria* is a place to taste wine and sample snacks.

Genuine small trattorias still abound as well as the increasingly rare *latterie* (dairies), which are small, crowded kitchens.

The Milan fish market is one of the best in Italy, and the city's excellent seafood restaurants guarantee superfresh fish.

At the lakes, much use is made of local fish such as carp, tench and shad, and you will also find regional specialities – in particular, Piedmontese, Valtellinese and Veneto cooking.

Gualtiero Marchesi's restaurant at Erbusco, Lago d'Iseo *(see p183)*

Raimondi del Villa Flori, Lake Como *(see p180)*

vine cellar in the famous Il Sole di Ranco rant, Lake Maggiore *(see p179)*

READING THE MENU

A classic Italian dinner begins with an *antipasto* or starter. The first course *(il primo)* is likely to be pasta or risotto but may be a hearty soup. The main course *(il secondo)* consists of meat or fish served with a side dish of vegetables *(contorno)*. Dessert *(il dessert)* follows and may consist of fruit, ice cream or pastries. Coffee *(il caffè)* comes next, and maybe a digestif.

A typical Milanese dinner might consist of *nervetti*, or *nervitt* (calf cartilage with oil, vinegar and onions), followed by *risotto alla milanese*, and then a veal cutlet *(cottoletta)*. Other classic dishes are *ossobuco* (a cut of veal including the bone and its marrow) and *casoeûla* (a dish of pork and cabbage served with polenta).

Vegetarians will find that many pasta dishes are meat-free. Autumn is good for non-meat eaters, as wild mushrooms and pumpkins start to appear on the menu. Cheeses are also a good option.

PAYING

Menus are usually posted outside restaurants, with prices. An unavoidable extra is the cover charge *(coperto)*, which is charged per person. In general Milanese restaurants accept major credit cards, except for some of the smaller, family-run trattorias, where you will need cash. Commonly accepted cards include Visa and MasterCard. Even restaurants in the smaller villages around the lakes now increasingly accept credit cards. When paying for a meal (the Italian for the bill is *il conto*), it is normal to leave a small tip.

WHEELCHAIR ACCESS

Unfortunately, not all Milanese restaurants have facilities for the disabled. Wheelchair access may be even more of a problem at the lakes, with restaurants often sited at the top of long slopes or paths with steps. Do telephone the restaurant beforehand for advice.

CHILDREN'S FACILITIES

Less expensive places such as trattorias and pizzerias are ideal for children. They may be less welcome in Milan's sophisticated restaurants. Restaurant owners at the lakes are more accustomed to families with children, and can often provide smaller portions if required.

he Flavours of Milan and the Lakes

As a powerhouse of industry, finance and fashion, Milan, more than any other Italian city, has embraced international cuisine. The Milanese are quick to adopt new culinary trends and food fads come and go. But there has also been a long-standing interest in rediscovering the historic cuisine of the region. Like the prosperous city itself, this traditional food is rich. Milanese risottos are laced with butter and Parmesan, and even the local asparagus is likely to arrive at the table topped with an egg and grated cheese. Increasingly chefs are now scaling down the fats and substituting olive oil to suit today's health-conscious palates.

Asparagus

Selection of salami at a delicatessen, Cremona

MILAN

The city is surrounded by vast agricultural plains that provide an abundance of fresh produce, including meat, cereals, cheese and vegetables. The Milanese are great meat-eaters – pork, veal and game are all very popular. The region's typical hearty casseroles were once the staples of the local peasant diet, combining whatever meat, grains and vegetables happened to be available. Filling *minestre* soups with added rice or pasta stem from the same tradition. A more elaborate cuisine also developed at the courts of the ruling Visconti and Sforza families. Recipes created there are still being prepared by Milanese chefs today. Spanish rule in the 16th century led to rice being grown with other crops along the Po valley. This was used to make risotto – a direct descendant of paella. Saffron, cultivated locally, was added to flavour Milanese risottos, giving them their characteristic yellow hue. Again, the grain was cooked with anything that was in season to make a filling meal –

Grana Padano   **Gorgonzola**   **Fontina**   **Bel Paese**   **Mascarpone**   **Taleggio**

Mouthwatering range of northeast Italy's excellent cheeses

LOCAL DISHES AND SPECIALITIES

Rich dishes with meat and offal are traditional Milanese fare. Meals often start with slices of cured meats or the fine-grained *salame di Milano*. Popular main courses include *cassouela*, a rich stew of pork, cabbage and sausage, served with polenta; *busecca alla Milanese*, tripe with onion, carrot, sage and celery; and *fritto misto alla Milanese*, fried mixed offal coated in breadcrumbs. Seasonal specialities are *fagiano alla Milanese*, braised spiced pheasant, and *rise spargitt*, rice and asparagus. From the lakes come *alborelle fritte*, tiny fish, floured and deep-fried, and *missoltini*, shad, air-dried then salted and flavoured with bay leaves. A selection of regional cheeses is usually served at the end of a meal.

Panettone

Risotto alla Milanese *Rice is cooked slowly with onion, stock, wine, butter, grated Parmesan and golden saffr[o]*

Fresh vegetables on sale at a Milanese greengrocer

vegetables, freshwater fish, meat and game. Milanese risottos still tend to have a seasonal twist. In the autumn, locally grown pumpkin is often added and, in summer, wild strawberries.

During the 18th century, maize (corn) was introduced into the region and polenta – made from maize flour and water – soon became an important staple food. Today, even though pasta is hugely popular, it is just as likely that polenta and rice will be found on the table in Milan.

Rule by Austria in the late 18th century has also left its mark on the Milanese diet. The popular bread-crumbed veal *Costoletta Milanese* is a version of *Wiener schnitzel*, and *panettone* is based on the rich yeast cakes of Central Europe.

THE LAKES

Although fishing on the region's deep glacial lakes is no longer a major industry, it still plays a central role in shaping the local diet. Pike, perch, trout, tench, bleak, shad, sardines and eel are

Shad, part of a catch of fish from the clear waters of Lake Como

plentiful, while carp is more elusive and prized. The catch served at lakeside restaurants is often simply fried, grilled or poached, although it is also popular marinated and is used in risottos, soups, pâtés and as a ravioli filling.

The land around Lake Garda is particularly suited for growing vines and olive trees. Light and delicate, Garda extra virgin olive oil is perfect in salad dressings and can be bought direct from oil mills. Other regional products include capers and a delicious honey sold by local bee-keepers.

WHAT TO DRINK

Franciacorta wines The reds and whites from the Lago d' Iseo area are held in high esteem by the Milanese, especially the *spumante*.

Oltrepo Pavese wines More than 70 different varieties, both still and sparkling, are produced in ancient vineyards to the south-west of Milan.

Valtellina wines From the Swiss border, north of Lake Como, these include reds and the unusual raisin-like *sforzato* made from semi-dried grapes.

Garda wines Made from a wide variety of grapes, the reds, whites and rosés from the area around Lake Garda include a light red Bardolino, Garda Classico Groppello and Garda Classico Chiaretto. The white Lugana goes particularly well with lake-fish dishes.

Minestrone *The Milanese add beef marrow and rice to their version of this hearty bean and vegetable soup.*

Osso Bucco *Veal shanks are braised very slowly in white wine. The bone marrow is considered a delicacy.*

Trota Ripiena *Lake trout are stuffed with mushrooms, onion and parsley then poached in red wine.*

Choosing a Restaurant

The restaurants in this guide have been selected across a wide price range for the high quality of their service, decor, value and location. They have been divided into six areas and listed by price category. Milan restaurants are further subdivided according to city areas. For Milan map references, see pages 224–37 and the inside back cover.

PRICE CATEGORIES
The price ranges are for a three-course meal for one, including a half-bottle of house wine, tax and service.
€ under €30
€€ €30–€45
€€€ €45–€55
€€€€ €55–€85
€€€€€ over €85

MILAN

CITY CENTRE Serendib €

Via Pontida 2, 20121 **Tel** *02 659 21 39* **Map** *3 B2*

This Sri Lankan restaurant in the Isola district is one of Milan's best ethnic eateries. Choose from a variety of delicate curry dishes. Serendib soup is a must, with meat broth, vegetables and mixed spices, as are the spicy fried artichokes and coconut milk, or try the chicken in spicy sauce. The decor is a combination of Italian and Sri Lankan styles.

CITY CENTRE Bistrot Duomo €€

Via San Raffaele 2, 20121 **Tel** *02 87 71 20* **Map** *7 C1, 10 D3*

Located at the top of the famous department store, La Rinascente, the view from Bistrot Duomo is unbeatable. It is a great place for a cappuccino or snack while shopping or for a full evening meal. In summer it opens a terrace which faces the spires of the cathedral. The menu is typically Milanese, with veal cutlets, salads, meat and fish dishes.

CITY CENTRE Hostaria Borromei €€

Via Borromei 4, 20123 **Tel** *02 86 45 37 60* **Map** *7 B1*

In the heart of Milan's business quarter is this unpretentious family-run tavern. It has a romantic courtyard setting in an old palazzo and in summer you can sit outside under the vines. Typical dishes include home-made pumpkin-filled pasta and a platter of boiled meats served with various spicy sauces. Closed Sat lunch, Sun.

CITY CENTRE Trattoria Milanese €€

Via Santa Marta 11, 20123 **Tel** *02 86 45 19 91* **Map** *7 B1, 9 B4*

This trattoria situated between the Duomo and the Basilica di Sant'Ambrogio is a classic institution in the city. With modest, sober decor and professional staff, it has served genuine Milanese food near the Stock Exchange for generations. Good classics include *ossobuco* (veal shank) and saffron risotto. Closed Tue; mid-Jul–Aug.

CITY CENTRE Boeucc €€€

Piazza Belgioioso 2, 20121 **Tel** *02 76 02 02 24* **Map** *4 D5, 10 D2*

This is possibly Milan's oldest restaurant, dating back to 1696. It is located near La Scala, on the ground floor of an old palazzo. Its name, pronounced "butch", is old Milanese for *buco* (hole). It offers classic Milanese dishes such as saffron risotto with sausages and *cassoeula* (a pork, cabbage and salami stew). Closed Sat & Sun lunch.

CITY CENTRE Le Noir €€€

Via San Raffaele 6, 20121 **Tel** *02 720 89 51* **Map** *7 C1, 10 D3*

The refined restaurant of The Gray hotel *(see p160)*, Le Noir is famous for its style. The wenge wood tables contrast with the Rosenthal porcelain tableware and are set off by the subtle changes of coloured lighting. The food is to as high a standard as the design. The menu offers creative Mediterranean and international cuisine. Closed Aug.

CITY CENTRE Marino alla Scala €€€€

Piazza della Scala 5, 20121 **Tel** *02 80 68 82 01* **Map** *3 C5, 10 D2*

Enjoy the view of Piazza della Scala from the stylish first-floor dining room in the Palazzo Trussardi. The fashion designer's shop is on the ground floor, alongside a more casual bistro, which is always busy at lunchtimes. On the menu is a refined Mediterranean cuisine rich in fish and vegetables. Excellent wines. Closed Sat lunch, Sun.

CITY CENTRE The Park €€€€

Via Tommaso Grossi 1, 20121 **Tel** *02 88 21 12 34* **Map** *7 C1, 9 C3*

Elegance, attention to detail and sophisticated cuisine make dining at the Park Hyatt hotel's restaurant a delight. The fare is modern Italian with Mediterranean flavours and regional dishes with a twist. Choose from a list of good wines. Fine glassware and Limoges china, leather seating and beige tones. Closed Sat lunch, Sun; Aug.

CITY CENTRE Cracco Peck €€€€€

Via Victor Hugo 4, 20123 **Tel** *02 87 67 74* **Map** *7 C1, 9 C3*

One of Milan's best restaurants, with a modern interior and the cuisine of master chef Carlo Cracco, not to mention a Michelin star. It is linked to the superb Peck delicatessen just around the corner. Delights include veal in breadcrumbs and suckling pig on a spit with artichokes. Exceptional desserts. Closed Sat lunch, Sun (Sat & Sun in Jun–Aug).

Key to Symbols *see back cover flap*

CITY CENTRE Savini

Galleria Vittorio Emanuele II, 20121 **Tel** *02 72 00 34 33*   **Map** *7 C1, 10 D3*

This elegant restaurant in the Galleria Vittorio Emanuele is favoured by older clients and business people. It is full of *belle époque* charm. The fare is high quality, with prices to match. The specials are typically Milanese dishes: ox muzzle fried with sweet red onions, balsamic vinegar and raisins, and *ossobuco* (veal shank). Closed Sun; 3 wks Aug.

NORTHWEST MILAN Tagiura

Via Tagiura 5, 20146 **Tel** *02 48 95 06 13*   **Map** *5 C2*

Known locally as *Il Bar Bello* (the beautiful bar), this pleasant bar-cum-restaurant is a great spot for lunch, or just a coffee and pastry during the day. In the evening it is open only on Thursdays and Fridays, so booking is essential. They serve traditional food from Piacenza, including meat and pasta, plus a wide selection of cured meats. Closed Sun.

NORTHWEST MILAN La Fermata

Via Saronno 3, 20154 **Tel** *02 345 15 96*   **Map** *2 E2*

La Fermata is a small, crowded and convivial restaurant with simple decor serving great Neapolitan cuisine. All the southern Italian dishes are good, providing an alternative from Milanese fare, but the fish is especially praiseworthy. Squid salad is a delicious speciality, as is ricotta cake. Closed lunch; Sun; 3 wks Aug.

NORTHWEST MILAN Osteria della Cagnola

Via D Cirillo 14, 20100 **Tel** *02 331 94 28*   **Map** *2 F3*

Situated in the Parco Sempione area, near the *Arco della Pace*, this cosy little restaurant dates back to 1940. It has a rustic feel and a simple, homely interior, but the clientele come here for the great food, not the design. It features an extensive menu with good antipasti, excellent meat and fish and home-made desserts. Closed Sun.

NORTHWEST MILAN Primo Novecento

Via Ruggero di Lauria 17, 20100 **Tel** *02 33 61 16 43*   **Map** *2 D1*

This restaurant serves classic Italian cuisine, mainly fish, influenced by Mediterranean touches. Turn-of-the-century black-and-white photos line the walls. Specialities include linguine with scampi in ginger and sherry, mixed fried seafood, and chocolate fondue Bourguignonne. Closed Sat lunch, Sun; 3 wks Aug; 26 Dec–7 Jan.

NORTHWEST MILAN Quattro Mori

Largo Maria Callas 1, 20121 **Tel** *02 87 84 83*   **Map** *3 B5, 9 B3*

Quattro Mori specializes in fish but also offers delicious grilled meats, vegetable and pasta dishes. The owners are friendly and welcoming, the pasta is home-made and the classic antipasti are a treat. Make sure you leave some room for the chef's fine desserts. In summer you can dine on the garden terrace. Closed Sat lunch, Sun; Aug.

NORTHWEST MILAN Taverna dela Trisa

Via Ferruccio 1, 20145 **Tel** *02 34 13 04*   **Map** *2 E2*

This typical trattoria specializes in Trentino cuisine. Close to the Fiera exhibition ground with a garden for summer dining. Good regional wines accompany the hearty Italian food, such as cured ham, dumplings and mushrooms. It has a homely and intimate atmosphere, subtle lighting and dark wood interior. Closed Mon, Sun; Aug.

NORTHWEST MILAN Alfredo Gran San Bernardo

Via Borgese 14, 20154 **Tel** *02 331 90 00*   **Map** *2 D1*

A traditional Milanese restaurant opened by veteran chef Alfredo Valli in 1964 in a residential area of the city, east of Piazza Firenze. Valli's breaded veal cutlet is legendary. Other dishes include risotto with sea salt, tagliatelle in meat sauce and beef in red wine. The dining rooms are smart and plainly decorated. Closed Sat–Sun in Jun–Jul.

NORTHWEST MILAN Da Leo

Via Trivulzio 26, 20146 **Tel** *02 40 07 14 45*   **Map** *1 B5*

This is an unpretentious restaurant with very good quality food. The owner visits the fish market daily to select the finest catch which is then fried or grilled. Seafood with spaghetti is also served. There are few tables, so book ahead. Ask the friendly waiters for the day's specials. Closed Mon, Sun dinner.

NORTHWEST MILAN Trattoria Franca

Viale Certosa 235, 20151 **Tel** *02 38 00 62 38*   **Map** *2 D1*

Franca is an excellent family-run trattoria in the northern outskirts of the city. The seasonal produce is carefully sourced throughout Italy and transformed into great Lombard dishes. Ask about the daily specials and try the excellent wine. This cosy and well-designed restaurant gets pretty busy, so book well ahead. Closed Sat, Sun.

SOUTHWEST MILAN L'Oca Giuliva

Viale Bligny 29, 20136 **Tel** *02 58 31 28 71*   **Map** *7 C4*

"The happy goose", as this restaurant is called, has a lively atmosphere and lots of goose-related images and ornaments. The popular Puglian cuisine has Mediterranean influences. Try the prawns in saffron or gnocchi made with chestnuts and cheese. The pizzas are good too. The kitchen stays open until 11pm. Closed Mon lunch; 2 wks Aug.

SOUTHWEST MILAN Pizzeria Tradizionale con Cucina di Pesce

Ripa di Porta Ticinese 7, 20144 **Tel** *02 839 51 33*   **Map** *6 D4*

This traditional pizzeria serves excellent Neapolitan-style wood-oven baked pizzas, plus pasta dishes with seafood and fish. The fresh fish dishes vary daily. The interior is styled in old Milanese fashion, and in the summer months you can sit outside by the canal. Book ahead. Closed Wed lunch.

SOUTHWEST MILAN Premiata Pizzeria

Via Alzaia Naviglio Grande 2, 20144 **Tel** *02 89 40 06 48*

Map *7 A4*

A great, affordable pizzeria in a central location near the canals. Tables are available in a lovely courtyard at the back when the weather is warm. Service can be hurried and the seating is communal on long tables, but they do serve good pizzas and pasta dishes. Alternatively, try the Parma ham focaccia or the rocket (arugula) salad.

SOUTHWEST MILAN Al Pont de Ferr'

Ripa di Porta Ticinese 55, 20143 **Tel** *02 89 40 62 77*

Map *6 D4*

Typical Milanese tavern on the Navigli blending traditional cuisine with modern flair. Good antipasti include courgette flower flans, salamis and bean soups. The restaurant is renowned for its great variety of cheeses, from taleggio to gorgonzola and fontina. Also recommended is the Argentine beef fillet. A wide selection of wines is available.

SOUTHWEST MILAN Aurora

Via Savona 23, 20144 **Tel** *02 89 40 49 78*

Map *5 B4*

Aurora serves Piedmontese cuisine in the heart of Milan. This local favourite offers specials such as wafer-thin veal in a creamy sauce, stuffed ravioli tossed in butter and sage and roast meat on skewers. In summer take advantage of the lovely vine-covered shady garden and in winter enjoy the cosy turn-of-the-century dining room. Closed Mon.

SOUTHWEST MILAN Osteria del Binario

Via Tortona 1, 20100 **Tel** *02 89 40 94 28*

Map *6 E3*

Located behind Porta Genova station in a *casa ringhiera* (a traditional Milanese dwelling with an open terrace), this informal restaurant offers genuine Lombard cuisine, from *ossobuco* (veal shank) to a wide range of cold meats. The service is friendly and efficient. Closed lunch; Sun.

SOUTHWEST MILAN Osteria di Via Pre

Via Casale 4, 20144 **Tel** *02 837 38 69*

Map *6 F4*

A simple, historic tavern serving Ligurian seafood specials that harness the delicate flavours of the coast. Try the stuffed vegetable antipasti, swordfish *carpaccio* (thin, raw slices), organic pesto from Albenga, *pansotti* (pasta filled with ricotta, lemon and herbs) with nut sauce or the fish ravioli. Excellent for seafood. Closed Mon.

SOUTHWEST MILAN Osteria Grand Hotel

Via A Sforza 75, 20136 **Tel** *02 89 51 15 86*

Map *7 A4*

Owner Fabrizio is head of one of Milan's Slow Food groups and he practices what he preaches. The ingredients are fresh, and the food is excellent. Try the gnocchi with smoked ricotta or the venison cutlet in apple and cheese sauce. Competent and courteous service, good wine list and traditional old-tavern atmosphere. Closed lunch; Mon; Aug.

SOUTHWEST MILAN Osteria Porta Cicca

Ripa di Porta Ticinese 51, 20143 **Tel** *02 837 27 63*

Map *6 D4*

This typical *osteria* (tavern) in Milan's canal district gives traditional Italian cuisine a creative slant. The menu offers good-quality meat and fish dishes and home-made pastas. Small but not over-crowded, the restaurant has well-placed tables and subtle music. A pleasant, welcoming ambience. Booking is advisable. Closed Sat lunch, Sun.

SOUTHWEST MILAN Pace

Via G Washington 74, 20146 **Tel** *02 46 85 67*

Map *5 C1*

An honest and unpretentious Tuscan trattoria with wood-panelled walls and white linen tablecloths. The menu focuses on traditional cuisine based on meat and fish. Specials include ravioli in broth, mushroom and bean soup and, on Mondays, *bollito* (boiled meats with spicy mustard). Closed Wed, Sat lunch.

SOUTHWEST MILAN Rifugio Pugliese

Via Boni 16, 20144 **Tel** *02 48 00 09 17*

Map *6 D2*

Rifugio Pugliese is a lively and pleasant restaurant just outside the centre of Milan, in the Universtiy district. Sample Puglian specialities like pasta with turnip tops, home-made *orecchiette* (a small, ear-shape pasta) with a variety of sauces or mozzarella served with cherry tomatoes. Book ahead. Closed Sun; Aug.

SOUTHWEST MILAN Noy

Via Soresina 4, off Via Mauri, 20144 **Tel** *02 48 11 03 75*

Map *6 E1*

Noy is part of the trendy *Habits Culti* complex, where a lifestyle store, spa and healthy restaurant with lounge and bar were designed in an old garage. The menu features contemporary cuisine with meat, fish and vegetables. The friendly ambience is dedicated to the feel-good factor, and the design is high-tech industrial. Closed Mon; 2 wks Aug.

SOUTHWEST MILAN Aimo e Nadia

Via Montecuccoli 6, 20147 **Tel** *02 41 68 86*

Map *5 A5*

Expect creative pan-Italian cuisine at Aimo e Nadia. Perfect pasta dishes and game in autumn, such as veal tenderloin or guinea fowl. The finest ingredients, from seafood to vegetables, are blended into superb culinary delights. Worth the trip out to the suburbs for the truffle risotto. Closed Sat lunch, Sun; Aug.

SOUTHWEST MILAN Al Porto

Piazzale Generale Cantore **Tel** *02 89 40 74 25*

Map *6 F3*

One of Milan's most popular seafood restaurants, Al Porto has been around since 1907. Some of the fish dishes include sea bass in white wine and olives, seafood risotto and the traditional *fritto misto*, a platter of mixed fried fish and seafood. The warm antipasti are good, as is the selection of Friulian wines. Closed Mon lunch, Sun; Aug.

Key to Price Guide *see p172* **Key to Symbols** *see back cover flap*

SOUTHWEST MILAN L'Assassino €€€€
Via Amedei 8, 20123 **Tel** *02 805 61 44* **Map** *7 C2, 9 C4*

This large trattoria has a vaulted, classic Italian kitchen. The menu is Tuscan, with well-prepared ingredients and fine wines. Good antipasti, meat stews and dessert trolley. Famous for its fiery *penne all'arrabbiata* (pasta with a spicy tomato sauce). Despite being an expensive restaurant, it has a laid-back, relaxed atmosphere. Book ahead. Closed Mon.

SOUTHWEST MILAN L'Ulmet €€€€
Via Disciplini, corner Via Olmetto, 20123 **Tel** *02 86 45 27 18* **Map** *7 B2, 9 C5*

L'Ulmet serves traditional Milanese fare, such as *ossobuco* (veal shank), risotto with asparagus and morels, or steak in a rich red wine sauce with shallots, in a formal, elegant dining room. Friendly ambience and pleasant decor, including wooden ceilings, matt green walls and an open fire. The menu is continually revised. Closed Mon lunch, Sun; Aug.

SOUTHWEST MILAN Marghera 37 €€€€
Via Marghera 37, 20149 **Tel** *02 481 43 86* **Map** *1 C5*

This smart, contemporary lounge/café/restaurant offers a great choice of grilled seafood, fish dishes, meats and antipasti. The refined dark atmosphere mixes gilt and African-inspired design with rattan, exotic plants and candlelight. It has three dining rooms and an indoor garden. A post-theatre meal is also available. Closed Wed; Aug.

SOUTHWEST MILAN Sadler €€€€€
Via Conchetta, corner Via Troilo 14, 20149 **Tel** *02 58 10 44 51* **Map** *7 A5*

Chef Claudio Sadler blends tradition with innovation at his well-run, elegant and informal restaurant and wine bar. Carefully sourced ingredients make up some original dishes, such as sea-bass strudel with olives and aubergines (eggplant), or desserts like iced melon with zabaglione and white port. Closed Sun lunch; Aug.

SOUTHEAST MILAN Dongio €
Via Corio 3, 20135 **Tel** *02 551 13 72* **Map** *8 F4*

Dongio is a typical simple trattoria, where the food is the highlight. The rustic, comfortable and intimate atmosphere is perfect for a romantic meal. Calabrian and Piacenza cuisines are both on offer, with plenty of salami, pasta, cheese and paprika. Try the Calabrian home-made gnocchi. Closed Sat & Sun lunch; Aug.

SOUTHEAST MILAN Pizzeria Napoletana La Taverna €
Via F Anzani 3, 20135 **Tel** *02 59 90 07 93* **Map** *8 F1*

Southern hospitality in the heart of Milan. This pizzeria's reputation is clear by the number of Neapolitans who favour it. The pizzas are the authentic thin and crispy variety. Other specialities include Neapolitan fried food. There is a convivial and popular atmosphere, so be sure to book ahead. Seating outdoors in summer. Closed Sun lunch, Mon; Aug.

SOUTHEAST MILAN Al Merluzzo Felice €€
Via L Papi 6, 20135 **Tel** *02 545 47 11* **Map** *8 F4*

This tiny restaurant specializes in Sicilian-style seafood and desserts. The owner rattles off the names of daily specials, created using the freshest ingredients – clams, prawns, garlic, lobster, ginger and fish. A simple, cosy atmosphere and a rich cuisine full of flavour and colour. Closed Mon lunch, Sun.

SOUTHEAST MILAN Cueva Maja €€
Viale Monte Nero 19, 20135 **Tel** *02 55 18 57 40* **Map** *8 F2*

A good Mexican restaurant with a warm, welcoming feel serving typical Mexican dishes. It has a white arched façade with a terrace and awning and the interior is decorated with objects from the Mayan culture. Try the brunch on Sundays for an alternative to Italian cuisine. Closed Mon; 1 wk Aug.

SOUTHEAST MILAN Masuelli San Marco €€
Viale Umbria 80, 20135 **Tel** *02 55 18 41 38* **Map** *8 F3*

Milanese cuisine is the pride of this trattoria, which has been in the same family since 1921. It has a contemporary feel, with terracotta floor tiles, a black ceiling and colourful Murano glass chandeliers. Excellent antipasti, risottos, soups, pasta with beans, veal cutlets, meat stews and desserts. Good wines too. Closed Mon lunch, Sun; 3 wks Aug.

SOUTHEAST MILAN Mauro €€
Via Colonnetta 5, corner Via Cesare Battisti, 20122 **Tel** *02 546 13 80* **Map** *8 E1, 10 F4*

Expect classic modern Italian cuisine with some great seafood at Mauro. This family-run affair serves smoked salmon with *scamorza* cheese, grilled fish, spaghetti with clams, and *pappardelle* with scampi in a curry sauce. The selection of wines and the service are good. Parking available. Closed Mon, Sat lunch.

SOUTHEAST MILAN Taverna degli Amici €€
Via Spartaco 4, 20100 **Tel** *02 55 19 40 05* **Map** *8 F2*

Rita and Ernesto's welcoming *locale* is situated in the southeast of the city and has a sister restaurant in Paris. The menu includes meats, rustic pâtés, grills and cold cuts. Booking is essential, and there is a choice of à la carte or three tasting menus. Fairly small, rustic and simple in style, with brickwork and murals. Closed Sat lunch, Sun; 3 wks Aug.

SOUTHEAST MILAN Trattoria dei Decemviri €€
Via Decemviri 14, 20100 **Tel** *02 70 10 24 42* **Map** *8 F1*

Set amid the greenery of Parco Forlanini, this lively spot is always busy in summer. Delicious spaghetti with seafood in large terracotta dishes for two or more is on offer. Ingredients include lobster, mussels, swordfish, grilled prawns and sea bass. Swift service and parking available. Closed Mon; mid-Jul–Aug.

SOUTHEAST MILAN Trattoria del Pescatore   €€€

Via Vannucci 3, 20100 **Tel** *02 58 32 04 52*   **Map** 8 E4

As the name suggests, this restaurant specializes in fish and seafood. It may not be directly in the centre, located in the Porta Romana zone, but the dishes are of high quality, and it is necessary to book ahead. The food is full of great flavours and scents. Try the Catalan lobster, or the spaghetti with squid and mullet roe. Closed Sun; Aug.

SOUTHEAST MILAN Da Giacomo   €€€€

Via Sottocorno 6, corner Via B Cellini, 20129 **Tel** *02 76 02 33 13*   **Map** 4 F5

A popular haunt for the well-heeled and fashionable Milanese. The stylish dining room is decorated with Art Deco lamps and photos of famous faces. House specialities include fish, such as swordfish steak *alla Giacomo*. The wine list offers a wide choice of quality vintages and desserts are a must. Closed Tue lunch, Mon; Aug, 10 days at Christmas.

SOUTHEAST MILAN Yar   €€€€

Via Mercalli 22, 20122 **Tel** *02 58 30 96 03*   **Map** 7 C3

An opulent and trendy Russian bistro with a bar full of endless varieties of vodka and a romantic, candlelit restaurant with velvet-lined walls. The menu offers caviar, meat, fish, potatoes, herring and traditional *borscht* and salmon ravioli. On Tuesdays the menu has a French theme. Closed lunch; Sun; Aug.

SOUTHEAST MILAN Da Giannino   €€€€€

Via Sciesa 8, 20135 **Tel** *02 55 19 55 82*   **Map** 8 F1

The place to go for a classic Italian meal with excellent service and high prices. The sophisticated atmosphere in the smart *belle époque* dining rooms is preferred by the city's influential figures. Giannino's Milanese veal cutlet is one of the best in the city, but also recommended are saffron rice, home-made pasta dishes, seafood and desserts.

NORTHEAST MILAN Massawa   €

Via Sirtori 6, 20129 **Tel** *02 29 40 69 10*   **Map** 4 F4

Massawa, with its typical Eritrean cuisine, lies on the streets behind Corso Buenos Aires which are rich in African smells and flavours. Choose between the affordable, Eritrean fixed menu or Italian dishes à la carte. Specials include *zighini* (meat with spicy vegetables and sourdough) and fish on Fridays. Closed Mon; Aug.

NORTHEAST MILAN Mykonos   €

Via Tofane 5, 20217 **Tel** *02 261 02 09*   **Map** 4 F1

This traditional Greek taverna is located in the Buenos Aires area, not far from Central Station, and overlooks the Martesana canal. It is advisable to book in advance. Among the classics are the starters and *tiropita*, a delicious goat's cheese quiche. The kitchen is open until 1am, which is rare in Milan. Closed lunch; Tue; 3 wks Aug.

NORTHEAST MILAN Princi   €

Piazza XXV Aprile 5, 20154 **Tel** *02 29 06 08 32*   **Map** 3 C2

This designer bakery is a recent chain in Milan. It is highly sophisticated and full of the *beau monde*, with a sleek, stylish atmosphere. It is perfect for a light snack, coffees and pastries and bread-based lunches, with pizza slices, tartlets and flans. You can also sit in and watch the bakers at work.

NORTHEAST MILAN Taiwan   €

Via Adda 10, 20124 **Tel** *02 670 24 88*   **Map** 4 E2

Authentic Chinese food is served here. Located near Gioia metro station, it has an elegant ambience and friendly owners. Choose from a variety of meat, fish, seafood, noodles and rice dishes. Higher prices than the majority of other Chinese restaurants, but with the quality to match. Closed Tue; 2 wks Aug.

NORTHEAST MILAN Vecchia Napoli   €

Via Chavez 4, 20131 **Tel** *02 261 90 56*   **Map** 4 F1

Vecchia Napoli is all about pizza. It gets popular and crowded, since the prices are low and the pizzas delicious. The restaurant's creations have won awards, and you can enjoy delightful toppings such as fried aubergine (eggplant) with Parmesan flakes, sweet pizzas laden with fruit or gluten-free soya-flour pizzas. Closed Mon.

NORTHEAST MILAN Fortunio   €€

Via del Carmine 3, 20121 **Tel** *02 72 00 31 85*   **Map** 3 B4, 9 C1

Fortunio offers a seasonal menu that changes on a monthly basis, featuring innovative, international cuisine. The decor is simple and stylish, with contemporary red leather seating but the food is the main attraction. Specials include pumpkin flowers stuffed with ricotta and pesto. Great value for money.

NORTHEAST MILAN Il Coriandolo   €€

Via dell'Orso 1, 20121 **Tel** *02 869 32 73*   **Map** 3 C5, 9 C2

Located in the heart of Brera, Milan's artistic quarter, Il Coriandolo is an elegant, charming place for dinner, with a tastefully decorated, if a little spartan, room. It is not far from La Scala opera house, and one of few restaurants to open in August. The emphasis is on excellent food and wine and dishes include a wonderful Milanese-style risotto.

NORTHEAST MILAN Il Doge di Amalfi   €€

Via Sangallo 41, 20133 **Tel** *02 73 02 86*   **Map** 4 F5

Warm and welcoming, this restaurant offers a real Neapolitan experience, from the pizzas and typical dishes, to the slightly chaotic ambience. Photos of Naples and fishing paraphernalia decorate the walls. Expect dishes such as linguine with lobster, Sicilian pasta specials and lots of *limoncello* (a traditional lemon liqueur). Closed Mon; Aug.

Key to Price Guide *see p172* **Key to Symbols** *see back cover flap*

NORTHEAST MILAN Malavoglia €€

Via Lecco 4, 20124 **Tel** *02 29 53 13 87* **Map** *4 E3*

This hospitable restaurant has been run by a Sicilian couple since 1973: she is in the kitchen and he is front of house. The seafood menu has Sicilian origins with a modern twist. Specials include spaghetti with tuna, pasta with swordfish and spicy tuna steak. There is a good wine list and booking is essential. Closed lunch; Sun; Aug.

NORTHEAST MILAN Matarel €€

Corso Garibaldi 75, 20121 **Tel** *02 65 42 04* **Map** *3 B3*

Traditional Milanese cuisine with lots of veal and saffron risotto is the order of the day at Matarel. The house special is *cazzoeula*, a simple but classic pork stew. This charming, homely restaurant does not look much from outside, but it is always packed with tables squeezed close together. A great choice in the heart of the city. Closed Tue.

NORTHEAST MILAN Osteria del Treno €€

Via San Gregorio 46, 20100 **Tel** *02 670 04 79* **Map** *4 E2*

Located in an old railway workers' club, this restaurant specializes in Italian cuisine with an innovative touch. Influenced by the Slow Food philosophy, the chef creates dishes such as gnocchi made with cocoa and gorgonzola in a thyme and pecorino sauce or tartare with onions, capers and anchovies. Closed Sun lunch, Sat.

NORTHEAST MILAN Piccola Cucina €€

Viale Piave 17, 20129 **Tel** *02 76 01 28 60* **Map** *4 F4*

This tiny restaurant is colourful and unpretentious, but still very chic and favoured by local architects, design and fashion people. The specials range from octopus and squid on chickpeas to a chocolate sponge filled with hot chocolate sauce. The small number of tables ensures an intimate ambience. Closed Sat lunch, Sun; Aug.

NORTHEAST MILAN Piero e Pia €€

Piazza Aspari 2, 20219 **Tel** *02 71 85 41* **Map** *4 F4*

Piero e Pia is a small, family-run establishment in the Città Studi, the smart area near Milan's polytechnic. Expect typical cuisine from the Piacenza area of Emilia-Romagna: fresh pasta parcels, roast pork and boiled meats. Cordial and informal ambience and good wine list. Closed Sun; 3 wks Aug.

NORTHEAST MILAN Ran €€

Via Bordoni 8–10, 20124 **Tel** *02 669 69 97* **Map** *4 D1*

Ran is a great choice for Japanese food in Milan. The tasting menu is one option; alternatively, the chefs and kimono-clad waitresses can prepare sushi in front of you. Specialities include sushi, *sashimi*, *tempura*, soups, and *sukiyaki* (cooked vegetables, meat, soya and noodles). A favourite of the local Japanese community. Closed Mon.

NORTHEAST MILAN Rigolo €€

Largo Treves, corner Via Solferino, 20121 **Tel** *02 86 46 32 20* **Map** *3 C3*

Rigolo is centrally located, near Milan's pretty bohemian district of Brera. It serves a predominantly Tuscan menu to the fashionable set. Choose from wild boar with *pappardelle*, rich local sausages, and steaming boiled meat (*bollito*), which is served on Thursdays. The service is excellent. Closed Mon; Aug.

NORTHEAST MILAN Valtellina €€

Via Taverna 34, 20134 **Tel** *02 756 11 39*

A refined, alpine-style restaurant offering Valtellina specialities. These rustic dishes include salamis, local hams, good meat and game with mushrooms and polenta. Also recommended are the antipasti and home-made pasta dishes. Round your meal off with a hearty home-made pudding. Parking is available nearby. Closed Sat lunch, Fri; Aug.

NORTHEAST MILAN 10 Corso Como €€€

Corso Como 10, 20154 **Tel** *02 29 01 35 81* **Map** *3 C2*

Carla Sozzani's designer empire 10 Corso Como is still a firm favourite in fashion circles. The Zen restaurant here is found on the ground floor, with a leafy and tranquil courtyard. The menu offers a selection of healthy dishes for those who are watching their figure. Fusion cuisine and a bistrot-style atmosphere. Closed Mon lunch.

NORTHEAST MILAN Bulgari Restaurant €€€€

Via Privata Fratelli Gabba 7b, 20122 **Tel** *02 80 58 03 28* **Map** *3 C4*

Join the stylish Milanese for an elegant dining experience, worth the expense. Bulgari is in a tranquil location at the edge of the Botanical Gardens, in a curvaceous space on two levels with an outdoor courtyard. A typical dish is lemon risotto with vanilla flowers accompanied by an excellent choice of wines. Sunday brunch is sublime.

NORTHEAST MILAN Centro Ittico €€€€

Via Martiri Oscuri 19, 20125 **Tel** *02 28 04 03 96* **Map** *4 F1*

This exceptional seafood restaurant is located right next to the fish market, so the freshest produce and excellent shellfish are always ensured for the creative dishes produced here. Centro Ittico is contemporary in design, with neon-lights shining through a long glass-tiled bar. Booking is essential. Closed Sun; Aug.

NORTHEAST MILAN Da Ilia €€€€

Via Lecco 1, 20124 **Tel** *02 29 52 18 95* **Map** *4 F3*

A classic north Italian restaurant with an ample antipasti buffet. Choose from delicious Tuscan cheeses and salamis, various meat dishes with *porcini* (cep) mushrooms, grilled monkfish with rosemary or ravioli with ricotta cheese and spinach in melted butter. All dishes are excellent and home-made. Closed Fri & Sat lunch; Aug.

NORTHEAST MILAN Il Baretto

Via Senato 7, 20121 **Tel** *02 78 12 55*

Map *4 E5, 10 E1*

Il Baretto al Baglioni is more a bar-cum-dining-room than a restaurant proper, though it offers traditional Italian fare of the finest quality. Try the truffle risotto or the seafood salad. As Italian law now dictates, there are seperate smoking and non-smoking rooms. Attentive service, extensive wine list and a sophisticated ambience.

NORTHEAST MILAN Il Pesce d'Oro

Via Nullo 14, corner Via Goldoni, 20129 **Tel** *02 70 12 34 76*

Map *4 F5*

A formal place with a reputation for good service. The typical setting for great seafood and fish specials includes a huge buffet display of hors d'oeuvres, an aquarium tank, sea-related decor and murals of old fishing scenes. Choose from Catalan prawns, mixed seafood platter, tuna, swordfish, sea bass, scampi and more. Closed Mon lunch, Sun.

NORTHEAST MILAN Joia

Via Panfilo Castaldi 18, 20124 **Tel** *02 29 52 21 24*

Map *4 E3*

Joia is a gourmet restaurant close to the Porta Venezia metro station. The dining room is minimalist and well lit. The food on offer is mostly vegetarian and includes vegetable foie gras with truffle sauce, greens layered with fontina cheese and herbs, and tuna and beans with balsamic vinegar and ginger oil. Closed Sat lunch, Sun; 3 wks Aug.

NORTHEAST MILAN La Briciola

Via Solferino 25, 20121 **Tel** *02 655 10 12*

Map *3 C3*

A warm atmosphere and a cheerful host welcomes you at La Briciola. Typical Mediterranean food made with seasonal produce is served. The bistro feel is echoed in the open vaulted rooms, plants and pillars. Try Parma ham and foie gras, gnocchi in a four-cheese sauce or toasted rice. Closed Mon lunch, Sun; Aug.

NORTHEAST MILAN La Terrazza di Via Palestro

Via Palestro 2, 20121 **Tel** *02 76 00 22 77*

Map *4 E4, 10 F1*

In a location overlooking the public gardens and contemporary art museums in the northeast of the city, La Terrazza serves innovative fish cuisine and seafood. Try the famous house special Mediterranean sushi. Lovely views from the terrace enhance the dining experience. Closed Sat, Sun; Aug.

NORTHEAST MILAN Le Langhe

Corso Como 6, 20154 **Tel** *02 655 42 79*

Map *3 C2*

Just a few doors down from the fabulous designer store 10 Corso Como is this restaurant with two rooms – the upstairs one for informal meals, and the one downstairs for more elegant dining. The menu comprises of classic Piedmont dishes including Barolo risotto and *tomini alle erbe* (goat's cheese flavoured with herbs). Closed Sun; 3 wks Aug.

NORTHEAST MILAN Nobu/Armani

Via Pisani 1, 20121 **Tel** *02 62 31 26 45*

Map *4 E2*

Within the white Armani megastore on Via Manzoni you can find Japanese master chef Nobuyuki Matsuhisa's famous Nobu restaurant. The menu is exquisite, unique and worth the expense. Enjoy the famous house special of black cod in miso sauce and sip saké with added gold leaf, all in a stylish, low-lit designer environment. Closed Mon lunch, Sun.

NORTHEAST MILAN Il Sambuco

Hotel Hermitage, Via Messina 10, 20154 **Tel** *02 33 61 03 33*

Map *3 A2*

One of Milan's top dining establishments, this restaurant is a must for fish. Its house special is ravioli stuffed with Mediterranean sea bass and sheep's cheese. Also worth a try are the black risotto with squid ink and the linguine with lobster, aubergine (eggplant) and cherry tomatoes. Closed Sat lunch, Sun; 3 wks Aug.

NORTHEAST MILAN Il Teatro (Four Seasons)

Four Seasons Hotel, Via Gesù, 20121 **Tel** *02 770 88*

Map *4 D5, 10 E2*

One of Milan's finest dining establishments, this award-winning restaurant treats guests like royalty, with excellent service, sophisticated table settings and a wonderful menu. Try the dried salt cod with artichokes and spinach infused with onions and wine or the medallion of veal with foie gras, black truffle and green vegetables.

LAKE MAGGIORE

ARONA Del Barcaiolo

Piazza del Popolo 23, 28041 **Tel** *0322 24 33 88*

In an ancient palazzo in the main square of Arona, under the medieval arches, is this cosy restaurant specializing in Piedmontese cuisine. It offers a rustic menu of good antipasti, chargrilled meats and fish and other hearty fare from the northern region. Seating outdoors in summer. Closed Wed; 2 wks Jan–Feb, 2 wks Dec–Jan.

ARONA La Vecchia Arona

Lungolago Marconi 17, 28041 **Tel** *0322 24 24 69*

Welcoming restaurant with imaginative Piedmontese cuisine. The atmosphere is comfortable, intimate and favoured by couples. Home-made pâtés, pasta with cheese or meat sauces, or Mediterranean fish dishes are all delicious. Leave room for the excellent desserts and cheeses. Good regional and international wines. Closed Fri; Jun, Nov.

ARONA Taverna del Pittore

Piazza del Popolo 39, 28041 **Tel** *0322 24 33 66*

This is one of the region's best restaurants, located in the main square in Arona. Spectacular lake views from the terrace only enhance the excellent menu. Simple Tuscan cuisine is mixed with more elaborate dishes using game, or fish caught on the lake. Sample the multicoloured pasta and excellent-quality fish. Closed Mon; Dec–21 Jan.

CANNOBIO Ca' Bianca

Via Casali Cà Bianca 1, 28822 **Tel** *0323 78 80 38*

Sitting on the shores of Lake Maggiore with views of the Malpaga castle ruins, on a rocky island in the lake, Cà Bianca is located between Cannobio and Cannero. This lovely garden restaurant serves home-made sage and butter ravioli and excellent perch from the lake, as well as great desserts. Closed Wed; Jan–mid-Feb.

CANNOBIO Porto Vecchio

Piazza Vittorio Emanuele III 6, 28822 **Tel** *0323 73 99 98*

Hotel Cannobio's lovely little restaurant has a central, peaceful location on the promenade. The stylish intimate interior has a warm atmosphere, with parquet flooring, large lamps, creamy decor, striped walls and rattan chairs. Excellent fish, seafood, salads and pasta. Reservations are not possible for the spectacular terrace at the lakeside.

CANNOBIO Del Lago

Via Nazionale 2, Località Carmine Inferiore, 28822 **Tel** *0323 705 95*

The refined Italian and international cuisine and the views of Lake Maggiore are the main draws for the faithful followers to this restaurant. The freshest ingredients are used to produce imaginative simple dishes, enhancing aromas and flavours. There is a lovely summer terrace surrounded by verdant gardens. Closed Wed lunch, Tue; Nov–Feb.

LAVENO Il Porticciolo

Via Fortino 40, 21014 **Tel** *0332 66 72 57*

The owner provides his guests with creatively cooked fish from the lake, while his wife will suggest a complementary wine. In summer the veranda overlooking the Laveno Gulf is open. Try the trout ravioli with prawns, thyme and mushrooms or whitefish with lemon sauce, capers and tomatoes. Closed Wed lunch, Tue; Jan–mid-Feb.

LESA L'Antico Maniero

Via alla Campagna 1, 28040 **Tel** *0322 74 11*

A wonderful setting in a pastel-coloured 18th-century renovated castle with acres of surrounding parkland. The period decor includes mirrors, chandeliers and antique furniture, as well as luxurious fabrics. The menu offers a range of well-prepared foods and delicately mixed flavours. Fish and vegetables feature mainly. Closed Sun dinner, Mon.

PALLANZA Dell'Angolo

Piazza Garibaldi 35, 28048 **Tel** *0323 55 63 62*

Located in a small square, Dell'Angolo is a typical regional tavern offering a variety of refined fish dishes, a mix of Piedmontese and Lombardy cuisine and good value for money. In the summer months, tables are also available outside on the square. There is limited space, so book ahead. Closed Mon; Jan.

PALLANZA Il Torchio

Via Manzoni 20, 28048 **Tel** *0323 50 33 52*

Il Torchio is a rustic restaurant with exposed wooden beams and pleasant decor. The cuisine is regional but creative and accompanied by a good selection of local wines. Lake Maggiore fish is served alongside other traditional Piedmontese meat dishes. The restaurant is small and popular. Book ahead. Closed Wed, Thu lunch.

PALLANZA Milano

Corso Zanitello 2, 28048 **Tel** *0323 55 68 16*

Milano is located in a Neo-Gothic building in the centre of Pallanza. It has a lovely terrace with views across Lake Maggiore and serves great fish from the lake, including perch and char accompanied by home-grown seasonal organic vegetables and great wines. Closed Mon dinner, Tue; 1 wk Jun, mid-Nov–Feb.

RANCO Il Sole di Ranco

Piazza Venezia 5, 20120 **Tel** *0331 97 65 07*

This excellent restaurant is surrounded by parkland and offers great panoramic views. Chef Carlo Brovelli uses only the freshest ingredients for his dishes, without smothering them with sauces or added flavours. In the summer months you can also eat alfresco. Closed Mon lunch, Tue; mid-Dec–mid-Feb.

SESTO CALENDE La Biscia

Piazza de Cristoforis 1, 21028 **Tel** *0331 92 44 35*

A light, airy restaurant in the centre of town, Biscia offers a menu based around regional dishes from the surrounding countryside and the lake, as well as some seafood. A house speciality is white bream cooked in rocket (arugula) or linguine with Sicilian red prawns. A rich picking of desserts complete the menu. Closed Sun dinner, Mon.

STRESA Piemontese

Via Mazzini 25, 28838 **Tel** *0323 302 35*

A good place for award-winning creative versions of traditional local cuisine. This intimate establishment in the centre of Stresa offers relaxed elegance and a pretty terrace under vines in the summer. An excellent selection of wines is also available. Try the spaghetti with chilli and onions, or the foie gras pâté with fondue. Closed Mon; Dec–Jan.

VERBANIA Boccon di Vino   🍴   €
Via Troubetzkoy 86, 28900 **Tel** *0323 50 40 39*

An elegant tavern with reliably good food. A local special of pasta with leeks is offered here and the desserts are also fine. Enjoy the lake views over other dishes, including home-made pastas, smoked fish or Piedmontese meat specials. The owner knows his wines, so just ask and he will pick the best. Closed Mon dinner, Sun; mid-Jan–mid-Feb.

LAKE COMO

BELLAGIO Silvio   🍽 ♿ 🏧   €
Via Carcano 12, 22021 **Tel** *031 95 03 22*

This restaurant's owner and his son are professional fishermen providing an abundant catch of fresh lake fish for their patrons. The catch ranges from perch, served with rice, Parmesan and sage, to lake trout, served in a fine parsley sauce. Visitors can even arrange a fishing trip with them. The views over Lake Como are enchanting. Closed Jan–Feb.

BELLAGIO Barchetta   🏧   €€€
Salita Mella 13, 22021 **Tel** *031 95 13 89*

A wide variety of fish fills the menu, and the home-made cakes come highly recommended. Local ingredients form the basis of the food here, which the chef deftly works into a creative Lombard and Mediterranean mixed menu. Established in 1887, Barchetta offers a lovely terrace in summer and nearby parking. Booking advisable. Closed Tue.

BRIENNO Crotto dei Platani   🏧 🍴   €€
Via Regina 73, 22010 **Tel** *031 81 40 38*

Set in a cave once used to preserve wine and food, hide smugglers and store ancient recipes, this atmospheric restaurant offers excellent lake fish, such as shad, as well as great regional wines and cheeses. Enjoy the renovated cave with a cosy open fire in winter or the pretty veranda and lake views in summer. Closed Wed lunch, Tue.

CERNOBBIO Trattoria del Vapore   ♿ 🍴   €€
Via Garibaldi 17, 22012 **Tel** *031 51 03 08*

This trattoria in the town centre has a pleasant atmosphere and plenty of local dishes full of flavour. Try the house special of risotto with carp and perch from the lake. The cosy atmosphere is partly due to the decor, which includes antique furniture, old stone walls and an open fire. There is also an excellent wine cellar. Closed Tue; mid Dec–Jan.

CERNOBBIO Al Musichiere   ♿ 🍴   €€€
Via Cinque Giornate 32, 22012 **Tel** *031 34 22 95*

A centrally located restaurant in Cernobbio with a sober but elegant decor. The menu offers classic local cuisine using meat, as well as lake and sea fish. There is limited space in the two rooms so book ahead. The decor is refined, romantic and antique. Closed Sat lunch, Sun; 2 wks Aug, Christmas and New Year.

CERNOBBIO Gatto Nero   🏧   €€€
Via Monte Santo 69, Località Rovenna, 22012 **Tel** *031 51 20 42*

Il Gatto Nero offers a stunning view over Lake Como, from the road to Monte Bisbino above Canobbio. The menu is kept to a few high-quality dishes, with such delicacies as tagliatelle with fresh truffles and chopped kidneys cooked in brandy. All dishes are regional specialities. Booking essential. Closed Mon, Tue lunch.

COMO La Forchetta d'Oro   €€
Via Borsieri 24, 22100 **Tel** *031 27 15 37*

Located near the medieval town walls, this restaurant occupies the former refectory of Saint Margaret's convent. It has a romantic, spacious, relaxing atmosphere with two dining rooms. Local specials include game salami, wild mushrooms or venison cutlets in ginger with *pizzoccheri* (buckwheat pasta). Closed Sun lunch, Mon.

COMO Locanda dell'Oca Bianca   🏧 🍴   €€
Via Canturina 251, 22100 **Tel** *031 52 56 05*

Housed in a renovated 17th-century farmhouse with a warm, intimate atmosphere, this restaurant is located outside Como, in the village of Trecallo. It offers a variety of Italian regional dishes with a French twist. Choose from lake fish, vegetable soups, meat dishes, cheeses and home-made desserts. The garden is open in summer. Closed Mon; Jan.

COMO Raimondi del Villa Flori   ♿ 🏧 📋 🍷 🍴   €€€
Via Cernobbio 12, 22100 **Tel** *031 338 20*

Raimondi is a romantic and refined restaurant with a splendid setting in a grand 19th-century hotel with lovely views of the lake and the gardens. Enjoy the elegant terrace in summer. The classic Italian regional cuisine offers a selection of Lombardy specials and excellent freshwater fish from the lake. Closed Mon; Dec–Feb.

COMO Sant'Anna 1907   ♿ 🏧 📋 🍴   €€€
Via Turati 3, 22100 **Tel** *031 50 52 66*

Creative local food is served at this traditional restaurant split into four elegant, soberly designed rooms. Typical fare includes veal in an olive crust, fillet of red tuna with chicory shoots and olives and risotto with fish and saffron. Artichokes and polenta also feature heavily on the menu. Closed Sat lunch, Sun; Aug.

Key to Price Guide *see p172* **Key to Symbols** *see back cover flap*

COMO Navedano €€€€
Via Pannilani, 22100 **Tel** *031 30 80 80*

This first-class restaurant has been in the same family for four generations. The menu is experimental gourmet with a floral influence, and the rooms in the 19th-century villa are filled with flowers and plants. Regional dishes include noodles with rabbit stew and pumpkin flowers. The wine cellar boasts more than 400 wines. Closed Tue; Jan.

ISOLA COMACINA Locanda dell'Isola Comacina €€€€
Sala Comacina, 22010 **Tel** *0344 567 55*

A unique experience on an island that is deserted except for this restaurant, which is reached by boat (pay on board). The same set menu of fish has survived since 1947 and still thrives today as a set-price option. It is necessary to book ahead. Wonderful at any time of the year. Closed Tue (in spring); 2 Nov–1 Mar.

LECCO Antica Osteria Casa di Lucia €€
Via Lucia 27, Località Acquate, 23900 **Tel** *0341 49 45 94*

This superb gourmet restaurant with a good reputation and loyal clientele is housed in a characteristic 17th-century house that also holds photographic exhibitions. Lake fish specialities, game, pasta dishes and a delicious home-made nut tart are some of the traditional Slow Food specials. Closed Sat lunch, Sun.

LECCO Al Porticciolo 84 €€€
Via Valsecchi 5–7, 23900 **Tel** *0341 49 81 03*

This restaurant serves high-quality fish and shellfish, with home-made pastas as well as excellent antipasti. The well-spaced room is welcoming, with an open fire in winter and outdoor terrace in summer. It is advisable to book in advance. Parking available. Closed lunch (except hols); Mon, Tue; 2 wks Jan, Aug.

LECCO Nicolin €€€
Via Ponchielli 54, 23900 **Tel** *0341 42 21 22*

This classic restaurant in the Località Maggianico Sud area of town has been in the Cattaneo family for some 30 years and is now run by a father-and-son team. The son, is the more creative chef, whereas the father specializes in traditional Lombardian dishes. The restaurant boasts a summer terrace and parking. Closed Tue; Aug.

MANDELLO OLCIO Il Ricciolo €€€
Via Statale 165, 23826 **Tel** *0341 73 25 46*

This cosy little restaurant serves a great light menu based around Lake Como freshwater fish (perch and eels, for example). Pick from the variety of specials such as fish soup or pasta with crayfish. There is also an impressive list of the restaurant's own oils and grappa. Parking available. Closed Mon, Sun dinner; 2 wks Sep, Christmas–Jan.

MOLTRASIO Imperialino €€€€
Via Antica Regina 26, 22010 **Tel** *031 34 66 00*

The restaurant is part of the Imperial hotel, a splendid villa overlooking Lake Como. The food served is regional, sourced from local ingredients and with a leaning towards seafood. There are three dining rooms with plenty of tables, but it is best to book ahead. Try the prawns and cannelloni. Closed Mon (except summer); Jan–mid-Feb.

SALA COMACINA La Tirlindana €€€€
Sala Comacina, 22010 **Tel** *0344 566 37*

This wonderful, elegant restaurant sits in a picturesque square that overlooks the lake and the landing stage where the boats leave for Isola Comacina. The menu offers fish from the lake and cuisine with a French slant. The house special is ravioli stuffed with a local lemon-flavoured cheese. Sit outside in summer. Closed Wed; Nov–Feb.

VARENNA Vecchia Varenna €€€
Contrada Scoscesca 10, 23828 **Tel** *0341 83 07 93*

This restaurant is right on the lake, near a tiny harbour, with terrace dining in summer. The menu mixes regional surf and turf. Some of the best dishes include rainbow trout baked with olives, capers and anchovies; lasagne with lake fish sauce and beef with rosemary and madeira. Closed Mon; Jan.

LAKE GARDA

DESENZANO Esplanade €€€
Via Lario 10, 25015 **Tel** *030 914 33 61*

Located close to the historic centre of Desenzano, Esplanade overlooks the lake. It has large windows in the dining room and a garden terrace which opens in summer. The elegant interior echoes the tone of the menu. Choose from dishes such as gnocchi with pumpkin flower and foie gras, or rabbit in rosemary with black olives. Closed Wed.

DESENZANO Cavallino €€€€
Via Gherla 30, corner Via Murachette, 25015 **Tel** *030 912 02 17*

Set in a courtyard, Cavallino serves a high-class menu of fish from the lake and the sea. A fine special is caviar risotto whisked with Franciacorta wine. The main dining room is light and pleasantly decorated and a smaller, more intimate room can also be booked. In the summer months, tables are set up on the terrace. Closed Sun dinner, Mon.

GARDONE Locanda Agli Angeli
*Piazza Garibaldi 2, 25083 **Tel** 0365 208 32*

Within the narrow streets of Upper Gardone Riviera, this cosy restaurant is a short walk from the lake. It is part of a charming hotel with arches and wooden beams on the ceiling. It serves homely Italian and Mediterranean cuisine. Try the risotto with trout from the lake and pumpkin or the sea bass with *porcini* (cep) mushrooms. Closed mid-Nov–Feb.

GARDONE Villa Fiordaliso
*Corso Zandarelli 150, 25083 **Tel** 0365 201 58*

Excellent-quality ingredients and fine flavours make the cuisine of Fiordaliso stand out. The Art Nouveau-style restaurant offers a creative menu of meat, seafood and fish from the lake. *Tagliolini neri ai crostacei* (black pasta with shellfish) is one of the chef's specials. The villa boasts wonderful grounds and a lovely terrace. Closed Tue; Jan–Mar.

GARGNANO Tortuga
*Via XXIV Maggio 5, 25084 **Tel** 0365 712 51*

A light, imaginative cuisine is offered at this refined, intimate lakeside restaurant. Despite serving dishes with foie gras, lobster and pasta, the meals are still light and delicate in flavour. The fish is excellent and the wine list superb. Guests travel here from miles around, so it is best to book ahead. Closed Mon dinner, Tue; mid-Jan–Mar.

MANERBA Capriccio
*Piazza San Bernardo 6, 25080 **Tel** 0365 55 11 24*

A sophisticated establishment with splendid views of Lake Garda and the surrounding hills. A high-quality cuisine with such delicacies as sea bass scallops with fennel cream with a grapefruit sauce, medallions of *ricciola* (greater amberjack fish), and prawns in fennel sauce. A highlight among the desserts is passion-fruit sorbet. Closed Tue; Jan–Mar.

PESCHIERA DEL GARDA Trattoria al Combattente
*Strada Bergamini 60, 37019 **Tel** 045 755 04 10*

Situated in the village of Bergamini, between Sirmione and Peschiera, this popular trattoria serves straightforward local specials, including a wide variety of Lake Garda fish. The true flavours of the ingredients, such as the simple grilled lake sardines or pike, are not hidden by rich extras. The antipasti is delicious. Closed Mon; Oct.

RIVA DEL GARDA Restel de Fer
*Via Restel de Fer 10, 38066 **Tel** 0464 55 34 81*

Located in a renovated country inn that has been in the same family since 1400, Restel de Fer is a stone's throw from the shores of the lake. The small restaurant has old vaulted rooms and a tasting cellar with great wines. All dishes are home-made and the specials include marinated salmon trout and sardines with onions. Closed Tue; Nov–Feb.

SALÒ Alla Campagnola
*Via Brunati 11, 25087 **Tel** 0365 221 53*

Angelo del Bon, of Slow Food fame, has made this one of the best-known restaurants in Lombardy. He uses fresh ingredients to produce refined regional, national and international dishes. He also offers some 600 wines. One of the oldest restaurants around Lake Garda, this is a popular spot, so book well ahead. Closed Mon, Tue lunch; Jan.

SALÒ Antica Trattoria Alle Rose
*Via Gasparo da Salò 33, 25087 **Tel** 036 54 32 20*

A young clientele flocks here for the innovative lakeside cuisine. This old trattoria offers local seasonal fresh produce from the market, freshwater fish from the lake and dishes such as *carpaccio* (wafer-thin slices) of *porcini* (cep) mushrooms, rabbit or delicious spaghetti with rocket (arugula), tomatoes and langoustines. Closed Wed.

SALÒ Osteria dell'Orologio
*Via Butturini 26, 25087 **Tel** 0365 29 01 58*

An old, beautifully restored inn in Salò's historic centre. It is always busy, so book in advance for delicious local specialities. The home-made dishes include game, such as partridge with *pappardelle* pasta. Great variety of wines by the glass or bottle and a young, informal atmosphere. Closed Wed; Jul–Nov.

SAN VIGILIO Locanda San Vigilio
*Località San Vigilio, 37016 **Tel** 045 725 66 88*

A noble tavern dating back to 1500, with medieval arches and spectacular views. As well as a romantic setting in a lovely garden, the restaurant offers regional specialities from the land and the lake. On Fridays and Saturdays, from June to August, there is a special candlelit supper with a grand buffet. Book well ahead. Closed Dec–mid-Mar.

SIRMIONE Al Porticciolo
*Porto Galeazzi, Via XXV Aprile 83, 25019 **Tel** 030 919 61 61*

This lakeside trattoria, located outside the town of Sirmione, is very popular. On the menu is a wide variety of dishes: fresh salads, seafood, lake fish and great pastas, all served in ample portions. Pick a table in the cosy indoor room, under the roof outdoors or on the open terrace under parasols. Closed Wed lunch; Nov–mid-Jan.

SIRMIONE La Rucola
*Via Strentelle 3, 25019 **Tel** 030 91 63 26*

Located in the historic centre of Sirmione, with ancient brick walls adding a certain charm, La Rucola serves innovative Mediterranean cuisine using both meat and fish. Specials include calamari in squid ink with potato cakes and prosciutto sticks, or lamb cutlets in onion glaze with potato purée. Compulsory booking at lunchtime. Closed Thu.

SIRMIONE Signori €€€€

Via Romagnoli 17, 25019 **Tel** *030 91 60 17*

This elegant restaurant close to the Castello Scaligero is the ideal destination for an intimate dinner. Get there a little early to enjoy the views of the sunset over the lake. The modern decor is highlighted by large artworks on the walls and the menu relies heavily on locally sourced products, reflecting seasonal variations. Closed Mon; Nov.

SOIANO DEL LAGO Aurora €€

Via Ciucani 1, 25080 **Tel** *0365 67 41 01*

A good, simple restaurant with a warm country feel to it. It is housed in an elegant villa decorated with taste and originality and features a lovely covered veranda in summer. House specials include pasta filled with squid and spinach, marinated smoked salmon and pasta with a ragout of fresh lake fish. Good value for money. Closed Wed.

LAGO D'ISEO

ERBUSCO Mongolfiera dei Sodi  €€€€

Via Cavour 7, 25030 **Tel** *030 726 83 03*

An excellent, cosy artisan restaurant offering local traditional game, meat, fish and vegetables, as well as rich, innovative cuisine. Try the famous Florentine steak, home-made pasta with pigeon sauce, courgette crêpes, baked lamb with sheep's cheese and prawns with a hot curry sauce. The drinks list includes local Franciacorta wines. Closed Thu.

ERBUSCO Gualtiero Marchesi €€€€€

Via Vittorio Emanuele II 23, 25030 **Tel** *030 776 05 62*

This place is a treat. It is run by one of Italy's most famous chefs, Gualtiero Marchesi, under the Relais gastronomy banner. It is also a wine estate in the heart of the Franciacorta region with exceptional food. For a taste of the house specials, try the saffron risotto, *porcini* (cep) casserole or roast turbot. Lovely views and stylish, luxurious decor.

ISEO Osteria Il Volto €€€€

Via Mirolte 33, 25049 **Tel** *030 98 14 62*

Il Volto is one of the lesser-known addresses around Lake Iseo. The interior is rustic, and the menu is regional and simple, but excellent quality. The best ingredients are cooked to perfection, unadultered by fancy blends of flavours. Highlights include pasta with a lake fish ragout, caviar in potato pastry and beef in olive oil. Closed Thu lunch, Wed.

MONTE ISOLA La Foresta €€€

Località Pescheria Maraglio 174, 25050 **Tel** *030 988 62 10*

What makes this a popular spot at the water's edge is the excellent menu, laden with fish from Lake Iseo. Good wines too, especially the sparkling Franciacorta. Salted pressed fish, dried in the sun and marinated in olive oil is a speciality, and is often prepared on the shore in front of the restaurant. Closed mid-Dec–Feb.

SARNICO Al Desco di Puledda Mario €€€€

Piazza XX Settembre 19, 24067 **Tel** *035 91 07 40*

In summer, expect Al Desco's terrace to be packed. People return to this elegant restaurant again and again – for the lakeside view, but also for the great choice of dishes. In addition to fresh fish, the menu has local and international meat dishes and home-made pastas. Good wine list. Closed Mon; Jan.

LAGO D'ORTA

ORTA SAN GIULIO Taverna Antico Agnello €€€

Olina 18, 28016 **Tel** *0322 902 59*

Set in a 17th-century building, this rustic family-run restaurant serves traditional Lombardian dishes, such as lake fish and venison, as well as great cheeses, home-made pasta dishes and desserts. Specials include pasta with goat's cheese, horse meat with garlic and rosemary and divine dishes using duck breast. Closed Tue; mid-Dec–mid-Feb.

ORTA SAN GIULIO Villa Crespi €€€€

Via G Fava 18, 28016 **Tel** *0322 91 19 02*

Villa Crespi's restaurant boasts one of the region's top chefs. The gourmet and regional menus on offer in this ornate Moorish villa comprise of highly acclaimed, innovative Mediterranean dishes, and the wines include some of the world's best. Try the lobster medallions with cheese and pepper sauce, or the *fusilli* (pasta) with crayfish, sea urchins and apples.

SORISO Al Sorriso €€€€€

Via Roma 18, 28018 **Tel** *0322 98 32 28*

A fine gourmet restaurant, with sober decor, high-quality cuisine and a fabulous wine cellar. The chef offers a skilled and imaginative menu of seasonal, fragrant Piedmontese dishes. Specials include egg and potato gratin with white truffles and saffron risotto with courgettes and San Remo prawns. Closed Mon & Tue lunch; Jan, Aug.

BARS AND CAFES

In general, Milanese bars and cafés are places to go for lunch or an aperitif. Breakfast for most Milanese office workers tends to consist of a cappuccino with a croissant, usually consumed at the bar counter. In the Brera quarter, cafés are lively and full of atmosphere. In the early evening they are popular places to relax in with colleagues and friends. Fashions come and go and a café that is "in" one month may be suddenly empty a few months later. To counteract such swings, many Milanese bars have initiated a "happy hour",

**Logo of Bar
Jamaica (see p187)**

when drinks are cheaper. Cafés are usually more crowded during the lunch break, when office workers stop for a quick salad or quiche. As well as cafés, Milan also has excellent cake shops and *pasticcerie*, where you can sample pastries and cakes. For a more formal afternoon tea there are tea rooms *(sala da thé)*, which are also packed at lunchtime. Many are historic places with period furniture. At the lakes, some of the more enterprising bars and cafés offer entertainment in the evening, either with a piano bar area or a small band.

WHERE TO LOOK

In Milan, there are plenty of places to choose from, whether you are going out for an aperitif or to eat snacks, and the choice will vary from area to area. In the atmospheric Brera quarter the bars usually have tables outside in summer. These places are popular with the fashion set and art students. **Jamaica** *(see p187)* is one established institution, an ideal place for a cocktail before dinner as well as for a chicken salad for lunch or an after-dinner drink. **Sans Égal** *(see p187)* is equally popular; on Sunday afternoons they show football (soccer) live on television, and in the evening the place is filled with young rock music buffs.

Around the Navigli, which is a pedestrian precinct, from

8pm in summer all the bars and cafés have tables set out outside, and it is possible to forget that Milan is a bustling commercial city altogether.

The Conca del Naviglio area is always busy. There are numerous places to try such as the **Caffé della Pusterla** *(see p187)*, located in the renovated medieval walls of the city, **Julep's New York** *(see p186)*, which is a good place to try for Sunday brunch, and the **Colonial Fashion Café** *(see p186)*, deservedly famous for its aperitifs.

In the Ticinese quarter **Coquetel** *(see p186)* is a popular place, especially during happy hour, when the young Milanese get together for an early evening drink.

For those with a sweet tooth who like croissants

Sans Égal business card *(see p187)*

and pastries for breakfast, the place to go is **Angela** *(see p186)*, near the Fiera, or **Sissi** *(see p186)*, where you can enjoy cream pastries. If you like brunch, a habit that is increasingly popular in Milan, you can choose from among **Café l'Atlantique** *(see p186)*, a favourite with VIPs, **Speak Easy** *(see p186)*, which also serves good salads, and the **Orient Express** *(see p186)*, with its appealingly old-fashioned look.

HISTORIC CAFES AND BARS

Some of Milan's most frequented cafés and pastry shops have a long tradition, and are housed in old palazzi with fine interiors. One interesting historic pasticceria is **Sant'Ambroeus** *(see p187)*, famous for its traditional panettone. Another ornate setting for breakfast and an aperitif is **Taveggia** *(see p187)*, which has been a favourite with the Milanese since 1910. Don't miss **Zucca**

Watching life go by at a café in Piazza del Duomo

in **Galleria** *(see p187)*, (formerly Camparino), a historic, old-fashioned bar and the place where the world-famous Campari drink was invented. Another must is **Cova** *(see p187)*, a café-pastry shop in Via Montenapoleone in business since 1817. In the heart of the fashion district, it is perfect for a cup of mid-afternoon hot chocolate or an evening aperitif. Lastly, the **Bar Magenta** *(see p186)* has been popular year in and year out and is now an evening haunt for the young Milanese crowd.

WHAT TO ORDER

A vast selection of beers, wines, aperitifs, excellent cocktails and non-alcoholic drinks is served in Milanese bars. A wide range of international beers is available as well as the Italian brands Peroni and Moretti. The current fashion is for Latin-American cocktails, which are gradually replacing classics like the Alexander and Bloody Mary. Almost every bar produces its own house aperitif.

A tray of savouries
served with aperitifs

Italy is a wine-producing country and the regions of Piedmont, Lombardy and the Veneto all have extensive areas under vine. Piedmont is best known for its red wines, Barolo and Barbaresco, and the more affordable Barbera and Dolcetto. Good reds are also made in Franciacorta in Lombardy, in the Valtellina and near Verona, where Bardolino and Valpolicella are made. These regions' white wines include Gavi, Soave, Bianco di Custoza and Lugana, and there are some very good sparkling wines.

The historic Cova pastry shop in Via Montenapoleone *(see p187)*

Most bars provide snacks to go with early evening drinks. These may be simple, such as peanuts, or more elaborate. For generous snacks, try **Honky Tonks** *(see p186)*, where they serve Ascoli olives and pasta salad, as well as the classic *pinzimoni* dips with raw vegetables and canapés, during happy hour.

USEFUL HINTS

It is best to get around by public transport as parking is notoriously difficult in Milan and popular bars are likely to be surrounded by scooters, motorbikes and cars. Most bars and cafés operate two price tariffs, with higher prices charged for sitting down at a table. Ordering and con-suming at the bar counter is the most economical option, but you may prefer to linger and "people-watch".

Many bars operate a "happy hour" from 6:30 to 9:30pm, when drinks such as cocktails are sold at half-price. As a result these places become extremely crowded. At bars attracting younger people the music can be very loud, so if peace and quiet are needed, "happy hour" may not suit.

BARS IN HOTELS

Unlike the other bars in town, those in the large hotels are mostly used as venues for business rendezvous. They are ideal for this purpose, splendidly furnished, and usually quiet. The discretion and privacy creates ideal conditions for discussing business matters.

Among the most distin-guished are the bar in the **Hotel Palace** *(see p163)*, with a fountain in the middle, and the Foyer, the bar in the **Hotel Four Seasons** *(see p163)*. The latter is decorated with theatre set designs. Extra charm is added by an antique fireplace, recreating the plush atmosphere of old Milanese palazzi.

The Foyer in the Hotel Four Seasons *(see p163)*

HAPPY HOUR

Colonial Fashion Café
Via De Amicis 12. **Map** 7 A2 (9 A5).
Tel 02-89 42 04 01.
⬚ *5pm–2am.*

Fitted out with furniture and objects from all over the world, many reminiscent of the colonial style, this café is very popular for its aperitifs and also offers a wide range of delicious snacks.

Coquetel
Via Vetere 14. **Map** 7 B3 (9 B5).
Tel 02-836 06 88. ⬚ *8am–2am Mon–Sat; 6pm–2am Sun.*

For years this establishment has been popular with young Milanese. It is especially busy in the summer, when people stroll around the grassy stretches of the adjacent Piazza della Vetra, and drop in for a beer and a chat. The cocktails are very good. Happy hour is from 6:30 to 8:30pm.

Honky Tonks
Via Fratelli Induno, corner of Via Lomazzo. **Map** 2 F1.
Tel 02-345 25 62.
⬚ *6pm–2am Mon–Sat.*

This establishment in a converted garage is famous for the variety and sheer quantity of the snacks offered during happy hour. The counter is laden with heaps of Ascoli olives, croquettes, stuffed *focaccia* (flat bread) and cured meats of every kind. A good choice of traditional and Caribbean cocktails.

Magenta
Via Carducci 13. **Map** 3 A5 & 7 A1 (9 A3). *Tel 02-805 38 08.*
⬚ *7am–3am Tue–Sun.*

This historic café is ideal for a light lunch snack or a beer in the evening. Try an aperitif at the counter with delicious savouries and *bruschetta*. The good atmosphere attracts smart young Milanese, as well as students from the Università Cattolica and the San Carlo secondary school, both of which are nearby.

Makia
Corso Sempione 28. **Map** 2 E2.
Tel 02-33 60 40 12.
⬚ *8am–3pm, 6pm–2am Mon–Sat.*
⬚ *Aug.*

This chic cocktail bar-restaurant offers tasty Italian/European dishes at lunch, dinner and Sunday brunch as well as a great selection of snacks served to your table so you avoid the crush at the bar during cocktail hour.

BRUNCH

Café L'Atlantique
Viale Umbria 42. **Map** 8 F4.
Tel 199-111 111.
⬚ *9pm–5am Tue–Sat (from 12:30pm Sun for brunch).*
www.cafeatlantique.com

This establishment boasts original, extravagant decor, including a famously huge chandelier. The Sunday brunch attracts many young locals. Atlantique is also a disco and a restaurant.

Julep's New York
Via Torricelli 21. **Map** 7 A5.
Tel 02-89 40 90 29. ⬚ *7pm–2am Mon–Sat; noon–4pm Sun.*

Great atmosphere and excellent service await at this American bar-restaurant. The interior is done out in stylish 1930's decor and the cuisine is typical North American. On Sundays you can enjoy brunch with a Tex-Mex twist.

Orient Express
Via Fiori Chiari 8. **Map** 3 C4 (9 C1).
Tel 02-805 62 27.
⬚ *11am–2am daily.*

The decor, atmosphere and service are all reminiscent of the good old days, when the famous Orient Express was in its heyday. Bar, restaurant and Sunday brunch.

Speak Easy
Via Castelfidardo 7. **Map** 3 C2.
Tel 02-65 36 45. ⬚ *noon–3pm, 6:30pm–2:30am daily; noon–5pm Sun.*

"Eat as much as you like" is the motto in this place in the Brera quarter, which offers a tantalizing, varied buffet and fresh salads.

BREAKFAST

Angela
Via Ruggero di Lauria 15.
Map 2 D1. *Tel 02-34 28 59.*
⬚ *8am–7:30pm Tue–Fri; 8.30–1.30pm, 3–7pm Sat & Sun.*

This small pastry shop near the Fiera has a counter where you can pause and enjoy breakfast. Go for the pastries with custard or whipped cream, the warm puff pastry with ricotta cheese and the fresh croissants with hot custard.

De Cherubini
Via Trincea delle Frasche 2.
Map 7 B3 & B4. *Tel 02-54 10 74 86.*
⬚ *6:45am–11pm daily.*

On the south side of Piazza XXIV Maggio, under a colonnade, lies this lovely café cum pastry shop. Good dishes at lunchtime, snacks with pre-dinner drinks and excellent croissants. Grab an outside table in good weather.

Leonardo
Via Aurelio Saffi 7. **Map** 2 F5.
Tel 02-439 03 02. ⬚ *7:15am–8:30pm Tue–Sun.*

This ice cream parlour and pastry shop is famous for its crème patissière. The pastry rolls and cream puffs are delicious. Try the home-made yogurt or vanilla ice cream.

Marchesi
Via Santa Maria alla Porta 11a.
Map 7 B1 (9 B3). *Tel 02-87 67 30.*
⬚ *8am–8pm Tue–Sat; 8:30am–1pm Sun.*

This historic pastry shop, in the centre between Via Meravigli and Piazza Cordusio, offers croissants, savouries, salads, a vast assortment of cakes and delicious tartlets.

San Carlo
Via Bandello 21, corner of Corso Magenta. **Map** 6 E1. *Tel 02-48 12 227.* ⬚ *6:30am–8:30pm Tue–Sun.*

A stone's throw from Santa Maria delle Grazie, this pastry shop features delicious chocolate-based delicacies and irresistible cream-filled pastries.

Sissi
Piazza Risorgimento 20.
Map 4 F5 & 8 F1. *Tel 02-76 01 46 64.* ⬚ *7am–8pm Wed–Mon.*
⬤ *Mon pm.*

A small pastry shop featuring a host of tempting morsels, including custard-filled croissants or raw ham savouries. The pretty courtyard with its pergola is ideal for Sunday afternoon tea.

SNACKS

Coin – The Globe
Piazza Cinque Giornate 1a.
Coin department store, 8th floor.
Tel 02-55 18 19 69.
⬚ *11:30am–8:30pm Mon; 11:30am–2am Tue–Sun.*

This restaurant, bar and food market, on the top floor of the Coin department store, is similar to those in Harrod's or Macy's. The restaurant offers light lunches and traditional dinners, both high quality. The bar offers fine aperitifs, and you will find delectable delicatessen specialities in the food market.

De Santis

Corso Magenta 9. **Map** 3 A5 & 6 F1 (9 A3). *Tel 02-87 59 68.*
◯ *noon–3pm, 8pm–1am Mon–Sat.* ◉ *Aug, Christmas.*

This compact place specializes in filled rolls. On the walls are banknotes from all over the world and signed photographs of celebrities who have enjoyed choosing from 150 types of sandwich, made with fresh, tasty ingredients.

El Tombon de San Marc

Via San Marco 20. **Map** 3 C3.
Tel 02-659 95 07. ◯ *12:30–2pm, 5pm–2am Mon–Sat.* ◉ *Aug.*

A historic establishment that has resisted passing fashions since the 1930s. A warm, intimate atmosphere. Sandwiches and salads as well as excellent soups and various hot and cold dishes.

Latteria di Via Unione

Via dell'Unione 6. **Map** 7 C1 (9 C4). *Tel 02-87 44 01.*
◯ *11:30am–4pm Mon–Sat.*

This dairy in the heart of town offers good vegetarian dishes. Get there early, because it is small and usually quite crowded.

Luini

Via Santa Radegonda 16.
Map 7 C1. *Tel 02-86 46 19 17.*
◯ *10am–8pm Mon–Sat.*

For over 30 years this baker's has featured Puglian *panzerotti* (ravioli) filled with tomatoes and mozzarella.

Salumeria Armandola

Via della Spiga 50. **Map** 4 D4 (10 E1). *Tel 02-76 02 16 57.*
◯ *8am–7pm Mon–Sat.*

People drop in here for a quick bite at the counter. The chef's specialities include baked pasta, roasted meat and a range of vegetable and side dishes.

BARS AND CAFES

Biffi

Corso Magenta 87.
Map 3 A5 & 6 F1 (9 A3).
Tel 02-48 00 67 02.
◯ *7:30am–8pm Tue–Sun.*

This historic bar-pastry shop dates from the end of the 19th century. Biffi is famous for its milk rolls with cured ham or butter and anchovies. The home-made *panettone*, made every year, is one of the best in Milan.

Caffè della Pusterla

Via De Amicis 24. **Map** 7 A2 (9 A5). *Tel 02-89 40 21 46.* ◯ *7am–2am Mon–Sat; 8am–2am Sun.*

This charming café is located in the former Pusterla, or minor gate, in Milan's medieval walls. A wide range of cocktails and a fine wine list too. The savouries served with the aperitifs are also very good.

Cova

Via Montenapoleone 8. **Map** 4 D5 (10 E2). *Tel 02-76 00 05 78.*
◯ *8am–8:30pm Mon–Sat.*

Founded in 1817, this elegant pastry shop is right in the heart of the fashion district and is an ideal place for a pause during your shopping spree. Cova is well-known for its chocolates and stuffed *panettone*.

Jamaica

Via Brera 32. **Map** 3 C4 (9 C1). *Tel 02-87 67 23.*
◯ *9am–2am daily.* ◉ *Aug.*

This historic Milanese café is the haunt of artists and intellectuals, who flock to this fascinating corner of the Brera quarter. Busy at all hours. Drinks as well as good huge salads.

Sans Égal

Vicolo Fiori 2. **Map** 3 B4.
Tel 02-869 30 96.
◯ *6:30pm–2:30am Mon; 10am–2:30am Tue–Sun.*

In an alley in the Brera quarter, this multi-faceted establishment is a sports pub on Sunday, a small lunch-time restaurant during the week, a drinks bar in the evening and a music pub at night.

Sant'Ambroeus

Corso Matteotti 7. **Map** 4 D5 (10 E2). *Tel 02-76 00 05 40.*
◯ *7:45am–8:15pm.* ◉ *Aug.*

The atmosphere in what is probably Milan's most elegant pastry shop is plush, with sumptuous window displays and slick service. The tarts, pralines and cakes are famous. There is a lovely tearoom inside and tables outside under the arcade opposite.

Taveggia

Via Visconti di Modrone 2. **Map** 8 E1 (10 F3). *Tel 02-76 02 12 57.* ◯ *7:30am–8:30pm Tue–Sun.*

Another historic Milanese pastry shop, inaugurated in 1910. Great rice pudding, many different types of croissants and various delicacies. Taveggia is also popular for its aperitifs.

Victoria Café

Via Clerici 1. **Map** 3 C5 (9 C2). *Tel 02-805 35 98.*
◯ *6:30pm–2am Mon–Sat.*

Behind Piazza della Scala is this Parisian-style *fin de siècle café* with red lamps on the tables, lace curtains and red leather seats. Popular for aperitifs and after dinner.

Zucca in Galleria

Piazza del Duomo 21. **Map** 7 C1 (10 D3). *Tel 02-86 46 44 35.*
◯ *7:30am–8:30pm Tue–Sun.*

This famous bar (formerly Camparino) in the Galleria has period decor and tables outside. The world-famous Campari drink was created here in the late 1800s.

LAKE BARS & CAFES

Matella (Lake Maggiore)

Via Ruga 1, Pallanza.
Tel 0323-50 19 88.
◯ *7:30am–8pm Wed–Mon (to midnight in summer).* ◉ *mid-Oct–mid-Nov.*

Bar-pasticceria shop in the 19th-century arcades of Palazzo Municipale featuring *amaretti* (macaroons). Nice tables for a drink outside.

Mimosa (Lake Garda)

Via RV Cornicello 1, Bardolino.
Tel 045-621 24 72. ◯ *8am–2am.* ◉ *mid Oct–May.*

The barman at Mimosa is a true cocktail "magician". There is also a garden where you can listen to the music from the piano bar while sipping your drink or enjoying good home-made ice cream.

Monti (Lake Como)

Piazza Cavour 21, Como.
Tel 031-30 11 65. ◯ *7am–1am Wed–Mon.* ◉ *Tue (in winter).*

Bar-pastry shop overlooking Piazza Cavour, with tables outside and a view of the lake. Perfect for sipping tea and tasting pastries in tranquil surroundings.

Vassalli (Lake Garda)

Via San Carlo 84, Salò.
Tel 0365-207 52.
◯ *8am–9pm Wed–Mon.*

This historic bar-pastry shop in Salò has been popular for over a century. The aperitifs and cocktails are good, but Vassalli is most well-known for its desserts, such as the exquisite bacetti di Salò chocolates and the lemon mousse.

SHOPS AND MARKETS

Whether buying or just looking, shopping is a real pleasure in Milan. As well as the window displays of the leading national and international fashion designers – whose outlets are all within the area between Via Manzoni, Via Montenapoleone, Via della Spiga and Via Sant'Andrea, the so-called "quadrilateral" – you can find small shops and stores throughout the city. Shops are generally smart and stylish, especially in the city centre, as good design is highly regarded in Italy, and Milan is one of the most affluent cities. For those who are interested in interior design there is plenty of choice among the specialist shops, while lovers of antiques will love the Brera and Navigli quarters, where regular outdoor antique markets are held. Milan also has some excellent *pasticcerie*, where you can purchase authentic delicacies and traditional Milanese confectionery. At the lakes the choice is widest in the bigger towns, and includes clothes shops, craft shops and wine shops selling local produce.

Shopping in Milan

OPENING HOURS

Shops in Milan are usually open from 9:30am to 1pm and then from 3:30 to 7:30pm. However, many shops in the city centre and the department stores stay open all day, without a break, and major bookshops stay open until 11pm.

Shops are closed on Sunday and Monday mornings, except over Christmas, when they are usually open every day of the week. Food shops, on the other hand, close on Monday afternoon, with the exception of supermarkets.

During the summer holiday period, shops generally close for most of August, apart from the department stores which maintain their normal opening hours, even during this rather inactive month.

Window shopping in fashionable Via Montenapoleone

The Coin department store in Piazza Cinque Giornate

DEPARTMENT STORES

There are not many department stores in Milan. One of the most central is **La Rinascente**, which is open seven days a week and stays open until 10pm. Opposite the Duomo, it is perhaps the most prestigious department store in the city, selling everything from clothing, perfumes, toys and stationery to food over eight floors. The restaurant has a view of the Duomo and an exhibition space.

In Piazza Cinque Giornate is the **Coin**, with quality products at medium-range prices, including clothes and household goods. **Upim**, in Piazza San Babila, is more down-market and sells clothes and other articles at really low prices. The **Centro Bonola** is a huge shopping centre with a Coop supermarket and an Upim department store, as well as 60 shops and many bars and cafés. Lastly, there is **Il Portello**, a new shopping centre with shops, boutiques and a large supermarket.

MARKETS

Italy's outdoor markets are always fun and Milan has some good specialist markets. The Mercatone dell'Antiquariato, held on the last Sunday of the month at the Alzaia Naviglio Grande, is an extensive antiques market with more than four hundred exhibitors offering antique objects and bric-a-brac. Every Saturday at the Darsena on Viale d'Annunzio there is the Fiera di Senigallia, where you can find almost anything, from clothing to records and ethnic handicrafts.

The Mercato dell'Antiquariato in the Brera area, between Via Fiori Chiari and Via Madonnina, is also worth a visit. Every third Saturday of

The Fiera di Senigallia along the Darsena

the month antiques, books, postcards and jewellery go on sale here. Lastly, don't miss the Mercato del Sabato on Viale Papiniano, which offers, great designer-label bargains, clothes, shoes and bags.

FOOD SHOPS

Gourmets will appreciate the well-stocked Milanese delicatessens and food shops. Perhaps the most famous is **Peck**, which since 1883 has been synonymous with fine food and delicacies. It is a large firm with 150 employees, and the shops are known for the high quality of the produce and the delicious recipes. Besides the main delicatessen in Via Spadari, selling hams, salami and cheeses of all kinds, there is also a popular Peck *rosticceria* in Via Cantù where you can buy the best ready-made dishes in Milan.

Another top-quality establishment is **Il Salumaio** on Via

Corso Vittorio Emanuele, a popular street for shopping

Montenapoleone, which is both a delicatessen and a restaurant offering international, impeccably prepared and presented dishes.

N'Ombra de Vin is one of Milan's most famous *enoteche*, where you'll find the best Italian wines. For those who love chocolate, **Neuhaus Maitre Chocolatier** is paradise. Its specialities are fresh praline and home-baked cakes – if you feel the need, Neuhaus will even deliver.

Garbagnati is the best-known baker in town, and is especially known for *panettone*. Garbagnati has been making this traditional Milanese cake with a natural leavening process since 1937.

Go to **Fabbrica di Marroni Giovanni Galli** for sweet things; this shop has made the best marrons glacés in Milan since 1898. Equally famous is **L'Angolo di Marco**, in the Brera quarter, a delightful *pasticceria* (pastry shop) offering delectable treats of all kinds. At **Ranieri** they make a *panettone* with pineapple, and sweets and pastries with fresh fruit. Last but not least, **Marchesi** is the best place to go for meltingly good chocolates, both milk and dark.

SALES

In Milan, sales *(saldi)* are held twice a year: in early July and then in January, immediately after Epiphany. Discounts may even be as much as 70 per cent, but check goods carefully before you buy, especially if the discount looks overgenerous. Shop-owners may use

the sales as an excuse to get rid of old stock or defective clothing. For all-year-round bargains, try the numerous outlet shops: Il Salvagente at Via Bronzetti 16 is the most famous shop to head for.

DIRECTORY

DEPARTMENT STORES

Centro Bonola
Via Quarenghi 23. **Tel** 02-33 40 06 25. www.centrobonola.it

Coin
Piazza Cinque Giornate 1. **Map** 8 F1. **Tel** 02-55 19 20 83.

La Rinascente
Piazza del Duomo. **Map** 7 C1 (10 D3). **Tel** 02-88 521.

Il Portello
Piazzale Accursio.

Upim
Piazza San Babila 5. **Map** 4 D5 (10 E2). **Tel** 02-76 02 07 36.

FOOD SHOPS

Fabbrica di Marroni Giovanni Galli
Corso di Porta Romana 2. **Map** 7 C2 (10 D5). **Tel** 02-86 45 31 12. Via Hugo. **Tel** 02-86 46 48 33.

Garbagnati
Via Hugo 3. **Tel** 02-87 53 01. Via Dante 13. **Tel** 02-86 46 06 72.

Il Salumaio
Via Montenapoleone 12. **Map** 4 D5 (10 E2). **Tel** 02-76 00 11 23.

L'Angolo di Marco
Piazza del Carmine 6. **Map** 3 B4 (9 C1). **Tel** 02-87 43 60.

Marchesi
Via Santa Maria alla Porta 13. **Map** 7 B1 (9 B3). **Tel** 02-86 27 70.

Neuhaus Maitre Chocolatier
Via San Vittore 6. **Map** 6 E1. **Tel** 02-72 00 00 96.

N'Ombra de Vin
Via San Marco 2. **Map** 3 C3. **Tel** 02-659 96 50. www.vinoplease.it

Peck
Via Spadari 9. **Map** 7 C1 (9 C3). **Tel** 02-86 08 42. Via Cantù 3 (restaurant/bar). **Map** 7 C1. **Tel** 02-869 30 17. www.peck.it

Ranieri
Via della Moscova 7. **Map** 3 B3. **Tel** 02-659 53 08.

Clothing and Accessories

The clothes shops of Milan are known all over the world because of their associations with famous Italian fashion designers. The city centre fashion district is stormed each year by Italians and foreigners alike in search of the latest top fashion items. However, Milan is not just about expensively priced goods, and the true secret of pleasurable shopping can lie in discovering the less well-known shops which offer good prices and still work to high standards of quality.

CLASSIC CLOTHING

Women in search of impeccable classic clothing for themselves and their children should seek out the **Pupi Solari** shop, which also makes wedding dresses to order. Lovers of colourful sports clothes, on the other hand, will be more than satisfied at **Urrà**. Elegant children's apparel and shoes can be found at **Gusella**, while **Host** features men's sports and informal clothes. Elegant, stylish clothes for men can also be found at **Bardelli** or **Gemelli**, and **Ravizza** is an ideal shop for those who prefer classic wear with a casual touch. **Ermenegildo Zegna** is the place to go for stylish men's classic clothing made of the best quality fabrics. **Brian & Barry** offers both classic and sports clothes at reasonable prices. Lastly, the recently renovated **Neglia** has two floors filled with fashionable menswear, from clothing to accessories.

DESIGNER WEAR

Almost all the shops that feature the latest in top designer clothes are in or near the city centre (see pp106–7). **Hugo Boss** is a recently opened shop of some size, selling elegant clothes for men. **Giò Moretti**, an institution in Via della Spiga, features articles by the top names as well as pieces by up-and-coming fashion designers. **Marisa** is a shop specializing in Italian and foreign designers and there is always something new and interesting, while **Fay** has clothes for the young and

sophisticated. **Biffi** is famous for its wide-ranging selection of top designer clothes.

Among non-Italian fashion designers **Jil Sander** is growing more and more popular. **Guess**, the well-known New York designer, is represented in the city and offers the latest lines.

The diffusion lines of the most famous designers can be found in the fashion district, where the main names have their own branches, from **Miu Miu** to **D&G** and **Emporio Armani**. Armani's Via Manzoni store also

houses an art gallery and Nobu sushi bar. Lastly, **Antonio Fusco** attracts an enthusiastic clientele.

ACCESSORIES

For good quality sports shoes there is **Tod's**. Less well-known but equally good is the **Stivaleria Savoia**, which features classic styles that can also be made to measure. **Gallo** is proud of its stylish high-quality hosiery.

Ferragamo, the Italian designer known all over the world for his top fashion styles, offers elegant classic shoes. More bizarre and unconventional articles can be found at **La Vetrina**, while **Camper** features classic shoes known for their fine workmanship. **Garlando** offers a vast range of styles and colours that aim at the young people's market.

Crocodile, ostrich and leather handbags can be found at **Colombo**, while **Valextra** features high-quality

SIZE CHART

Children's clothing

Italian	2–3	4–5	6–7	8–9	10–11	12	14	14+	(age)
British	2–3	4–5	6–7	8–9	10–11	12	14	14+	(age)
American	2–3	4–5	6–6X	7–8	10		12	14	16	(size)

Children's shoes

Italian	24	25½	27	28	29	30	32	33	34
British	7½/	8	9	10	11	12	13	1	2
American	7½	8½	9½	10½	11½	12½	13½	1½	2½

Women's dresses, coats and skirts

Italian	38	40	42	44	46	48	50	52
British	6	8	10	12	14	16	18	20
American	4	6	8	10	12	14	16	18

Women's blouses and sweaters

Italian	40	42	44	46	48	50	52
British	30	32	34	36	38	40	42
American	6	8	10	12	14	16	18

Women's shoes

Italian	36	37	38	39	40	41
British	3	4	5	6	7	8
American	5	6	7	8	9	10

Men's clothing

Italian	44	46	48	50	52	54	56	58
British	34	36	38	40	42	44	46	48
American	34	36	38	40	42	44	46	48

Men's shirts

Italian	36	38	39	41	42	43	44	45
British	14	15	15½	16	16½	17	17½	18
American	14	15	15½	16	16½	17	17½	18

Men's shoes

Italian	40	41	42	43	44	45	46
British	7	7½	8	9	10	11	12
American	7½	8	8½	9½	10½	11	11½

suitcases and briefcases. For something original head for the **Atelier Anne Backhaus**, where they make handbags and accessories using different materials.

The **Mandarina Duck** shops have stylish sports bags, luggage, casual handbags and knapsacks. **Borsalino** is the place to go for top-quality classic hats. **Giusy Bresciani** has more original designs, as well as gloves and other highly stylish accessories. **Cappelleria Melegari** deals in hats imported from all over the world and they can do hat alterations in their workshop if a customer requires. A wide range of ties and knitwear can be found at **Fedeli** and at **Oxford**, where you can also find good ranges of men's shirts.

JEWELLERY

Elegant, classic jewellery is featured at **Calderoni**, which has designed jewels for smart Milanese women since 1840, and **Cusi**, which has been in business since 1885. **Tiffany & Co** is known for high-class jewellery, while Mario Buccellati has gold and silver pieces of elegant workmanship. Another historic shop is **Bulgari**, known for its beautiful jewellery and watches. **Mereú** features original and modern hand-crafted jewels. Jewellery dating from the 19th century to 1950 is to be found at **Mirella Denti**. For modern costume jewellery, you will find a good collection at **Donatella Pellini**, and **Sharra Pagano** also has a good choice of the latest costume jewellery and jewellery styles, made of original materials.

DIRECTORY

CLASSIC CLOTHING

Bardelli
Corso Magenta 13.
Map 3 A5 (9 A3).
Tel 02-86 45 07 34.

Brian & Barry
Via Durini 28.
Map 8 D1 (10 E3).
Tel 02-76 00 55 82.

Ermenegildo Zegna
Via Verri 3. **Map** 4 D5 (10 E2). *Tel* 02-76 00 64 37.

Gemelli
Corso Vercelli 16. **Map** 2 D5. *Tel* 02-48 00 00 57.

Gusella
Corso V Emanuele II 37b.
Map 8 D1 (10 E3).
Tel 02-79 65 33.

Host
Piazza Tommaseo 2. **Map** 2 E5. *Tel* 02-43 60 85.

Neglia
Corso Venezia 2.
Map 4 E4 (10 F2).
Tel 02-79 52 31.

Pupi Solari
Piazza Tommaseo 2. **Map** 2 E5. *Tel* 02-46 33 25.

Ravizza
Via Hoepli 3. **Map** 4 D5 (10 D3). *Tel* 02-869 38 53.

Urrà
Via Solferino 3. **Map** 3 C2. *Tel* 02-86 43 85.

DESIGNER WEAR

Antonio Fusco
Via Sant'Andrea 11.
Map 4 D5 (10 E2).
Tel 02-76 00 29 57.

Biffi
Corso Genova 6. **Map** 7 A2 (9 A5). *Tel* 02-831 16 01.

D&G
Corso Venezia 7.
Map 4 E4 (10 F2).
Tel 02-76 00 40 91.

Emporio Armani
Via Durini 24. **Map** 8 D1 (10 E3). *Tel* 02-76 02 03 06.
Via Manzoni 31. **Map** 3 C5 (10 D2). *Tel* 02-62 69 07 29. www.armani-viamanzoni31.com

Fay
Via della Spiga 16.
Map 4 D4 (10 E2).
Tel 02-76 01 75 97.

Giò Moretti
Via della Spiga 4.
Map 4 D4 (10 E2).
Tel 02-76 00 31 86.

Guess
Piazza San Babila 4b.
Map 4 D5 (10 E2).
Tel 02-76 39 20 70.

Hugo Boss
Corso Matteotti 11.
Map 4 D5 (10 E2).
Tel 02-76 39 46 67.

Jil Sander
Via P Verri 6. **Map** 4 D5 (10 E2). *Tel* 02-777 29 91.

Marisa
Via della Spiga 52.
Map 4 D4 (10 E2).
Tel 02-76 00 20 82.

Miu Miu
Corso Venezia 3.
Map 4 E4 (10 F2).
Tel 02-76 01 44 48.

ACCESSORIES

Atelier Anne Backhaus
Corso di Porta Vigentina 10. **Map** 8 D3.
Tel 02-58 30 27 93.

Borsalino
Galleria Vittorio Emanuele II. **Map** 7 C1 (10 D3).
Tel 02-86 45 72 42.

Camper
Via Torino 15. **Map** 7 B1 (9 C4). *Tel* 02-805 71 85.

Cappelleria Melegari
Via P Sarpi 19. **Map** 3 A2. *Tel* 02-31 20 94.

Colombo
Via della Spiga 9.
Map 4 D4 (10 E2).
Tel 02-76 02 35 87.

Fedeli
Via Montenapoleone 8.
Map 4 D5 (10 E2).
Tel 02-76 02 33 92.

Ferragamo
Via Montenapoleone 3.
Map 4 D5 (10 E2).
Tel 02-76 00 00 54.

Gallo
Via Durini 26. **Map** 8 D1 (10 E3). *Tel* 02-76 00 20 23.

Garlando
Via Madonnina 2. **Map** 3 B4 (9 C1). *Tel* 02-87 46 65.

Giusy Bresciani
Via Ciovasso 5.
Map 3 C4 (9 C2).
Tel 02-89 01 35 05.

La Vetrina
Via Statuto 4. **Map** 3 B3.
Tel 02-65 42 78.

Mandarina Duck
Corso Europa. **Map** 8 D1 (10 E3). *Tel* 02-78 22 10.

Oxford
Via Verri 2. **Map** 4 D5 (10 E2). *Tel* 02-76 02 34 04.

Stivaleria Savoia
Via Petrarca 7. **Map** 2 E4.
Tel 02-46 34 24.

Tod's
Via della Spiga 22.
Map 4 D4 (10 E2).
Tel 02-76 00 24 23.

Valextra
Piazza San Babila 1.
Map 4 D5 (10 E2).
Tel 02-76 00 29 89.

JEWELLERY

Bulgari
Via della Spiga 6.
Map 4 D4 (10 E2).
Tel 02-77 70 01.

Calderoni
Via Montenapoleone 23.
Map 4 D5 (10 E2).
Tel 02-76 00 12 93.

Cusi
Via Montenapoleone 21a. **Map** 4 D5 (10 E2). *Tel* 02-76 02 19 77.

Donatella Pellini
Via Santa Maria alla Porta 13. **Map** 7 B1 (9 B3).
Tel 02-72 01 05 69.

Mario Buccellati
Via Montenapoleone 4.
Map 4 D5 (10 E2).
Tel 02-76 00 21 53.

Mereú
Via Solferino 3. **Map** 3 C3. *Tel* 02-86 46 07 00.

Mirella Denti
Via Montenapoleone 29.
Map 4 D5 (10 E2).
Tel 02-76 02 25 44.

Sharra Pagano
Corso Garibaldi 35. **Map** 3 B3. *Tel* 02-29 51 41 73.

Tiffany & Co
Via della Spiga 19a.
Map 4 D4 (10 E2).
Tel 02-76 02 23 21.

Design and Antiques

Milan is the acknowledged capital of modern design and a paradise for enthusiasts, who can spend their free time browsing in the numerous shops and showrooms throughout the city. Every spring the Salone del Mobile, the famous Milan furniture fair, attracts all the top designers and trade buyers. During the fair, many of Milan's interior design shops extend their opening hours and put on various events for trade experts and visitors.

INTERIOR AND INDUSTRIAL DESIGN

At **De Padova**, elegant, studiously avant-garde objects for the home, including furniture, are made of the finest materials. For stylish lighting there is **Artemide**, which is known for its superb modern designs, created by well-known names, and **Flos**, in Corso Monforte, which features sleek ultra-modern lighting of all kinds.

Fontana Arte is a kind of gallery and a leading light in the field of interior design. Founded in 1933, its displays include splendid lamps, mostly crystal.

Da Driade, located in the heart of the fashion district, features objects created in the last 30 years which have since become collectors' items. **Galleria Colombari**, on the other hand, offers modern antiques as well as a range of contemporary design objects.

Spazio Cappellini is a show room for informal and elegant furniture, while **Zani & Zani** features interior design accessories, displayed in a chessboard pattern to show off the individual objects at their best.

Kartell stocks various articles for the home and the office, while **Arform** specializes in Scandinavian design. **Venini** is an institution in the production of blown Venetian glass vases, while **Barovier & Toso** offers extremely high-quality chandeliers and vases, and **Cassina** features products by leading designers.

Spazio 900 has fabulous furniture and interior objects by top designers from the 1950s to the 1980s, as well as vintage and end-of-line pieces at discount prices.

Officina Alessi, in Corso Matteotti, specializes in interior design pieces and kitchenware in stainless steel and colourful plastic.

Those who love stylish period furniture should stop by **L'Utile e il Dilettevole**, where 19th-century taste prevails, and **Dimorae**, where the furniture is beautifully displayed in welcoming settings.

MEGASTORES

The Megastore, where you can purchase almost anything under the sun, from the tiniest household article to a large piece of furniture, is now becoming the rage in Milan as well as in other Italian cities. These large establishments (*empori*) are usually open late in the evening and on Sunday and are frequently able to offer their customers various additional services.

High Tech was one of the first to offer this new mode of shopping. Come here for exotic furniture, fabrics and wallpaper for the home, kitchenware, perfume and accessories imported from all over the world.

Visit **Cargo Hightech's** warehouse store for beautiful Chinese laquered chests or ultra modern Italian design lighting. Alternatively, browse their clothing in fabulous cloth from India and bamboo furniture from the Philippines.

Emporio 31 is another interesting place built in the old industrial district near the Navigli. It offers everything for the interior designer, accurately selected for the discerning eye. There are three spacious floors, often with design exhibitions thrown in for free.

Corso Como 10 is an unusual place featuring designer articles and objects from the Middle and Far East. It also has a gallery and an interesting café/bar.

The ultramodern and unconventional **Moroni Gomma** offers boots, raincoats, kitchenware and interior design and household articles, all made of plastic or rubber (*gomma*).

FABRICS AND LINEN FOR THE HOME

For elegance and high-class interior design, Milan cannot be beaten. There are many shops which specialize in fabrics and linen which can be made to order.

Etro, in Via Pontaccio, is famous for its fabrics and stylish accessories. In the same street is **KA International**, a sales outlet for a Spanish chain of fabric shops, offering excellent value for money. Among the many other articles, **Lisa Corti** features original Indian cotton and cheesecloth fabrics with floral and stripe decorative patterns. **Mimma Gini** has characteristic fabrics from India, Japan and Indonesia; **Castellini & C** is known mostly for its linen articles.

Original and exclusive fabrics can be found at **Fede Cheti**. Among the shops featuring household linen, **Pratesi**, in the heart of the fashion district, is known for its classic and elegant ranges, while **Jesurum** is famous for its embroidered materials and fine lace cloth. **Zucchi** is a very well-known name in Italy for beautifully made fabrics.

Bed linen and table linen in both modern and practical styles are featured at **Mirabello**. Since 1860 **Frette** has been a guarantee of high quality bed linen, table linen and articles for the bathroom such as towels and bathrobes. They also offer delivery throughout the world as well as advice and help from an interior designer.

ANTIQUES

Milan has numerous antique shops and workshops. Subert, in Via della Spiga, specializes in 18th-century furniture and scientific instruments. In the same street is **Mauro Brucoli**, where they specialize in 19th-century furniture and objects as well as splendid jewellery dating from the same period. At Franco Sabatelli, which is also a furniture restorers, you can find picture frames of all periods, some even dating to the 16th century.

Lovers of 18th- and 19th-century British furniture must head for Old English Furniture, which also has a fine stock of medical and scientific instruments. If you prefer the unusual and even bizarre object, try **L'Oro dei Farlocchi**, a historic antique gallery in the Brera area.

Galleria Blanchaert is one of Milan's best-known shops for antique glass, with Murano chandeliers and Venini vases.

At **Antichità Caiati** you will find stunning 17th- and 18th-century Italian paintings, Valuable canvases are also sold at **Walter Padovani** as well as decorative art, sculpture and precious stones. **Carlo Orsi** has exclusive antiques, including bronze sculpture, splendid paintings, fine furniture, delicate ivory pieces and precious stones.

DIRECTORY

INTERIOR AND INDUSTRIAL DESIGN

Arform
Via della Moscova 22.
Map 3 B3.
Tel 02-655 46 91.

Artemide
Corso Monforte 19.
Map 4 E5 (10 F2).
Tel 02-76 00 69 30.

Barovier & Toso
Via Manzoni 40. **Map** 4 D5. **Tel** 02-76 00 09 06.

Cassina
Via Durini 16.
Map 8 D1 (10 E3).
Tel 02-76 02 07 58.

Da Driade
Via Manzoni 30.
Map 4 D5 (10 D2).
Tel 02-76 02 30 98.

De Padova
Corso Venezia 14. **Map** 4 E4 (10 F2). **Tel** 02-77 72 01. www.depadova.it

Dimorae
Corso Magenta 69.
Map 3 A5 (9 A3).
Tel 02-48 01 18 03.

Flos
Corso Monforte 9.
Map 4 E5 (10 F2).
Tel 02-76 00 36 39.

Fontana Arte
Via Santa Margherita 4.
Map 3 C5 (9 C3).
Tel 02-86 46 45 51.

Galleria Colombari
Via Maroncelli 10. **Map** 3 B1. **Tel** 02-29 0025 33.

Kartell
Via Turati (corner of Corso Porta 1). **Map** 4 D3.
Tel 02-659 79 16.

L'Utile e il Dilettevole
Via della Spiga 46.
Map 4 D4 (10 E2).
Tel 02-76 00 84 20.

Magazzini Cappellini
Via S Cecilia 4.
Tel 02-76 00 29 56.

Officina Alessi
Corso Matteotti 9. **Map** 4 D5 (10 E2). **Tel** 02-79 57 26.

Spazio 900
Corso Garibaldi 42. **Map** 3 B2. **Tel** 02-70 12 57 37. www.spazio900.com

Venini
Via Montenapoleone 9.
Map 4 D5 (10 E2).
Tel 02-76 00 05 39.

Zani & Zani
Via San Damiano (corner of Corso Venezia). **Map** 4 E4 (10 F2). **Tel** 02-79 80 96.

MEGASTORES

Cargo-Hightech
Via Meucci 39.
Tel 02-27 22 131.
www.cargomilano.it

Corso Como 10
Corso Como 10. **Map** 3 C2. **Tel** 02-29 00 26 74.

Emporio 31
Via Tortona 31. **Map** 6 D3.
Tel 02-42 22 577.

High Tech
Piazza XXV Aprile 12.
Tel 02-624 11 01.

Mondadori Multicenter
Via Marghera 28. **Map** 1 C5. **Tel** 02-48 04 71.

Moroni Gomma
Corso Matteotti 14.
Map 4 D5 (10 E2).
Tel 02-76 00 68 21.
Via Giusti 10. **Map** 3 A2.
Tel 02-33 10 65 65.

FABRICS AND LINEN FOR THE HOME

Etro
Via Montenapoleone 5.
Map 4 D5 (10 E2).
Via Bigli 2. **Map** 4 D5 (10 D2). **Tel** 02-76 00 50 49.

Fede Cheti
Via Manzoni 23.
Map 3 C5 (10 D2).
Tel 02-86 46 40 05.

Frette
Via Montenapoleone 21.
Map 4 D5 (10 E2).
Tel 02-76 00 37 91.
Via Manzoni 11.
Map 3 C5 (10 D2).
Tel 02-86 45 06 46.
Corso Vercelli 23–25.
Map 2 D5.
Tel 02-498 97 56.

Jesurum
Via Verri 4. **Map** 4 D5 (10 E2). **Tel** 02-76 01 50 45.

KA International
Via Pontaccio 3. **Map** 3 B4 (9 C1). **Tel** 02-86 45 12 44. Via Marghera 14. **Map** 1 C5. **Tel** 02-48 00 63 53.

Lisa Corti
Via Conchetta 6. **Map** 7 A5. **Tel** 02-58 10 00 31.

Mimma Gini
Via Santa Croce 21. **Map** 7 B3. **Tel** 02-89 40 07 22.

Mirabello
Via Montebello (corner of Via San Marco). **Map** 4 D3. **Tel** 02-65 48 87.

Pratesi
Via Montenapoleone 27e. **Map** 4 D5 (10 E2).
Tel 02-78 35 74.

Zucchi
Via Ugo Foscolo 4.
Tel 02-89 01 14 14.

ANTIQUES

Antichità Caiati
Via Gesà 17. **Map** 4 D5 (10 E2). **Tel** 02-79 48 66.

Carlo Orsi
Via Bagutta 14.
Tel 02-76 00 22 14.

Galleria Blanchaert
Piazza Sant'Ambrogio 4.
Map 7 A1 (9 A3).
Tel 02-86 45 17 00.

L'Oro dei Farlocchi
Via Madonnina, opposite No. 5. **Map** 3 B4 (9 C1).
Tel 02-86 05 89.

Mauro Brucoli
Via della Spiga 17.
Map 4 D4 (10 E2).
Tel 02-76 02 37 67.

Walter Padovani
Via della Spiga 25.
Map 4 D4 (10 E2).
Tel 02-76 31 89 07.

Books and Gifts

Milan is well supplied with good bookshops, many offering foreign-language publications as well as books in Italian. The larger bookstores in the centre are usually open late in the evening and also on Sunday. They have plenty of space where you can quietly browse through the books on display at your leisure. In addition there are plenty of small bookshops, many stocking rare or out-of-print books. Around the University there are many specialist bookshops. Music fans can head for the megastores and the many music shops in town, while the specialist gift article shops will help those interested in buying presents to take home.

BOOKSHOPS

The **Mondadori Multicenter** is centrally located, open every day until 11pm and on Sunday as well. It spreads out over two floors. On the ground floor, next to the newspapers and periodicals (including international ones), are the new releases, both fiction and non-fiction for visitors who read Italian. The mezzanine contains books of all kinds.

Computer buffs should head for the recently opened **Mondadori Informatica**, which is a paradise for anyone interested in IT.

Another large, well-stocked and very popular bookstore is **Rizzoli** in the Galleria Vittorio Emanuele, which has a fine arts section.

Feltrinelli has six bookshops in Milan, which are open every day including Sunday. The brand-new main bookshop in Piazza del Duomo, almost 500 sq m (5,380 sq ft) in size, has more than 60,000 books and offers various services, such as wedding lists, to its customers.

Five-floor **Hoepli** is a serious bookstore steeped in tradition. It specializes particularly in scientific publications and subscriptions to foreign periodicals. The **American Bookstore** and **English Bookshop** specialize in English-language literature and the **Libreria Francese Ile de France** has a good selection of publications in French. For second-hand books,

go to **Il Libraccio**, which has a number of branches. Besides school textbooks, it has various books, comic books and even CDs.

A small shop where opera fans can find interesting publications is **Il Trovatore**. Out-of-print editions, scores and libretti are offered together with valuable rarities such as facsimiles of scores by Donizetti or Verdi with the composers' signatures. This music store also provides a catalogue of its publications.

Books Import specializes in art show catalogues and art history books, and books on architecture, design and photography, almost all of which are published abroad. Their section on hobbies is particularly good.

L'Archivolto, which specializes mostly in architecture and design, also has a section on antiques with books from the 1500s to the present. This shop also has modern design objects on display. The **Libreria della Triennale** also deals mainly in books on architecture and design, but has a well-stocked children's book section as well.

Art lovers will also enjoy the **Libreria Bocca**, in the Galleria Vittorio Emanuele. The **Libreria dei Ragazzi** is the only bookshop in town entirely given over to children's books, with games and educational books. The **Libreria del Mare**, as its name suggests, offers a wide range of prints and books on the sea (*il mare*), while the **Libreria Milanese** has books (including photographic

ones), prints, posters and gadgets concerning Milan. **Milano Libri**, always up with the latest trends, has a section on high fashion and another on photography. **Luoghi e Libri** specializes in travel books, novels and non-fiction, and the **Libreria Magenta** offers a good range of foreign newspapers and periodicals. Comic-book fans should visit **La Borsa del Fumetto**, which also has rare and old editions.

Besides travel guides, the **Libreria dell'Automobile** has handbooks and illustrated books on cars and motorcycles. **Libreria dello Sport** features books and videos on all sports, and **Libreria dello Spettacolo** specializes in theatre and biographies of famous actors and actresses.

MUSIC, CDs & RECORDS

A good music shop in the city is the **Ricordi Media Store**, which has parts and scores as well as books on composers and their works. It is open even on Sunday (until 8pm), offers discounts on items at least once a month and also has a ticket office for concerts. Another good destination for music lovers is **Messaggerie Musicali**. Located over three floors, it boasts a vast range of records, tapes and CDs, as well as a well-stocked section with books on music in various foreign languages.

The **Bottega Discantica** is a paradise for lovers of opera and church and symphonic music, while **Supporti Fonografici** is a shop with a British flavour: besides the latest trends in music, there are records that are almost impossible to find elsewhere and a wide range of Italian and foreign periodicals as well as rare music-themed T-shirts. **Buscemi Dischi** is one of the best-stocked and low-priced music shops and is especially recommended for jazz lovers.

Rasputin, in Piazza Cinque Giornate, specializes in rock music, particularly from

American bands, and offers a good assortment of the latest chart releases at reasonable prices.

GIFTS

Visitors in search of gifts would do well to try **MacKenzy Gadgets** in the Galleria for Italian branded merchandise or **Co Import** for household goods and funky items. For something special try **Penelopi 3**. If circumstances call for a more sophisticated gift, head for **Albrizzi**, a famous

bookbinder's dealing in quality notebooks, albums and other handcrafted articles. Another good alternative in this field is **La Piccola Legatoria**, where visitors will find excellent handcrafted stationery, including writing paper and cardboard articles.

Smokers will love **Lorenzi** which, besides a vast assortment of knives, scissors and toilet and gift articles, has high-quality pipes and accessories for smokers. Again for the smoker, **Savinelli** is an institution

in Milan. Since 1876 it has sold pipes of all kinds, at all prices, up to unique and extremely expensive ones.

For toys or games, try the **Città del Sole**, which stocks Milan's largest assortment of traditional wooden toys, educational games and board games for both children and adults. **Movo**, in business since 1932, is the domain of model-making enthusiasts, while **Pergioco** specializes in video games and DVDs, as well as computer games.

DIRECTORY

BOOKSHOPS

American Bookstore
Via Camperio 16. **Map** 3 B5 (9 B2). **Tel** 02-87 89 20.

Books Import
Via Maiocchi 11.
Tel 02-29 40 04 78.

English Bookshop
Via Mascheroni 12. **Map** 2 E4 **Tel** 02-469 44 68.
www.englishbookshop.it

Feltrinelli
Megastore: Piazza Piemonte 2. **Map** 1 C5.
Tel 02-43 35 41,
Via Manzoni 12.
Map 3 C5 (10 D2).
Tel 02-76 00 03 86.
Via Foscolo 1–3.
Tel 02-86 99 68 97.
Corso Buenos Aires 33.
Map 4 F3.
Tel 02-20 23 361.
Via P Sarpi 15. **Map** 3 A2. **Tel** 02-349 02 41.

Hoepli
Via Hoepli 5. **Map** 4 D5 (10 D3). **Tel** 02-86 48 71.

Il Libraccio
Via Arconati 16.
Tel 02-55 19 08 97.
Via Corsico 9. **Map** 6 F3.
Tel 02-837 23 98.
Via Santatecla 5.
Tel 02-87 83 99.
Viale Vittorio Veneto 22.
Map 4 E3.
Tel 02-655 56 81.

Il Trovatore
Via Carlo Poerio 3.
Tel 02-76 00 16 56.

L'Archivolto
Via Marsala 2. **Map** 3 C3.
Tel 02-659 08 42.

La Borsa del Fumetto
Via Lecco 16. **Map** 4 E3.
Tel 02-29 51 38 83.

Libreria Bocca
Galleria Vittorio Emanuele II 12. **Map** 7 C1 (10 D3).
Tel 02-86 46 23 21.

Libreria dei Ragazzi
Via Tadino 53. **Map** 4 F2.
Tel 02-29 53 35 55.

Libreria del Mare
Via Broletto 28. **Map** 3 B5 (9 C2). **Tel** 02-89 01 02 28

Libreria dell'Automobile
Corso Venezia 43.
Map 4 E4 (10 F2).
Tel 02-76 00 66 24.

Libreria della Triennale
Viale Alemagna 6. **Map** 2 F3 **Tel** 02-89 01 34 03.

Libreria dello Spettacolo
Via Terraggio 11.
Map 7 A1 (9 A3).
Tel 02-86 45 17 30.

Libreria dello Sport
Via Carducci 9. **Map** 3 A5 (9 A3). **Tel** 02-805 53 55.

Libreria Francese Ile de France
Via San Pietro all'Orto 10.
Map 4 D5 (10 E2).
Tel 02-76 00 17 67.

Libreria Magenta
Corso Magenta 65.
Map 3 A5 (9 A3).
Tel 02-49 84 611.

Libreria Milanese
Via Meravigli 18. **Map** 3 B5 (9 B3). **Tel** 02-86 45 31 54.

Luoghi e Libri
Via M Melloni 32. **Map** 4 F5. **Tel** 02-738 83 70.

Milano Libri
Via Verdi 2. **Map** 3 C5 (9 C2). **Tel** 02-87 58 71.

Mondadori
Corso Vittorio Emanuele II 34. **Map** 8 D1 (10 E3).
Tel 02-76 00 58 33.

Mondadori Informatica
Corso di Porta Vittoria.
Map 8 F1 (10 F4).
Tel 02-55 19 22 10.

Rizzoli
Galleria Vittorio Emanuele II 79. **Map** 7 C1 (10 D3).
Tel 02-86 46 10 71.

MUSIC

Buscemi Dischi
Corso Magenta 31.
Map 3 A5 (9 A3).
Tel 02-80 41 03.

La Bottega Discantica
Via Nirone 5. **Map** 7 A1 (9 A3). **Tel** 02-86 29 66.

Messaggerie Musicali
Galleria del Corso 2.
Tel 02-76 05 54 31.

Rasputin
Piazza Cinque Giornate 10. **Map** 8 F1.
Tel 02-59 90 20 40.

Ricordi Media Store
Galleria Vittorio Emanuele II. **Map** 7 C1 (10 D3).
Tel 02-86 46 02 72.

Supporti Fonografici
Corso di Porta Ticinese 106. **Map** 7 B2 (9 B5).
Tel 02-89 40 04 20.

GIFTS

Albrizzi
Via Bagutta 8.
Tel 02-76 00 12 18.

Città del Sole
Via Orefici 13. **Map** 7 C1 (9 C3). **Tel** 02-86 46 16 83.

Co Import
Piazza Diaz. **Map** 7 C1 (10 D4). **Tel** 02-86 98 40 84.

Lorenzi
Via Montenapoleone 9.
Map 4 D5 (10 E2).
Tel 02-76 02 28 48.

MacKenzy Gadgets
Galleria Vittorio Emanuele II. **Map** 7 C1 (10 D3).
Tel 02-87 50 85.

Movo
Piazzale Principessa Clotilde 8. **Map** 4 D2.
Tel 02-655 48 36.

Penelopi 3
Via Palermo 1. **Map** 3 B3.
Tel 02-72 00 06 52.

Pergioco
Via San Prospero 1.
Tel 02-86 46 34 14.

La Piccola Legatoria
Via Palermo 11. **Map** 3 B3. **Tel** 02-86 11 13.

Savinelli
Via Orefici 2. **Map** 7 C1 (9 C3). **Tel** 02-87 66 60.

ENTERTAINMENT IN MILAN

The entertainment scene is lively in Milan and there is plenty of choice for those who love night life, given the hundreds of clubs that animate the Brera and Navigli quarters in particular. Pubs, discos and nightclubs with live music, as well as late-night bistros, are filled every evening with people who come from all corners of Italy. The theatres offer the public a rich and varied programme: La Scala represents the top in opera and ballet. Major music concerts are usually held in the Palavobis arena (formerly

PalaTrussardi) or at the Filaforum at Assago. Milan is equally generous to sports lovers. Every Sunday from September to May the San Siro stadium plays host to the matches of local football teams Inter and Milan. It also stages national and international championship matches. Sometimes matches are also scheduled during the week. Horse racing takes place all year round at the Ippodromo racecourse Milan's many sports and leisure clubs cater to those who like to play as well as watch sports.

Javier Zanetti, defender for Inter club

INFORMATION

In order to find out the latest information on the many evening events in Milan, check the listings in *ViviMilano*, a Wednesday supplement to the newspaper *Corriere della Sera*. Every Thursday the daily paper *La Repubblica* publishes *Tutto Milano*, which is also full of useful information.

The IAT tourist offices in Piazza del Duomo and the Stazione Centrale (main railway station) provide free copies of the brochure *Milano Mese*, containing information on art shows, light and classical music concerts, jazz and other cultural events. Alternatively, pick up a copy of *Easy Milano*. You can also log on to the *Inmilano* or *Easy Milano* websites: (www.rcs.it/quotidiani/inmilano/benven.htm or

www.easy milano.it) for information on Milanese nightlife, exhibitions and other forms of entertainment.

BUYING TICKETS

Tickets for the theatre and various concerts can be purchased in specialist booking offices such as **Ricordi Box Office**, **Ticket Web** (telephone reservations and online www.ticketweb.it), **Ticket One, Easy Tickets** and **Prenofacile**. However, note that for performances at La Scala, you have to go in person to the box office at the theatre or book through the theatre's website (www.teatroallascala.org).

Tickets for football (soccer) matches can be purchased directly from the stadium box offices. Alternatively tickets for Inter matches

Alcatraz, one of the trendiest discos in Milan *(see p199)*

can be bought from the Banca Popolare di Milano, Banca Briantea, Banca Agricola Milanese and Ticket One. Tickets for AC Milan matches are sold by Cariplo bank, various businesses (40 bars and shops) and Milan Point, whose listings are shown at the Milan Club.

Tickets for the annual Formula 1 Grand Prix, held in September at the Autodromo Nazionale in Monza, are sold at the **Automobile Club Milano**, **Acitour Lombardia** and **AC Promotion**. The Monza race track is usually open to visitors at weekends when there are no other events going on. Cars and motorbikes can be driven on the track when it is free. For more information, enquire at the **Autodromo Nazionale**.

The auditorium of La Scala, Milan's premier theatre

The Filaforum at Assago is a sports arena which is also used for concerts *(see p199)*

CHILDREN

Families visiting Milan with children should be warned that the city does not have extensive specialist entertainment available for them. However, some of the museums and galleries are quite child-friendly. To stimulate the young imagination and provide lots of interesting educational material, there are the Planetarium *(see p120)* and the Science and Technology Museum *(see p88)*, as well as the Civic Aquarium *(see p68)*.

As far as shows and spectacles are concerned, the **Cinema Arti** motion picture theatre shows children's films, and the **Teatro delle Marionette** is a children's puppet theatre.

If on the other hand you opt for pure entertainment,

young tourists enjoying an ice cream

the amusement park at the **Idroscalo** is a good choice.

From June to September **Aquatica** is a popular place to take children: slides, pools and shows make this aquatic park a children's paradise that will entertain both the youngsters and adults alike.

Children over the age of 12 who are keen on video games can try out one of the numerous amusement arcades in the city.

A good place for entertaining smaller children only is the **Play Planet**. This is a recreation centre where the kids can let off some steam and use up a lot of energy or become involved in some of the creative workshops that are on offer. Play Planet is open all year round, and there are also two rooms in which birthday parties can be held.

In sunny weather there are always local public parks to take children to. The most suitable parks for children are the ones at Porta Venezia and Via Palestro, where theoretically no one is allowed to enter unless they are accompanied by a child. There is also a large play area with an electric train in Parco Sempione (between Piazza Castello and Piazza Sempione), near the Arco della Pace.

DIRECTORY

TICKET AGENCIES

Acitour Lombardia
Corso Venezia 43. **Map** 4 E4.
Tel 02-76 00 63 50.

ACP & Partners
Piazza E Duse 1. **Map** 4 F4.
Tel 02-76 00 25 74.

Autodromo Nazionale
Parco di Monza.
Tel 039-248 21.
www.monzanet.it

Automobile Club Milano
Corso Venezia 43.
Map 4 E4 (10 F2).
Tel 02-77 451.

Easy Tickets
Tel 899-899 811.
www.tkts.it

Italian Tickets
www.italiantickets.com

La Scala
Tel 02-86 07 75.
www.teatroallascala.org

Prenofacile
Tel 199-158 152.
www.prenofacile.it

Ricordi Box Office
Galleria Vittorio Emanuele II.
Map 7 C1 (10 D3).
Tel 02-86 90 683.

Ticket One
Tel 899-500 022.
www.ticketone.it

Ticket Web
Tel 02-48 85 73 32.
www.ticketweb.it

CHILDREN

Aquatica
Via G Airaghi 61.
Tel 02-48 20 01 34.

Cinema Arti
Via Mascagni 8.
Map 4 E5 (10 F3).
Tel 02-76 02 00 48.

Idroscalo (Fun Park)
Via Rivoltana 64.
Tel 02-756 03 93.

Play Planet
Via Veglia 59.
Tel 02-668 88 38.
www.playplanet.it

Teatro delle Marionette
Via Tullio Ostilio 1.
Tel 02-46 82 60.

Nightlife

One of the characteristics that distinguishes Milan from other Italian cities is the way in which the city really comes alive at night. From Tuesday to Saturday the city's pubs, bars, restaurants, cafés and discotheques are generally packed, though there are fewer Milanese and more people from outside the city on Saturdays. Monday and, to a certain extent, Sunday, are the quiet days, offering only rare occasions for entertainment. During the week clubs and discos organize theme evenings, and some of them operate a strict door policy. Places offering live music are also very popular; they often feature promising performers. The majority are located in the Navigli district, one of Milan's most vibrant areas.

DISCOS AND CLUBS

For the energetic on the lookout for new trends in music and dance, Milan is a great place to be. The many discos and clubs in town offer different types of music and are so popular that they attract young people from all over Italy. The scene is quite volatile and with rare exceptions – some places have become positive institutions – Milan discos change their name, management and style periodically. It is quite common for a wildly popular club to fall out of favour, only to return to popularity once again some time later.

Some places charge an entrance fee; others are free but you are obliged to pay for drinks. Prices vary quite a lot; the so-called drinkcard system, whereby you pay for your drinks at the entrance, is fairly common.

One disco that has adopted this method is **Alcatraz**, a former factory converted into a multi-purpose venue for concerts, fashion shows and even conventions. Friday is given over to 1970s–80s revival dance music.

Next door is **Zenith**, which is more formal. There is a restaurant and also a private club called **De Sade**.

La Banque attracts a chic crowd to its good restaurant. The clientele stay on to dance to music mixed by hip DJs. **Colony Dine & Dance** has live music and a students' night on Mondays. Sunday is cocktail evening with dancing.

Currently drawing in the fashion crowd is **Hollywood**. This is the place to go if you fancy celebrity spotting. The **Magazzini Generali**, which is also used for concerts and exhibitions, attracts a mixed crowd. The week opens on Wednesday and themed evenings include new musical trends and popular DJs. Friday is usually international night, with the latest music from around the world. Saturdays focus on the best of new dance, rock and contemporary pop music.

The **Shocking Club** is crowded every night from Monday to Saturday, and has become a Milanese institution. There is a strict door policy. A trendy multi-purpose disco is the **Café Atlantique**, which is a café, bar, restaurant and disco in one. **Rolling Stone** is a historic address where rock music reigns supreme. Thanks to its size, concerts are often held here.

The **Old Fashion**, inside the Triennale, is a disco with popular theme evenings. (The restaurant is also a big draw, especially for Sunday brunch.)

One of the largest discos in Milan is **Limelight**. The place is also used for television programmes and music concerts.

For an alternative spot, try the **Rainbow**: it features rock and pop and on Friday and Saturday is mainly the haunt of teenagers. **Il Ragno d'Oro**, near the Spanish walls overlooking Porta Romana, is jam-packed in the summer.

NIGHTSPOTS WITH LIVE MUSIC

Listening to live music is a popular activity in the city and the choice of venues is wide. **Scimmie** is one of the city's historic nightspots. In the 1980s it was the place to go for live jazz, but recently has concentrated more on rock, blues and ethnic music. The place gets very crowded and it can be difficult to find a table unless you go early.

In the Navigli area, **Grillo-parlante** is worth checking out for up-and-coming bands. **Ca' Bianca** is the place to hear jazz and cabaret. You can sit outside in the summer, and there is also a restaurant.

Nidaba is small, dark and smoky, but people love the atmosphere and it is always full. Promising young bands often perform here.

Lastly, concerts of current music are held at the **Tunnel**, a converted warehouse under the Stazione Centrale (main railway station). Tunnel also functions as a cultural centre, hosting shows and exhibitions as well as book launches for new publications.

DISCOPUBS

For those who want to dance without going to a disco there are so-called discopubs. In the early evening, these places are ideal for a relaxing drink and quiet conversation. Later in the evening, the atmosphere livens up considerably. **Loolapaloosa**, for example, is an Irish pub with a happy hour extending from 5 to 9pm. Late at night it transforms into a totally different creature: the volume is turned up and every available spot is used for dancing, including the tables and the counter.

The **Indian Café**, in the Brera area, has a happy hour from 6 to 8pm, and turns into a discopub in the evening.

There are three floor levels, and concerts are put on for very reasonable prices. Music tends to be rock-oriented.

A great place for followers of fashion is the **Grand Café Fashion**, which is popular with celebrities and models. Happy hour runs from 6:30 to 9:30pm, after which you can dance downstairs. The house aperitifs are excellent.

Stonehenge is a bar and disco on two floor levels, inspired by Celtic culture. It is popular for theme evenings, live music and Latin-American dance courses. Happy hour extends from 6 to 9pm.

LATIN-AMERICAN

Latin-American dance is increasingly popular in Milan. The place to go for uninhibited dancing is the **Tropicana**. It attracts mostly the over-thirty crowd and the best evenings to go are Thursday, Friday and Saturday.

If you find Cuban atmosphere intriguing and feel like trying out some Creole cuisine, the place to go is **Bodeguita del Medio**. Live music is on offer late at night and you can try salsa and merengue dancing.

A disco with Latin-American music only is **Etoile**, where entry is free but drinks are obligatory.

Oficina do Sabor, on the other hand, alternates rock and blues evenings with nights entirely given over to Latin-American music. They also offer courses in salsa-merengue dancing, and anyone who wants to celebrate a special occasion can rent the club.

El Tropico Latino is a great place to try Mexican food while listening to music and sampli. of tequila. W best evening t.

MAJOR CONCE.

Milan's largest conce. are sometimes perform. places normally associat. with football. The stadiun. San Siro *(see p202)* is some-times used, but the usual venue is the **Filaforum**, an ultra-modern sports arena with a seating capacity of 12,000. Other venues are the **Mazda Palace**, the former Palavobis, which can hold 9,000 people, and the **Pala-lido**, with 5,000 seats Al-though space is limited at the **Leoncavallo** social centre, interesting concerts are put on. In the summer, concerts are also held at the Idroscalo or under the Arco della Pace. Sponsored by the Milan city council, entry is free.

DIRECTORY

DISCOS AND CLUBS

Alcatraz
Via Valtellina 21.
Tel 02-69 01 63 52.

Café Atlantique
Viale Umbria 42.
Tel 199-111 111.

Colony Dine & Dance
Piazza XXIV Maggio 8.
Tel 02-58 10 27 66.

Hollywood
Corso Como 15.
Tel 02-659 89 96.

Il Ragno d'Oro
Piazzale Medaglie d'Oro.
Tel 02-54 05 00 04.

La Banque
Via Porrone 6.
Tel 02-86 99 65 65.

Limelight
Via Castelbarco 11.
Tel 02-58 31 06 82.

Magazzini Generali
Via Pietrasanta 14.
Tel 02-55 21 13 13.

Old Fashion
Viale Alemagna 6.
Tel 02-805 62 31.
www.oldfashion.it

Rainbow
Via Besenzanica 3.
Tel 02-404 83 99.

Rolling Stone
Corso XXII Marzo 32.
Tel 02-73 31 72.

Shocking Club
Piazza XXV Aprile 10.
Tel 02-657 50 73.

Zenith – De Sade
Via Valtellina 21.
Tel 02-688 88 98.

NIGHTSPOTS WITH LIVE MUSIC

Ca' Bianca
Via Lodovico il Moro 117.
Tel 393-84 61 607.

Grilloparlante
Alzaia Naviglio Grande 36.
Tel 02-89 40 93 21.

Indian Café
Corso Garibaldi 97–99.
Tel 02-29 00 03 90.

Nidaba
Via Gola 12.
Tel 02-89 40 86 57.

Scimmie
Via A Sforza 49.
Tel 02-89 40 28 74.

Tunnel
Via Sammartini 30.
Tel 02-66 71 13 70.

DISCOPUBS

Grand Café Fashion
Via Vetere 6.
Tel 02-89 40 29 97.

Loolapaloosa
Corso Como 15.
Tel 02-655 56 93.

Stonehenge
Viale Pasubio 3.
Tel 02-655 28 46.

LATIN-AMERICAN

Bodeguita del Medio
Viale Col di Lana 3.
Tel 02-89 40 05 60.

El Tropico Latino
Via G Romano 15.
Tel 02-58 30 45 16.

Etoile
Via Corelli 62.
Tel 340-38 93 570.

Oficina do Sabor
Via Gaetana Agnesi 17.
Tel 02-58 30 49 65.

Tropicana
Viale Bligny 52.
Tel 02-58 43 65 25.

MAJOR CONCERT VENUES

Filaforum
Via Di Vittorio 6,
Assago.
Tel 02-48 85 71.

Leoncavallo
Via Watteau 7.
Tel 02-670 51 85.

Mazda Palace
Via Elia 33.
Tel 02-33 40 05 51.
www.mazdapalace.it

Palalido
Piazza Stuparich.
Tel 02-39 26 61 00.

...atre and Cinema

...son in Milan is undoubtedly one of ...ost varied in Italy. Visitors interested ... performance (especially if it is being put ...ell-known theatre such as the Scala or the ...should book well in advance, either directly ...n the theatre box office or by contacting one ...e booking agencies in the city centre (see p197). ...or those who prefer films to the stage, Milan has a ...eat number of cinemas. A bonus is that new releases are shown in Milan ahead of most other Italian cities. Many of the cinemas are multiplexes with plenty of screens, and the majority are concentrated in the city centre. Foreign-language films are also screened at some cinemas on specific days of the week.

OPERA, BALLET & THEATRE

It would be a shame to leave Milan without having seen an opera at **La Scala** (see pp52–3). The season begins on 7 December, the feast day of Sant'Ambrogio, the city's patron saint. Lovers of ballet and classical music can also enjoy performances at the highest level from the theatre's ballet company and Filarmonica orchestra. It is important to book as far ahead of performances as possble, as, inevitably, there is much competition for seats at one of the world's most famous opera houses.

No less prestigious and world-famous is the **Teatro Grassi**. Founded just after World War II by Giorgio Strehler as "an arts theatre for everyone", its productions are known for their excellence. The **Teatro Strehler**, opened in 1998, was dedicated to the maestro, who had planned a state-of-the-art theatre worthy of his company's quality productions for over 40 years. The new theatre, with a seating capacity of 974, hosts the major Piccolo Teatro productions.

The **Teatro Studio** was originally meant to be a rehearsal hall for the Piccolo Teatro, but later became an independent company. Though interesting from an architectural standpoint, it is not all that comfortable.

The **Manzoni**, a favourite with the Milanese, presents a very eclectic programme,

ranging from musicals to drama and comedy, always with top-level directors and actors.

Another historic theatre is the **Carcano**, first opened in 1803. It was restructured in the 1980s and has a capacity of 990 people. Its repertoire is classical, and dance is sometimes offered as well. For comedy, head for the **Ciak**, which usually stars leading comic actors.

For lovers of experimental and avant-garde theatre there are the **Teatridithalia-Elfo** and **-Leonardo da Vinci** theatres, which are dedicated to performing original works that are always fascinating and may sometimes shock. The **Out Off** is also dedicated to avant-garde productions.

Milanese experimental theatre is performed at the **CRT Teatro dell'Arte**, which recently increased its seating capacity to 800.

The **San Babila** theatre offers a programme of more traditional theatre. Here the fame of the directors and actors attracts a large number of spectators, so that getting hold of a ticket may be hard.

The largest theatre in Milan is the **Smeraldo**, which can seat 2,100 people. Besides famous musicals, it plays host to dance performances, straight theatre and concerts.

Recently associated with the Smeraldo theatre is the **Nazionale**, which always features famous actors and has been concentrating more and more in recent years on dance and operettas.

The **Litta**, in Corso Magenta, is an elegant theatre which usually presents classic 20th-century plays. Another fascinating theatre is the **Teatro Franco Parenti**, which has a seating capacity of 500. The programme is quite varied, with particular attention being paid to new international works and music.

The small, intimate **Filo-drammatici**, next to La Scala, presents a repertoire of classical works that also includes contemporary plays. The **Nuovo**, with its 1,020 seats, presents different kinds of theatrical productions, including musicals, comedies and dance, usually with famous actors. The recently renovated **Teatro Dal Verme** is also worth checking out.

CINEMAS

Most of the leading cinemas in Milan are concentrated in the city centre, around Corso Vittorio Emanuele II. Most of these are multiplexes, which means there is plenty of choice. Ticket prices are reduced on Wednesday evening and in almost all cinemas on week-day afternoons as well. When popular new films are being shown there are always long queues, so go early.

Most non-Italian films are dubbed into Italian, without subtitles, so they will be difficult for anyone unfamiliar with the language. Visitors who want to see a film with the soundtrack in the original language (in lingua originale) can try **Anteo Spazio Cinema** on Mondays, or **Arcobaleno** on Tuesdays, **Mexico** on Thursdays or the **Odeon Cinema 5**, where they have all-day showings of films in the original language on Mondays.

The **San Lorenzo**, with 170 seats, promotes various cultural events and pro-grammes, such as the African Cinema Festival. The **Auditorium San Fedele** is the home of three film clubs which offer different screening schedules and subject matter. The **Odeon Cinema 5**, a multiplex, is the largest cinema in Milan, with ten theatres. On Corso Vittorio Emanuele II there are the **Pasquirolo**, with a seating capacity of 490, the **Mediolanum**, with 500 seats.

The **Excelsior** is situated in the Galleria del Corso. Another popular venue is the **San Carlo** in Via Morozzo della Rocca. The **Anteo Spazio Cinema** houses three theatres and also presents children's films.

The **Plinius Multisala**, in Viale Abruzzi, is a multiplex with five screens, while the **Colosseo**, in Viale Montenero, has three: the Visconti, Allen and Chaplin. The **President** cinema in Largo Augusto can seat 250 people

and is very comfortable. On Corso Garibaldi the **Brera Multisala** has two theatres. The **Ducale**, in Piazza Napoli, is an old cinema which has been converted into a multiplex with four theatres.

A popular newcomer on the scene is the **Arcadia Multiplex**, just outside Milan at Melzo. The six cinemas here include Energia, the biggest in Italy.

The renovated **Gloria** now has two theatres (Garbo and Marilyn), huge screens and a good audio system. The Cinema Arti *(see p197)* in Via Mascagni is entirely given over to programmes of children's cinema. Fans

of arthouse films can head for the recently reno-vated **Ariosto**, the **Nuovo Corsica** or the **Sempione**. At the **De Amicis** cinema Milan city council organizes themed seasons of films, debates and film club showings.

Every year the Milan city council organizes cinema festivals, one of the best of which is the Panoramica di Venezia, held in September, when previews of the films competing in the Venice Film Festival are shown.

Many cinemas in Milan do provide wheelchair access, but it is always a good idea to telephone the box office beforehand for advice.

DIRECTORY

THEATRES

Carcano
Corso di Porta Romana 63. **Map** 8 E3 (10 D5). **Tel** 02-55 18 13 77. www.teatro carcano.com

Ciak
Via Sangallo 33. **Tel** 02-76 11 00 93 www.teatrociak.it

CRT Teatro dell'Arte
Viale Alemagna 6. **Map** 2 F3. **Tel** 02-88 12 98. www.teatrocrt.org

Filodrammatici
Via Filodrammatici 1. **Map** 3 C5 (9 C2). **Tel** 02-869 36 59. www. teatrofilodrammatici.it

Litta
Corso Magenta 21. **Map** 3 A5 (9 A3). **Tel** 02-86 45 45 46. www.teatrolitta.it

Manzoni
Via Manzoni 42. **Map** 4 D4 (10 D1). **Tel** 02-76 36 901. www.teatromanzoni.it

Nuovo
Piazza San Babila 37. **Map** 4 D5. **Tel** 02-79 40 26. www.teatronuovo.it

Out Off
Via MacMahon 16. **Tel** 02-34 53 21 40. www.teatrooutoff.it

San Babila
Corso Venezia 2/a. **Map** 4 E4 (10 F2). **Tel** 02-79 54 69. www. teatrosanbabila.it

Smeraldo
Piazza XXV Aprile 10. **Map** 3 C2. **Tel** 02-29 00 67 67. www. teatrosmeraldo.it

Studio Teatro
Via Rivoli 6. **Map** 3 B4 (9 B1). **Tel** 02-72 33 32 22.

Teatridithalia Elfo
Via C Menotti 11. **Tel** 02-71 67 91. www.elfo.org

Teatridithalia-Leonardo da Vinci
Via Ampere 1. **Map** 7 C2. **Tel** 02-26 68 11 66.

Teatro Franco Parenti
Via Tertulliano 19. **Tel** 02-55 18 70 56.

Teatro Grassi
Via Rovello 2. **Map** 3 B5 (9 B2). **Tel** 02-72 33 32 22. www.piccoloteatro. org

Teatro alla Scala
Via Filodrammatici 2. **Tel** 02-72 00 37 44. www.teatroallascala.org

Teatro Strehler
Largo Greppi 1. **Tel** 02-72 33 32 22.

Teatro Ventaglio Nazionale
Piazza Piemonte 12. **Map** 1 C5. **Tel** 02-48 00 77 00. www.teatronazionale. com

Teatro Dal Verme
Via Sangiovanni sul Muro. **Map** 3 B5 (9 B2). **Tel** 02-87 90 52 91. www.dalverme.org

CINEMAS

Anteo Spazio Cinema
Via Milazzo 9. **Map** 3 C2. **Tel** 02-659 97 75.

Arcadia Multiplex
Via Martiri della Libertà 5, Melzo. **Tel** 02-95 41 64 44.

Arcobaleno
Viale Tunisia 11. **Map** 4 E2. **Tel** 199 199 166.

Ariosto
Via Ariosto 16. **Map** 2 F4. **Tel** 02-48 00 39 01.

Auditorium S Fedele
Via Hoepli 3b. **Map** 4 D5 (10 D3). **Tel** 02-86 35 22 30.

Brera Multisala
Corso Garibaldi 99. **Map** 3 B2. **Tel** 02-29 00 18 90.

Centrale
Via Torino 30. **Map** 7 B1 (9 C4). **Tel** 02-87 48 26.

Cinema Cavour
Piazza Cavour 3. **Map** 4 D4 (10 E1). **Tel** 02-659 57 79.

Colosseo
Viale Montenero 84. **Tel** 02-59 90 13 61.

Corallo
Largo Corsia dei Servi 9. **Tel** 199 105 300.

De Amicis
Via Caminadella 15. **Map** 7 A2 (9 A4). **Tel** 02-86 45 27 16.

Ducale
Piazza Napoli 27. **Map** 5 C3. **Tel** 199-199 166.

Excelsior
Galleria del Corso 4. **Tel** 199 199 166.

Gloria
Corso Vercelli 18. **Map** 2 D5. **Tel** 02-48 00 89 08.

Mediolanum
Corso Vittorio Emanuele II 24. **Map** 8 D1 (10 E3). **Tel** 02-76 02 08 18.

Mexico
Via Savona 57. **Map** 5 B3. **Tel** 02-48 95 18 02.

Nuovo Corsica
Viale Corsica 68. **Map** 6 F3. **Tel** 02-70 00 61 99.

Odeon Cinema 5
Via Santa Radegonda 8. **Tel** 199 757 757.

Pasquirolo
Corso Vittorio Emanuele II 28. **Map** 8 D1 (10 E3). **Tel** 02-76 02 07 57.

Plinius Multisala
Viale Abruzzi 28–30. **Tel** 199 199 166.

President
Largo Augusto 1. **Map** 8 D1 (10 E3). **Tel** 02-76 02 21 90.

San Carlo
Via Morozzo della Rocca 4. **Map** 6 F1. **Tel** 02-481 34 42.

San Lorenzo alle Colonne
Corso di Porta Ticinese 45. **Map** 7 B2 (9 B5). **Tel** 02-58 11 31 61.

Sempione
Via Pacinotti 6. **Tel** 02-39 21 04 83.

Sports and Outdoor Activities

People visiting Milan on business may want to continue with a routine of practising a sport or exercising. If so, there are many facilities in the city, including health clubs and gymnasiums, that will suit the purpose. These centres often offer a range of activities under one roof so that you can make the most of your free time. Visitors preferring to spectate rather than participate can go and see the local football (soccer), basketball and hockey teams. All are in the first division and offer top-quality sport.

SPORTS FACILITIES

Football (soccer) fans should go to a match at the **Meazza** (or **San Siro**) **Stadium** *(see p203)* at least once in their lifetime. Called the "Scala of football", this stadium has a seating capacity of over 80,000. One particularly popular competition from both the sporting and the theatrical point of view is the local derby between the city's two teams, Inter and AC Milan. However, it is best to plan attendance in advance as tickets sell out pretty quickly.

For horse-racing fans there is the **Ippodromo**, where races are held all year long, except for December. Night races are held from June to September.

The Filaforum arena at Assago *(see p199)* is the home of the local basketball (Pallacanestro Olimpia) and volleyball (Gonzaga) teams. The arena also plays host to various tennis tournaments, first and foremost the Internazionale di Milano, which takes place in spring.

Ice-hockey buffs can follow the matches of the Vipers, who play at the **PalAgorà** arena. They have won the Italian championship for the last four years.

FIVE-A-SIDE FOOTBALL

One of the most popular sports at the moment in Milan is *calcetto* – five-a-side football (soccer). Those wishing to play should go to the **Centro Peppino Vismara**, where they play 11-, 7- and 5-a-side. Another good leisure facility is the **Palauno**, where there are five pitches.

GOLF

There are several golf courses in the Milan area. The closest one to the city is **Le Rovedine Golf Club–Sporting Mirasole**, which is about 7 km (4 miles) from the city centre. There is also a restaurant for the use of players at the club.

SWIMMING

For a relaxing swim, one good swimming pool is the **Piscina Solari**, which has five lanes. A good alternative is the **Piscina Giovanni da Procida**, which boasts a half-size Olympic pool with six lanes. There is also a gym at this site which is ideal for warming up.

The **Lido** is the city's most popular outdoor swimming pool. Visitors who are not daunted by large crowds and enjoy slides can come here to swim during the heat of the Milanese summer.

SKATING

Those keen on roller skating will enjoy themselves at the multi-purpose **24 Sport Village**, which has rinks for roller skating, roller hockey and aerobic roller skating. They also offer facilities for many other sporting activities, including tennis, basketball, swimming and mountain biking. Ice-skaters can go to the **PalAgorà**, which has an indoor rink where people can skate at their leisure on Friday and Saturday nights (9:30pm–12:30am) and Sunday mornings (10am–noon). It is also open in the afternoon at the weekends from 3 to 6pm.

The PalAgorà welcomes ice skaters from Wednesday to Saturday in the evening and also from 3 to 6pm at weekends. All the rinks have skates for rent. During the Christmas season an ice-skating rink is usually set up in Piazza del Duomo enabling people to skate by starlight.

SQUASH

This sport is ideal for fitness, and players are welcome at the **Squash Vico**. There are ten courts. Private and group lessons are available, and equipment can be hired. The centre is open every day, including the evening. However, to use these facilities visitors must buy a membership card, valid for two months.

TENNIS

Tennis players can play in an ideal setting at the **Associazione Sporting Club Corvetto**. The Club does not operate a membership card scheme, and there are 13 indoor courts as well as a gymnasium, bar and restaurant and parking space reserved for customers.

The **Centro Sportivo Mario Saini** has 12 courts, either covered or open to the air, depending on the season. It is best to book ahead by telephone. Another place where it is possible to play in peace and quiet, in a sporting club reserved exclusively for this sport, is the **Tennis Club 5 Pioppi**, in the Fiera district. There are four courts that can be used both in summer and winter.

JOGGING

The best and healthiest place for running is the Monte Stella park (also known as the "Montagnetta"), near the San Siro Stadium. This large area of greenery is a good place to jog, following marked paths, or even for cycling around on mountain bikes. In the summer the park is often filled with numbers of apartment-dwelling Milanese, catching some sun.

DIRECTORY

SPORTS FACILITIES

Ippodromo
Via Piccolomini 2.
Tel 02-48 21 61.
www.trenno.it

Meazza Stadium (San Siro)
Piazzale Axum.
Tel 02-622 81
or 848-89 21 01.

PalAgorà
Via dei Ciclamini 23.
Tel 02-48 30 09 46.

FOOTBALL

Centro Peppino Vismara
Via dei Missaglia 117.
Tel 02-826 58 23.

Palauno
Largo Balestra 5.
Tel 02-423 53 15.
www.palauno.it

GOLF

Le Rovedine Golf Club – Sporting Mirasole
Via C Marx 16,
Noverasco di Opera.
Tel 02-57 60 64 20.

SWIMMING

Lido
Piazzale Lotto 15.
Tel 02-39 26 61 00.

Piscina Giovanni da Procida
Via Giovanni da Procida 20. **Map** 2 D2.
Tel 02-33 10 49 70.

Piscina Solari
Via Montevideo 11.
Map 6 E2.
Tel 02-469 52 78.

SKATING

PalAgorà
Via dei Ciclamini 23.
Tel 02-48 30 09 46.

24 Sport Village
Via Assietta 19.
Tel 02-662 16 11.

SQUASH

Squash Vico
Via GB Vico 38.
Tel 02-48 01 08 90.

TENNIS

Associazione Sporting Club Corvetto
Via Fabio Massimo 15/4.
Tel 02-53 14 36.

Centro Sportivo Mario Saini
Via Corelli 136.
Tel 02-756 12 80.

Tennis Club 5 Pioppi
Via Marostica 4.
Map 5 A1. *Tel* 02-404 85 93. www.tennis-cinquepioppi.it

SAN SIRO STADIUM

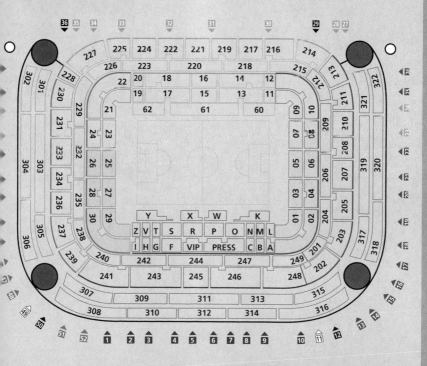

KEY

○ ticket office

■ stadium entrances

area for Milan guests

area for Inter guests

— block of seats

— block of seats

— block of seats

— block of seats

GETTING THERE

Avoid going by car, as parking space is very hard to find. The best way to get there is to take line 1 of the metro to the Lotto stop; from there a shuttle bus goes to the stadium. At the end of the match the No. 16 trams (under the blue area) go to the city centre. Another option is taking a taxi (from the Lotto metro as well).

ENTERTAINMENT AT THE LAKES

At the lakes it is possible to devote a considerable amount of leisure time to entertainment and sport. At Lake Garda in particular, you will be able to practise any type of aquatic sport, have a go at trekking in the hinterland and dance the night away at the discos. Of the lakes, Garda also has the liveliest nightlife and is the most popular with young people. Lake Como, Lake Maggiore and the smaller lakes still offer a variety of opportunities for entertainment. In recent years the enterprising local IAT

The logo of the Caneva aquatic amusement park

tourist offices, sponsored by the town administrations, have been quite successful in promoting initiatives aimed at making holidays more interesting for visitors. Outdoor markets, feasts, festivals and other events have therefore become more and more frequent. The lakes offer breathtaking scenery, an entertainment in itself, and every year there are programmes of cultural events. In addition there are fine architectural and artistic works to be seen, lovely gardens to explore, and nature reserves to wander through.

SPORTS

If keeping in top physical shape is a priority, there are plenty of activities that serve the purpose at the lakes. Lake Garda is the domain of windsurfing; Torbole and Riva in particular being the most popular places for surfers both in summer and winter. Sailing fans will enjoy the Centomiglia, an annual regatta organized by the Circolo Vela Gargnano sailing club and held on the second weekend of September. For a more relaxing time, there are also opportunities to go fishing.

In the Garda hinterland, hiking has become very popular, and touring the area on a mountain bike is the most recent vogue. More adventurous souls can take lessons in paragliding.

Lake Maggiore offers not only many aquatic sports but is quite popular with golf enthusiasts. There are state-of-the-art golf courses in lovely natural settings that are enjoyed by Italian and foreign golfers alike.

The hills and valleys around the lake are ideal places for horse riding, hiking, mountaineering, free climbing, hang-gliding and paragliding and, in the winter, when snow covers the high ground, skiing and snowboarding.

The most popular sports at Lake Como are sailing and water skiing. Lessons are available from qualified instructors, whatever your age and experience.

Another enjoyable activity is canoeing. All the lakes have clubs where you can rent canoes and equipment.

A water skiing instructor and his pupil at Lake Como

For the more sedentary, there are many spas *(terme)* at the lakes or in the vicinity. These centres offer a variety of treatments.

OTHER ACTIVITIES

Visitors to Lake Garda, especially families with children, might want to visit the Gardaland amusement park *(see pp152–3)*. It is recommended for children and adults alike, the ideal place to enjoy yourselves and even experience the occasional thrill. However, in peak season, be prepared for a very long wait at the most interesting attractions.

About 2 km (1 mile) from Gardaland is **Caneva**, the

A group of windsurfers in action at Lake Garda

Camels in the Natura Viva zoological park, at Bussolengo-Pastrengo near Lake Garda

largest water amusement park in Italy. Shows, water games and other displays, plus an area reserved for small children, make this a big aquatic attraction.

To take a closer look at some rare and endangered animal species, visit the **Parco Natura Viva**, a zoo located at Bussolengo-Pastrengo. A pleasant walk among ancient oak trees and plants takes visitors around the home of the 1,000 specimens in this lovely park. Cars are also allowed into the safari park, where a 6-km (4-mile) tour brings you into closer contact with some of the wild animals of the savannah.

Logo of the Natura Viva zoological park

Another popular place for lovers of interesting plants is the **Giardino Botanico della Fondazione André Heller** at Gardone Riviera: 1.5 ha (3.7 acres) of land with over 8,000 plants from every climatic zone in the world.

The **Parco Giardino Sigurtà** lies 8 km (5 miles) from Peschiera. This 50-ha (123-acre) garden is a temple to ecology. At Lake Maggiore the Villa Pallavicino park *(see p137)* has a lovely 20-ha (49-acre) botanic garden with 40 different species of animals.

NIGHTLIFE

The best area for nightlife is Lake Garda, which boasts internationally known nightspots. Desenzano, in particular, has a number of pubs and other spots for evening entertainment, while in the outskirts are some of the largest discotheques in Italy. The undisputed king is **Dehor**, a gigantic and extremely popular place, especially in the summer. Another famous and very popular nightspot is **Fura**, a multimedia disco where theme evenings feature. On Friday there is funk, soul and "rare groove" music, while the other evening (and night) programmes are more unconventional.

At Lake Como the most popular disco is **Mascara**, where live music is played until midnight, after which there is dancing with a disc jockey. For live music, go to **L'Ultimo Caffè**.

At Lake Maggiore, do not miss **La Rocchetta**, a disco situated in a splendid Art Nouveau villa with a view of the lake, and **Dancing Mirage**.

At Verbania, go to **Tam Tam**; **Byblos**, at Arizzano, is another lively spot.

DIRECTORY

ACTIVITIES

Caneva
Località Fossalta 1, Lazise.
Tel 045-69 69 900.
www.canevaworld.it

Giardino Botanico della Fondazione André Heller
Via Roma, Gardone Riviera.
Tel 033-65 52 02 47.

Parco Giardino Sigurtà
Via Cavour 1, Valeggio sul Mincio. *Tel* 045-637 10 33.
www.sigurta.it

Parco Natura Viva
Località Figara 40, Bussolengo-Pastrengo, Varenna.
Tel 045-717 01 13.
www.parconaturaviva.it

NIGHTLIFE

Byblos
Via Nuova Intra Premeno 0, Arizzano.
Tel 0323-533 03.

Dancing Mirage
Viale Baracca 1, Arona.
Tel 0322-443 31.

Fura
Via Lavagnone 13, Lonato.
Tel 030-913 06 52.
www.fura.it

Dehor
Via Fornace dei Gorghi 2, Lonato.
Tel 030-991 99 48.
www.dehor.it

L'Ultimo Caffè
Via Giulini 32, Como.
Tel 031-27 30 98.

La Rocchetta
Via Verbano 1, Arona.
Tel 0322-83 26 89.

Mascara
Via Sant'Abbondio 7, Como.
Tel 031-26 83 56.

Tam Tam
Piazza Flaim 16, Verbania.
Tel 0323-40 32 10.

One of the bars at the Dehor discotheque at Lake Garda

SURVIVAL
GUIDE

PRACTICAL INFORMATION 208–213

TRAVEL INFORMATION 214–223

1784

CASE D

casa d

PRACTICAL INFORMATION

Logo of the City of Milan

Milan is one of Italy's most efficient and business-like cities, with an excellent public transport network and good public services. In the capital of fashion, appearances do matter, and you are likely to receive better service and attention if you are smartly dressed. Milan has its share of petty crime, and it is advisable to take some basic precautions in order to enjoy your stay to the full. Keep bags and cameras close to you at all times, and take extra care travelling on public transport, where pickpockets may be operating. The public transport system is, however, the best way to get around the city. Walkers should stay alert in the chaotic traffic, and take particular care crossing streets. Tourist offices are the best places to go for practical information including maps. At the lakes, brochures are available from IAT offices, with information on local festivals and other entertainment. Information can be obtained ahead of your visit from the Italian tourist office (ENIT) in your home country.

TOURIST INFORMATION

The Italian tourist board, the Ente Nazionale Italiano per il Turismo (ENIT) has offices in many major capital cities including London, New York and Montreal, where maps and information on hotels, etc. are available. In Milan itself, the Informazione e Accoglienza Turistica (IAT) tourist offices provide detailed information about the city, including free lists of hotels and restaurants as well as information on cultural events.

At the lakes, look for IAT offices in larger towns, or Pro Loco offices in smaller towns and villages (usually in the town hall). English is spoken and understood in most hotels and shops and frequently used on planes and tour buses. However, a few words of Italian will always be welcome.

Logo of the IAT in Milan

PASSPORTS AND VISAS

European union nationals need a full passport to enter Italy, but can then stay as long as they like. Citizens of the US, Canada, Australia and New Zealand in possession of a full passport can stay in Italy for up to three months. For longer stays, special visas are needed from an Italian embassy.

All visitors must declare their presence to the police within eight days of arrival. If you are staying in a hotel, this will be done for you.

The *Milano è Milano* listings guide

USEFUL PUBLICATIONS

Every week the daily newspapers *Corriere della Sera* and *La Repubblica* publish a special supplement (*Vivi-Milano* and *Tutto Milano* respectively) packed with up-to-date information about cultural activities in the city and the surroundings.

The Milan daily newspapers such as *Il Corriere* have local news sections, which also include theatre and music entertainment and venues and a cinema guide.

The IAT office distributes free copies of *Milano Mese*, a brochure with listings of the various cultural events.

Another publication, *Milano è Milano* is a practical guide that will help you to get around the city. It is also obtainable from the Milan

The main IAT tourist office in Milan (on the left)

IAT office. People with access to the Internet will find these websites useful: www. itwg.com and www.milano infotourist.com.

MUSEUMS, MONUMENTS AND TOURS

Milan's artistic and architectural masterpieces are housed in a variety of institutions, from art galleries and churches to palazzi and castles. In general, most state-owned museums are open from Tuesday to Sunday, churches are open daily. Privately owned museums will operate their own individual timetables.

Discounts are available for residents of the EU under 18 and over 60 in the majority of state-run places.

A good way of gaining an overview of the city is to travel on the **Tram Turistico**, a tour tram that departs from Piazza Castello. The tour lasts for about 1 hour 45 minutes, and audio tapes provide recorded descriptions of sights in Italian, English, French, German and Japanese.

Another tour is the **Giro della Città**, which begins at Piazza del Duomo in the centre. This tour is available from Tuesday to Sunday and covers all the main monuments of Milan in about 3 hours.

In recent years the local administrations at the lakes have also been involved in a variety of cultural promotions. The Associazione Albergatori della Provincia di Varese (Varese hotel owners' association) has introduced a Welcome Card. Distributed free at hotels locally, it allows visitors to obtain a 10 per cent discount on the admission charge at many museums and sights in the area.

INFORMATION FOR STUDENTS

The Centro Turistico Studentesco (CTS) offers discount tickets to young people under 26, which can be used for travel not only in Milan, but in the rest of Italy and Europe as well.

There are two youth hostels in Milan, the **Ostello della Gioventù P Rotta** where you need to present an annual membership card (which can be bought at the hostel). **La Cordata (Casa Scout)**

Membership cards of the CTS, or Centro Turistico Studentesco

has three dorms and is centrally located. For detailed information on youth hostels around the lakes, contact the Associazione Italiana Alberghi per la Gioventù (Italian Youth Hostelling Association).

ITALIAN TIME

Milan is one hour ahead of Greenwich Mean Time. This means New York and Los Angeles are 6 and 9 hours behind Italian time, and Moscow is 2 hours ahead. Tokyo and Sydney are 8 and 9 hours ahead respectively.

DIRECTORY

TOURIST OFFICES

ENIT UK
1 Princes Street,
London W1R 8AY.
Tel 020 7408 1254.
www.enit.it

ENIT US
499 Park Avenue,
NY 10021.
Tel (212) 843 6884.

TOURIST INFORMATION

IAT Milan
Via Marconi 1. **Tel** 02-72 52 43 01. **www.** milaninfotourist.com

Lake Maggiore
IAT di Varese
Via Carrobbio 2.
Tel 0332-28 36 04.
www.turismo.provincia.varese.it

IAT di Laveno
Palazzo Municipale.
Tel 0332-66 66 66.

Lake Como
IAT di Cernobbio
Largo L Visconti 4.
Tel 031-34 97 30.

IAT di Como
Piazza Cavour 17.
Tel 031-33 00 111.
www.lakecomo.com

IAT di Lecco
Via Nazario Sauro 6. **Tel** 0341-36 23 60. **www.** turismo.provincia.lecco.it

Uff. Inf. di Bellagio
Piazza G Mazzini 12. **Tel** 031-95 02 04. **www.** bellagiolakecomo.com

Uff. Inf. di Tremezzo
Via Regina 3.
Tel 0344-404 93.

Uff. Inf. di Varenna
Piazza Venini 1.
Tel 0341-83 03 67.

Lake Garda
IAT di Desenzano
Via Porto Vecchio 34.
Tel 030-914 15 10.

IAT di Sirmione
Viale Marconi 8.
Tel 030-91 61 14, 91 62 45.

IAT di Gardone
Corso Repubblica 8.
Tel 0365-203 47.

IAT di Toscolano Maderno
Via Lungolago Zanardelli 18. **Tel** 0365-64 13 30.

Lake Iseo
Cooptur Lago d'Iseo
Via Duomo 5.
Tel 030-98 11 54.

IAT di Iseo
Lungolago Marconi 2c.
Tel 030-98 02 09.

TOURS OF MILAN

Giro della Città
Via Marconi 1.
02-72 52 43 00.

Tram Turistico
Piazza Freud 3.
Map 3 C1.

EMBASSIES AND CONSULATES

UK
Via San Paolo 7.
Tel 02-72 30 01.

US
Via Principe Amedeo 2/10.
Tel 02-29 03 51 41.

INFORMATION FOR STUDENTS

La Cordata (Casa Scout)
Via Burigozzo 11.
Tel 02-58 31 46 75.
@ ostello@lacordata.it

Ostello della Gioventù P Rotta
Via Bassi 2.
Tel 02-39 26 70 95.
www.ostellionline.org

Personal Security and Health

Italian pharmacy sign

In Milan, there is widespread petty crime, a problem common to all large cities. Stay wary and keep a close eye on your personal property such as bags or cameras, especially in the evening and, in some quarters, during the day as well. The towns and villages around the lakes are very safe areas however, and there should be no cause for concern. Should you fall ill during your stay, Italian pharmacists can advise on minor ailments.

A municipal policewoman directing traffic in Milan

HINTS FOR TRAVELLERS

It is not advisable to walk around alone in the evening in poorly lit streets far from the city centre. Unaccompanied women should take particular care.

Petty theft is a perennial problem, so keep a tight grip on your bag or case in crowded places, particularly in trams and on the metro. Pickpockets work their way around the public transport system and can operate un-noticed in crowds of people. Always keep handbags closed and do not carry haversacks (backpacks) or shoulder bags on your back. It is always best to keep valuables such as a wallet or mobile phone well out of sight.

When walking along the street, keep handbags on the inside, away from the road, and be aware of pickpockets who target tourists. Visitors who are getting about

by car should take all the usual precautions appropriate in a big city. Do not leave personal belongings or car radios visible inside the car, since they might attract potential thieves. It is best to try to leave your car in an attended parking space *(parcheggio custodito)*. Make sure you have adequate travel insurance before you leave.

HEALTH AND MEDICAL ASSISTANCE

The city has state-of-the-art health facilities, should you become ill during your stay in Milan. All EU citizens should be armed with the European Health Insurance Card (EHIC), available from post offices, which entitles the holder to free emergency treatment and reciprocal health care in Italy. It is wise, however, for visitors to have health insurance.

If the ailment is minor, go to a pharmacy *(farmacia)*. Italian pharmacists

are well trained to deal with routine problems. Each pharmacy can be identified by a neon green cross over the door. There is also a free emergency number: 800–80 11 85. A list of pharmacies open at night *(servizio notturno)* and on public holidays will be on display. A useful chemist (drugstore) is the **Farmacia della Stazione Centrale**, at the main railway station, open 24 hours a day. If you need urgent medical assistance, call the **Emergenza Sanitaria/Ambulanze** (Ambulance/Health Emergencies), or go straight to the *Pronto Soccorso* (Casualty Department/Emergency Room) at the nearest hospital.

If you need a doctor at your hotel, call the **Guardia Medica** (Night Duty Physician). In the unlikely event of poisoning, contact the **Centro Antiveleni** (Poison Control Centre).

MOSQUITOES

In summer mosquitoes *(zan-zare)*, which appear at the first sign of warm weather, can be a real pest. Despite the various anti-mosquito devices, such as citronella candles or electrical gadgets which burn insect-repellent tablets, it is difficult to fend them off altogether, especially when sitting at outdoor cafés (the Navigli quarter is fairly bad). People who are particularly allergic to mosquito bites should always apply insect repellent cream or spray.

Milanese police at a road block

Tap water is safe to drink in Italy, but many people prefer to drink bottled water *(acqua minerale)*, which may be either fizzy *(frizzante* or *con gas)* or still *(naturale)*.

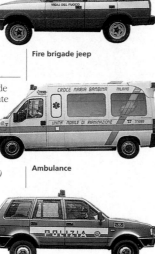

Fire brigade jeep

EMERGENCIES

The police and fire brigade emergency services operate 24 hours a day. The various police stations *(Questura)* and hospitals *(Ospedale)* with a casualty unit/emergency room *(Pronto Soccorso)* are shown in the Street Finder *(see pp224–37)*. There are several different police forces in Italy. State police *(la Polizia)* wear blue, traffic police *(Vigili Urbani)* wear blue and white in winter, white in summer, and are responsible for traffic and parking. *Carabinieri* deal with general crime, public order and drug-related offences.

Ambulance

Police van

LOST PROPERTY

If you lose documents or other personal property, it is advisable to report the loss immediately at the nearest police station. An official report will be needed for insurance claims. It may be worth contacting the city **Ufficio Oggetti Smarriti** (Lost Property Office). If you lose items on a train or in a station, contact the Left Luggage office *(Deposito)* in the Stazione Centrale.

Should an interpreter be needed, ask at your hotel or try the Yellow Pages *(Pagine Gialle)*, where agencies will be listed (there is also a website at www.paginegialle.it). The Associazione Italiana di Traduttori e Interpreti (AITI) has a list of qualified translators and interpreters. The various embassies should also be able to provide interpreters. It is wise to take photocopies of all important documents, including passport pages, before travelling.

SAFETY OUTDOORS

Milan has a number of green open spaces, but the city air is still quite polluted. In certain weather conditions this produces a high concentration of smog, and people are advised to wear anti-pollution masks.

The air is much cleaner and fresher at the lakes, and visitors are unlikely to experience anything more alarming than the odd mosquito. The more adventurous keen to practise watersports should follow certain guidelines. At Lakes Maggiore and Como, cold water and strong currents challenge even experienced swimmers. On Lake Garda, windsurfers may be taken by surprise by sudden gusts of wind, particularly in the areas around Torbole and Riva (the northern part of the lake).

DIRECTORY

EMERGENCY NUMBERS

General Emergencies
Tel 113.

Carabinieri
Tel 112.

Fire
Tel 115.

Emergenza Sanitaria/ Ambulanze (Health Emergencies/Ambulance)
Tel 118.

Municipal Traffic Police
Tel 02-772 71.

Guardia Medica
Tel 02-345 67.

Centro Antiveleni (Poison Control Centre)
Tel 02-66 10 10 29.

Farmacia della Stazione Centrale
Tel 02-669 07 35.

Pronto Farmacia
Tel 800-80 11 85 (free).

ACI – Accidents and Breakdowns
Tel 116.

LOST PROPERTY

Ufficio Oggetti Smarriti
Via Friuli 30. **Map** 8 F4.
Tel 02-88 45 39 00.
☐ 8:30am–4pm Mon–Fri.

Stazione Centrale (Left Luggage)
Piazza Duca d'Aosta.
Map 4 E1. *Tel 02-63 71 26 67.*
☐ 7am–1pm, 2–8pm daily.

Canoeing, one of the most popular outdoor activities in the lakes in Lombardy

Banking and Communications

Milan has very good public services. There is a bank on almost every corner of the city, and almost all of them have automatic cash dispensers. In general the post offices are well organized and run smoothly, despite the fact that the Italian postal system has a reputation for notoriously slow delivery. Public telephones can be operated by coins or phone cards and are well maintained. Business visitors may find it useful to know that it is possible to hire a mobile phone. At the lakes there are fewer banks and post offices because of the small size of the towns and villages, but the service is good.

Telecom Italia phone cards, now collectors' items

USING TELEPHONES

Telecom Italia runs the network of public telephones throughout Italy, including Milan and around the lakes. Milan is well supplied with telephone booths, which usually operate with telephone cards *(schede telefoniche)* (sold at tobacconists or newsstands). Public phones take coins although cards are widely used. There are also public phones at Telecom offices. The largest branch is in Galleria Vittorio Emanuele II and it is open every day from 8am to 9:30pm. The Telecom bureau also offers a fax service.

The Telecom office in the Stazione Centrale (main station) is usually open from 8am to 8pm daily. From here you can telephone anywhere in the world. You can also receive faxes, and consult telephone directories for the whole of Italy, the rest of Europe and countries around the Mediterranean basin.

The cheapest phone rates are between 10pm and 8am Monday to Saturday, and all day on Sunday. It is convenient to make calls from your hotel room, but the charges will be much higher than at a public phone.

The area code *(prefisso)* for Milan is 02. The code should be included even when phoning within Milan. It is now necessary to dial numbers in full throughout Italy, even for local calls.

For information concerning international calls, dial 176; to make an international reverse charge (collect) call, the number to dial is 170.

New telecommunications companies such as Infostrada and Wind now compete with Telecom Italia, and telephone rates have become much more competitive.

Logo of Telecom Italia

GSM mobile phones work in Italy (but make sure they are turned off on aeroplanes). It is possible

to rent a mobile phone. These are available from three firms: TIM (Telecom Italia Mobile), Omnitel and Wind, all of which use the GSM network. Be careful, as charges can vary quite a bit. Another useful place should you need to hire a mobile phone, is the **Euro Business Centre** at Malpensa airport.

The Telecom office in Galleria Vittorio Emanuele II

Main branch of the Credito Italiano, in Piazza Cordusio

BANKS

Milanese banks are open from Monday to Friday from 8:30am to 1:30pm, and in the afternoon from 3 to 4pm, though this may vary by about quarter of an hour from bank to bank. Almost all banks have cashpoint machines, or ATMs, which take all major credit cards, including American Express and Visa.

CURRENCY EXCHANGE

The euro came into circulation in Italy on 1 January 2002. Cash will be needed in smaller shops, in bars and for items like taxis, but it is better not to carry large amounts on you. The safest way to carry money is to buy euro travellers' cheques, which can be refunded if unused.

It is a good idea to bring some euros with you, but it is possible to change money at the airports. At Linate, **Eurochange Linate**, at international arrivals, is open daily from 7am–midnight, and the office at international departures is open from 6am–10pm.

Departures at Malpensa airport has a branch of **Eurochange Malpensa**, open daily from 7am–11pm. The **Banca Ponti** in Piazza del Duomo has an automatic exchange machine. **CIT** travel agents in the centre can also offer exchange facilities from Monday to Saturday.

CREDIT CARDS

Both in Milan and at the lakes, businesses accept major credit cards such as American Express, Visa, Diners Club International and MasterCard (Access).

Most banks have automatic cash dispensers *(bancomat)* where you can obtain money with credit cards or bank cards, using a PIN number. In the event of the loss or theft of your credit card, you should immediately contact the numbers listed in the directory below.

POSTAL SERVICES

Post offices in Milan are open from Monday to Friday from 8am to 2pm and on Saturday from 9:30am to

Logo of cashpoint machines *(bancomat)*

1pm. There are also 13 post offices that have extended trading hours: weekdays from 8am to 7pm and on Saturday from 9:30am to 1pm. The **Ufficio Centrale** (central post office) is open all day and also has a poste restante *(Fermo Posta)* and express service *(Postacelere)*.

At **Linate Airport Post Office** you can send parcels, letters and registered letters, and a telegram office is open from 8am to 2pm every day.

This service is also offered at the **Ufficio Stazione Centrale** (main railway station) from Monday to Friday from 8am to 7pm and on Saturday from 9:30am to 1pm. Throughout Italy, stamps can be bought at post offices and also at tobacconists *(tabaccai)*.

E-MAIL

E-mail is a convenient way to keep in touch when travelling through Italy. Telecom Italia is setting up Internet services in major train stations and public phone centres. Time is purchased using a regular phone card.

Some Internet access chains sell cards with credit that can be used in any of their Italian stores. Internet points can often be found around train stations and university areas. Users can often buy wcomputer time in blocks as short as 15 minutes, and there are usually student discounts available.

DIRECTORY

MOBILE HIRE

Euro Business Centre
Malpensa airport.
Tel 02-58 58 10 74.

INTERNET CAFES

Internet Enjoi
Via Medici 6. **Map** 7 B2.
Tel 02-86 68 00.

Mondadori
Via Marghera 28.
Map 1 C5.
Tel 02-48 04 73 03.

CURRENCY EXCHANGE

Eurochange Linate
International arrivals.
Tel 02-756 13 72.

Eurochange Malpensa
International departures T2.
Tel 02-58 58 13 16.

Banca Ponti
Piazza Duomo 19.
Map 7 C1 (10 D3).
Tel 02-72 27 71.

CIT Travecafe
Via Dante 6.
Map 3 B5 (9 B2).
Tel 02-86 37 01.
www.citonline.it

CREDIT CARDS (MISSING/STOLEN)

American Express
Tel 800-86 40 46.

Diners Club
Tel 800-86 40 64.

MasterCard
Tel 800-87 08 66.

Visa
Tel 800-87 72 32.

POSTAL SERVICES

Ufficio Centrale
Via Cordusio 4. **Tel** 02-72 48 20 65. **www**.poste.it

Other Post Offices
Tel 02-58 58 66 31 (Malpensa).
Tel 02-71 78 47 (Linate).
Tel 02-67 39 51.
Via Sammartini 2 (Central Railway Station).

TRAVEL INFORMATION

Three airports link Milan with the rest of the world. Linate airport is only a few kilometres from the city centre and connects the capital of Lombardy with the main Italian and European cities. Malpensa is an intercontinental airport about 50 km (30 miles) from Milan, while Orio al Serio is located 45 km (27 miles) away. There are car hire offices at all the airports though it is usually cheaper to book a fly-drive deal ahead rather than arrange hire on arrival. For those travelling by train, there are excellent train links between Milan and

An Alitalia airplane

other cities in Italy. The city is also well connected to the rest of Europe, with fast, easy routes to France and Switzerland, and to Austria and Germany via Verona. Visitors arriving by car will use the excellent road and motorway networks. Exits from the ringroad around Milan are clearly marked. However, these roads are always congested with traffic, so journey times can be slow. In the early morning, when commuters begin to make their way into the centre, getting into town may take twice as long as you expect.

ARRIVING BY AIR

Visitors arriving in Milan by air are likely to fly into Linate or Malpensa airports. Frequent flights between London and Milan are operated by Alitalia and British Airways. Many low-cost airlines, such as Ryan Air and easyjet, fly to Orio al Serio in Bergamo. Alitalia offers the best choice of direct flights from the US, linking Milan with Boston, New York, Chicago, Miami and Los Angeles. Alitalia also has good connections from Toronto, Vancouver and Sydney.

LINATE AIRPORT

This airport has always been popular with the Milanese because of its proximity to the city centre. However business has been

scaled down since the government renovated and enlarged Malpensa airport in 1998. At present Linate handles the Milan–Rome flights of all carriers except Meridiana; two daily Alitalia and AirOne flights to Naples; two Alitalia flights to Sicily and Sardinia; three to five daily flights to London, Paris, Amsterdam, Madrid and Frankfurt.

The airport has Left Luggage facilities, car rental offices including Avis and Hertz, and plenty of car parking space.

In the future the majority of international flights will be handled at Malpensa.

Getting from Linate airport to the centre of Milan is very straightforward. Visitors unfamiliar with the city and burdened with a great deal

A view of modern Malpensa airport

of luggage would do best to take a taxi. Official taxis are white and line up at the taxi stand right in front of the airport exit. In general, the service is prompt.

An alternative is going by bus, which is perfectly comfortable and a much cheaper option: tickets cost only €1 and are sold at the vending machine near the bus stop.

There are two bus lines serving Linate airport. ATM bus number 73 passes at regular intervals from 5:30am to 0:20am and connects the airport with the city centre, going as far as Piazza San Babila. The STAM bus runs from 5:40am to 7pm every 20 minutes and from 7 to 9pm every 30 minutes, connecting Linate and the main station.

The Milan airport, Linate

The ring road *(tangenziale)* around Milan, often congested with traffic

MALPENSA AIRPORT

The Malpensa Express runs on the line connecting Malpensa airport with Milan's city centre. The train arrives and departs from Stazione Nord in Piazza Cadorna, stopping at Stazione Bovisa and Sarona on the way. The journey time is 50 minutes. Trains depart from the airport every 30 minutes from 6:45am to 9:45pm, then a direct shuttle bus takes over until 1:30am; trains from Milan depart from 5:50am to 8:20pm, with the bus taking over until

11:10pm. An adult ticket costs €9.

Two efficient coach lines also offer a good airport service. The Malpensa Shuttle is scheduled as follows: Malpensa–Stazione Centrale every 20 minutes from 6:20am to 10:30pm; Stazione Centrale–Malpensa every 20 minutes from 5:15am to 10:30pm. Journey time is one hour, and tickets cost €4.50. Airpullman runs coaches between Linate and Malpensa airports. Phone for times.

The Malpensa Bus Express also runs to and from

Stazione Centrale every 20 minutes from 6:20am to 10:30am.

ORIO AL SERIO AIRPORT

Autostradale runs an efficient bus service between the airport and Stazione Centrale, leaving every 30 minutes during the day. Journey time is one hour and costs €6.70.

ARRIVING BY CAR

Visitors arriving in Milan from the *autostrada* (motorway) will approach the city via the ring roads, *tangenziale est* (east) and *tangenziale ovest* (west), which are often congested with heavy traffic. Approaching the centre, it is best to look for an official car park *(see p219)* and then use public transport. The alternative is to use the ATM parking areas *(see chart below)*, which are on the outskirts but are well served by the metro. These are open from 7am to 8pm, cost one euro for half a day and two euros for a whole day up to 8pm. On Sundays and public holidays (and after 8pm), ATM parking is free *(see pp220–21)*.

ARRIVING FROM	MOTORWAY EXITS	CAR PARK	NUMBER OF CARS	METRO AND BUS	DISTANCE FROM CITY CENTRE
	Cavenago/Cambiago	Gessate	500	M 2 (30/35 min.)	23 km
Trieste Venice Verona Brescia	Sesto San Giovanni/V.le Zara	Sesto Marelli	250	M 1 (20 min.)	8 km
	Tang. est/Cologno Monzese	Cologno Nord	500	M 2 (30 min.)	9 km
	Tang. est/Viale Palmanova	Cascina Gobba/ Crescenzago	800 600	M 2 (20 min.)	6 km
	Tang. est/Viale Forlanini	Forlanini	650	12 73	6 km
Turin Aosta Como Chiasso Varese Gravellona	Viale Certosa	Lampugnano	2,000	M 1 (20 min.)	5 km
	Pero	Molino Dorino	450	M 1 (25 min.)	8.5 km
	Tang. ovest/Milano Baggio	Bisceglie	900	M 1 (20/25 min.)	6 km
Ventimiglia Genoa	Viale Liguria/Centro Città/ Filaforum	Romolo/ Famagosta	250 560	M 2 (20 min.)	4–5 km
Naples Rome Florence Bologna	Milano/Piazzale Corvetto	Rogoredo/ San Donato	350 2,400	M 3 (20 min.)	5–7 km

An ETR departing from the Stazione Centrale in Milan

ARRIVING BY TRAIN

The main railway station in Milan is the **Stazione Centrale**, where all the major domestic and international trains arrive. Connections with your destination in town can be made by taxi, metro (underground) lines 2 and 3 and many trams and buses, all of which are just outside the entrance. **Porta Garibaldi**, in the Centro Direzionale area, and Milano Lambrate (near Città Studi), are much smaller railway stations. Both can be reached via metro line 2. Metro line 3 links the **Rogoredo** station, near San Donato Milanese, with central Milan.

A regional train service connects the city with Como, Varese and the Brianza region, run by the Ferrovie Nord Milano. Trains depart from Piazzale Cadorna, where metro lines 1 and 2 converge.

There is also the recently opened Passante Ferroviario, a suburban railway link network that connects various metro lines with the Porta Garibaldi station, run by the Ferrovie dello Stato (state railway), and the Milano-Bovisa station, run by Ferrovie Nord.

A number of different types of train operate on Italy's railways. The fastest train linking Milan and the main national and international cities is the **ETR Eurostar**, which is first-class only. The ticket price includes a supplement and obligatory seat reservation. Free drinks and newspapers are provided. **Eurocity** trains also offer fast links between Milan and major European cities such as Paris and Barcelona. **Intercity** trains link Milan and the main cities within Italy such as Florence and Rome. On both Eurocity and Intercity services tickets should be booked ahead. A supplement is charged.

The other types of train are slower, but the fares are reasonable, and calculated by the kilometre. Espresso trains stop at main stations, Diretto trains at most stations, and the Locale stops at every single station on the route.

There are also trains with sleeping cars for people travelling at night. A *cuccetta* (bunk bed) in a compartment can be reserved. Compartments hold 6 or 4 beds. A more expensive but more private alternative are the Wagons-Lits carriages *(vagoni letto)*. Compartments have washing facilities, and breakfast is provided. A first-class ticket is obligatory for a one-bed cabin.

Train tickets can be purchased at railway stations or in travel agencies. Tickets must be validated before departure, by date-stamping them at the station. This is done at small yellow stamping machines which are found normally at the entrance to each platform *(binario)*.

Tickets are valid for two months from the time of purchase, but once date-stamped, they are only good for 24 hours. If you are adversely affected by a railway strike, tickets for travel should be stamped by a ticket inspector or cashier in order to claim a refund. Seats, *cuccette* and sleeping car bunks can be booked at railway stations or at any travel agency with terminals linked to the stations. Reservations can be made two months before departure time. Should your travel plans change and you need to alter a ticket, there is a charge. Cancellations cost 20 per cent of the price of the ticket if you cancel 24 hours before departure; after this you will be charged 50 per cent of the price.

The Ferrovie dello Stato logo

The ticket counters at the Porta Garibaldi railway station

Coaches parked at Autostazione Garibaldi in Milan

ARRIVING BY COACH

Coach travel is a common means of getting about in Italy. Coaches (in Italian, *pullman*) arriving in Milan end their journey at the coach terminus at Autostazione Garibaldi in Piazza Freud.

The most important coach carrier connecting Milan with northern, central and southern Italy, including Sicily, is **Autostradale Viaggi**, with direct connections with the motorway.

SGEA, **SIA** and **STIE** cover many key destinations in Lombardy, including most of the major holiday centres around the lakes. For destinations in the rest of Europe, the principal firm is **Eurolines**.

Long-distance coaches are comfortable, with reclining seats, air conditioning, toilets and television. There are regular stops at motorway service stations.

Tickets for coach travel can be purchased directly at the Autostazione Garibaldi in Piazza Freud.

Timetables and rates vary according to the length of the journey and the seasons. Reductions are sometimes available for small children and those over 60.

DIRECTORY

AIRPORTS

**Information
Linate – Malpensa**
Tel 02-74 85 22 00.
www.sea-
aeroportimilano.it

**Lost Luggage
(Linate & Malpensa)**
*Tel 800-96 46 92 or
0039 02-74 85 22 00
(from abroad).*
sosbagagli@sea-
aeroportimilano.it

Lost and Found
*Tel 02-70 12 44 51.
(7:30am–9pm).*

Left Luggage
Tel 02-71 66 59.

First Aid
Tel 02-74 85 22 22.

Lost and Found
*Tel 02-74 86 83 31 (T1).
Tel 02-74 85 42 15 (T2).*

Left Luggage
*Tel 02-58 58 02 98 (T1).
Tel 02-40 09 93 63.*

First Aid
*Tel 02-74 86 24 08 (T1).
Tel 02-74 85 44 44 (T2).*

Orio al Serio
📞 *035-32 62 87.*
www.orioaeroporto.it

CONNECTIONS
WITH MALPENSA

Malpensa Express
From Milan
(Piazzale Cadorna).
📞 *02-202 22.*
www.ferrovienord.it

Malpensa Shuttle
From Milan
(Stazione Centrale).
📞 *02-58 58 31 85.*

**Airpullman
Linate – Malpensa**
📞 *02-58 58 32 02.*
www.airpullman.com

AIRLINES

Air France
*Tel 848-88 44 66.
Tel 02-76 07 323.*
www.airfrance.co.uk

Air One
Tel 199-20 70 80.
www.flyairone.it

Alitalia
Tel 06-22 22.
www.alitalia.it

British Airways
*Tel 02-72 41 61.
Tel 199 71 22 66.*
www.ba.com

Easyjet
Tel 848 88 77 66.
www.easyjet.com

Lufthansa
Tel 199-400 044 030.
www.lufthansa.it

Meridiana
Tel 199-111 388.
www.meridiana.it

Qantas
Tel 02-86 45 01 68.
www.qantas.com

Ryan Air
Tel 899 67 89 10.
www.ryanair.com

RAILWAY STATIONS

Stazione Centrale
*Tel 89-20 21
(state railway call centre).*
www.trenitalia.com

*Tel 02-63 71 20 16
(reception centre).*

*Tel 02-63 71 22 12
(left luggage).*

*Tel 02-669 45 35
(railway police).*

**Ferrovie Nord
(Cadorna)**
Tel 02-202 22.

Porta Garibaldi
*Tel 02-63 71 62 75
(information).*

Rogoredo
*Tel 02-63 711 or
89-20 21.*

COACHES

Autostradale Viaggi
Piazza Freud 3.
Buses to Orio al Serio
leave from Stazione
Centrale.
Tel 02-63 79 01.
www.autostradale.com

Eurolines
c/o Autostradale Viaggi,
Piazza Freud 3.
*Tel 02-63 79 01.
Tel Florence: 055-35 71 10
(main office &
information).*
www.eurolines.com

SGEA Lombardia
Tel 02-72 02 32 98.
www.sgea.it

SIA
Piazza Freud 3.
Tel 02-63 79 01.
www.sia.it

STIE
Via Paleocapa 1.
Tel 02-86 45 06 14.
www.stie.it

GETTING AROUND MILAN

Although there are some traffic-free areas in Milan, such as the Brera and the historic centre, where you can stroll in relative peace and quiet, the city is not really very pedestrian-friendly. Milanese traffic is always heavy and often chaotic. This, combined with the great difficulty in finding parking space, would discourage anybody from using a car in Milan. Double parking, collisions and traffic jams are everyday matters, to

Ticket for a car park in Milan

say the least. Public transport *(see p220)* and, for the brave, scooters, offer the best solution to the problem of getting around. The tram, bus and metro network is efficient and purchasing tickets is straightforward, with a flat fare operating in the city centre. One-day tickets offer good value. Tickets should be bought in advance and must be date-stamped before use. Fines are imposed on anyone caught having a "free ride".

WALKING IN MILAN

Some areas of Milan are very pleasant to walk around. Strolling around the fashion district, for example, window shopping, is always an enjoyable aspect of Milan. Another good area for people on foot is the Navigli quarter, which is a pedestrian zone after 8pm in summer. However, oases like these are few and far between in Milan, and the pedestrians' lot is by no means an easy one.

The main problem is the heavy traffic. Drivers tend to treat the streets as race tracks, and even where people crossing the streets are using the zebra crossings, the road markings may be ignored by motorists. An additional problem is that the chronic lack of parking space means that cars are

Looking down Corso Vittorio Emanuele to Piazza del Duomo

Corso Buenos Aires on a weekday

usually parked on the pavements (sidewalks), leaving pedestrians very little room to manoeuvre. This is a particular problem for those trying to get around with prams or pushchairs.

DRIVING AROUND MILAN

Visitors should try to avoid getting around Milan by car if possible. The heavy, chaotic traffic, motorists who sound their car horns for no apparent reason, one-way streets and no-entry areas are enough to turn a tour of the city into a nightmare. However, if you absolutely must use a car, it is possible to park (for a fee) without risking a fine.

The authorized ATM sales points, usually tobacconists, bars and newsstands, sell SostaMilano cards, which are pay-ahead car parking tickets. They are also sold

by the ATM personnel near the official car parks. The price varies according to the length of time: a 1-hour ticket costs €1.50, the 2-hour one €3. Both can be used from 8am to 8pm. In the evening from 8pm to midnight you can use the 2-hour ticket. Just scratch off the gilded part of the ticket so that the year, month, day, hour and minute of the beginning of your parking time is clearly visible and then place it either over the dashboard or on the rear-view mirror. SostaMilano cards are also used in those areas marked and bordered by blue lines.

Areas with yellow lines are reserved for residents only. From 8am to 8pm parking is allowed for a maximum of two hours in the blue areas. An alternative is the garages *(autorimesse), (see p219).*

Ask the staff at the car parks if you need help.

Motorbikes and scooters parked in Piazza Cordusio

SCOOTERS, MOPEDS AND BICYCLES

Scooters and mopeds *(moto)* are certainly a good means of getting around Milan. They are fast and agile, allowing you to avoid long queues and traffic jams.

Bicycles *(biciclette)* can also provide an alternative,

provided you are confident and keep your wits about you. The tram tracks can be a nuisance for bicycle wheels. A number of companies offer moped or bicycle hire (rent).

TAXIS

One of the most common means of transport used in Milan, particularly for business purposes, is the taxi. Official taxis are generally white, but you may see yellow ones or taxis with the livery of their sponsors. Taxi stands are located throughout the city; all taxis have telephones and the numbers are listed in the telephone directory. At the beginning of the ride the meter should read €3, to which is added a supplement for holidays and night runs and for luggage. To call a taxi, ring the radio taxi service.

DIRECTORY

BICYCLES AND SCOOTERS FOR HIRE

AWS

(bicycles)

Via Ponte Seveso 33.

Tel 02-67 07 21 45.

@ awsbici@fastwebnet.it

Bianco Blu

(scooters)

Via Gallarate 33.

Tel 02-308 24 30.

www.biancoblu.com

RADIO TAXI

Tel 02-85 85;

02-40 40; or

02-6969.

CAR PARKS IN THE CITY CENTRE

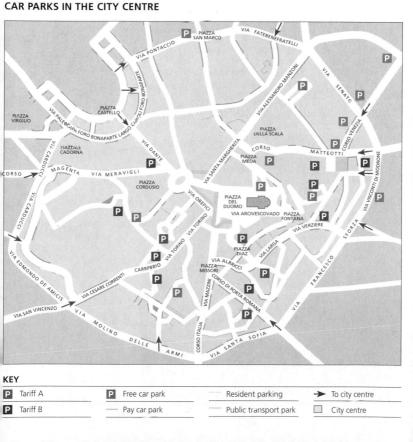

KEY

P Tariff A	**P** Free car park	— Resident parking	→ To city centre
P Tariff B	— Pay car park	— Public transport park	▢ City centre

Travelling by Public Transport

Logo of the Azienda Trasporti Municipali

To avoid stressful driving and parking problems, the best and least expensive way to get around town is to use public transport. Milan has a very efficient city transport system, run by the Azienda Trasporti Municipali (ATM), which comprises trams, buses, trolleybuses, and the three lines of the underground railway *(metropolitana)*.

TRAMS AND BUSES

Trams and buses in Milan are all orange – except for the tourist trams *(see p209)*, which are green – and virtually serve the entire city. They are always extremely crowded, especially during rush hour, and generally pass by every ten minutes.

Bus and tram stops are easy to recognize. Each has a yellow sign displaying the route taken. Stops are often located on islands with seats for waiting passengers.

The yellow signs also have a timetable, but be careful to distinguish the summer *(estate)* from the winter *(inverno)* schedules, as they are posted side by side. Italian timetables always use the 24-hour clock.

The doors of trams and buses have signs indicating which to use to get on and off (*uscita* means exit), but they are often ignored, so do not be surprised if you see someone getting off where you are getting on, and vice versa.

Tickets should be bought before you get on, and your ticket should be date-stamped on the bus or tram. There is a small machine to validate *(convalidare)* your ticket; it is usually at the front, behind the driver, but on longer vehicles there are at least two, one in the front and one at the back.

When you want to get off, press the red button. A sign saying *"fermata prenotata"* will flash until the next stop is reached.

The ATM runs a night bus called Radiobus. Call ahead to book a pick-up at your nearest stop. It costs €3 a ride.

Keep a close eye on your personal belongings, including luggage, when travelling on public transport, particularly on a crowded bus or tram. Pickpockets may be on the lookout for handbags, mobile phones and wallets, and you must be wary.

THE METRO

There are three underground railway (subway) lines: number 1 (red) was inaugurated in 1964, while 2 (green) and 3 (yellow) are newer. Stations all have

An escalator at the exit of a Milan metro station

escalators (some have lifts/elevators for the disabled) and are usually located close to tram and bus stops. The trains run approximately every five minutes from about 6am to 12:30am and are often crowded. Once stamped, tickets can also be used for other means of public transport.

MILAN UNDERGROUND RAILWAY (METRO)

CERTOSA F.S.

Vill

M1
RHO FIERA — Molino Dorino

P S. Leonardo
Bonola
Uruguay
P Lampugnano
QT8
Lotto
Amendola Fi
Buona
M1
BISCEGLIE Inganni Primaticcio Bande Nere Gambara De Ang

M

A tramcar going through the Navigli quarter

One of the Milan tourist trams *(see p209)*, painted green

PASSANTE FERROVIARIO

This train service links the northwest of Milan with the metro. The line goes from Porta Venezia to Bovisa, with intermediate stops at Piazza della Repubblica, Stazione Garibaldi and Via Lancetti.

TICKETS AND TIMETABLES

All tickets can be used for above-ground transport, the metro and the new Passante. Tickets are valid for 75 minutes on all lines. However, they cannot be used twice on the metro.

Tickets should be bought in advance as you cannot buy them on board. They are sold at newsstands, tobacconists and automatic vending machines, which operate with both coins and banknotes. The tourist tickets are good value. They cost from €2 and are valid for 24 hours, or about €4 (48 hours).

(see p209)

DIRECTORY

ATM (Public Transport)
Linea Verde ATM
Tel 800-80 81 81.
www.atm.mi.it

Season Ticket and Travel Pass Sales
Duomo ATM station.
◯ 7:45am–8:15pm Mon–Fri.
Cadorna ATM, Centrale FS, Loreto and Romolo stations.
◯ 7:45am–7:15pm Mon–Sat.

Radiobus
Tel 02-48 03 48 03 (between 1pm and 1am) to book time and route (runs 8pm–2am).

Weekly and monthly passes *(abbonamenti)* are also available.

Milanese public transport, including the metro, usually operates from 6am to midnight, but some buses and trams stay in service until 1:30am. For detailed information, make enquiries at the ATM information bureaux.

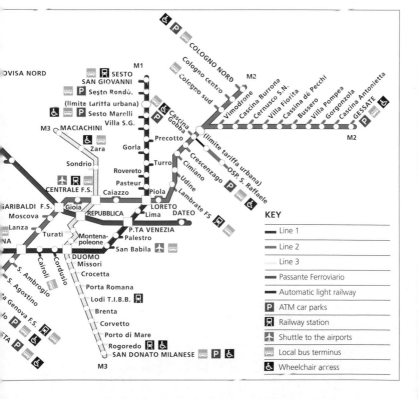

KEY

▬	Line 1
▬	Line 2
▬	Line 3
▬	Passante Ferroviario
▬	Automatic light railway
P	ATM car parks
R	Railway station
✈	Shuttle to the airports
▭	Local bus terminus
♿	Wheelchair access

Arriving at the Lakes

The funicular at Como in 1894

The lakes are easily accessible from Milan, both by car and by train. Visitors arriving by car will take the Autostrada dei Laghi motorway or the Valassina *superstrada*. There are good train links with all the lakes using either the Ferrovie dello Stato (FS) or the Ferrovie Nord (FNM) railways. Both offer frequent services. Bus services link the various towns and villages around the lakes, or you may well prefer to use the hydrofoils or ferries in order to avoid traffic jams on the crowded roads, especially at weekends.

A Ferrovie dello Stato regional train

LAKE MAGGIORE

To get to lake Maggiore from Milan by car, take the A8 autostrada and then the exit for Sesto Calende. From here take the road to Angera to go to the Lombardy side of the lake, or the road to Arona to go to the Piedmontese side.

To get to the upper part of the lake, proceed northwards, turn off at Gravellona Toce and then follow the signs for Fondotoce and Verbania.

Should you decide to go to Lake Orta, take the Borgomanero turnoff and follow the signs for Gozzano-Orta San Giulio. The A8 autostrada is also the easiest way to get to Lake Varese from Milan: take the Varese exit and continue to Gavirate.

The lake is also accessible by train from the Porta Garibaldi railway station in Milan, where the local trains go as far as Luino, via Gallarate. Another rail company, the **Ferrovie Nord** railway operates from the station in Piazzale Cadorna. There are frequent daily train services to Laveno.

The most enjoyable way of travelling from one town to another on Lake Maggiore is to use the hydrofoils and ferries. The main towns are connected by the **Navigazione Lago Maggiore** service, which has a fleet of 30 vessels, including steamboats, motor boats and ferries. The timetables are posted at local hotels, restaurants and all the ports, and are subject to seasonal changes.

If you are travelling to Lake Maggiore from outside Italy, the Malpensa 2000 airport (about 50 km, 30 miles from Milan) (*see p215*) is the closest to Lake Maggiore.

LAKE COMO

The shortest route from Milan to Lake Como by car is to take motorway (*autostrada*) A9, better known as Milano-Laghi, and exit at the Como Nord signs. To get to the western side of the lake, from Como take the statale 340 road, the ancient Via Regina, which goes as far as Sorico. If however you are headed for the other side, you have to go up the state road 583, which passes through Bellagio and goes as far as Lecco.

Traffic can be very heavy during the weekend, and as there is not much parking space around, the best solution may be to use a combination of car followed by one of the frequent hydrofoil or car ferry services. The hydrofoils are particularly frequent on the Como–Colico line, with intermediate stops, while the ferries stop only at Cadenabbia, Bellagio, Menaggio and Varenna. For detailed information, make enquiries at **Navigazione Lago di Como**.

The town of Como is also served by the Ferrovie dello Stato and Ferrovie Nord railways. The FS trains go to Como along the Milan–Chiasso line. The Nord trains leave from Piazzale Cadorna in Milan and arrive in the centre of town at Piazza Cavour. If you travel by air, the Malpensa 2000 airport is the closest one to Lake Como.

A ferry connecting the main towns around Lake Como

LAKE GARDA

Verona is the nearest main town to the lake. It is on routes linking Milan with Venice, both road and rail. To reach Salò from the Milan–Venice A4 motorway, exit at the Brescia Centro signs and then go eastwards on the *tangenziale* (ring road) until you see signs for the Salò *superstrada* (highway). Alternatively you can exit at the Desenzano sign 118 km (73 miles) from Milan, cross the town and then go up the *statale* 572 road for 20 km (12 miles).

A few kilometres past Salò is Gardone. Sirmione can be reached from Desenzano by following the southern side of Lake Garda for 9 km (6 miles), or by turning off the autostrada at the Sirmione-San Martino della Battaglia exit.

Navigarda tickets

To get to the Veneto side of the lake, take the A22 autostrada to Brennero and then exit at Affi.

To get to Lake Idro from Milan, take the A4 autostrada to Brescia Ovest and then proceed to Lumezzane.

Those coming from the east should take the state road that goes from Salò to Barghe, and then follow the signs for Madonna di Campiglio.

Lake Garda is also well served by trains. Desenzano and Peschiera del Garda are stops on the Milan–Venice line and coaches will take you onwards from these stations to Sirmione, Salò, Gardone and Limone. For more information, contact the **Azienda Provinciale Trasporti**.

A pleasant alternative is to travel on the lake: 21 boats offer continuous service on Lake Garda. The hydrofoils are the fastest means of crossing the lake and will save you time, while ferries go directly from Maderno to Torri del Benaco and back, for those who do not want to stop at every town on the route. Boat services are run by **Navigazione Lago di Garda (Navigarda)**; consult the website for seasonal variations on timetables and trips.

The nearest airport is Catullo in Verona Villafranca. Other possibilities are Orio al Serio in Bergamo, Linate in Milan and Marco Polo in Venice.

LAKE ISEO

The easiest way to get to Lake Iseo by car is to take the A4 Milan–Venice motorway. Come off at the Ponte Oglio and Palazzolo exits to get to Sarnico, and at the Rovato, Ospitaletto and Brescia Ovest exits to get to Iseo. If you go to the lake by train, the state railway takes you to Brescia, and from there you can go on the Ferrovie Nord Brescia-Iseo-Edolo line; passengers can take bicycles with them if required.

The best way to get to Sarnico and Lovere is to take a boat from Iseo. **Navigazione Lago Iseo** will provide information on timetabling. In the summer (from June to September) there is a train service to Sarnico on the Palazzolo-Paratico-Sarnico line, run by the Ferrovia del Basso Sebino, which operates in the Oglio River Regional Park in cooperation with the WWF and other environmental associations.

DIRECTORY

RAILWAYS

Ferrovie Nord
Piazzale Cadorna 14, Milan.
Map 3 A5. *Tel* 02-202 22.
www.ferrovienord.it

BUS SERVICE

Azienda Provinciale Trasporti
Via Lungadige Galtarossa 5, Verona. *Tel* 045-805 78 11.
www.apt.rr.it

FERRY AND BOAT SERVICES

Navigazione Laghi Maggiore–Garda–Como
Via Ariosto 21, Milan.
Tel 800-55 18 01.

Navigazione Lago Maggiore
Isola Bella, Stresa.
Tel 0323-303 91 or 800-55 18 01.
Viale F Baracca 1, Arona.
Tel 0322-23 32 00.
www.navigazionelaghi.it

Navigazione Lago di Como
Via Cernobbio 18, Como.
Tel 031-57 92 11.
www.navigazionelaghi.it

Navigazione Lago di Garda (Navigarda)
Plazza Matteotti 2, Desenzano.
Tel 800-55 18 01.
Tel 030 91 49 511.
www.navigazionelaghi.it

Navigazione Lago Iseo
Via Nazionale 16, Costa Volpino.
Tel 035-97 14 83.
www.navigazionelagoiseo.it

The redeveloped Ferrovie Nord railway station, Milan

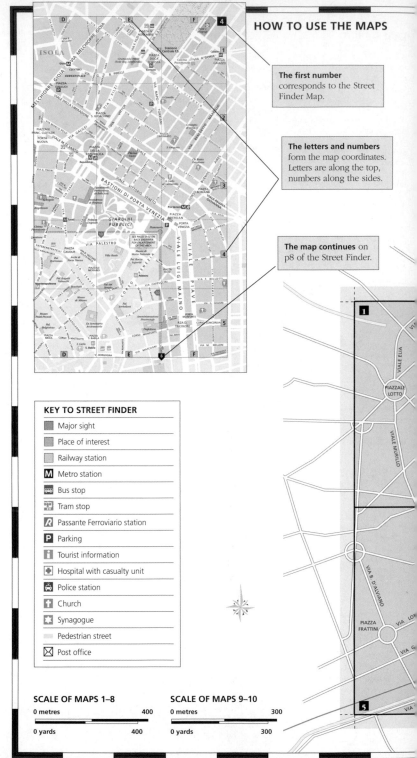

HOW TO USE THE MAPS

The first number corresponds to the Street Finder Map.

The letters and numbers form the map coordinates. Letters are along the top, numbers along the sides.

The map continues on p8 of the Street Finder.

KEY TO STREET FINDER

▪	Major sight
▪	Place of interest
▪	Railway station
M	Metro station
🚌	Bus stop
🚊	Tram stop
R	Passante Ferroviario station
P	Parking
i	Tourist information
✚	Hospital with casualty unit
🚓	Police station
✝	Church
✡	Synagogue
	Pedestrian street
⊠	Post office

SCALE OF MAPS 1–8

0 metres	400
0 yards	400

SCALE OF MAPS 9–10

0 metres	300
0 yards	300

MILAN STREET FINDER

All the map references in this guide, both in the *Milan Area by Area* and in the *Travellers' Needs* sections, refer to the maps in this *Street Finder*. The page grid superimposed on the *Area by Area* map below shows which parts of Milan are covered by maps in this section. Besides street names, the maps provide practical information, such as metro stations, tram and bus stops, post offices, hospitals and police stations. The key on the opposite page shows the scale of the map and explains the symbols used. The main sights are shown in pink. On page 219 there is a map of the Milan metro system, including the Passante Ferroviario.

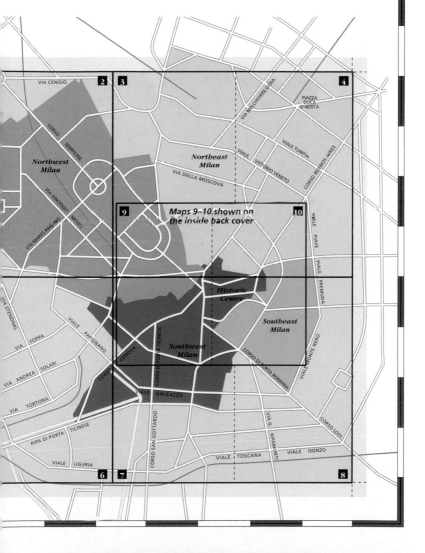

Street Finder Index

A

Abbiati Filippo (Via)	1 A4
Acquario	3 B4
Adda (Via)	4 D1
Adige (Via)	8 F4
Affari (Piazza degli)	7 B1
Africa (Largo)	1 C3
Agnello (Via)	8 D1
Agnesi Gaetana Maria (Via)	8 E4
Agudio Tommaso (Via)	2 E2
Alatri (Via)	1 B4
Albani Francesco (Via)	1 B2
Albertinelli (Via)	1 A3
Albertini Alfredo (Via)	2 F2
Alberto Mario (Via)	1 B4
Albricci Alberico (Via)	7 C2
Alcamo (Via)	1 A2
Alcuino (Via)	2 D2
Aleardi Aleardo (Via)	2 F1
	& 3 A2
Alemagna Emilio (Viale)	2 F3
Alessandria (Via)	6 F3
Alessi Galeazzo (Via)	7 A3
Alfieri Vittorio (Via)	3 A2
Algardi Alessandro (Via)	1 B1
Algarotti Francesco (Via)	4 D1
Allegranza Giuseppe (Via)	6 D2
Allori (Via)	1 A3
Altaguardia (Via)	8 E4
Altamura (Via)	1 A5
Altino (Via)	6 E2
Amedei (Via)	7 C2
Amendola–Fiera (metro station)	1 C4
Amendola Giovanni (Piazza)	1 C4
Amministrazione Provinciale	4 E5
Anco Marzio (Via)	6 F2
Anelli Luigi (Via)	8 D3
Anfiteatro (Via)	3 B3
Anfiteatro Romano	7 A2
Anfossi Augusto (Via)	8 F2
Angelicum	4 D3
Angioli (Via degli)	3 B4
Anguissola Sofonisba (Via)	5 A1
Annunciata (Via dell')	3 C4
Antonello da Messina (Via)	1 A5
Appiani Andrea (Via)	4 D3
Aquileia (Piazzale)	6 E1
Archimede (Via)	8 F1
Arco della Pace	2 F3
Arcole (Piazza)	6 F4
Arduino (Piazzale)	1 C3
Arena	3 A3
Arena (Via)	7 A2
Argelati (Piscina)	6 F4
Argelati Filippo (Via)	6 F4
Ariberto (Via)	6 F2
Ariosto Ludovico (Via)	2 E4
Arona (Via)	2 D1
Arzaga (Via)	5 A3
Asti (Via)	1 C5
Augusto (Largo)	8 D1
Aurispa Giovanni (Via)	7 B3
Ausonio (Via)	6 F2
	& 7 A2
Autari (Via)	6 E4
Avogadro (Via)	5 A5
Azario Pietro (Via)	6 F2
APT (Azienda di Promozione Turistica)	7 C1

B

Bach JS (Viale)	8 D4
Baiamonti Antonio (Piazza)	3 B2
Balbo Cesare (Via)	8 D2
Balestrieri Domenico (Via)	3 A3
Balilla (Via)	7 B4
Bandello Matteo (Via)	6 E1
Bande Nere (metro station)	5 A5
Baracca Francesco (Piazzale)	2 E5
Baracchini Flavio (Via)	7 C1
Baravalle Carlo (Via)	5 C3
Barbaro di San Giorgio Ramiro (Viale)	3 A3
Barbavara Francesco (Via)	6 F3
Barce (Via)	5 C3
Barinetti Giovanni Battista (Via)	2 E3
Barozzi Michele (Via)	4 E4
Barsanti Eugenio (Via)	6 E4
Bartolomeo d'Alviano (Via)	5 A3
Barzilai Salvatore (Via)	5 A3
Basiliche (Parco delle)	7 B3
Bassi Martino (Via)	1 A1
Battisti Cesare (Via)	8 E1
Bazzi Carlo (Via)	7 C5

Bazzi Giovanni Antonio (Piazza)	6 D2
Bazzoni Gian Battista (Via)	2 E5
Beatrice d'Este (Viale)	7 C4
Beauharnais (Viale)	3 A4
Beccaria Cesare (Piazza)	8 D1
Beccaria Cesare (Via)	8 D1
Beethoven Ludwig Van (Largo)	8 D5
Belfanti Serafino (Piazza)	6 F5
Belfiore (Via)	2 D5
Bellani Ettore (Via)	4 D1
Bellezza Giovanni (Via)	8 D4
Bellini Gentile (Via)	5 A4
Bellini Vincenzo (Via)	8 E1
Bellisario (Via)	2 D4
Bellotti Felice (Via)	4 F4
Berengario (Viale)	1 C3
Bergamo (Via)	8 F2
Bergognone (Via)	6 E3
Bertacchi Giovanni (Via)	7 B4
Bertani Agostino (Via)	3 A3
Bertarelli Luigi Vittorio (Piazza)	7 C2
Bertieri Raffaello (Via)	5 B3
Bertini Giovanni Battista (Via)	2 F2
Bertinoro (Via)	1 A1
Besana Enrico (Via)	8 F2
Bettinelli Fratelli Angelo e Mario (Via)	7 A4
Bezzi Ergisto (Viale)	5 B1
Bianca di Savoia (Via)	7 C3
Biancamano (Piazzale)	3 B3
Bianca Maria (Viale)	8 F1
Biancardi G (Via)	1 B3
Bianchi Mosè (Via)	1 B3
Biancospini (Via dei)	5 A4
Bibbiena (Piazza)	7 B5
Bigli (Via)	4 D5
Bilbao (Piazza)	6 D5
Binda Ambrogio (Via)	5 C5
Biondi Ezio (Via)	2 D1
Bisleri (Via)	1 A5
Bixio Nino (Via)	4 F4
Bligny (Viale)	7 C4
Bobbio (Via)	6 F3
Boccaccio Giovanni (Via)	2 E5
Bocchetto (Via)	7 B1
Bocconi (Università Commerciale)	7 C4
Bocconi Ferdinando (Via)	7 C4
Boezio Severino (Viale)	2 D2
Boito Arrigo (Via)	3 C5
Bolivar Simone (Piazza)	5 C3
Boni Giacomo (Via)	6 D2
Bonnet Nino (Via)	3 B2
Bonzagni Aroldo (Via)	1 B4
Bordone Paris (Via)	1 B4
Bordoni Antonio (Via)	4 D1
Borelli Giovanni Alfonso (Via)	5 A2
Borgazzi (Via)	7 C3
Borghetto (Via)	4 F4
Borgogna (Via)	4 D5
Borgonuovo (Via)	3 C4
Borromeo (Piazza)	7 B1
Borromini Francesco (Via)	7 B5
Borsa	7 B1
Borsieri Pietro (Via)	3 C1
Borsi Giosuè (Via)	7 A5
Boschetti	4 E4
Boschetti (Via)	4 E4
Boscovich Ruggero (Via)	4 E2
Boselli Antonio (Via)	8 D5
Bossi (Via dei)	3 C5
Botta Carlo (Via)	8 F3
Braccio da Montone (Via)	3 A2
Bragadino Marco A (Via)	6 F2
Brahms Giovanni (Viale)	7 C5
Braida (Via della)	8 E3
Bramante Donato (Via)	3 A2
Breguzzo (Via)	1 A1
Brembo (Via)	8 F5
Brentonico (Via)	1 A1
Brera (Via)	3 C4
Brescia (Piazzale)	1 B4
Brin Benedetto (Via)	1 C3
Brioschi (Via)	7 B5
Brisa (Via)	7 B1
Broletto (Via)	3 B5
Brugnatelli Luigi (Via)	6 D5
Brunacci Vincenzo (Via)	7 A5
Brunelleschi Filippo (Via)	5 B5
Bruno Giordano (Via)	3 A2
Bruzzesi Giacinto (Via)	5 B4
Buenos Aires (Corso)	4 F3
Bugatti Gaspare (Via)	6 E3

Buonarroti metro station	1 C4
Buonarroti Michelangelo (Piazza)	1 C4
Buonarroti Michelangelo (Via)	1 C4
Buozzi Bruno (Piazza)	8 F4
Burchiello (Via del)	2 D5
Burigozzo Marco (Via)	7 B3
Burlamacchi Francesco (Via)	8 F4
Bussa Eugenio (Cavalcavia)	3 B1
Bussola Dionigi (Via)	6 D5
Byron (Via)	3 A3

C

Caboto Sebastiano (Via)	6 D1
Caccialepori (Via)	1 A5
Cadamosto Alvise (Via)	4 F3
Cadorna (metro station)	3 A5
Cadorna Luigi (Piazzale)	3 A5
Cagnola Luigi (Via)	2 F3
Cagnoni (Via)	5 A1
Caiazzo (Piazza)	4 F1
Caiazzo (metro station)	4 F1
Caimi (Piscina)	8 F3
Caimi Giuseppe (Via)	7 B5
Cairoli (metro station)	3 B5
Cairoli Benedetto (Largo)	3 B5
Calabiana Arcivescovo (Via)	8 F5
Calatafimi (Via)	7 B3
Calco Tristano (Via)	6 F2
Caldara Emilio (Viale)	8 E2
California (Via)	6 D2
Calliano (Via)	1 A1
Camera del Lavoro	8 E1
Caminadella (Via)	7 A2
Campanini Alfredo (Via)	4 D1
Camperio Manfredo (Via)	3 B5
Campobasso (Via)	2 E1
Campo Lodigiano (Via)	7 B3
Camus Alberto (Largo)	2 D4
Caneva Generale Carlo (Piazzale)	2 D1
Canonica Luigi (Via)	2 F2
Canottieri Milano	5 B5
Canottieri Olona	5 C5
Canova Antonio (Via)	2 F3
Cantoni Giovanni (Via)	6 D1
Cantore Generale Antonio (Piazzale)	6 F3
Cantù Cesare (Via)	7 C1
Cappellini Alfredo (Via)	4 E2
Capponi Pier (Via)	2 D5
Cappuccini (Via)	4 E5
Cappuccio (Via)	7 A1
Caprera (Via)	6 D2
Caprilli (Via)	1 A2
Carabinieri d'Italia (Largo)	2 E4
Caradosso (Via)	2 F5
Caravaggio (Via del)	6 E2
Carcano Filippo (Via)	1 B3
Carceri Giudiziarie	6 E1
Carchidio (Via)	6 F3
Carducci Giosuè (Via)	3 A5
	& 7 A1
Carità (Strada della)	8 F4
Carmine (Via)	3 B4
Carracci (Via dei)	1 B3
Carretto Aminto (Via)	4 E2
Carriera Rosalba (Via)	5 A4
Carrobbio (Largo)	7 B2
Carroccio (Via del)	6 F2
Cartesio (Via)	4 D2
Casale (Via)	6 F4
Casanova Luigi (Via)	4 E1
Casati Felice (Via)	4 E2
Cassala (Viale)	6 D5
Cassino (Via)	1 A1
Cassiodoro (Via)	2 D3
Cassolo (Via)	8 D3
Castaldi Panfilo (Via)	4 E2
Castelbarco Gian Carlo (Via)	7 C4
Castelfidardo (Via)	3 C2
Castello (Piazza)	3 A4
Castello Sforzesco	3 A4
Castelvetro Lodovico (Via)	2 E1
Castiglioni Cardinale (Via)	7 C5
Caterina da Forlì (Viale)	5 A2
Cavalcabò Pietro (Via)	5 C1
Cavalieri Bonaventura (Via)	4 D3
Cavalieri di Malta (Largo)	4 A3
Cavallotti Felice (Via)	8 D1
Cavenaghi Luigi (Via)	1 B4
Cavour Camillo Benso, Conte di (Piazza)	4 D4

Cecchi Antonio (Via)	5 C2
Cellini Benvenuto (Via)	8 F1
Cenacolo Vinciano	2 F5
Cenisio (Via)	2 E1
Centrale (Stazione FS)	4 E1
Centrale (metro station)	4 E1
Centro Direzionale	4 D1
Centro Sportivo Cappelli	7 C5
Cerano (Via)	6 E3
Ceresio (Via)	3 B1
Cernaia (Via)	3 C4
Cerva (Via)	8 E1
Cervantes Michele (Via)	3 A3
Cesare da Sesto (Via)	6 F2
Cesariano Cesare (Via)	3 A3
Cèzanne P (Via)	6 E5
Cherubini Francesco (Via)	2 D5
Chiesa Anglicana	4 D3
Chiesa Damiano (Piazzale)	2 D1
Chiesa Protestante	4 D3
Chiesa Russa Ortodossa	4 F3
Chieti (Via)	2 E1
Chiossetto (Via)	8 E1
Chiostri (Via dei)	3 B3
Chiusa (Via della)	7 B2
Chizzolini Gerolamo (Via)	2 E1
Cimabue (Via)	1 A1
Cimarosa Domenico (Via)	6 D1
Cimitero Monumentale	3 A1
Cimitero Monumentale (Piazzale)	3 A1
Cincinnato (Piazza)	4 E2
Cinque Giornate (Piazza)	8 F1
Ciovassino (Via)	3 C4
Ciovasso (Via)	3 C4
Circo (Via)	7 A1
Cirillo Domenico (Via)	2 F3
Città di Messico (Via)	1 B2
Claudiano (Via)	1 C3
Clefi (Via)	5 B1
Clerici (Via)	3 C5
Clusone (Via)	8 F2
Cola da Montano (Via)	3 B1
Cola di Rienzo (Via)	5 C3
Col del Rosso (Via)	7 B4
Col di Lana (Viale)	7 B4
Col Moschin (Via)	7 B4
Collecchio (Via)	1 A1
Colleoni Bartolomeo (Via)	1 C1
Colletta Pietro (Via)	8 F4
Colombo Cristoforo (Corso)	6 F3
Colonna Marco Antonio (Via)	1 C1
Colonna Vittoria (Via)	1 B5
Comerio Luca (Via)	2 E3
Comizi di Lione (Viale)	3 A3
Commenda (Via della)	8 E3
Como (Corso)	3 C2
Conca del Naviglio (Via)	7 A2
Conchetta (Via)	7 A5
Conciliazione (Piazza)	2 E5
Conciliazione (metro station)	2 E5
Conconi Luigi (Via)	1 B5
Concordia (Corso)	4 F5
Confalonieri Federico (Via)	3 C1
Coni Zugna (Viale)	6 E2
Conservatorio (Via)	8 E1
Conservatorio di Musica Giuseppe Verdi	8 F1
Consiglio di Zona 4	4 F2
Consiglio di Zona 5	7 B5
Copernico (Via)	4 E1
Coppi (Piazza)	1 A3
Cordusio (Piazza)	7 C1
Cordusio (metro station)	3 B5
Corio Bernardino (Via)	8 F4
Coriolano (Piazza)	3 A1
Corleone (Via)	2 D2
Cornalia Emilio (Via)	4 D1
Cornelio (Via)	5 C1
Coronelli (Via)	5 A4
Corpus Domini (Church)	2 F3
Correggio Antonio (Via)	1 B4
Correnti Cesare (Via)	7 A2
Corridoni Filippo (Via)	8 E1
Corsico (Via)	6 F3
Costanza (Via)	5 C2
Cozzi (Piscina)	4 E2
Crema (Via)	8 E4
Cremona Tranquillo (Via)	2 D4
Cremosano Marco (Via)	1 A2
Crespi Daniele (Via)	7 A2
Crispi Francesco (Viale)	3 B2
Cristo Re (Church)	1 C2
Crivelli Carlo (Via)	8 D3
Crivellone Angelo Maria (Piazzale)	1 B4
Crocefisso (Via)	7 B2

Crocetta (Largo della) 8 D3
Crocetta (metro station) 8 D3
Crociate (Piazza delle) 3 B4
Crollalanza (Via dei) 6 E5
Cuneo (Via) 1 C5
Curie Pietroß e Maria (Viale) 2 F4
Curio Dentato (Via) 5 A4
Curtatone (Via) 8 E2
Curti Antonio (Via) 7 C5
Cusani (Via) 3 B5
Custodi Pietro (Via) 7 B4

F

Fanti Manfredo (Via) 8 E2
Faraday Michele (Via) 5 B5
Fara Generale Gustavo (Via) 4 D1
Faravelli Luigi Giuseppe
  (Via) 1 C1
Farini Carlo (Via) 3 B1
Faruffini Federico (Via) 1 B5
Fatebenefratelli (Via) 3 C4
Fatebenesorelle (Via) 3 C3
Favretto Giacomo (Via) 5 C2
Fedro (Via) 7 B5
Ferdinando di Savoia (Viale) 4 D2
Ferrari Cardinale Andrea
  (Piazza) 8 D3
Ferrari Gaudenzio (Via) 7 A3
Ferrari Giuseppe (Via) 3 B1
Ferrario E (Via) 6 D1
Ferruccio Francesco (Via) 2 E2
Festa del Perdono (Via) 8 D1
Fezzan (Via) 5 B2
Fieno (Via) 7 C2
Fiera di Milano 1 C2
Filangeri Gaetano (Piazza) 6 F2
Filarete (Via) 2 E3
Filargo Pietro (Via) 6 D5
Filelfo Francesco (Via) 2 E2
Filippetti Angelo (Viale) 8 E4
Filzi Fabio (Via) 4 E1
Finocchiaro Aprile Camillo
  (Via) 4 E2
Fioravanti Aristotele (Via) 3 A2
Fiori Chiari (Via) 3 C4
Fiori Oscuri (Via) 3 C4
Firenze (Piazza) 2 D1
Fogazzaro Antonio (Via) 8 F2
Fontana (Piazza) 8 D1
Fontana (Via) 8 F1
Fontanesi Antonio (Via) 5 A1
Fonzaso (Via) 1 A3
Foppa Vincenzo (Via) 5 C2
Foppette (Via) 6 D4
Forcella Vincenzo (Via) 6 E3
Fornari Pasquale (Via) 5 A1
Foro Buonaparte 3 A4
Forze Armate (Via delle) 5 A1
Fra' Bartolomeo (Via) 5 C2
Fra' Galgario (Via) 5 A1
Franchetti Raimondo (Via) 4 E2
Frascati (Via) 1 B5
Frassinetti (Via) 1 A4
Frattini Pietro (Piazza) 5 A4
Freguglia Carlo (Via) 8 E1
Freud Sigmund (Piazza) 3 C1
Frisi Paolo (Via) 4 F3
Friuli (Via) 8 F4
Frua Giuseppe (Via) 5 B1
Fumagalli Angelo (Via) 6 F4
Fusaro (Via del) 5 C1
Fusetti Mario (Via) 7 A4

G

Gadda Carlo Emilio (Largo) 2 F2
Gadio Gerolamo Bartolomeo
  (Via) 3 A4
Galeazzo Gian (Viale) 7 B3
Galilei Galileo (Via) 4 D2
Galli Riccardo (Via) 1 A2
Galvani Luigi (Via) 4 D1
Gambara (Piazza) 5 A1
Gambara (metro station) 5 A1
Garian (Via) 5 C2
Garibaldi (metro station) 3 C1
Garibaldi Giuseppe (Corso) 3 B2
Gattamelata (Via) 1 C1
Gavirate (Largo) 1 A3
Gavirate (Via) 1 A3
Genova (Corso) 7 A2
Gentili Alberico (Via) 5 C1
Gentilino (Via) 7 B4
Gerusalemme (Piazza) 2 E1
Gessi Romolo (Via) 5 C2
Gesù (Via) 4 D5
Gherardini (Via) 2 F3
Ghiberti Lorenzo (Via) 1 B3
Ghirlandaio Domenico
  (Piazza) 1 B5
Ghisleri Arcangelo (Via) 6 F2
Giambellino (Largo) 5 A5
Giambellino (Via) 5 A4
Giambologna (Via) 7 B5
Giannone Pietro (Via) 3 A2
Giardini (Via dei) 4 D4
Giardini Pubblici 4 E4
Gigante (Via) 1 A4
Gignese (Via) 1 A3
Gignous Eugenio (Via) 1 B4
Gioberti Vincenzo (Via) 2 F5
Gioia (metro station) 4 D1
Gioia Flavio (Via) 1 C2
Gioia Melchiorre (Via) 3 C1

Giorgione (Via) 3 B2
Giorza Paolo (Via) 6 E4
Giotto (Via) 2 D5
Giovanni da Procida
  (Via) 2 D2
Giovanni XXIII (Piazza) 2 E3
Giovenale (Via) 7 B4
Giovine Italia (Piazza) 2 F5
Giovio Paolo (Via) 6 D1
Giuliano Savio (Via) 5 C2
Giusti Giuseppe (Via) 3 A2
Gnocchi VO (Via) 6 D3
Gobbi Ulisse (Via) 7 C4
Goethe (Via) 3 A3
Goito (Via) 3 C4
Gola Emilio (Via) 7 A4
Goldoni Carlo (Via) 4 F5
Gonzaga Maurizio (Via) 7 C1
Gorani (Via) 7 B1
Gorizia (Viale) 7 A3
Gracchi (Via dei) 5 B1
Gramsci Antonio (Piazza) 2 F2
Grancini Angelo Michele
  (Via) 2 D4
Grattacielo Pirelli (Sede
  Regione Lombardia) 4 E1
Grimani (Via dei) 5 C2
Griziotti Giacomo (Via) 2 D4
Grossi Tommaso (Via) 7 C1
Guastalla (Giardino) 8 D2
Guastalla (Via) 8 E1
Guercino (Via) 3 B2
Guerrazzi FD (Via) 2 E3
Guicciardini Francesco
  (Via) 4 F5
Guintellino (Via) 5 A5

H

Hoepli Ulrico (Via) 4 D5

I

Ibsen Enrico (Viale) 3 A4
Illica Luigi (Via) 3 A5
Immacolata Concezione
  (Church) 5 B1
Intendenza di Finanza 4 D3
Irnerio Carlo (Piazza) 5 C1
Isarco (Largo) 8 F5
Ischia (Via) 6 D1
Isola (Quartiere) 4 D1
Isonzo (Viale) 8 E5
Istituto delle Missioni Estere 8 F3
Istituto Ortopedico Gaetano Pini
  8 D3
Istituto Sieroterapico Milanese
  7 A5
Italia (Corso) 8 C2
Italico (Via) 8 F3

J

Jacopo della Quercia (Via) 1 B3

K

Kramer Antonio (Via) 4 F4

L

La Foppa (Largo) 3 B3
Laghetto (Via) 8 D1
Lagrange Giuseppe L (Via) 7 A4
Lamarmora Alfonso (Via) 8 E2
Lambro (Via) 4 F4
Lambro Meridionale
  (Fiume) 6 D5
Lanino Bernardino (Via) 6 D2
Lanza (metro station) 3 B4
Lanza Giovanni (Via) 3 B4
Lanzone (Via) 7 A1
Larga (Via) 8 D1
Lattuada Serviliano (Via) 8 F3
Lauro (Via del) 3 B5
Laveno (Via) 1 A3
Lazio (Viale) 8 F3
Lazzaretto (Via) 4 E2
Lazzati Antonio (Via) 2 D1
Lecco (Via) 4 E3
Lega Lombarda (Piazza) 3 B3
Legnano (Via) 3 B3
Lentasio (Via) 7 C2
Leone XIII (Via) 2 D3
Leoni Pompeo (Via) 8 D5
Leopardi Giacomo (Via) 2 F5
  & 3 A5
Lepetit Roberto (Via) 4 F1
Lesmi (Via) 7 A1
Letizia (Via) 6 E2
Leto Giunio Pomponio
  (Via) 5 C2
Liberazione (Viale della) 4 D2
Libia (Piazzale) 8 F3
Lido di Milano 1 A2

Liguria (Viale) 6 F5
Lincoln Abramo (Via) 8 F1
Linneo Carlo (Via) 2 E3
Lipari (Via) 6 D1
Litta Pompeo (Via) 8 F1
Livenza (Via) 8 E4
Livorno (Via) 4 E5
Lodi (Corso) 8 E4
Lodi (Piazzale) 8 F5
Lodi Tibb (metro station) 8 F5
Lodovico il Moro (Via) 5 A5
Lomazzo Paolo (Via) 2 F1
Lombardini Elia (Via) 6 E4
Londonio Francesco (Via) 2 F2
Lorenteggio (Via) 5 A3
Lorenzini Giovanni (Via) 8 E5
Loria Moisè (Via) 6 D2
Losanna (Via) 2 E1
Lotto (metro station) 1 A2
Lotto Lorenzo (Piazzale) 1 A2
Lovanio (Via) 3 C3
Lovere (Via) 1 A1
Luini Bernardino (Via) 7 A1
Lusardi Aldo (Via) 7 C3

M

Macchi Mauro (Via) 4 F1
Machiavelli Niccolò (Via) 2 E3
Maddalena (Via) 7 C2
Madonnina (Via) 3 B4
Madre Cabrini (Via) 8 E3
Madruzzo Cristoforo (Via) 1 B2
Maffei Andrea (Via) 8 F2
Magenta (Corso) 3 A5
  & 6 F1
Maggi Carlo Maria (Via) 2 E5
Maggiolini Giuseppe e
  Carlo Francesco (Via) 4 F5
Magnasco Alessandro (Via) 1 B4
Magolfa (Via) 7 A4
Maino Giason del (Via) 5 C1
Majno Luigi (Viale) 4 F4
Malaga (Via) 6 D5
Malpighi Marcello (Via) 4 F3
Malta (Viale) 3 A3
Manara Luciano (Via) 8 E1
Mancini Lodovico (Via) 8 F1
Mangili Cesare (Via) 4 D3
Mongone Fabio (Via) 8 F2
Manin Daniele (Via) 4 D3
Mantegazza Laura (Via) 3 B3
Mantegna Andrea (Via) 2 E1
Mantova (Via) 8 F4
Manusardi (Corso) 7 A4
Manuzio Aldo (Via) 4 E2
Manzoni Alessandro
  (Casa del) 4 D5
Manzoni Alessandro (Via) 3 C5
Maratta (Via) 1 A4
Marcello Benedetto (Via) 4 F2
Marcona (Via) 8 F1
Marconi Guglielmo (Via) 7 C1
Marcora Giuseppe (Via) 4 D3
Marenco Romualdo (Via) 6 D1
Marengo (Piazzale) 3 B4
Marghera (Via) 1 C5
Mar Jonio (Viale) 1 A3
Maroncelli Pietro (Via) 3 B1
Marostica (Via) 5 A1
Marradi G (Via) 7 A1
Marsala (Via) 3 C3
Martinitt (Via dei) 1 B5
Martiri Triestini (Via) 1 A4
Marussig Pietro (Via) 2 E1
Marziale (Via) 8 E1
Masaccio (Via) 1 B2
Mascagni Paolo (Via) 4 F4
Mascagni Pietro (Via) 4 E5
Mascheroni Lorenzo (Via) 2 E4
Massarenti Giuseppe (Via) 1 A4
Massaua (Via) 5 B2
Massena Andrea (Via) 2 E3
Mater Amabilis (Church) 1 C4
Matteotti Giacomo (Corso) 4 D5
Mauri Angelo (Via) 6 D1
Mayr Giovanni (Via) 4 F5
Mazzini Giuseppe (Via) 7 C1
Meda Filippo e Luigi
  (Piazza) 4 D5
Meda Giuseppe (Via) 7 A5
Medaglie d'Oro (Piazzale) 8 E4
Medici (Via) 7 B2
Medici Luigi (Largo) 2 F2
Melegnano (Via) 7 C3
Mellerio Giacomo (Via) 7 A1
Melloni Macedonio (Via) 4 F5
Meloria (Via) 1 B1
Melzi D'Eril Francesco (Via) 2 F3
Melzo (Via) 4 F3
Mentana (Piazza) 7 B1
Meravigli (Via) 3 B5

Name	Ref
Mercalli Giuseppe (Via)	7 C3
Mercanti (Via dei)	7 C1
Mercato (Via)	3 B4
Messina (Via)	3 F1
	& 3 A1
Metauro (Via)	5 B4
Micca Pietro (Via)	8 E2
Migliara Giovanni (Viale)	1 A3
Milazzo (Via)	3 C2
Milizie (Piazzale delle)	6 D4
Milton (Via)	2 F4
Minghetti Marco (Via)	3 A5
Mirabello Carlo (Piazza)	3 C3
Missori (metro station)	7 C2
Missori Giuseppe (Piazza)	7 C1
Misurata (Viale)	5 C2
Modestino (Via)	6 F2
Modigliani Amedeo (Via)	6 D3
Mogadiscio (Via)	5 B2
Molière (Viale)	2 F4
Molino delle Armi (Via)	7 B2
Moncalvo (Via)	5 A1
Mondadori Arnoldo (Piazza)	7 C3
Moneta (Via)	7 B1
Monferrato (Via)	6 D1
Monforte (Corso)	4 E5
Monreale (Via)	1 A3
Monte Amiata (Via)	1 C3
Monte Asolone (Via)	2 F1
Montebello (Via)	4 C3
Monte Bianco (Via)	1 B3
Montecatini (Via)	6 D3
Monte Cervino (Via)	1 C3
Monte di Pietà (Via)	3 C5
Monte Falterona (Piazza)	1 A4
Monte Grappa (Viale)	3 C2
Monte Leone (Via)	1 C3
Montello (Viale)	3 B2
Montenapoleone (metro station)	4 D4
Montenapoleone (Via)	4 D5
Monte Nero (Viale)	8 E2
Monte Rosa (Via)	1 B3
Monte Santo (Viale)	4 D2
Montevideo (Via)	6 E2
Monti Vincenzo (Via)	2 E3
	& 3 A5
Montorfano Donato (Via)	1 B4
Monviso (Via)	2 F1
Mora Gian Giacomo (Via)	7 A2
Morandi Rodolfo (Piazzale)	4 D4
Morazzone (Via)	2 F2
Morbelli Angelo (Via)	1 B4
Morigi (Via)	7 B1
Morimondo (Via)	5 B5
Morivione (Quartiere)	7 C5
Morone Gerolamo (Via)	3 C5
Moroni Giovanni Battista (Via)	5 A1
Morosini Emilio	8 F3
Morozza della Rocca Enrico (Via)	6 F1
Mortara (Via)	6 F3
Moscati Pietro (Via)	2 F2
Moscova (metro station)	3 B3
Moscova (Via della)	3 B3
Motta Emilio (Via)	6 E1
Mozart (Via)	4 E5
Muratori Lodovico (Via)	8 F4
Murillo (Via)	1 A3
Museo Archeologico	7 A1
Museo del Risorgimento	3 C5
Museo di Milano	4 D5
Museo di Storia Naturale	4 E4
Museo Nazionale della Scienza e della Tecnica	6 F1
Museo Poldi Pezzoli	4 D5
Mussi Giuseppe (Via)	2 E2

N

Name	Ref
Nago (Via)	1 A1
Napoli (Piazza)	5 C3
Naviglio Grande	5 A4
Naviglio Grande (Alzaia)	5 A4
Naviglio Pavese	7 A4
Naviglio Pavese (Alzaia)	7 A4
Necchi Lodovico (Via)	7 A1
Negrelli (Piazzale)	5 A5
Negri Gaetano (Via)	7 B1
Neri Pompeo (Via)	5 B3
Niccolini GB (Via)	3 A2
Nievo Ippolito (Via)	2 D3
Nirone (Via)	7 A1
Novegno (Via)	1 C3
Novi (Via)	6 E3
Numa Pompilio (Via)	6 F2

O

Name	Ref
Oberdan Guglielmo (Piazza)	4 F3
Oderzo (Via)	1 A1
Olivetani (Via degli)	6 E1
Olmetto (Via)	7 B2
Olona (Via)	6 F2
Omboni Giovanni (Via)	4 F3
Omenoni (Casa degli)	3 C5
Ore (Via delle)	8 D1
Orefici (Via)	7 C1
Organdino Giuseppe (Via)	5 C1
Oriani Alfredo (Via)	8 D3
Orobia (Via)	8 F5
Orseolo Pietro (Via)	6 F3
Orso (Via dell')	3 C5
Orti (Via)	8 E3
Orto Botanico	3 C4
Osoppo (Via)	1 A5
Ospedale	8 E2
Ospedale dei Bambini Vittore Buzzi	2 E1
Ospedale Fatebenefratelli	3 C2
Ospedale Maggiore di Milano (Policlinico)	8 D2
Ospedale Regina Elena	8 E2
Ospedale San Giuseppe	6 F1
Ottolini Giordano (Via)	7 B5

P

Name	Ref
Pace (Via della)	8 E2
Pacioli Fra' Luca (Via)	6 F3
Pagano (metro station)	2 D5
Pagano Mario (Via)	2 E3
Pagliano Eleuterio (Via)	1 B3
Palazzetto dello Sport (Palalido)	1 A2
Palazzi Lazzaro (Via)	4 E3
Palazzo Archinto	8 E1
Palazzo Arcivescovile	8 D1
Palazzo Bagatti Valsecchi	4 D4
Palazzo Belgioioso	4 D5
Palazzo Borromeo	4 D4
Palazzo Clerici	3 C5
Palazzo Cusani	3 C4
Palazzo della Ragione	7 C1
Palazzo dell'Arte	3 A4
Palazzo delle Stelline	6 F1
Palazzo del Senato	4 E4
Palazzo di Brera	3 C4
Palazzo di Giustizia	8 E1
Palazzo Dugnani	4 D3
Palazzo Durini	8 E1
Palazzo Litta	3 A5
Palazzo Marino	3 C5
Palazzo Reale	7 C1
Palazzo Rocca Saporiti	4 E4
Palazzo Serbelloni	4 E5
Palazzo Sormani	8 D1
Palazzo Stanga	7 A1
Paleocapa Pietro (Via)	3 A5
Palermo (Via)	3 B3
Palestro (metro station)	4 E4
Palestro (Via)	4 D4
Palladio Andrea (Via)	8 E4
Pallavicino Giorgio (Via)	2 D4
Palma Jacopo (Via)	5 A1
Pandino (Via)	5 A5
Panizza Bartolomeo (Via)	6 E1
Panizzi (Via)	5 A3
Pantano (Via)	7 C2
Panzacchi (Via)	7 A1
Panzeri Pietro (Via)	7 A3
Panzini Alfredo (Via)	2 D4
Paoli Pasquale (Via)	6 F4
Papi Lazzaro (Via)	8 F4
Papiniano (Viale)	6 E2
Papini Giovanni (Via)	1 C1
Parini Giuseppe (Via)	4 D3
Parmigianino (Via)	1 B5
Paselli Ernesto (Via)	7 B5
Passeroni Gian Carlo (Via)	8 F4
Passione (Via)	8 E1
Passo Buole (Via)	8 F4
Pastorelli Giovanni (Via)	6 D5
Pastrengo (Via)	3 C1
Pasubio (Viale)	3 B2
Patellani Carlo (Via)	8 D4
Pattari (Via)	8 D1
Pavia (Via)	7 A5
Pecorari Francesco (Via)	7 C1
Pellegrini (Via dei)	8 D3
Pellico Silvio (Via)	7 C1
	& 7 C1
Pepe Guglielmo (Via)	3 B1
Perosi (Via)	5 A3
Peschiera (Via)	2 F3
Pestalozzi Giovanni Enrico (Via)	5 C5
Pesto (Via)	5 C4
Petitti Carlo Ilarione (Via)	1 C1
Petrarca Francesco (Via)	2 E4
Petrella Enrico (Via)	4 F1
Piacenza (Via)	8 E4
Piatti (Via dei)	7 B2
Piave (Viale)	4 F4
Piccolo Teatro	3 B5
Pichi Mario (Via)	7 A4
Piemonte (Piazza)	1 C5
Pier della Francesca (Via)	2 D1
Pier Lombardo (Via)	8 F3
Piermarini Giuseppe Francesco (Via)	2 F3
Pietrasanta (Via)	8 D5
Pinacoteca Ambrosiana	7 B1
Pinacoteca di Brera	3 C4
Pinamonte da Vimercate (Via)	3 B2
Pini Gaetano (Via)	8 D3
Pio Albergo Trivulzio	5 B1
Pioppette (Via)	7 B2
Pirandello Luigi (Via)	6 D1
Pirelli Giovanni Battista (Via)	4 D1
Pisanello (Via)	1 A5
Pisani Vittor (Via)	4 E2
Planetario	4 E4
Plutarco (Via)	2 D3
Po (Piazza)	6 D1
Podgora (Via)	8 E1
Poggibonsi (Via)	1 A5
Pogliaghi (Via)	5 A5
Poldi Pezzoli (Via)	1 A3
Polibio (Via)	6 D1
Politecnico (Università)	6 D1
Poliziano Angelo (Via)	2 E1
Polo Marco (Via)	4 D2
Pompeo (Via)	2 D3
Pontaccio (Via)	3 B4
Ponte Vetero (Via)	3 B5
Ponti Andrea (Via)	6 D5
Pontida (Via)	3 B2
Porrone Bassano (Via)	3 C5
Porta Carlo (Via)	4 D4
Porta Garibaldi	3 C2
Porta Garibaldi (Stazione FS)	3 C1
Porta Genova (Via)	6 F3
Porta Genova (Stazione FS)	6 F3
Porta Genova (metro station)	6 F3
Porta Lodovica (Via)	7 C4
Porta Monforte (Via)	4 F5
Porta Nuova (Via)	4 D2
Porta Nuova (Archi di)	4 D4
Porta Nuova (Bastioni)	3 C2
Porta Nuova (Corso di)	3 C2
Porta Romana (Via)	8 E3
Porta Romana (Corso di)	7 B3
Porta Ticinese (Via)	7 B2
Porta Ticinese (Corso di)	7 B2
Porta Venezia (Via)	4 F4
Porta Venezia (Bastioni di)	4 E3
Porta Venezia (metro station)	4 F3
Porta Vercellina (Viale di)	6 E1
Porta Vigentina (Via)	8 D4
Porta Vigentina (Corso di)	8 D3
Porta Vittoria (Via)	8 F1
Porta Vittoria (Corso di)	8 E1
Porta Volta (Via)	3 B2
Porta Volta (Bastioni di)	3 B2
Poste e Telegrafi	4 F1
Poste Telegrafo e Telefoni	7 B1
Pozzi Antonia (Via)	1 B3
Pozzobonelli (Cascina)	4 F1
Praga Emilio e Marco (Via)	2 D3
Prati Giovanni (Via)	2 D3
Preda (Via)	7 B5
Prefettura	4 E5
Premuda (Viale)	8 F1
Presolana (Via)	8 F2
Previati Gaetano (Via)	1 B4
Primule (Via delle)	5 A4
Prina Giuseppe (Via)	2 F2
Principe Amedeo (Via)	4 D3
Principessa Clotilde (Piazzale)	4 D2
Procaccini Giulio C (Via)	2 E1
Procopio (Via)	5 C3
Properzio (Via)	8 F3
Provveditorato agli Studi	8 D5
Pucci Marcello (Via)	2 E3

Q

Name	Ref
Quadrio Maurizio (Via)	3 B1
Quadronno (Via)	7 C3
Quarnero (Via)	5 C1
Quattro Novembre (Piazza)	4 E1
Questura	4 D4
Quinto Alpini (Largo)	2 E4

R

Name	Ref
RAI (Radio Televis ione Italiana)	2 E2
Randaccio Giovanni (Via)	2 E3
Ranzoni Daniele (Viale)	1 B5
Rasori Giovanni (Via)	2 E5
Rastrelli (Via)	7 C1
Ravizza (Parco)	8 D4
Ravizza Carlo (Via)	1 B4
Razza L (Via)	4 E2
Reale (Villa)	4 E4
Redaelli Piero (Via)	5 A3
Reggimento Cavalleria Savoia (Via)	2 E4
Reggio (Via)	8 E3
Regina Giovanna (Viale)	4 F3
Regina Margherita (Viale)	8 F1
Rembrandt (Via)	1 A5
Repubblica (Piazza della)	4 D2
Repubblica (metro station)	4 D3
Resistenza Partigiana (Piazza della)	7 A2
Respighi Ottorino (Via)	8 E1
Restelli Francesco (Viale)	4 D1
Revere Giuseppe (Via)	2 F4
Ricciarelli Daniele (Via)	1 A4
Richard (Via)	5 B5
Richini Francesco (Largo)	8 D2
Ripa di Porta Ticinese	6 D4
Ripamonti Giuseppe (Via)	8 D4
Riva Rocci Scipione (Via)	5 B3
Riva Villasanta Alberto (Via)	2 E2
Romagnoli Ettore (Via)	5 B3
Romagnosi Gian Domenico (Via)	3 C5
Romana (Piazza)	4 F3
Romana (metro station)	8 E4
Romano Giulio (Via)	8 E4
Romolo (metro station)	6 E5
Romolo (Via)	6 E5
Roncaglia (Via)	5 C2
Ronchetti Anselmo (Via)	4 E5
Rondoni Pietro (Via)	5 A3
Rontgen Guglielmo (Via)	7 C4
Ronzoni Gaetano (Via)	7 A3
Rosales Gaspare (Via)	3 C2
Rosario (Piazza del)	6 E3
Rosmini Antonio (Via)	3 A2
Rossetti Dante Gabriel (Via)	2 D4
Rossini Gioacchino (Via)	4 F5
Rotonda di Via Besana	8 F2
Rotondi Giovanni (Via)	2 D3
Rovani Giuseppe (Via)	2 F5
Rovello (Via)	3 B5
Rubens Pier Paolo (Via)	1 A5
Ruffini Fratelli (Via)	2 F5
Rugabella (Via)	7 C2
Russi (Via)	1 A1

S

Name	Ref
Sabbatini Liopoldo (Via)	7 C4
Sabotino (Viale)	8 E4
Sacchi Giuseppe (Via)	3 B5
Sacco Luigi (Via)	5 C1
Sacra Famiglia (Church)	1 C4
Sacro Volto (Church)	3 C1
Saffi Aurelio (Via)	2 F5
Salaino Andrea (Via)	6 E2
Sala Luigi (Via)	6 D5
Salasco (Via)	8 D4
Salmini Vittorio (Via)	8 E4
Salmoiraghi (Via)	1 A1
Salutati Coluccio (Via)	6 D1
Salvini Tommaso (Via)	4 E4
Sambuco (Via)	7 B3
Sammartini Giovan Battista (Via)	4 E1
San Babila (Piazza)	4 D5
San Babila (metro station)	4 D5
San Barnaba (Via)	8 D2
San Benedetto (Church)	5 B2
San Bernardino alle Monache (Church)	7 A2
San Calimero (Church)	8 D3
San Calimero (Via)	8 D2
San Calocero (Via)	7 A2
San Camillo (Church)	4 E2
San Carlo (Church)	4 D5
San Carlo al Lazzaretto (Church)	4 F3
San Celso (Church)	7 C3
San Cipriano (Church)	6 E5
San Cristoforo Church	5 C5
San Cristoforo (Quartiere)	5 C5
San Cristoforo (Via)	5 C4
San Damiano (Via)	4 E5
San Fedele (Church)	3 C5
San Fedele (Piazza)	3 C5
San Fermo della Battaglia (Via)	3 C3
San Francesco d'Assisi (Via)	3 C3
San Gioachino (Piazza)	4 D2
San Giorgio al Palazzo (Church)	7 B1

San Giovanni di Dio (Via) 6 F1
San Giovanni sul Muro (Via) 3 B5
San Gottardo (Church) 8 D1
San Gottardo (Corso) 7 A4
San Gottardo al Corso (Church) 7 A4
San Gregorio (Via) 4 F2
San Gregorio (Via) 4 E2
San Lorenzo Maggiore (Basilica) 7 B2
San Luca (Via) 7 B3
San Mansueto (Via) 8 D4
San Marco (Church) 3 C4
San Marco (Piazza) 3 C4
San Marco (Via) 3 C3
San Martino della Battaglia (Via) 7 C3
San Maurilio (Via) 7 B1
San Maurizio (Church) 7 A1
San Michele del Carso (Viale) 6 E1
San Nazaro Maggiore (Church) 8 D2
San Nicolao (Via) 3 A5
San Paolo (Via) 4 D5
San Paolo Converso (Church) 7 C2
San Pietro all'Orto (Via) 4 D5
San Pietro dei Pellegrini (Church) 8 E3
San Pietro in Gessate (Church) 8 E1
San Pietro in Sala (Church) 2 D5
San Pio V (Via) 7 A1
San Primo (Via) 4 E4
San Raffaele (Via) 7 C1
San Rocco (Via) 8 E4
San Satiro (Basilica) 7 C1
San Sebastiano (Church) 7 B1
San Senatore (Via) 7 C2
San Sepolcro (Church) 7 B1
San Sepolcro (Piazza) 7 B1
San Simpliciano (Church) 3 B4
San Simpliciano (Via) 3 B4
San Siro (Ippodromo) 1 A2
San Siro (Via) 1 C4
San Sisto (Via) 7 B1
San Tomaso (Via) 3 B5
San Vincenzo (Via) 7 A2
San Vincenzo in Prato (Via) 7 A2
San Vito (Church) 5 B4
San Vito (Via) 7 B2
San Vittore (Via) 6 E1
San Vittore al Corpo (Church) 6 F1
Sangiorgio Abbondio (Via) 3 E2
Sant'Agnese (Via) 7 A1
Sant'Agostino (Church) 7 A1
Sant'Agostino (Piazza) 6 F2
Sant'Agostino (metro station) 6 F2
Sant'Alessandro (Church) 7 C2
Sant'Ambrogio (Basilica) 7 A1
Sant'Ambrogio (Piazza) 7 A1
Sant'Ambrogio (Pusterla di) 7 A1
Sant'Ambrogio (metro station) 6 F1
Sant'Andrea (Church) 8 E4
Sant'Andrea (Via) 4 D5
Sant'Angelo (Church) 4 D3
Sant'Angelo (Piazza) 3 C3
Sant'Anna (Church) 1 B2
Sant'Antonio (Via) 8 D1
Sant'Antonio di Padova (Church) 3 B1
Sant'Eufemia (Church) 7 C2
Sant'Eufemia (Via) 7 C2
Sant'Eusebio (Via) 6 D1
Sant'Eustorgio (Church) 7 B3
Sant'Eustorgio (Piazza) 7 A3
Sant'Ildefonso (Church) 1 C1
Sant'Orsola (Via) 7 B1
Santa Cecilia (Via) 4 E5
Santa Croce (Via) 7 B3
Santa Lucia (Via) 7 C3
Santa Margherita (Via) 3 C5
Santa Maria Addolorata (Church) 5 A2
Santa Maria alla Porta (Via) 7 B1
Santa Maria degli Angeli e San Francesco (Church) 1 A5
Santa Maria dei Miracoli, (Santuario) 7 C3
Santa Maria del Carmine (Church) 3 B4
Santa Maria della Pace (Church) 8 E2

Santa Maria della Passione (Church) 8 E1
Santa Maria della Visitazione (Church) 7 C2
Santa Maria delle Grazie (Church) 2 F5
Santa Maria delle Grazie (Piazza) 2 F5
Santa Maria delle Grazieal Naviglio (Church) 6 F4
Santa Maria del Rosario (Church) 6 E3
Santa Maria di Caravaggio (Church) 7 B5
Santa Maria Fulcorina (Via) 7 B1
Santa Maria Incoronata (Church) 3 C2
Santa Maria Nascente (Church) 1 A1
Santa Maria Segreta (Church) 2 E5
Santa Maria Segreta (Via) 7 B1
Santa Marta (Via) 7 B1
Santa Sofia (Via) 7 C2
Santa Teresa del Bambino Gesù (Church) 1 C1
Santa Valeria (Via) 7 A1
Santi Angeli Custodi (Church) 8 F4
Santi Barnaba e Paolo (Church) 8 E2
Santi Protaso e Gervaso (Church) 1 B4
Santissima Trinità (Piazza) 3 A2
Santo Spirito (Via) 4 D4
Santo Stefano (Piazza) 8 D1
Sanzio Raffaello (Via) 1 C5
Sardegna (Via) 5 C1
Sarfatti Roberto (Via) 7 C4
Saronno (Via) 2 E2
Sarpi Paolo (Via) 3 A2
Sartirana (Via) 6 F3
Sassetti Filippo (Via) 4 D1
Savarè Manlio e Gioachino Gerosati (Via) 3 A5
Sebenico (Via) 3 C1
Segantini Giovanni (Via) 6 F4
Segesta (Piazzale) 1 A3
Sei Febbraio (Piazza) 2 D3
Selinunte (Piazzale) 1 A4
Seminario Arcivescovile (Ex) 4 D5
Sempione (Corso) 2 D4
Sempione (Parco) 3 A4
Sempione (Piazza) 2 F3
Sempione (Porta) 2 F3
Senato (Via) 4 D4
Seneca (Via) 8 F3
Senofonte (Via) 2 D3
Seprio (Via) 1 C5
Serao Matilde (Via) 6 D1
Serbelloni Gabrio (Via) 4 E4
Serra Renato (Viale) 1 B1
Servio Tullio (Via) 6 F2
Sesto Calende (Via) 1 A1
Settala Lodovico (Via) 4 E2
Settembrini Luigi (Via) 4 F1
Settimio Severo (Largo) 2 E5
Settimo Ruggero (Via) 6 C1
Sforza Cardinale Ascanio (Via) 7 A4
Sforza Francesco (Via) 8 D2
Shakespeare William (Viale) 3 A4
Sicilia (Piazza) 5 C1
Signora (Via della) 8 D1
Signorelli Luca (Via) 2 F2
Signorini Telemaco (Via) 1 C1
Silva Guglielmo (Via) 1 B2
Simonetta Cicco (Via) 7 A3
Sinagoga (Synagogue) 8 E2
Sirte (Via) 5 C3
Sirtori Giuseppe (Via) 4 F3
Soave Francesco (Via) 8 D5
Società Umanitaria 8 E2
Soderini (Via) 5 A3
Sofocle (Via) 2 D4
Solari (Parco) 6 E2
Solari Andrea (Via) 6 D3

Soldati Giacomo (Via) 2 F1
Solferino (Via) 3 C2
Soperga (Via) 4 F1
Soresina Giovanni Battista (Via) 6 E1
Sormani (Via dei) 6 D2
Sottocorno Pasquale (Via) 4 F5
Spadari (Via) 7 C1
Spagnoletto Ribera Giuseppe (Via) 1 B4
Spallanzani Lazzaro 4 F3
Spartaco (Via) 8 F2
Speri Tito (Via) 3 B2
Spiga (Via della) 4 D4
Spinola Ambrogio (Via) 1 C3
Sraffa Angelo (Largo) 7 C4
Stampa (Via) 7 B2
Statuto (Via) 3 B3
Stazione Ferrovie Nord (Milano) 3 A5
Stazione Porta Genova (Piazzale) 6 F3
Stelline (Via delle) 5 B1
Stendhal (Via) 6 D2
Stromboli (Via) 5 B2
Strozzi Piero (Via) 5 A2
Stuparich Carlo (Piazza) 1 A1
Sturzo Luigi (Viale) 3 C1
Svetonio (Via) 8 F3

T

Tabacchi Odoardo (Via) 7 B5
Tadino Alessandro (Via) 4 F2
Tagiura (Via) 5 B2
Tamburini Pietro (Via) 2 E4
Tantardini A (Via) 7 B5
Tarchetti (Via) 4 D3
Tarquinio Prisco (Via) 6 F2
Tarra Giulio (Via) 4 E1
Tartaglia Nicolò (Via) 2 F1
Tasso Torquato (Via) 2 E4
Tazzoli Enrico (Via) 3 B1
Teatro alla Scala 3 C5
Teatro Carcano 8 D2
Teatro Dal Verme 3 B5
Teatro Fossati 3 B4
Teatro Nazionale 1 C5
Teatro Studio (Ex Fossati) 3 B4
Telesio Bernardino (Via) 2 E4
Tempesta Pietro (Via) 1 B3
Tenaglia (Via) 3 B3
Tenca Carlo (Via) 4 E2
Teodorico (Viale) 1 C1
Terraggio (Via) 7 A1
Teuliè Pietro (Via) 7 C4
Tibaldi (Via) 7 B5
Tintoretto Jacopo (Via) 1 B4
Tiraboschi Gerolamo (Via) 8 F3
Tito Lucrezio Caro (Piazza) 7 B4
Tivoli (Via) 3 B4
Tiziano (Via) 2 D4
Tobruk (Via) 5 C3
Tocqueville (Via di) 3 B2
Tolstoi Leone (Via) 5 B3
Tombone di San Marco 3 C2
Tommaseo Nicolò (Piazza) 2 E5
Toniolo G (Via) 7 C4
Tonoli Rita (Via) 2 E3
Torchio (Via del) 7 A2
Torino (Via) 7 B1
Torre Carlo (Via) 6 E5
Torriani Napo (Via) 4 E1
Torricelli E (Via) 7 A5
Tortona (Via) 6 D3
ToscanaViale 7 C5
Tosi Arturo (Via) 6 E5
Tosi Franco (Via) 6 D5
Traiano Marco Ulpio (Via) 1 C1
Tranchedini N (Via) 1 C2
Trebazio (Via) 2 E2
Trebbia (Via) 8 E4
Trento (Piazza) 8 E5
Treves Claudio (Largo) 6 D3
Trezzo d'Adda (Via) 4 F5
Tricolore (Piazza del) 4 F5
Trieste (Via) 5 C1
Tripoli (Piazzale) 5 B2
Trivulzio AT (Via) 1 B5
Troya Carlo (Via) 5 C4
Tulipani (Via dei) 5 A4
Tunisia (Viale) 4 E2
Turati (metro station) 4 D3
Turati Filippo (Via) 4 D3
Türr Stefano (Piazzale) 1 C1

U

Uccello Paolo (Via) 1 B2
Uffici della Provincia 8 E1
Ulpiano Domizio (Via) 5 C2

Soldati Giacomo (Via) 2 F1
Umanitaria (Piazza) 8 E2
Unione (Via dell') 7 C1
Università Cattolica 7 A1
Università degli Studi di Milano (Ex Ospedale Maggiore) 8 D2

V

Vacani (Via) 1 A3
Vaina (Via) 8 E3
Valenza (Via) 6 F4
Val Lavizzana (Via) 5 A1
Val Leventina (Via) 1 A5
Valparaiso (Via) 6 E2
Val Vigezzo (Via) 1 C1
Vannucci Atto (Via) 8 D4
Varazze (Via) 1 A4
Varese (Via) 3 B2
Vasari Giorgio (Via) 8 F3
Vasto (Via) 3 B3
Vecchio Politecnico (Via del) 4 D4
Vegezio Flavio (Via) 1 C3
Velasca (Torre) 7 C2
Velasquez (Piazzale) 1 A5
Venafro (Via Privata) 2 F2
Venezia (Corso) 4 E4
Veniero S (Via) 1 B2
Venticinque Aprile (Piazza) 3 C2
Ventimiglia (Via) 6 F3
Ventiquattro Maggio (Piazza) 7 A3
Venti Settembre (Via) 2 E5
Vepra (Via) 6 D2
Vercelli (Corso) 2 D5
Verdi Giuseppe (Via) 3 C5
Verga Andrea (Via) 6 D1
Verga Giovanni (Via) 3 A2
Verona (Via) 8 E4
Veronese Paolo (Via) 2 D4
Verri Pietro (Via) 4 D5
Verziere (Via) 8 D1
Vesio (Via) 1 A1
Vespri Siciliani (Via) 5 B3
Vespucci Amerigo (Via) 4 D2
Vesuvio (Piazza) 6 D2
Vetere (Via) 7 B3
Vetra (Piazza della) 7 B2
Vetta d'Italia (Via) 6 D2
Vico Gian Battista (Via) 6 E1
Viganò F (Via) 3 C2
Vigevano (Via) 6 F3
Vigliani PO (Viale) 1 B2
Vigna (Via) 7 A1
Vignola (Via) 8 D4
Vignoli Tito (Via) 5 B3
Vigoni Giuseppe (Via) 7 C3
Vigorelli (Ex Velodromo) 2 D2
Villoresi Eugenio (Via) 6 E4
Virgilio (Piazza) 2 F5
Visconti di Modrone (Via) 8 E1
Visconti Venosta Emilio (Via) 8 F2
Vitruvio (Via) 4 F2
Vittadini Carlo (Via) 8 D4
Vittorio Emanuele II (Corso) 8 D1
Vittorio Emanuele II (Gall.) 7 C1
Vittorio Veneto (Viale) 4 E3
Vivaio (Via) 4 F5
Viviani Vincenzo (Via) 4 D2
Vodice (Via) 1 A3
Voghera (Via) 6 E3
Volta Alessandro (Via) 3 B2
Volterra (Via) 5 C1
Volturno (Via) 3 C1

W

Wagner (metro station) 1 C5
Wagner Riccardo (Piazza) 2 D5
Washington Giorgio (Via) 5 C1
Watt Giacomo (Via) 5 A5
Winckelmann GG (Via) 5 B3

Z

Zaccaria Sant'Antonio Maria (Via) 8 E2
Zamenhof LL (Via) 7 B5
Zandonai Riccardo (Largo) 2 D4
Zanzur (Via) 5 C2
Zarotto A (Via) 4 E3
Zavattari Fratelli (Piazzale) 1 A3
Zenale Bernardino (Via) 6 F1
Zezon Achille (Via) 4 E1
Zola Emilio (Viale) 2 F4
& 3 B4
Zuara (Via) 3 B4
Zuccaro (Via) 5 A4

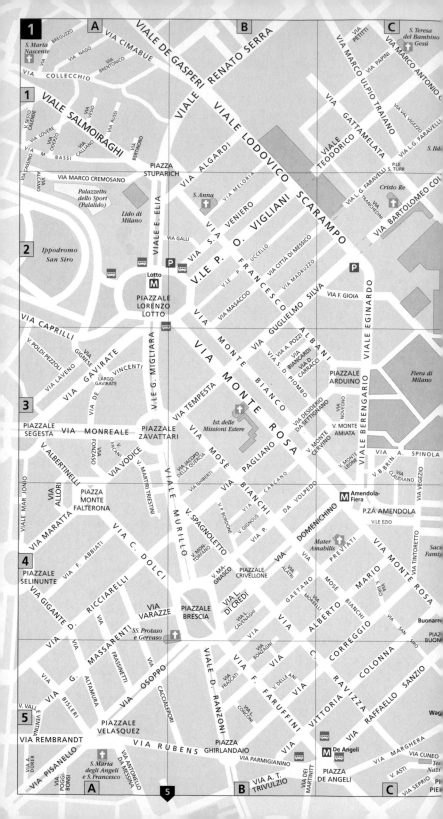

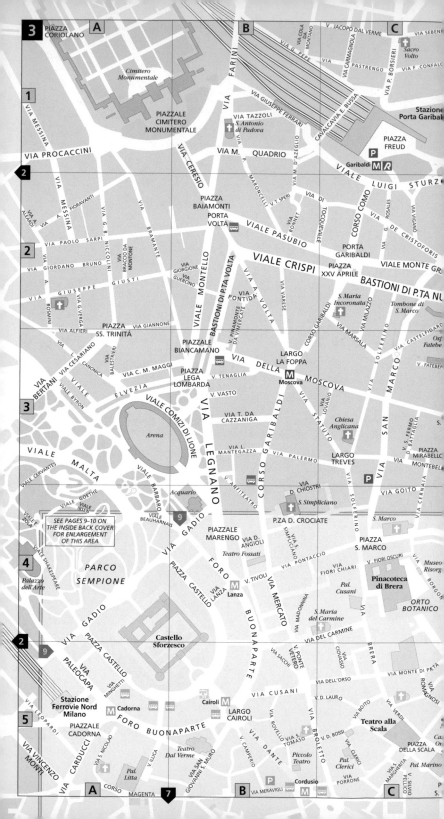

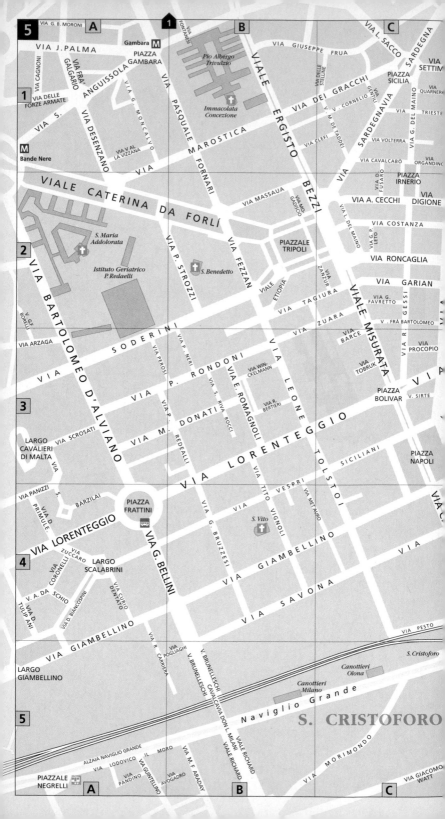

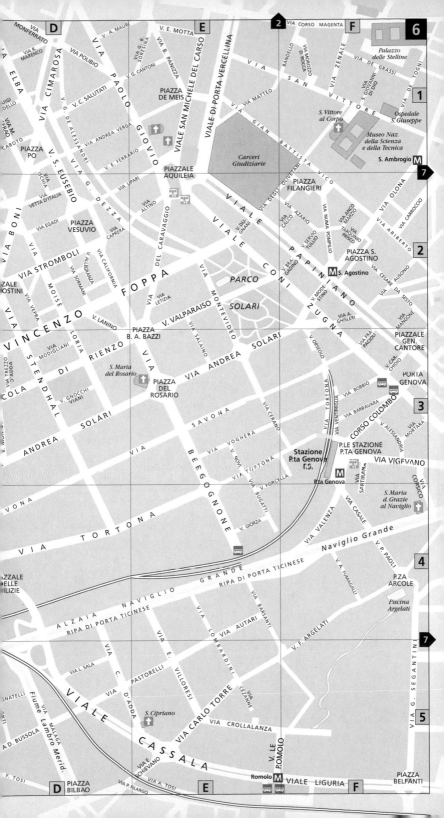

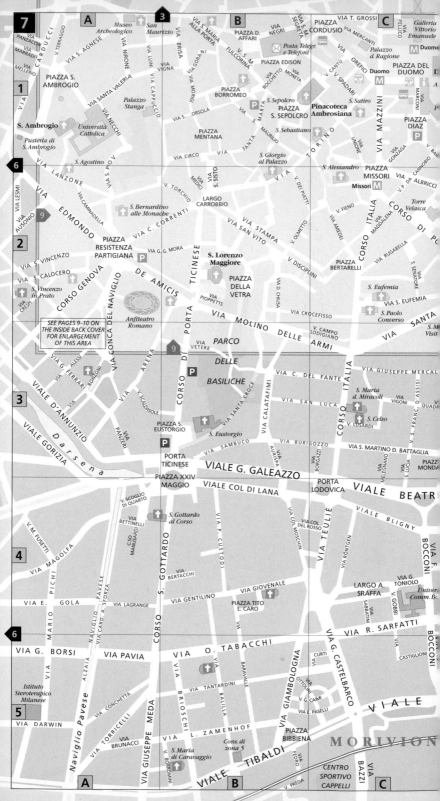

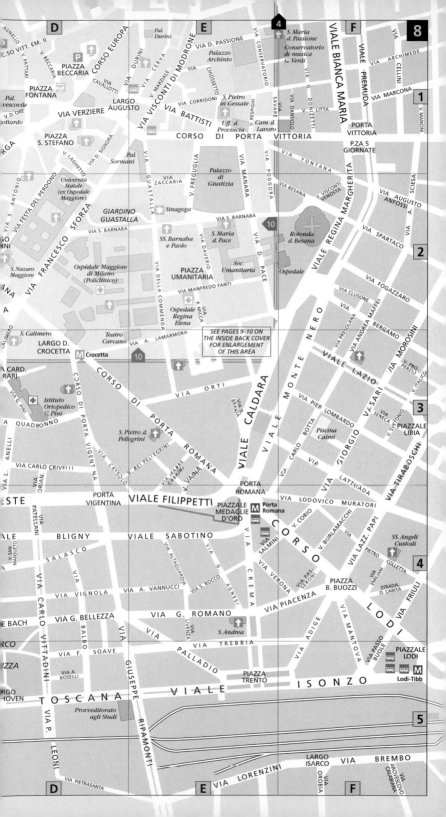

SEE PAGES 9–10 ON
THE INSIDE BACK COVER
FOR ENLARGEMENT
OF THIS AREA

General Index

The numbers in **bold type**
refer to main entries.

A

Abbazia di Chiaravalle 15, **102–3**
Abbazia di Piona **144**
Abbiati, Filippo 87, 91
Accademia di Belle Arti 110, 114, 116
Acquafredda Abbey 143
Acquario Civico **68**
  Street-by-Street map 63
Adaloaldo, King 83
Adda, Isabella d' 134
Adda river 141, 144
Adoration of the Magi (Titian) 56, 58
Agilulf, King 18
Agostino di Duccio 66–7
Agrate, Marco d' 49
Air France 217
Air One 217
Air pollution 211
Air travel **214**, 217
Airpullman Linate - Malpensa 217
Albergo (hotels) 158
Albertolli, Giocondo 142, 145
Alboin, King 18
Alemagna, Emilio 62, 68, 120
Alessi, Galeazzo 50, 88, 91, 98
Alitalia 217
Alps 137
Ambrogio, Sant' (St Ambrose) 49, 58, 66, 91, 99
  feast day 52, 78
  Museo Diocesano 90
  Sant'Ambrogio 17, 78, 84–7
  San Lorenzo alle Colonne 14, 17
  San Nazaro Maggiore 17, 94, 96
  San Simpliciano 17, 110, 113
  statues of 33, 48, 55
Ambrosian Republic 19, 21, 64
Angel Musicians (A. Luini) 113
Angeliche di San Paolo convent 91
Angilberto, Archbishop 86
Anguissola, Count 145
Anspert da Biassono, Archbishop 84, 86
Antelami, Benedetto 54, 66
Antique shops 193
Appiani, Andrea 59, 91, 101, 117, 121, 143
Archi di Porta Nuova **109**, 125
  Street-by-Street map 106
Architecture
  Milan's Best: Churches and
    Basilicas **32–3**
Arcimboldi brothers 49
Arco della Pace 23, 61, **69**
  Street-by-Street map 62
Arena Civica 23, **68**
  Street-by-Street map 62
Arese, Count Bartolomeo 74
Arianteo 37
Ariberto d'Intimiano, Archbishop 18, 19, 48
Aristotle 59
Arona 11, 135, **136**
Arp, Hans 121
Art Nouveau 70, 119
Atellani family 74
ATM (Public Transport) 221
Attila 18
Augustine, St 49, 55, 87
Ausonius 55
Authari, King 18
Autostradale Viaggi 217
Autumn in Milan 38
Azienda Provinciale Trasporti 223

B

Bagatti Valsecchi, Fausto 107, 109
Bagatti Valsecchi, Giuseppe 107, 109
Bagolino 155
Bagutta-Pittori all'Aria Aperta 36
Baldo, Monte 150
Balduccio, Giovanni di 54, 66, 90, 112
  *Madonna and Child with St
    Ambrose Proffering the Model of the
    City* 82
Balla, Giacomo 54, 121
Ballet 200
Ballet School, Teatro alla Scala 53
Balzaretto, Giuseppe 120, 143
Il Bambaia (Agostino Busti) 59, 66, 67
Banca Commerciale Italiana 108
Banks 213
Bar Magenta 10, 74
Bardolino **151**
Barnabas 90
Barnabiti family 91
Bars and cafés **184–7**
  historic cafés and bars 184–5
  in hotels 185
  what to order 185
Bartholomew, St 49
Barzaghi, Francesco 68
Baschenis, Evaristo 59, 117
Basilicas in Milan
  Milan's Best: Churches and
    Basilicas **32–3**
  Sant'Ambrogio 11, 17, 32, 78, **84–7**, 124, 126
  Sant'Eustorgio 32, 79, **90**
  San Lorenzo alle Colonne 17, 32, 78, 79, **80–81**
  San Nazaro Maggiore 17, 33, 94, **96**
  San Simpliciano 17, 110, **113**
Basket of Fruit (Caravaggio) 57, 58–9
Bassano, Jacopo 58
Bassi, Martino 33, 50, 81, 91, 100
Bastioni di Porta Venezia **119**
Battagio, Giovanni 100
Battle at Porta Tosa (Canella) 24–5
Bava Beccaris, Fiorenzo 26
Baveno **137**
Beauharnais, Eugenio di 100
Beccaria, Cesare 23, 31, 143
Bedoli, Mazzola Girolamo 59
Belgioioso, Count Lodovico Barbiano
  di 96, 121
Belgioioso d'Este, Prince Alberico XII
  di 51
Belgirate **136**
Bellagio 11, 140, **145**
Bellano **144**
Bellini, Gentile 116
Bellini, Giovanni 67, 106, 108, 109, 116, 126
  Pietà 108
Bellini, Jacopo 155
Bellini, Vincenzo 100
Bellotto, Bernardo 67, 117
Beltrami, Luca 50, 62, 64, 65, 67, 75, 98, 118, 119
Bembo, Bonifacio 65, 67
Benedict, St 88
Benedictines 84, 86, 88
Bergognone, Ambrogio da Fossano
  58, 90, 91, 99, 101, 108, 113, 115, 116, 136
  The Risen Christ 87
Bernard, St 102
Bernardino da Siena 83
Bertini, Giuseppe 59
Bertini brothers 46, 49
Bianchi, Mosè 59
Bianchi, Federico 91

Biandronno 154
Biassono, Anspert da, Archbishop 55
Biblioteca Ambrosiana 22, **59**
Biblioteca Civica di Milano 95
Bicycles
  cycling in Milan 219
  mountain bikes 204
Biffi, Giovanni Battista 23
Binago, Lorenzo 91
Bini, Giuseppe
  La Madonnina 15, 46, 118
Birago, Daniele 100
Bistolfi, Leonardo 118
BIT 36
Boat services, on the Lakes 223
Boccaccino 117
Boccaccio, Giovanni 59, 67
Boccioni, Umberto 118, 121
  The City Rises 116
  *Unique Forms of Continuity in
    Space* 54
Bogliaco 146
Boiola spring 148
Bolli, Bartolomeo 74
Bonino da Campione
  Mausoleum of Bernabò Visconti 66
Bonino da Campione 117
Bordone, Paris 71, 91
Borgia, Lucrezia 59
Borromean Islands (Isole Borromee)
  11, 137
Borromeo, Princess Bona 139
Borromeo, San Carlo 22, 48, 49, 50, 56, 98, 123
  Santuario della Pietà (Cannobio)
    138
  statues of 11, 135, 136
Borromeo, Charles III 134
Borromeo, Federico 22, 34, 56, 58
Borromeo family 55, 134, 135, 136, 137, 139
Borromeo gulf 138
Borsa Valori (Stock Exchange) 75
Bossi, Giovan Battista 119
Botta, Mario 52
Botticelli, Sandro 108
  Madonna del Padiglione 56, 58
  Pietà 108
Brabbia marsh nature reserve 154
Bramante, Donato di Angelo 64, 90
  Abbazia di Chiaravalle 102, 103
  Casa Fontana-Silvestri 123
  Christ at the Pillar 117
  Sant'Ambrogio 78, 84, 87
  Santa Maria delle Grazie 19, 32, 71
  Santa Maria presso San Satiro 55
  Università Cattolica del Sacro
    Cuore 87
Bramantino, Bartolomeo Suardi 58, 64, 66, 67, 75, 94, 96, 101, 115, 116
Branca, Giulio 138
Brasa torrent 150
Brentani, Pietro 144
Brera, Pinacoteca di *see* Pinacoteca di
  Brera
Brera Quarter 10
  Street-by-Street map 110–11
Bresci, Gaetano 26
Bril, Paul 59
British Airways 217
Brivio, Giovanni Stefano 90
Broggi, Luigi 75
Broletto 82
Bronzino (Agnolo di Cosimo) 117
Brueghel, Jan 59
Brueghel, Pieter the Elder 117
Brunate 142
Burgundians 18
Burri, Alberto 54
Buses 220

Buses (cont.)
airport 214, 215
at the Lakes 223
Butinone, Bernardino 71, 99
Butti, Enrico 118
Buzzi, Carlo 46, 98
Byron, George Gordon 131, 134, 145

C

Ca' Granda (Ospedale Maggiore) 19, 94, **97**
Street-by-Street map 95
Caccia Dominioni, Luigi 108
Caesar, Julius 139
Cafés see Bars and cafés
Il Caffè 23, 31
Caffè Greco 31
Caffè Zucca 10, 125
Cagnola, Luigi 55, 69, 95, 98
Caimi, Protaso 90
Cairo, Francesco 59
Calderara Collection of Contemporary
Art (Vacciago di Ameno) 154
Camaldolite Hermitage (Lake Garda) 147
Campari, Davide 118
Campi, Antonio 75, 91, 99, 113
Campi, Bernardino 50, 67, 94
Campi, Giulio 91, 101
Canaletto 67, 117, 146
Canals see Navigli
Canella, Carlo
Battle at Porta Tosa 24–5
Caneva 204–5
Cannobio 132, **138**
Canonica, Luigi 68
Canova, Antonio 11, 59, 121, 155
Cupid and Psyche 141, 143
Statue of Napoleon 105
Cantoni, Simone 122, 142
Caravaggio 34, 111, 114
Basket of Fruit 57, 58–9
Supper at Emmaus 117
Carlo Alberto, King of Sardinia 24, 25
Carloni, Carlo Innocenzo 108, 143
Carlotta, Princess of Prussia 141
Carnevale Ambrosiano 36, 39
Carpaccio, Vittore 116
Carrà, Carlo 54, 116, 121
Carracci, Agostino 117, 137
Carracci, Annibale 117, 137
Carracci, Ludovico 94, 117, 137
Carroccio 19, 113
Cars
breakdown services 211
driving in Milan 218
driving to Milan 215
parking 215, 218, 219
safety 210
Casa Bettoni 96
Casa Campanini 101
Casa del Fascio (Como) 142
Casa Fontana-Silvestri 123
Casa Galimberti 119
Casa Manzoni **51**
Casa Natale di Manzoni (Caleotto) 145
Casa degli Omenoni 44, **51**, 125
Casa Toscanini 98
Casati, Isabella 118
Castiglioni, Giannino 119
Castles
Castello degli Oldofredi (Iseo) 155
Castello di Porta Giovia see
Castello Sforzesco
Castello Sforzesco 10, 14, 19, 21, 24, 62, 66, **64–7**, 103, 126
Castello di Vezio 141
Castello Visconti di San Vito 136

Castles (cont.)
Malpaga castles 134
Scagliero (Malcesine) 150, 151
Torri del Benaco 151
Cathedrals see Duomo
Catherine of Alexandria, St 49
Catherine of Siena, St 71
Cattaneo, Carlo 23, 24, 118
Catullus 146, 148
Caves, Lake Como 141
Cavour, Count Camillo di 109, 118
Cazzago Brabbia 154
Cazzaniga, Francesco 71
Cazzaniga, Tommaso 71, 90
Celesti, Andrea 150
Celso, St 91
Celts 17
Centomiglia 146
Il Cerano (Giovan Battista Crespi) 50, 67, 71, 91, 112, 117, 137
Certosa di Garegnano **70**
Ceruti, Giovanni 120
Cesa Bianchi, Paolo 123
Cézanne, Paul 121
Chagall, Marc 121
Charles V, Emperor 19, 22, 83, 138
Chiari, Walter 118
Chierici Regolari di San Paolo College 98
Children
entertainment 197
in hotels 159
in restaurants 169
Chirico, Giorgio de 54, 68
Churches in Milan
Milan's Best: Churches and
Basilicas **32–3**
Chiesa dell'Annunciata 97
Sant'Alessandro **91**
Sant'Angelo **113**
Sant'Antonio Abate 94
San Babila 122, 123
Santi Barnaba e Paolo 98
San Bernardino alle Monache 78, **83**
San Bernardino alle Ossa 95, **98**
San Carlo al Corso 45
San Celso 91
San Cristoforo al Naviglio 89
San Donnino alla Mazza 106
Sant'Eustorgio 11, 127
San Fedele 33, 44, **50**, 125
San Giorgio al Palazzo **55**
San Giovanni in Conca 91
San Gottardo in Corte **54**
San Lorenzo alle Colonne 11, 14, **84–7**
San Marco 33, 111, **112**
Santa Maria del Carmine 111, **112**
Santa Maria delle Grazie 10, 19, 32, **71**, 72, 89, 103, 126
Santa Maria Incoronata **113**
Santa Maria Maddalena al Cerchio 78
Santa Maria della Passione **100–101**, 101
Santa Maria della Sanità 98
Santa Maria della Scala 52
Santa Maria presso San Celso **91**
Santa Maria presso San Satiro **55**, 125
San Maurizio **75**, 83
San Michele ai Nuovi Sepolcri 100
San Paolo Converso **91**
San Pietro in Gessate **99**
San Sepolcro **55**, 57, 58
San Sisto 79, 82–3
Santo Stefano Maggiore 95, **98**
San Vittore al Corpo **88**

Churchill, Winston 145
Cimitero Monumentale **118**
Cinema 200–201
Museo del Cinema 120
Cinque Giornate di Milano 23, **24–5**
"Ciribiciaccola" bell tower (Abbazia di
Chiaravalle) 103
Cistercians 87, 102
The City Rises (Boccioni) 116
Civic Museums (Castello Sforzesco) 34, **66–7**
Civiche Raccolte Storiche 109
Civico Mausoleo Palanti 118
Civico Museo Archeologico **74–5**
Civico Museo d'Arte Contemporanea
(CIMAC) 54
Clothes
shops 190–91
size chart 190
Clubs 198, 199
Cluniacs 155
Coaches 215, 217
Colà 151
Colico 140
Comacina 133
Como 11, 140, **142**
Como, Lake 131, 140, **140–45**
Day out **11**
hotels 165–6
restaurants 180–81
travel 222
Concert venues 199
Confalonieri, Federico 23
Conservatorio di Musica Giuseppe
Verdi **100**
Constance, Treaty of (1183) 18
Constantine I, Emperor 17, 49, 90
statue of 80
Corot, Jean-Baptiste-Camille 121
Corrado II 19
Correggio, Antonio Allegri 51, 67, 117
*Madonna and Child with the
Young St John the Baptist* 34
Corso
Magenta **74**
di Porta Romana 22, 94, **96**
Sempione 62, **69**
Venezia 23, **122–3**
Vittorio Emanuele II 22, 44, **51**
Corteo dei Re Magi 39
Cortona, Pietro da 117
Cossa, Francesco del 117
Counter-Reformation 22, 44, 48, 50
Cova 125
Cranach, Lucas 108
Portrait of Martin Luther 35, 108
Credit cards 213
in hotels 158
in restaurants 169
Credito Italiano 75
Crespi, Daniele 59, 70, 88, 91, 100, 101
Crime 210
Cristoforis, Giuseppe de 120
Crivelli, Carlo 67
Madonna della Candeletta 117
Croce, Francesco 98–9
Crucifixion (Montorfano) 72
Cupid and Psyche (Canova) 141, 143
Currency exchange 213
Cusani brothers 112
Cycling
cycling in Milan 219
mountain bikes 204

D

Dance
ballet 200
Latin-American 199

D'Annunzio, Gabriele 146
  portrait of 149
  Vittoriale degli Italiani (Gardone
   Riviera) 149
Dante Alighieri 59, 108, 146, 151
Danusso, Arturo 118
Darsena 127
Dead Christ (Mantegna) 115
Dell'Orto, Egidio 118
Della Scala, Mastino I 148
Della Scala, Regina 52
Della Torre, Giacomo 71
Demìo, Giovanni 71
Department stores 188, 189
Desenzano del Garda 146, **148**
Dialling codes 212
Dickens, Charles 134
Disabled travellers
  in restaurants 169
Discopubs 198–9
Discos 198, 199
Dogs, in hotels 159
Dolcebuono, Gian Giacomo 75, 91
Dominicans 139
Dongo 144
Donizetti, Gaetano 100
Drinks *see* Food and drink
Duchino, Paolo Camillo Landriani 101
Duomo (Como) 11, 142
Duomo (Desenzano del Garda) 148
Duomo (Milan) 10, 15, 19, 33, **46–9**,
  103, 112, 125
  Floorplan 48
  Museo del Duomo **49**
  Street-by-Street map 45
Duomo (Salò) 149
Durini, Cardinal 142–3
Duse, Eleonora 96

E

E-mail 213
easyjet 217
Einstein, Albert 118
Einstein, Hermann 118
Elisi family 118
Emergencies 211
Enotecas 169
Entertainment
  for children 197
  at the Lakes **204–5**
  in Milan **196–203**
  nightlife 198–9
  opera, theatre and cinema **200–201**
  sports and outdoor activities **202–3**
  tickets 196
Erba, Carlo 118
Eruli 18
Estate all'Idroscalo 36
Estate all'Umanitaria 37
Este, Beatrice d' 17, 71, 72
Etruscans 17
Eugene of Savoy, Prince 23
Eurolines 217
Eustorgius, St 90

F

Fabrics
  shops 192–3
  silk production **142**
Falck 26, 144
Falck, Giorgio Enrico 118
Fascism 26, 30
Fashion District 125
  Street-by-Street map 106–7
Fashion Week 36
Fattori, Giovanni 117, 121
Fedeli, Stefano de 65, 67
Ferdinand, Archduke of Austria 54, 78
Ferdinand I 69
Ferramola, Floriano 155
Ferrari, Cardinal 48
Ferrari, Daniele 50

Ferrari, Gaudenzio 71, 87, 91, 101,
  113, 116, 136, 138, 142
Ferries, on the Lakes 223
Ferrini 64
Ferrovie Nord railway 139, 217, 223
Festa di Sant'Ambrogio 39
Festa del Naviglio 37
Festival Latino-Americano 37
Festivals **36–9**
Fiammenghino brothers 112, 143, 144
Fiera di Chiaravalle 38
Fiera dei Fiori 36
Fiera di Milano 26, **70**
Fiera Milano (Rho) 70
Fiera degli *Oh bej Oh bej* 39, 78
Fiera di Senigallia 39
Figino, Giovanni Ambrogio 49, 67, 88
Filarete (Averulino Antonio) 19, 64, 97
Filippino degli Organi 49
Film *see* Cinema
Finding of the Body of St Mark
  (Tintoretto) 114
Fire services 211
Fishing 204
Five-a-side football 202
Fo, Dario 27
Foix, Gaston de 59, 67
Fondutis, Agostino de 55, 91
Fontana, Angelo 123
Fontana, Annibale 91
Fontana, Lucio 54, 118
  Woman at the Mirror 35
Food and drink
  shops 189
  What to Eat **170–71**
  see also Restaurants
Football 38, 70, 203
  five-a-side football 202
Foppa, Vincenzo 75, 83, 90, 108, 115,
  116, 127
Fornaroli, Antonio 118
Foro Buonaparte 23
  Street-by-Street map 63
Foscolo, Ugo 145
Fotoshow 37
Fourth Estate (Pelizza da Volpedo) 11
Fracci, Carla 53
Francis I, Emperor of Austria 62, 69
Franciscans 149
Franks 18
Frederick Barbarossa, Emperor 18, 19,
  36, 90, 96, 112, 113, 142
Futurism 26

G

Gadda, Carlo Emilio 30
Gadio, Abbot 100
Gaffurio, Franchino 56
Galgario, Fra (Vittore Ghislandi) 59,
  67, 108, 117
Galizia, Fede 67
Galleria dell'Accademia Tadini (Lago
  d'Iseo) 155
Galleria Vittorio Emanuele II 10, 26,
  43, **50**, 125, 137
  Street-by-Street map 44
Galleries *see* Museums and galleries
Gallio, Cardinal Tolomeo 144
Gallio family 142
Garavaglia, Carlo 99, 102
Garda **151**
Garda, Lake 131, **146–53**
  hotels 166–7
  restaurants 181–3
  travel 223
Gardaland **152–3**, 204
Gardens *see* Parks and gardens
Gardone Riviera 133, 146, **149**
Gargnano 150
Garibaldi, Giuseppe 51, 118, 138
Gauguin, Paul 121
Gemelli, Agostino 87
Genga, Girolamo 117

Genovesino (Luigi Miradori) 112
Gentile da Fabriano
  Valle Romita Polyptych 116
Gervasio, St 87
Ghirlandaio, Domenico 58
Giampietrino 109
Giardini di Villa Taranto (Pallanza)
  138
Giardini Pubblici 109, 119, **120**, 125
Giardino Botanico della Fondazione
  André Heller (Gardone Riviera)
  205
Giardino Botanico Hruska (Gardone
  Riviera) 149
Giardino della Guastalla **98**
  Street-by-Street map 95
Gift shops 194–5
Giordano, Luca 117
Giorgione
  Portrait of a Young Man 58
Giotto 19, 54, 151
Giovan Pietro da Cemmo 155
Giovanni d'Alemagna 116
Giovanni da Milano 116
Giulino di Mezzegra 143
Giunti, Domenico 91, 113
Goethe, Johann Wolfang von 131,
  146, 150
Golasecca 136
Golf 202, 203, 204
Gonzaga, Ferrante 96, 119
Gonzaga, Vincenzo I 150
Gonzaga family 150
Gozzano 154
Gozzano, Guido 136
Gran Premio di Monza 38
Grand Hotel et de Milan 125, 108
Grand Prix motor racing 38
Grand Tour 131
Grandi, Giuseppe 100
Grassi, Gino 121
Grassi, Nedda 121
Grassi, Paolo 30, 39
Gratian, Emperor 85
Gravedona 141, **144**
El Greco 117
Gregory, St 88
Grifo, Ambrogio 99
Grossi, Tommaso 51
Grotte di Catullo (Sirmione) 148
Guardi, Francesco 117
Guercino 97, 117

H

Habsburg dynasty 23
Hayez, Francesco 11, 59, 118, 121,
  143, 155
  The Kiss 114, 117
  Matilda Juva Branca 35
Health and medical assistance **210–
  11**
Helena, St 49
Hemingway, Ernest 131
Henry II, King of France 58
Hesse, Hermann 131
Hiking 204, 218
Historic Centre **43–59**
  area map 43
  Street-by-Street map: Piazza del
   Duomo 44–5
History **17–27**
Hoepli, Ulrico 118, 120
Holidays, public 38
*Holy Family with St Anne and the
  Young St John the Baptist* (Luini) 58
Holy Nail of the Cross **49**
Honorius, Bishop 18
Hospitals 210, 211
Hotels **158–67**
  bars in 185
  booking 158–9
  children in 159
  choosing a hotel 158

Hotels (cont.)
  grading 159
  Lago d'Iseo 167
  Lago d'Orta 167
  Lake Como 165–6
  Lake Garda 166–7
  Lake Maggiore 164–5
  Milan 160–64
  pets 159
  prices 159
Huns 18

I
Idro, Lago d' 131, **155**
Indian Café
  Street-by-Street map 110
Inganni, Angelo
  Teatro alla Scala in 1852 **52**
Inquisition 71
Insect bites 210
Interior design shops 192–3
Interpreters 211
Intra 138
Iseo 155
Iseo, Lago d' 131, **155**
  hotels 167
  restaurants 183
  travel 223
Isimbardi family 101
Isola Bella 11, 134, 137
Isola Comacina **143**, 144
Isola di Garda 149
Isola Madre 11, 137
Isola dei Pescatori 11, 137
Isola di San Giulio 154
Isole Borromee 11, 134,
  137
Isolino di San Giovanni 138
Isolino Virginia 154

J
Jamaica Café 110
Jan, Giorgio 120
Jesi, Emilio and Maria 116
Jesuits 50, 114
Jewellery shops 191
Jogging 202
John the Good, St 49
Julius (deacon) 154
Juvarra, Filippo 142

K
Kennedy, John F 145
The Kiss (Hayez) 114, 117
Klee, Paul 35, 131
Knoller, Martin 51, 54, 74

L
La Scala *see* Teatro alla Scala
Labienus, Titus 139
Labò, Oreste 68
Lagoni di Mercurago Regional Park
  136
Lakes *see individual lakes*
Lambrate 66
Landriani, Camillo 112
Lanino, Bernardo 87, 96
Lanino, Gerolamo 138
Largo Augusto 95, **98**
Largo Carrobbio **82–3**
  Street-by-Street map 79
Last Supper (Leonardo da Vinci) 10,
  19, 30, 71, **72–3**, 74, 126
Latin-American dance 199
Latterie (dairies) 169
Laveno **139**
Lazise **151**
Lazzaretto 22, 119
Lazzaro, San 82
Lecco 140, **145**

Lega, Silvestro 117, 121
The Legend of Maria (Polacco) 150
Leggiuno 139
Legnanino, Stefano Maria 91, 113
Legnano, Battle of (1176) 113
Lenno **142–3**
Leonardo da Vinci 30, 57, 116–17, 124
  Castello Sforzesco 64, 65, 66
  Codex Atlanticus 30, 34, 51, 59
  Last Supper 10, 19, 30, 71, **72–3**,
    74, 126
  Museo della Scienza e della
    Tecnica 11, 88, 126
  navigli (canals) 89, 124, 127
  Portrait of a Musician 56, 58
  statue of 43, 50
Leoni, Leone 49, 51
Lesa **136**
Leyva, Marianna de 50
Ligurians 17
Limone sul Garda 147, **150**
Lingeri, Pietro 69
Linate airport **214**, 217
Litta, Duchess 74
Locanda (hotels) 158
Locati, Sebastiano 68
Loggia degli Osii 55
Loggia Rambaldi (Bardolino) 151
Lomazzo, Paolo 112
Lombard League 18, 19, 36
Lombardi, Franco 87
Lombardo, Cristoforo 96, 100
Lombards 18
Londonio, Francesco 59
Longo, Alfonso 23
Longoni, Emilio 59
Lorenzetti, Ambrogio 116
Lorenzi, Stoldo 91
Lorenzo, San 80
Lost property 211, 217
Lotto, Lorenzo 67, 108, 116
Louis XII, King of France 19
Loveno 143
Lovere 155
Lufthansa 217
Luini, Aurelio 98
  Angel Musicians 113
Luini, Bernardino 55, 74, 75, 87, 90,
  98, 108, 115, 142, 143
  Benefactory Christ 58
  Deposition 101
  *Holy Family with St Anne and the
    Young St John the Baptist* 58
  Madonna della Buonanotte 103
  Madonna del Roseto 117
  Passion of Jesus 96
  San Pietro in Campagna frescoes
    (Luino) 138
Luino **138**
Luther, Martin 35, 108

M
Macchiaioli 117, 121
McEacharn, Neil 134, 138
Maciachini, Carlo 112, 113, 118
*Madonna and Child with St Ambrose
  Proffering the Model of the City*
  (Giovanni di Balduccio) 82
Madonna della Buonanotte (Luini)
  103
Madonna di Campagna 138
Madonna della Candeletta (Crivelli)
  117
Madonna del Carmine sanctuary 149
Madonna della Ceriola sanctuary
  (Monte Isola) 155
Madonna del Frassino sanctuary
  (Peschiera del Garda) 151
Madonna del Ghisallo Sanctuary 145
Madonna in Glory and Saints
  (Mantegna) 67
Madonna del Padiglione (Botticelli)
  56, 58

Madonna del Sasso sanctuary (Isola
  di San Giulio) 154
La Madonnina 15, 46, 118
Magatti, Pietro Antonio 59
Maggiolini, Giuseppe 54, 67, 143
Maggiore, Lake 131, **134–9**
  Family day out **11**
  hotels 164–5
  restaurants 178–80
  travel 222
Magi, relics of **90**
Magnasco, Alessandro 59, 108
Malcesine **150–51**
Malpaga castles 134
Malpensa airport 214, **215**, 217
Malpensa Express 217
Malpensa Shuttle 217
Mandello del Lario 144
Manerba del Garda 148–9
Mangone, Fabio 58
"Mani Pulite" 99
Mantegazza, Antonio 67
Mantegna, Andrea 106, 108, 111, 114,
  116, 126
  Dead Christ 115
  Madonna in Glory and Saints 67
Manzoni, Alessandro 26, 30, 31, 143
  The Betrothed **22**, 31, 38, 44, 50,
    51, 140, 145
  Casa Manzoni **51**
  Casa Natale di Manzoni (Caleotto)
    145
  Museo Manzoniano di Villa Stampa
    (Lesa) 136
  portrait of 145
  statue of 50
  tomb of 118
  Via Manzoni **108**
Manzoni, Piero 54
Manzù, Giacomo 118
Maps
  car parks in the city centre 219
  Central Milan 14–15
  Europe 12
  Exploring the Lakes 132–3
  Growth of Milan 21
  Historic Centre 43
  Lake Como 140–41
  Lake Garda 146–7
  Lake Maggiore 134–5
  Metro 220–21
  Milan 12–13
  Milan and environs 13
  90-minute walk around Milan's
    hidden glories 125
  Northeast Milan 105
  Northwest Milan 61, 62–3
  Piazza del Duomo 44–5
  Southeast Milan 93
  Southwest Milan 77
  Two-hour walk around the Milan
    of yesteryear 126–7
Marcellus, Claudius 17
Marchesi, Pompeo 122
Maria Theresa, Empress of Austria 23,
  93, 114, 122
Marinetti, Filippo Tommaso 26
Marini, Marino 116
  Marino Marini Museum 121
Marino, Tommaso 50
Mark, St 112
Markets *see* Shops and markets
Maroncelli, Piero 23
The Marriage of the Virgin (Raphael)
  115, 117
Martin V, Pope 46
Martini, Arturo 54, 116, 138
Martini, Simone 59
Master of the Borromeo Games 55
Matilda Juva Branca (Hayez) 35
Matisse, Henri 121
Maximian, Emperor 17, 75, 83
Maximilian, Emperor 21
Mazzardites 134

Mazzucotelli, Alessandro 101
Meazza, Giuseppe 70
Meazza (San Siro) stadium 68, **70**, **203**
Meda, Giuseppe 49, 66, 98
Medical assistance **210–11**
Medici, Gian Giacomo 49
Megastores 192
Menaggio **143**
Mengoni, Giuseppe 26, 44, 50
Mercato dell'Antiquariato 89
Mercato dell'Antiquariato di Brera 39
Meridiana 217
Merlo, Carlo Giuseppe 74
Messina, Francesco 82–3
Metanopoli 27
Metro 220–21
Mezzanotte, Paolo 75
Mezzola, Lake 141
Michelangelo Buonarroti 49, 58, 126
Rondanini Pietà 65, 67
Michelino da Besozzo, school of 139
Michelozzi, Michelozzo 67
Milan, Edict of (313) 17, 80
Milano Cortili Aperti 36
Milano d'Estate 37
Milano-SanRemo race 36
Minguzzi, Luciano 110
Mobile phones 212
Modigliani, Amedeo 54
Portrait of Moïse Kisling 114, 116
MODIT-Milanovendemoda 36, 38
Monasteries
 Certosa di Garegnano **70**
 Santa Caterina del Sasso Ballaro **139**
Moncalvo (Guglielmo Caccia) 88, 91, 94, 98, 99
Mondadori, Arnoldo 118
Money 213
Moniga del Garda 148
Montalto 91, 113
Monte Isola 155
Montecastello Sanctuary (Limone sul Garda) 150
Montefeltro, Federico da 115, 117
Montefeltro Altarpiece (Piero della Francesca) 115, 117
Monti, Cardinal 101
Montinelle 149
Montorfano, Giovanni Donato da 71, 99
 Crucifixion 72
Monza 18, 37
Mopeds 219
Morandi, Giorgio 54, 116, 121
Morazzone (Pier Francesco Mazzucchelli) 59, 67, 113, 117
Moretti, Cristoforo 108
Moretto (Alessandro Bonvicino) 59, 91, 155
Morgagni family 118
Morigi family 83
Moroni, Giovan Battista 59
Mosquitoes 210
Moto Guzzi factory 144, 145
Motor racing 38
Motorways 215
Mottarone, Monte 11, 137, 139, 154
Mozart, Wolfgang Amadeus 54, 100
Museums and galleries 209
 Milan's Best: Museums and Galleries **34–5**
 Bagatti Valsecchi 10
 Belgiojoso Bonaparte - Museo dell'Ottocento 35, **121**
 Calderara Collection of Contemporary Art (Vacciago di Ameno) 154
 Casa Manzoni **51**
 Casa Natale di Manzoni (Caleotto) 145
 Civic Museums (Castello Sforzesco) 34, **66–7**

Museums and galleries (cont.)
 Civico Museo Archeologico **74–5**
 Civico Museo d'Arte Contemporanea (CIMAC) 35, 54
 Civico Museo Marinaro Ugo Mursia 109
 Civico Museo del Risorgimento 109, 111
 Galleria dell'Accademia Tadini (Lago d'Iseo) 155
 Galleria Comunale d'Arte (Varenna) 145
 Marino Marini Museum 35, 121
 Museo dell'Acquario 68
 Museo Archeologico 10, 126
 Museo Archeologico (Salò) 149
 Museo Archeologico della Valtènesi (Montinelle) 149
 Museo Bagatti Valsecchi 35, 107, **109**, 125
 Museo della Bambola (Doll Museum, Rocca di Angera) 135, 139
 Museo della Basilica di Sant'Ambrogio 87
 Museo del Castello (Torri del Benaco) 151
 Museo del Cinema 120
 Museo Civico (Riva del Garda) 150
 Museo Civico Archeologico (Desenzano del Garda) 148
 Museo di Criminologia e delle Armi Antiche 86
 Museo Diocesano 11, **90**
 Museo del Duomo 35, **49**
 Museo Etnografico e dello Strumento a Fiato (Quarna) 154
 Museo Francesco Messina 79, 82–3
 Museo Manzoniano di Villa Stampa (Lesa) 136
 Museo di Milano 109
 Museo Minguzzi 110
 Museo Moto Guzzi della Motocicletta (Varenna) 144, 145
 Museo del Nastro Azzurro (Salò) 149
 Museo Nazionale della Scienza e della Tecnica 34, **88**
 Museo del Paesaggio (Pallanza) 138
 Museo Poldi Pezzoli 10, 35, 106, **108**
 Museo Preistorico (Isolino Virginia) 154, 155
 Museo del Rubinetto (San Maurizio d'Opaglio) 154
 Museo della Scienza e della Tecnica 11, 126
 Museo della Seta (Silk Museum, Como) 142
 Museo Settala 57, 120
 Museo di Storia Contemporanea 109
 Museo di Storia Naturale **120**
 Museo di Storia Naturale (Lecco) 145
 Museo di Storia Naturale del Garda e del Monte Baldo (Malcesine) 150
 Museo Teatrale alla Scala 10, 52, 74, 125
 Pinacoteca Ambrosiana 10, 34, **56–9**
 Pinacoteca di Brera 10, 111, **114–17**
 Vittoriale degli Italiani (Gardone Riviera) 149
Music
 nightlife 198, 199
 shops 194–5
Mussolini, Benito 26, 30, 118, 137, 143, 149, 150
Muzio, Giovanni 51, 69, 78
Muzio, Lorenzo 51

N

Napoleon Buonaparte 59, 74, 78
 Abbazia di Chiaravalle 102
 Arco della Pace 62, 69
 Arena Civica 68
 Arona 136

Napoleon Buonaparte (cont.)
 coronation 23, 46
 Duomo 23, 33, 46
 Isola Bella 137
 Palazzo Serbelloni 122
 statue of 105
 Villa Belgiojoso Bonaparte 121
Napoleon III, Emperor 68
Narses 18
Nava, Cesare 81
Navigazione Laghi Maggiore-Garda-Como 223
Navigazione Lago di Como 223
Navigazione Lago di Garda (Navigarda) 223
Navigazione Lago Iseo 223
Navigazione Lago Maggiore 223
Navigli (canals) 19, 62, 77, 96, 124, 127
Naviglio della Martesana
 Street-by-Street map 110
Naviglio Grande 77, **89**, 127
Naviglio Pavese 77, 127
Nazaro, St 91, 96
"Needle, Thread and Knot" sculpture 27
Nervi, Pier Luigi 118
Newspapers 208
Nicola da Verdun 49
Nietzsche, Friedrich 131
Nightlife
 Milan 198–9
 at the Lakes 205
Northeast Milan **105–23**
 area map 105
 Street-by-Street map: Brera Quarter 110–11
 Street-by-Street map: Fashion District 106–7
Northwest Milan **61–75**
 area map 61
 Street-by-Street map: Around the Castello Sforzesca 62–3
Notarial Acts Archive 99
Nuvolone, Carlo Francesco 112
Nuvolone, Panfilo 101

O

Oggi Aperto 36
Oggiono, Marco d' 67, 100
Oldofredi, Giacomo 155
Olivetans 88
Olona river 126, 127
Omegna 154
Omm de Preja 51
Opening hours
 museums and galleries 209
 restaurants 168
 shops 188
Opera 200
Order of the Knights of the Holy Sepulchre 100
Orio al Serio Airport **215**, 217
Orrido di Bellano 144
Orrido di Sant'Anna (Val Cannobina) 138
Orta, Lago d' 131, **154**
 hotels 167
 restaurants 183
Orta San Giulio 154
Orticola 37
Ospedale Maggiore *see* Ca' Granda
Ossuccio 140
Osteria (restaurant) 169
Ostrogoths 18

P

Padenghe 148
Padiglione del Caffè 120
Palazzetto della Comunità (Orta San Giulio) 154
Palazzi, Lazzaro 119

Palazzina del Serraglio (Toscolano Maderno) 150
Palazzos
Acerbi 96
Anguissola 108
Annoni 96
dell'Arte 63, 69
Belgioioso (Lecco) 145
Belgioioso (Milan) 125
Bigli 107
Borromeo **55**, 139
Borromeo d'Adda 108
Brentani 108
del Capitano (Garda) 151
Carlotti (Garda) 151
Castiglioni 122
Citterio 116
Cusani 111, **112**
Dugnani (Milan) 120
Dugnani (Pallanza) 138
Durini 22, 98
Fantoni (Salò) 149
Gallarati Scotti 108
Gallio (Gravedona) 144
dei Giornali 109
dei Giureconsulti 55
di Giustizia **99**
Isimbardi **101**
Liberty 51
Litta 61, **74**, 126
Litta Biumi 83
Litta Modignani 98
Marino **50**, 125
Mellerio 96
Melzi di Cusano 106
Morando Attendolo Bolognini 109
Moriggia 109, 111
Parrasio *see* Palazzo della Ragione (Cannobio)
della Permanente 54, 119
della Prefettura 101
Pretorio (Riva del Garda) 150
del Provveditore (Riva del Garda) 150
Radice Fossati 83
della Ragione (Cannobio) 138
della Ragione (Milan) 54
Reale 23, **54**, 143
Rocca-Saporiti 122
delle Scuole Palatine 55
Serbelloni 122
Sormani Andreani 95, **98–9**
Stampa 83
delle Stelline 74
Terzi-Martinengo (Barbarano) 149
Trivulzio 91
Vescovile (Gozzano) 154
del Vescovo (Isola di San Giulio) 154
Pallanza 138
Palma il Giovane 112, 150, 151
Pandiani, Giovanni
The Soldier's Widow 25
Panoramica di Venezia 38
Parco Giardino Sigurtà (Peschiera) 205
Parco Natura Viva (Bussolengo-Pastrengo) 205
Parini, Giuseppe 91
Parking 215, 218, 219
Parks and gardens
Giardini Pubblici 109, 119, **120**, 125
Giardini di Villa Taranto (Pallanza) 138
Giardino Botanico della Fondazione André Heller (Gardone Riviera) 205
Giardino Botanico Hruska (Gardone Riviera) 149
Giardino della Guastalla 95, **98**
Isola Bella 137
Isola Madre 137

Parks and gardens (cont.)
Parco Giardino Sigurtà (Peschiera) 205
Parco Sempione 62, **68**
Parco Sormani 98
Parco di Villa Pallavicino 137, 205
Piazza della Vetra **82**
Via Manzoni 108
Villa Carlotta (Tremezzo) 143
Villa Taranto 134
Pascal, Blaise 88
Passante Ferroviario 221
Passports 208
Pataria movement 19
Pavia 18
Pecis, Giovanni Edoardo de 57, 59
Pecorari, Francesco 54, 103
Peglio 144
Pelizza da Volpedo, Giovanni 117
Fourth Estate 121
Pellico, Silvio 23
Penna, Francesco 118
Pensiones 158
Perego, Giovanni 122
Peressutti, Enrico 96
Personal security 210
Pertini, Sandro 108
Peschiera del Garda **151**
Petacci, Claretta 26, 143
Peter Martyr, St 90
Peterzano, Simone 70
Petrarch 59
Pets, in hotels 159
Pharmacies 210
Piacentini, Marco 99
Piazzas
Affari **75**
Belgioioso **51**
Cinque Giornate 100
Cordusio **75**
del Duomo 10, 44–5
Fontana 27, 45
del Liberty 45, **51**
Meda 45
Mercanti **54–5**
Missori 91
San Sepolcro 26
della Vetra 79, **82**
Piazza, Callisto 75, 87, 117
Piazzale Loreto 26–7
Piazzetta, Gian Battista 117, 150
Picasso, Pablo 35, 121
Piccio (Giovanni Carnovali) 121
Piccolo Teatro *see* Teatro Grassi
Pickpockets 210
Piermarini, Giuseppe 23, 45, 51, 52, 54, 112, 120
Piero della Francesca 106, 108, 111, 114
Montefeltro Altarpiece 115, 117
Pietà (Botticelli) 108
Pinacoteca Ambrosiana 10, **56–9**
Biblioteca Ambrosiana 59
Borromeo Collection 58–9
De Pecis Collection 59
Galbiati Wing 59
Museo Settala 59
Sculpture 59
Visitors' Checklist 57
Pinacoteca di Brera 10, 34, **114–17**
Jesi Collection 116
Street-by-Street map 111
Visitors' Checklist 115
Pioverna 144
Piramidi di Zone (Lago d'Iseo) 155
Pirelli, Giovan Battista 118
Pirelli Building 27, **118**
Pisis, Filippo de 121
Pisogne 155
Il Pitocchetto (Giacomo Ceruti) 117
Pittori sul Naviglio 36
Pius IV, Pope 48, 49
Pizzerias 169
Plague 22

Planetarium **120**
Pogliaghi, Ludovico 47
Polacco, Martino Teofilo
The Legend of Maria 150
Poldi Pezzoli, Gian Giacomo 106, 108
Police 211
Pollack, Leopold 121
Pollaiolo, Antonio
Portrait of a Young Lady 106, 108
Pollution, air 211
Polpenazze del Garda 149
Pomodoro, Arnaldo 45
Ponti, Gio 68, 118
Porta, Carlo 31
Porta Garibaldi station 217
Porta Nuova 82
Porta Orientale *see* Porta Venezia
Porta Romana 22, 96, 109
Porta Ticinese (medieval) 79, **82**, 126
Porta Ticinese (19th century) 127
Porta Tosa 24, 25
Porta Venezia **119**
Porta Vercellina 74
Porta Vittoria 24, 25
Portaluppi, Piero 74, 120
Portico del Lattèe
Street-by-Street map 106
Portinari, Pigello 90, 99
Portrait of Moïsè Kisling (Modigliani) 114, 116
Portrait of a Musician (Leonardo da Vinci) 56
Portrait of a Young Lady (Pollaiolo) 106, 108
Portrait of a Young Man (Giorgione) 58
Postal services 213
Preda, Carlo 87
Predis, Ambrogio de 58, 117
Premier league football 38
Premio Bagutta 38
Previati, Gaetano 90
Procaccini, Camillo 49, 67, 88, 91, 98, 101, 112, 113, 138
Procaccini, Ercole 112
Procaccini, Giulio Cesare 59, 101, 112
Protasio, St 87
Provaglio d'Iseo 155
Puegnago sul Garda 149
Punta Belvedere 149
Punta San Fermo 149
Punta San Vigilio 147, 151
Pusterla di Sant'Ambrogio 126

Q

Qantas 217
Quadrilatero (fashion district) 10, 106–7
Quadrio, Gerolamo 88, 112
Quarna 154
Quasimodo, Salvatore 118

R

Radetzky, Count Joseph 23, 24, 25, 121
Raffagno, Francesco 100
RAI (Italian State TV) 69
Railways *see* Trains
Rainfall 38
Rambaldi family 151
Rangone, Tommaso 116
Raphael 34, 111, 114
Cartoon for *The School of Athens* 57, 58
The Marriage of the Virgin 115, 117
Rembrandt van Rijn 117
Reni, Guido 59, 117, 146
Republic of Salò 149
Restaurants **168–83**
children's facilities 169
choosing a restaurant 168

Restaurants (cont.)
  eating hours 168
  etiquette 168
  Lago d'Iseo 183
  Lago d'Orta 183
  Lake Como 180–81
  Lake Garda 181–3
  Lake Maggiore 178–80
  Milan 172–8
  paying 169
  reading the menu 169
  types of restaurants 168–9
  What to Eat **170–71**
  wheelchair access 169
Ricci, Sebastiano 98
Richard, Jules 118
Richard-Ginori 68, 118, 139
Richini, Francesco Maria 33, 46, 50, 55, 74, 81, 96, 97, 98, 115, 123
The Risen Christ (Bergognone) 87
Ristorante (restaurant) 169
Riva del Garda **150**
Roberti, Ercole de' 117
Rocca di Anfo (Lago d'Idro) 155
Rocca di Angera 135, 136, **139**
Rocca Oldofredi (Monte Isola) 155
Rocca Scaligera (Sirmione) 148
Rodari, Jacopo 142
Rodari, Tommaso 142
Rogers, Nathan 96
Rogoredo station 217
Roman columns 79, 80
Romanino (Gerolamo Romani) 67, 149, 155
Romans 17, 18, 83, 131, 142, 144, 146, 148, 151
Rondanini Pietà (Michelangelo) 65, 67
Rosa, Monte 139
Rosmini, Antonio 136, 137
Rosselli, Alberto 118
Rossi, Aldo 108
Rossi, Giovanni Jacopo de 101
Rossini, Gioacchino 100, 145
Rosso, Medardo 116, 118
Rothari, Edict of (643) 18
Rotonda di Via Besana **100**
Rubens, Pieter Paul 96, 117
Ruggeri, Giovanni 91, 112
Rusca, Grazioso 122
Rusnati, Giuseppe 100
Ryan Air 217

S
Sacro Monte (Isola di San Giulio) 154
Sagra del Carroccio 36
Sagra di San Cristoforo 37
Sagra di San Giovanni (Monza) 37
Sailing 204
Sala Comacina 143
Salaino 58
Sales 189
Salmeggia, Enea 113
Salò 148, **149**
Saluzzo, Antonio da 46
San Donato 136
San Felice del Benaco **148–9**
San Giulio, Isola di 154
San Maurizio d'Opaglio 154
San Pietro in Lamosa monastery (Provaglio d'Iseo) 155
San Sigismondo oratory 87
San Siro stadium *see* Meazza stadium
San Vittore monastery 88
Sanagra river 143
Sangiorgio, Abbondio 69
Sanmicheli, Michele 151
Sansovino (Jacopo Tatti) 149
Santa Caterina del Sasso Ballaro 135, **139**
Santa Maria Maddalena al Cerchio convent 83
Santuario della Pietà (Cannobio) 138

Saponaro, Salvatore 101
Sarnico 155
Sasso del Ferro 139
Savignano, Luciana 53
Savini 50
Savoy family 50
Scaligeri family 148, 150, 151
Scapigliatura 121
Schuster, Cardinal 48
Scipio, Cnaes Cornelius 17
Scooters 219
Scuole Arcimbolde 91
Sebino *see* Iseo, Lake
Security 210
Seminario Arcivescovile 123
Seregni, Vincenzo 70, 88, 91, 123
Sesto, Cesare da 67
Sesto Calende 135, **136**
Settala, Lanfranco 112
Settala, Manfredo 59, 120
Severus, Septimius 62
Sforza, Ascanio 21
Sforza, Bianca Maria 21
Sforza, Bona 21
Sforza, Ercole Massimiliano 21
Sforza, Francesco I 19, 20, 21, 64, 97, 113
Sforza, Francesco II 21, 22
Sforza, Galeazzo Maria 21, 54, 65, 66
Sforza, Gian Galeazzo Maria 21
Sforza, Lodovico il Moro 19, 20, 21, 30, 74
  Castello Sforzesco 64, 66
  and the *Last Supper* 72
  Lazzaretto 22, 119
  navigli (canals) 89, 127
  Sforzesca Altarpiece 17, 116
  tomb of 71
Sforza, Muzio Attendolo 21
Sforza family 14, 19, **20–21**, 63, 68, 84, 142
Sforzesca Altarpiece 17, 116
SGEA Lombardia 217
Shops and markets **188–95**
  antiques 193
  books 194–5
  clothing and accessories 190–91
  department stores 188, 189
  design 192–3
  fabrics 192–3
  food shops 189
  gifts 195
  jewellery 191
  markets 188–9
  music 194–5
  opening hours 188
  sales 189
SIA 217
Silk production **142**
Simonetta, Angelo 112
Simpliciano, San 113
Simplon Pass 134
Singer, Isaac 88
Sirmione 146, **148**
Sironi, Mario 99, 109
Skating 202
SMAU 36, 38
Società Ceramica Italiana Richard-Ginori 139
Società Umanitaria 100
Soiano del Lago 149
Solari, Cristoforo 71
Solari, Guiniforte 19, 32, 71, 99, 113
Solari, Pietro Antonio 67, 83, 100
Solarolo 149
The Soldier's Widow (Pandiani) 25
Sommaruga, Giuseppe 122, 155
Sottocorno, Pasquale 25
Southeast Milan **93–103**
  area map 93
  Street-by-Street map: San Nazaro to Largo Augusto 94–5
Southwest Milan **77–91**
  area map 77

Southwest Milan (cont.)
  Street-by-Street map: From Sant'Ambrogio to San Lorenzo 78–9
Spas
  Sirmione 148
Sports
  at the Lakes **204**
  in Milan **202–3**
Spring in Milan 36
Squash 202, 203
Stacchini, Ulisse 119
Stadio Civico Giuseppe Meazza *see* Meazza stadium
Stampa, Massimiliano 83
Stazione Centrale **119**, 217
Stefano da Verona 116
Stendhal 95, 99, 108, 131, 134, 145
STIE 217
Stilicho, Sarcophagus of 85, 86, 87
Storer, Gian Cristoforo 80
Strada Regina 140
Stramilano 36
Stravinsky, Igor 121
Strehler, Giorgio 30, 39, 200
Stresa 11, 134, **137**
Strozzi 155
Student information 209
Summer in Milan 37
Sunshine 37
Supper at Emmaus (Caravaggio) 117
Swimming 202, 203

T
Tabacchi, Odoardo 109, 118
Tancredi 54
Tanzio da Varallo 100
Taurini, Giovanni 50
Taveggia pastry shop 99
Taxis
  airport 214
  in Milan 219
Tazzini, Giacomo 101
Teatro alla Scala in 1852 (Inganni) **52**
Telephones 212
Temperatures 39
Tempio Civico di San Sebastiano 91
Tempio della Vittoria
  Street-by-Street map 78
Tempio Voltiano (Como) 142
Tennis 202, 203
Terme di Catullo (Sirmione) 148
Terme di Villa Cedri (Colà) 151
Terragni, Giuseppe 69
Terrorism 27
Theatres 200, 201
  Teatro dell'Arte 69
  Teatro Carcano 96
  Teatro Grassi (formerly Piccolo Teatro) 39, 200
  Teatro Litta 74
  Teatro alla Scala 10, 23, 27, 39, 44, **52–3**, 108, 125, 200
  Teatro della Società (Lecco) 145
  Teatro Dal Verme 61
Theft 210
Theme parks
  Gardaland **152–3**, 204
Theodolinda 18
Theodora, Empress 66
Tibaldi, Pellegrino 33, 46, 48, 50, 91, 142, 143, 144, 145
Ticino river 127, 134
Tickets
  entertainments 196, 197
  travel 221
Tiepolo, Gian Battista 59, 87, 101, 108, 112, 117, 120, 137, 148, 155
Tignale 150
Time 209
Tintoretto 49, 116
  Finding of the Body of St Mark 114

Tipping, in restaurants 169
Titian 22, 51, 67, 116
  Adoration of the Magi 56, 58
Toce river 134
Tombone di San Marco 110
Torbiere d'Iseo 155
Torbole 147, 150
Torelli della Guastalla, Countess
  Ludovica 98
Torno **145**
Torre di Buccione 154
Torre del Comune 55
Torre dei Gorani 83
Torre dell'Orologio (Garda) 151
Torre di San Marco (Gardone Riviera)
  131
Torre Velasca **96**
  Street-by-Street map 94
Torri del Benaco 147, **151**
Torriani, Napo 55
Torriani family 19, 20
Toscanini, Arturo 27, 52, 98, 118, 131,
  138
Toscolano Maderno **150**
Tourist offices 208, 209
Traballesi, Giuliano 54
Trains **216**, 217
  from airport 215
  at the Lakes 223
  Passante Ferroviario 221
  stations **216**, 217
  Stazione Centrale **119**
Trams 220
Trattoria 169
Travel **214–23**
  air **214**, 217
  at the Lakes **222–3**
  buses 220
  cars 218
  coaches 217
  Exploring the Lakes 132
  Historic Centre 43
  Metro 220–21
  Northeast Milan 105
  Northwest Milan 61
  scooters, mopeds and bicycles 219
  Southeast Milan 93
  Southwest Milan 77
  tickets 221
  trains **216**, 217
  trams 220
  walking in Milan 218
Tremezzo 11, 141, **143**
Tremosine 150
Tresseno, Oldrado da 54
Trezzi 81
Triennale di Milano **69**
  Street-by-Street map 63
Trivulzio, Gian Battista 46
Trivulzio, Gian Giacomo 96
Trotti, Giovanni Battista 67
Tura, Cosmè 117

U

Umberto I, King 26
Umiliate di Sant'Erasmo 108
Unique Forms of Continuity in Space
  (Boccioni) 54
Università Cattolica del Sacro Cuore
  87
  Street-by-Street map 78
Università Statale 97

V

Vacciago di Ameno 154

Val Camonica 74, 155
Val Cannobina 138
Valentinian II, Emperor 88
Valle Romita Polyptych (Gentile da
  Fabriano) 116
Valtènesi **148–9**
Valtolina, Giuseppe 118
Van Dyck, Anthony 96, 117
Van Gogh, Vincent 121
Varenna 11, 141, **144**
Varese 139
Varese, Lago di 131, **154–5**
Varone river falls 150
Vasari, Giorgio 73
Vedova, Emilio 54
Veneziano, Lorenzo 116
Veneziano, Paolo 150
Venice 148, 150, 151
Verbania **138**
Verdi, Giuseppe 23, 26, 30, 31, 51,
  100, 108, 118, 125
Vermiglio, Giuseppe 143
Veronese, Paolo 116, 150
Verri, Alessandro 23, 31
Verri, Pietro 31
Verziere Column 98
Vezzio castle 141
Via
  Bigli 106
  Brisa **75**
  Carducci 74
  Circo 78, **83**
  Dante 63
  della Spiga 106
  Durini **98**
  Fatebenefratelli 27
  Festa del Perdono 94
  GG Moro 126
  Manzoni 105, 106, **108**, 125
  Montenapoleone 14, 105, 106, 107,
    125
  Sant'Andrea 106
  Sant'Antonio 94
  Torino **82–3**
Vicolo dei Lavandai 89, 127
Victoria, Queen of England 137
Villas
  Alba (Gardone Riviera) 149
  Albertini (Garda) 151
  del Balbianello (Lenno) 142–3
  Belgiojoso Bonaparte - Museo
    dell'Ottocento 35, **121**
  Bettoni (Bogliaco) 146
  Carlotta (Tremezzo) 11, 141, 143
  Cipressi (Varenna) 11, 144
  Ducale (Stresa) 137
  Erba (Cernobbio) 142
  d'Este (Cernobbio) 140, 142
  Faccanoni (Sarnico) 155
  Feltrinelli (Toscolano Maderno) 150
  Fiordaliso (Gardone Riviera) 149
  Frua (Laveno) 139
  Guarienti (Punta San Vigilio) 151
  Melzi d'Eril (Bellagio) 145
  Milyus-Vigoni (Loveno) 143
  Monastero (Varenna) 11, 144
  Olmo 142
  Pallavicino 137, 205
  Pliniana (Torno) 145
  Ponti (Arona) 136
  Romana (Desenzano del Garda)
    148
  Serbelloni (Bellagio) 11, 145
  Stampa 136
  Taranto 134, 138
  Trivulzio (Bellaggio) 145
  Trotti (Bellaggio) 145

Vineria 169
Vineyards, Valtanèsi 149
Virgil 17, 59
Visas 208
Visconti, Andreotto 20
Visconti, Azzone 20, 54, 82, 145
Visconti, Bernabò 20, 52, 66
Visconti, Bianca Maria 20, 21
Visconti, Caterina 20
Visconti, Filippo Maria 20, 21, 64
Visconti, Galeazzo I 20
Visconti, Galeazzo II 20, 64
Visconti, Gian Galeazzo 19, 20, 46,
  48, 64
Visconti, Gian Maria 20
Visconti, Giovanni 20, 70
Visconti, Luchino 20
Visconti, Marco 20
Visconti, Matteo 20, 55
Visconti, Matteo II 20
Visconti, Obizzo 20
Visconti, Ottone 19, 20
Visconti, Stefano 20
Visconti, Tebaldo 20
Visconti, Umberto 20
Visconti family 14, 19, **20**, 33, 63, 67,
  90, 142, 139
Vittoriale degli Italiani (Gardone
  Riviera) 146, 149
Vittorio Emanuele I, King 122
Vittorio Emanuele II, King 50
Vittorio Emanuele III, King 54
Vivarini, Antonio 116
Volta, Alessandro 11, 142
Voltorre di Gavirate 155
Volvinius 85, 86

W

Waldensian church 91
Walking
  hiking 204, 218
  in Milan 218
  90-minute walk around Milan's
    hidden glories 125
  Two-hour walk around the Milan
    of yesteryear 126–7
Water, drinking 211
Water sports 204
Weather 36–9
Wenceslaus, Emperor 20
Wheelchair access, restaurants 169
Wildlife
  Brabbia marsh nature reserve 154
  Lagoni di Mercurago Regional Park
    136
  Lake Mezzola 141
Wildt, Adolfo 118
Windsurfing 204
Wines
  Valtanèsi 149
  What to Drink 171
Winter in Milan 39
World War I 78
World War II 26, 27, 43, 68, 84
WWF 151

Z

Zenale, Bernardino 87, 99, 109, 113
Zoo
  Parco Natura Viva (Bussolengo-
    Pastrengo) 205
Zucca in Galleria 79
  Street-by-Street map 44

Acknowledgments

Dorling Kindersley would like to thank all the people, organizations and associations whose contributions and assistance have made the preparation of this book possible. Special thanks are due to the following organizations and individuals: APT di Como (Sig. Pisilli), Silvia Dell'Orso, Direzione Civiche Raccolte d'Arte del Castello Sforzesco (Walter Palmieri), Giorgio Facchetti, Diana Georgiacodis, Alberto Malesani (Gardaland), Enrico Pellegrini, chef of the *Locanda degli Angeli* (Gardone), Augusto Rizza, Silvia Scamperle, Carla Solari, Crisca Sommerhoff, Valentina Tralli.

Design and Editorial Assistance
Gillian Allan, Douglas Amrine, Michelle Clark, Michelle Crane, Vivien Crump, Conrad van Dyk, Louise Bostock Lang, Annette Jacobs, Sands Publishing Solutions, Ellie Smith, Mary Sutherland.

Additional Assistance
Reid Bramblett, Sally Bloomfield, Susi Cheshire.

Picture Credits
Key: t = top; tl = top left; tlc = top left centre; tc = top centre; trc = top right centre; tr = top right; cla = centre left above; ca = centre above; cra = centre right above; cl = centre left; c = centre; cr = centre right; clb = centre left below; crb = centre right below; cb = centre below; bl = bottom left; br = bottom right; b = bottom; bc = bottom centre; bcl = bottom centre left; bcr = bottom centre right; (d) = detail.

Every effort has been made to trace the copyright holders. The publisher apologizes for any unintentional omissions and would be pleased, in such cases, to add an acknowledgment in future editions.

All the photographs reproduced in this book are from the Image Bank, Milan, except for the following:

Alamy Images: CuboImages srl/Bluered 170cl; Tibor Bognar 10cra; Adam Eastland 124clb; John Warburton-Lee Photography/Ian Aitken 11tr; Jon Arnold Images 42; CuboImages srl/Dario Mainetti 171cb; David Sanger photography/Sam Bloomberg-Rissman 171tl.

Archivio Fotografico del Teatro alla Scala: 52bl, 53tl, 53br, 53bl; Andrea Tamoni 52cl.

Archivio Fotografico Electa: 56-57 (all the photographs), 58tr, 58tl, 58c, 58bl, 59tr, 59c, 64cr(d), 146tl, 146tr, 148cr, 149tl, 149cr.

Archivio Fotografico Storico Achille Bertarelli: 41tc, 157tc, 207tc.

Simonetta Benzi: 36tl, 51tr, 51cl, 51cr, 68cr, 69cr, 74br, 75tr, 75cl, 78tr, 80br, 82tc, 85br, 87br, 88cr, 88br, 90c, 90bl, 97tl, 97cr, 97cb, 98cl, 100tl, 100br, 101br, 112tl, 113br, 122tr, 122cs, 122br, 123tr, 123cl, 123br, 212c, 212br.

Boeucc Antico Ristorante: 168bl.

Corbis: Massimo Listri 143t.

Discoteca Dehor: 205cb.

Dorling Kindersley Photo Library: Paul Harris and Anne Heslope 140tr; Ian O'Leary 170tr/cb/bl/br, 171bl/bc/br; 164 *(Risotto alla milanese)*, 165 (Ossobuco alla milanese and panettone), 197bl.

Empics: 196t.

Fabio De Angelis: 29tl, 29cl, 32br, 33tl, 33tr, 33bl, 35br (d), 44tl, 45br, 49tl, 49c, 80tr, 83tr, 83cr, 83bl, 84tl, 85tc, 85bl, 88tm, 90tc, 96c, 96br, 98br, 99tr, 100c, 102tr, 111br, 112cr, 112br, 119bl, 119cr, 121tl, 149bl, 185br, 188bl, 196cr, 211 (ambulance, fire brigade and police vans).

Gardaland: 152-3.

Giovanni Francesio: 32bl.

Grand Hotel Villa Serbelloni (Bellagio): 145tr, 159tl.

Grazia Neri: Archivio Marcello Mencarini/La Scala Theatre Museum, Milan, Angelo Inganni (1852) The Theater in a painting 124tc; Archivio Marcello Mencarini/La Scala Theatre Museum, Milan Ulisse Surtini Portrait of Maria Callas 125tr; Barbara Seghezzi 124br, 126clb, 126tr, 127tc.

Hotel Du Lac (Varenna): 141cr.

Hotel Four Seasons (Milan): 158cr, 185br.

Hotel Regency (Milan): 158bl.

Hotel Villa Crespi (Orta San Giulio): 159br.

IAT di Como: 144tr, 144bl.

INDEX, Firenze: Alberti 127crb; Pizzi 126c.

Krizia: 36c.

Marka, Milan: 196bl, 223b; Roberto Benzi 125bl; Danilo Donadoni 10bl; Nevio Doz 11bl; Giovanni Rivolta 10tc; Alessandro Villa 217tl.

Museo Diocesano: 90tl;

Museo del Risorgimento: 8–9c.

Omega Fotocronache: 27cl, 30tr, 30cl, 30bl.

Pasticceria Cova (Milan): 185tr.

Laura Recordati: 32cl, 54tl, 55br, 78br, 91br, 96tl, 98tl, 101c.

Ristorante Il Sole (Ranco): 169bl.

Ristorante L'Albereta (Erbusco): 169tl.

Ristorante La Briciola (Milan): 168tl.

Ristorante Pierino Penati (Vigan Brianza) 164 *(Gnervitt con cipolle and cotoletta alla milanese)*.

Ristorante Villa Flori (Como): 169tl.

Augusto Rizza: all the photographs on pages 164–5 except those from the Dorling Kindersley Picture Library.

Marco Scapagnini: 146cl, 158tc, 159cr, 168tc, 188tc.

Versace: 106tl.

FRONT ENDPAPERS
Alamy Images: Jon Arnold Images cr.
JACKET
Front - Alamy Images: Art Kowalsky main image; Laura Recordati: bl; Back - Alamy Images: Art Kowalsky tl;World Pictures Ltd bl; DK Images: Paul Harris cla; John Heseltine clb; Spine - Alamy Images: Art Kowalsky t; Fabio de Angelis: b.

SPECIAL EDITIONS OF DK TRAVEL GUIDES

DK Travel Guides can be purchased in bulk quantities at discounted prices for use in promotions or as premiums. We are also able to offer special editions and personalized jackets, corporate imprints, and excerpts from all of our books, tailored specifically to meet your own needs.

To find out more, please contact:

(in the United States) **SpecialSales@dk.com**

(in the UK) **Sarah.Burgess@dk.com**

(in Canada) DK Special Sales at **general@tourmaline.ca**

(in Australia) **business.development@pearson.com.au**